TO SAVE HER LIFE

TO SAVE HER LIFE

DISAPPEARANCE, DELIVERANCE, AND THE UNITED STATES IN GUATEMALA

Dan Saxon

UNIVERSITY OF CALIFORNIA PRESS
BERKELEY   LOS ANGELES   LONDON

University of California Press, one of the most distinguished university presses in the United States, enriches lives around the world by advancing scholarship in the humanities, social sciences, and natural sciences. Its activities are supported by the UC Press Foundation and by philanthropic contributions from individuals and institutions. For more information, visit www.ucpress.edu.

University of California Press
Berkeley and Los Angeles, California

University of California Press, Ltd.
London, England

A Caravan Book
For more information, visit www.caravanbooks.org.

Library of Congress Cataloging-in-Publication Data

Saxon, Dan, 1958–.
 To save her life : disappearance, deliverance, and the United States in Guatemala / Dan Saxon.
  p.   cm.
 Includes bibliographical references and index.
 ISBN 978-0-520-24597-6 (cloth : alk. paper)
 ISBN 978-0-520-25245-5 (pbk. : alk. paper)
  1. Disappeared persons—Guatemala.   2. Political persecution—Guatemala.   3. Human rights—Guatemala.   4. United States—Foreign relations—Guatemala.   5. Guatemala—Foreign relations—United States.   I. Title.
HV6322.3.G9S29   2007
972.8105'3—dc22
                                    2006022578

Manufactured in the United States of America

15   14   13   12   11   10   09   08   07
10   9   8   7   6   5   4   3   2   1

This book is printed on New Leaf EcoBook 50, a 100% recycled fiber of which 50% is de-inked post-consumer waste, processed chlorine-free. EcoBook 50 is acid-free and meets the minimum requirements of ANSI/ASTM D5634–01 (Permanence of Paper).

To the memory of
Jimmy Blum and Barbara Ford

If you can look into the seeds of time,
And say which grain will grow and which will not,
Speak then to me, who neither beg nor fear
Your favors nor your hate.

William Shakespeare, *Macbeth*, Act 1, scene 3

Contents

Photographs follow page 132

Map of Guatemala   xi

List of Abbreviations   xiii

Preface   xv

PART ONE: THE DISAPPEARANCE

1 Thursday, July 23, 1992   3

2 Thursday Morning and Afternoon   22

3 Friday, July 24, 1992   35

4 Saturday and Sunday, July 25–26, 1992   52

5 The Catholic Church in Guatemala, 1524–1992   65

6 Monday and Tuesday, July 27–28, 1992   80

7 Wednesday, July 29, 1992   94

8 Thursday, July 30, 1992   116

PART TWO: THE VISA

9 Friday, July 31, 1992   135

10 Saturday, August 1, 1992   144

11 Sunday, August 2, 1992   154

12 Monday, August 3, 1992   166

13 Tuesday, August 4, 1992   178

14 Wednesday, August 5, 1992   190

15 Thursday, August 6, 1992   205

    The Aftermath   227

    Epilogue   238

    Acknowledgments   245

    Notes   249

    Selected Bibliography and Further Reading   287

    Index   295

Map of Guatemala showing locations mentioned in the text.

Abbreviations

AID	Agency for International Development
CIA	Central Intelligence Agency
COPAZ	Comisión de Paz (Guatemalan Government's Commission for Peace Negotiations with the URNG)
COPREDH	Comisión Presidencial de los Derechos Humanos (Guatemalan Government's Presidential Commission for Human Rights)
DEA	Drug Enforcement Agency
EGP	Ejército Guerillero de los Pobres (Guerrilla Army of the Poor); the Organización
FAR	Fuerzas Armadas Rebeldes (Rebel Armed Forces)
G-2 or D-2	Guatemalan Army Intelligence Department
INM	Bureau for International Narcotics Matters of the U.S. Department of State
INS	Immigration and Naturalization Service of the United States
MLN	Movimiento de Liberación Nacional (Action for National Liberation; Movement for National Liberation)

ODHA   Oficina de Derechos Humanos del Arzobispado de Guatemala (Human Rights Office of the Archdiocese of Guatemala)

ORPA   Organización Revolucionaria del Pueblo en Armas

PGT   Partido Guatemalteco de los Trabajadores (Guatemalan Communist Party)

PUA   Partido de Unidad Anti-comunista (Party of Anti-Communist Unity)

URNG   Unidad Revolucionaria Nacional Guatemalteca (Guatemalan National Revolutionary Union)

USAC   Universidad de San Carlos de Guatemala (National University of San Carlos)

WOLA   Washington Office on Latin America

Preface

GUATEMALA CITY

October 20, 1944 Most of the city was asleep. Just after midnight, residents who lived along Twelfth Avenue heard the coughs and rumbles of a long parade of motor vehicles, and later the unmistakable cadence of troops on the march. From their windows the neighbors could see the silhouettes of passing motorcycles, of trucks loaded with armed men, and of tanks and cannon. The rebel Guatemalan army units placed their artillery on the large parade ground, the Campo Marte, and along the railroad tracks. Infantrymen and machine gunners took up their positions at strategic locations around the city, many within striking distance of the government's most formidable redoubts: the two forts known as Matamoros and San José. Within hours, groups of students, teachers and workers would join the rebellious soldiers, all determined to overthrow Guatemala's dictator, General Federico Ponce Vaides.[1]

The Urrutia family, Ester and Manuel and their seven children, were asleep in their home on Avenida Castellana when the shooting began just before 2:00 A.M. The house, modest but nearly half a block long, stood on a ridge that ran above the main thoroughfares of the city and just a kilometer or two south of the imposing gray stone walls of the San José fort, with its panoramic view of the city below. When the night was broken by the crash and boom of cannon fire and the staccato of machine guns and rifles, the Urrutias climbed out of bed to watch the drama. Tracer bullets filled the air and shell bursts lit up the cold sky as the rebels concentrated their fire on the San José. The loyal soldiers manning the fort vigorously returned the fire with cannon and mortars.

The Urrutias supported the revolt and were apprehensive about the consequences of its potential failure. What happens, they asked themselves, if the movement doesn't succeed?[2]

As dawn began to break over the city, thousands of residents from all walks of life took to the streets to support the rebellion. Many of them crept through the deep ravines in the south end of town and reached the Guardia de Honor, an army base now in rebel hands. There, the civilians were issued rifles and instructed where to take up positions against the loyalist forces. At 10:00 A.M. Oscar Urrutia, just fourteen, slipped away from home to fight with the revolutionaries.[3]

As the battle continued, women left the shelter of their homes to assist wounded rebels and to provide food and water to the combatants. "A single ideal united soldiers and civilians," the press later reported: "the overthrow of a tyrannical regime."[4] It was probably the last time unity would flourish and prevail in Guatemala.

Sometime during the morning a rebel artillery battery under the command of Captain Luis Valdes Peña fixed its sights on the towering San José. The first shot struck the fort, and the second did as well; a direct hit on its ammunition supply. Soon the fort was burning and smoke and flames climbed into the sky. Desperate soldiers abandoned their posts and jumped from the fort's high walls to escape the flames and exploding projectiles. Fearing reprisals from the hostile civilian population, many of these conscripts threw away their rifles and cartridge belts, their knee-high laced boots and broad-brimmed caps, and stripped down to their underwear in a vain attempt to conceal their identity.

As the San José began to burn, rumors flew among the residents who lived in the streets below it that there was a great deal of gunpowder stored in the fort; soon the entire redoubt would blow up. Eventually, whole families began to stream along the rutted dirt road past the Urrutias' house, seeking refuge further away from the carnage. Ester de Urrutia opened her home to a number of these displaced persons, served them coffee, and cooked up a huge pot of vegetable soup to keep them from going hungry. When the pathetic, nearly naked young conscripts ran or limped past the house, Ester took pity on them as well and rummaged through the clothing of her husband and sons to provide them with something to wear. "Poor kids. They're going naked."[5] Then she sent them on their way.

Loyalist forces from army bases outside Guatemala City arrived to reinforce their comrades in the urban redoubts, but the rebel units and their civilian allies prevented a counterattack. On the outskirts of the city Captain Braulio Laguardia, a dashing rebel officer driving a tank, led a group of soldiers and armed civilians who captured truckloads of government soldiers on their way to defend the dictatorship of General Ponce.[6]

Ester de Urrutia's twenty-one-year-old daughter, Julia, was listening to the radio that morning. The government's National Radio station was broadcasting only music, primarily military marches, a sign that a coup was under way. Periodically, however, the rebels broke into the government's broadcast to describe their progress. On one of these occasions, Julia learned that Captain Laguardia was driving a tank down Bolivar Avenue, just a few blocks above the Urrutia home, heading for the San José fort. Hundreds of civilians followed the intrepid captain in support of the revolution.

Julia grabbed her younger brother Edmundo, then sixteen, and the two siblings sneaked out of the house. Their mother had forbidden them to leave, but they were just going up to Bolivar to watch Captain Laguardia pass by in his tank. Then they'd come right back home.

When Julia and Edmundo reached the avenue at the corner of Twenty-fifth Street, they immediately were forced to take shelter inside a doorway. They hadn't counted on the snipers, loyal to General Ponce, who were shooting at Captain Laguardia and his followers along Bolivar Avenue. Moments later Captain Laguardia drove by on top of his tank, "like it was his chariot," smiling, with hundreds of people running behind him, urging him on with shouts of "Down with Ponce! Down with Ubico!"[7] Jorge Ubico was the dictator who had ruled Guatemala for thirteen years before General Ponce replaced him in mid-1944.

Swept up by the passion of the moment, Julia and Edmundo joined the crowd following Captain Laguardia down the avenue toward the San José. Several blocks later, the situation turned more serious. Loyalist soldiers close to the fort were firing at the oncoming crowds. As Julia and her younger brother approached the San José near Eighteenth Street, they were warned: "Be careful because they're firing from the fort!"[8] Moments later, a sniper shot and killed a man half a block away.

Thus cautioned, the two siblings took shelter in a doorway to reevaluate the situation. "We'd better go back," Julia told her brother. "What do you say?"

"Let's go on!" replied Edmundo. And so they sprinted past the bodies of several soldiers and into the burning fort.

Inside, the scene was Dantesque. Flames from the burning munitions lit up the sky as Julia and Edmundo ran past stone walls ripped open by shellfire, past headless bodies lying in rubble. They slipped and nearly fell as they crossed a patio whose floor was completely covered by small bits of black shrapnel.

Other civilians were busy looting whatever they could from the fallen bastion of General Ponce. Julia and Edmundo watched as men and women hauled away hundred-pound sacks of sugar and beans, mattresses, and iron beds. Finally Julia turned to her younger brother: "Let's go, 'Mundo, because it's getting late." But first they had a discussion: "What should *we* carry away?"

Edmundo grabbed a big bass drum painted with the blue and white national colors of Guatemala that lay in the debris and hung it from his shoulders. He spotted a rifle and grabbed that too while Julia picked up a large framed portrait of General Rufino Barrios, who ruled Guatemala during the nineteenth century. Then they started for home. At other points in the city, government forces were hoisting the white flag. The rebels had won!

As the siblings headed up Castellana Avenue toward their house, Julia began to worry about her mother's reaction to their unauthorized expedition to the fort. Ester de Urrutia had a quick temper and did not hesitate to demonstrate it to her children. "Our mother is gonna give us—" she started to tell Edmundo. "To you!" he interrupted, understanding that, as the older sibling, Julia would be held responsible for their exploits. And so they marched home, with Edmundo proudly beating his drum.

Julia was right; her worried mother *was* furious at Julia's imprudence. "You let me down!" Ester scolded her daughter. "Why did you take the kid? If you were curious, why didn't you go *alone*? You're *older!* If something had happened to the kid, what would your father and I have done?"[9]

Stung by her mother's rebuke, Julia went inside the house and right to bed, while Edmundo hid his loot. And so began, for the Urrutia family, the Guatemalan Revolution.

March 1996 Decades later, an old and dusty black file lies on a shelf inside the Argentine Embassy in Guatemala City. The papers inside the dossier, a mixture of dry diplomatic correspondence, emotional letters, and terse instructions, speak from 1954, when hundreds of desperate people sought refuge inside the embassy grounds. The United States government and a small group of Guatemalan exiles had just driven President Jacobo Árbenz, leader of the Guatemalan revolution, from office and quickly formed a new military regime. If the refugees left the embassy they would be imprisoned, perhaps killed, for their support of Árbenz.

I visited the Argentine Embassy in 1996, during the course of my research for this book. Ambassador Jorge Taiana, himself a former political prisoner, gave me permission to review the 1954 file concerning those who took refuge in the embassy after the Central Intelligence Agency drove Jacobo Árbenz from power. Among the diplomatic cables and the lists of suspected Communists, I found a letter that Ester de Urrutia (my wife's paternal grandmother, a political activist and loyal supporter of Árbenz) wrote from exile nearly forty-two years earlier, which I quote extensively in this story. Ester apparently sent the letter intended for her daughter Julia via diplomatic channels from Buenos Aires to Guatemala City, where it languished unread and undelivered in an embassy cabinet for more than four decades: "Give many kisses to my little ones, regards to Alfredo and to you, adored daughter—receive the blessings of your mother, who doesn't forget you for a minute."[10]

In July 1992 Ester's granddaughter Maritza was "disappeared" after taking her four-year-old son to school in Guatemala City. Maritza was an underground member of an insurgent organization when members of an army intelligence unit dragged her off the streets of Guatemala's capital. Very quickly, the disappearance of this unknown woman set off a cascade of challenges to the struggling Guatemalan democracy and the institutions committed to supporting it. What was the value of Maritza's life? Was it worth a blow to the pride and reputation of Guatemala's president? Was it worth a disruption of the counternarcotics activities of the United States? Could Maritza still contribute to what was, after all, a failed revolution?

When I began writing this book, I believed that Maritza's story was about the collision of humanitarianism and politics. By the time I finished writing—nearly twelve years later—I understood that humanitarianism *is* politics. An understanding of the political interests that envelop these issues becomes a fundamental ingredient of effective humanitarian work.

Many people participated in the efforts to save Maritza. In Guatemala, journalists, student groups, revolutionaries, the Catholic Church, human rights organizations, even the distrusted U.S. Embassy assisted Maritza. In the United States and in Europe, many more human rights activists mobilized to pressure the Guatemalan government to keep Maritza alive.

Yet as Maritza's circumstances changed, the other players' interests also evolved. An extraordinary "human rights machine" eventually emerged to help Maritza, but at times parts of the machine were out of sync. This book explores Maritza's disappearance and the efforts that saved her life.

Maritza's story is a tale of the complex and often cruel politics of human rights, which often seem more Machiavellian than humanitarian. But the broader lessons of Maritza's story transcend the actions and interests of individuals or institutions: lessons of endurance, intelligence, and courage as a single family, repeatedly torn apart by forty years of brutal war, came together one last time to fight for one of its own.

When Maritza disappeared, I was the legal advisor to the Archdiocese of Guatemala's Human Rights Office. After Maritza reappeared alive, my colleagues and I protected her inside the archbishop's residence while we struggled to find a way to take Maritza safely out of Guatemala. After several days of tense negotiations and international pressure, U.S. Embassy officials took Maritza's passport and her son's, promising to return them later that day with U.S. entry visas stamped inside them. When I went to the embassy to pick up the documents, embassy officials told me that the visas would not be forthcoming for several days. After a heated discussion with the U.S. ambassador and several of his aides, I returned to my office without the visas, without the passports, and despondent that Maritza and her little boy were unable to travel. In spite of her own exhaustion and trauma, Maritza noticed how upset I was. She came close, looked up at me with those big brown eyes, and said, in her soft voice: "Daniel, I want you to know that I'm very grateful for everything you've done for me and I believe you are a marvelous person. Don't feel bad about what happened at the embassy. I have faith that everything's going to be OK. Don't worry."

Maritza helped me to save her life, and we were married in 1999. Over the years spent researching and writing this book, during my moments of self-doubt or indecision, Maritza and I often discussed the potential costs of telling this story. Would there be reprisals against family members, former colleagues, or ourselves? Wouldn't it be safer to let this story remain in the darkness, along with the men who tortured her? Perhaps, but Maritza would gently remind me that when torture remains hidden in darkness and fear, then the torture perpetuates itself. The disappeared remain disappeared. Maritza returned from the darkness and for that reason alone this story should be told.[11]

As an optimist, I would like Maritza's story to offer some measure of hope and humanity amidst the checkered history of the United States within Guatemala. But perhaps this is naive. Her experience demonstrates that power, even in the hands of the most benevolent leader, becomes a mix of good intentions and selfish interests. And good intentions, even when exercised by committed human rights activists and government officials, are a poor substitute for sharp political insight. When a victim faces her torturer, the moral dynamics of the situation usually seem relatively simple. We usually know which party represents "evil" and which represents "good." Little room exists for moral ambiguity or shades of gray. But the efforts we make to resolve and heal human rights violations may say more about our disparate, flawed humanity than the abuse itself. *These* efforts expose our courage and cowardice, our virtue and hypocrisy.

I hope this book will provoke more discussion about what it means to be involved, from Guatemala to Guantánamo to Iraq, in that spiderweb of values and interests known as "human rights." Perhaps in the future those who are already involved, including the United States government, may provide more effective assistance to victims of human rights violations.

The Hague
September 2006

PART I

THE DISAPPEARANCE

The human rights issue has become a game,
played strictly for political advantage.

**CIA Guatemala Station secret cable, "The D-2
Conducts Human Rights Investigations,"
November 1989**

ONE

THURSDAY

July 23, 1992

GUATEMALA CITY

Maritza did not look like a revolutionary. She was just one of the young mothers walking their children to school in the morning. Her *organización*, the Guerrilla Army of the Poor—an insurgent group commonly known by its Spanish acronym EGP and referred to here as the Organización—had trained Maritza about the importance of blending in with the crowd so as to avoid detection by the Guatemalan army. She wore no uniform and carried no weapon. A white sweater protected Maritza from the early morning chill and underneath she wore a T-shirt from Albuquerque, New Mexico, where her brother, Edmundo René, had studied political science. Maritza had loafers on her feet and in the pockets of her green pants only her house keys and the thirty cents she would need to make a telephone call after dropping off Sebastián. She carried nothing that could fall into the hands of *el enemigo*.

Perhaps the most striking physical characteristic of this petite woman was her hair: a mass of long, unruly coffee-colored curls that flowed past Maritza's shoulders, with a streak of gray above her forehead. Sebastián, a precocious four-year-old with dark hair and his mother's large dark eyes, liked nothing better than to play with his toy cars and trucks or to color with crayons. That morning he was dressed in his school uniform of red pants, white shirt, and red sweater.

As they neared Boulevard de Liberación, the broad avenue that separates zone eight from zone thirteen of Guatemala City, just a few blocks from Sebastián's school, another mother waved to Maritza. She had already dropped off her daughter and was returning to her home in zone eight, not far from where Maritza lived with her parents. Would Maritza like to come by her house that afternoon? The woman sold jewelry from her home and had some earrings she wanted to show to Maritza. Of course! Maritza promised to drop by later that day.

Mother and son crossed the broad boulevard just after 8:00 A.M., and as they walked up Fifth Avenue toward Third Street, dozens of people filled the muddy thoroughfare. Men and women left their homes for work; mothers walked their children to school; young maids stood in the doorways of their employers' homes; shopkeepers hung out in front of their stores, chatting with the passersby. The sounds of planes taking off from the nearby airport and the heavy morning traffic filled the air.

Maritza was alert as she walked down Third Street with her little boy and neared Walt Disney Nursery School. Just outside the school on the previous day, Maritza had spotted the men who kept her under surveillance. The first man followed Maritza for almost four blocks after she said good-bye to Sebastián. Then he stopped and spoke to another man. A third man observed Maritza as she arrived at her bus stop. He stayed on the corner when Maritza boarded the number forty bus. Maritza didn't know at the time that her house was also under surveillance.

Later that day Maritza spoke with her superiors in the Organización. They agreed that Maritza should start to change her daily routine and move out of her parents' house. But there was no need to panic. Maritza could make these changes gradually over the next month.

As Maritza and Sebastián walked the final few blocks to the school, she was relieved to see that the men were not there. Maritza did not want to accept the fact the she had been identified, and so she minimized the significance of the surveillance. The men were gone. She could relax. And so, like every morning, Maritza kissed Sebastián's cheek at the nursery school entrance and told him that she would take him home again at noon.

But the men were not gone. There were nearly ten of them that day, hidden in three separate cars parked some distance from the nursery school. One of the vehicles, parked among other automobiles outside a nearby factory, had a clear view of the entrance to Walt Disney School. As Maritza bade her son farewell and started back toward her home, the men inside this vehicle radioed her position to their commander, "Don

Chando."* He sat in a Toyota Corolla with tinted windows that was parked around the corner on Fifth Avenue, just up the street from the route that Maritza would take on her way home.

Maritza was still alert as she walked away from the school up Third Street to the corner of Fifth Avenue, and then down the slope toward Boulevard de Liberación. Older children were walking to school and more men and women hurried off to catch the bus to work. After crossing Second Street, Maritza passed "Diana," who was walking her daughter to Walt Disney School.[1] From another automobile, "El Chino" radioed to Don Chando that Maritza was coming toward them now.

As Maritza approached First Street, she was surprised to see the jewelry vendor walking toward her, the same woman she had spoken to earlier that morning. But now the woman was on the opposite side of the street. Strange, because the jewelry vendor had already left her child at the school. The woman hailed Maritza again and spoke to her from across the street, briefly distracting Maritza as she continued to walk toward her home.

Perhaps that explains why Maritza never saw the large man who fell on her and covered her mouth with his hand and held her arms against her ribs. Or why she never noticed the second man, who almost simultaneously rushed up behind her and grabbed her arms.

Maritza screamed and tried in vain to free herself. "Oh no!" Her scream was a realization rather than a protest. She'd come to her end. There was no return. A white car with darkened windows pulled up and the back door flew open. The two men who held Maritza threw her onto the backseat, knocking one of her shoes off into the road. The men climbed in after her as the car rolled forward. A third man, his skin very pale, sat in the passenger seat next to the driver. The fair-skinned man glanced at Maritza and spoke into a radio: "We've got her. Go for the other."[2] Maritza was terrified. Later she realized that he was the same man who had followed her the day before.

TEGUCIGALPA, HONDURAS

February 1954 Two sisters stood by the side of the dusty airstrip, waiting to board the plane that would take them to a secret destination. Sonia Orellana was eighteen and Sara just one year older. Full of adoles-

---

*A pseudonym or alias—set inside quotation marks at first mention only—is used (as here) to protect the security of particular Guatemalan sources.

cent passion, the girls knew a great quest lay ahead of them that morning, although they didn't know specifically what it was. They were going to save Guatemala from the claws of Communism.

A slender man with a mustache and dark skin approached them and the sisters recognized him instantly. He was Colonel Carlos Castillo Armas, a Guatemalan army officer living in exile in Honduras, and the CIA's chosen leader of the "liberation movement" to oust the government of Jacobo Árbenz.

"Are you calm?"

"Yes, Colonel."

"You're not sad?"

"No," they replied, although the two girls had no idea where they were going or why. But they would do anything to help the "liberation movement." "You're going to be well cared for and you're going to do a good job," Castillo Armas reassured them. "You're going to write a page in the country's history."[3]

Sonia and Sara flew first to San Salvador, and then on to Miami. Waiting for them at the Miami airport was a "Mr. López," who had visited their father many times in their home-in-exile in Tegucigalpa. Mr. López was a North American who spoke bad Spanish and whose real name was Davis. Mr. López brought the girls to a palatial estate in Florida where they would spend the next few months.[4] There was a recording studio on the grounds of the estate, and every morning beginning at 9:00 A.M. and working into the evening, Sonia, Sara, and a small group of other young Guatemalans prepared their *escrips* and produced radio programs attacking the Árbenz government:

> This is the voice of Clandestine Radio—the radio of liberation. . . .
> The heroic people of Guatemala, who for more than ten years have endured the savage oppression of international Communism, have lost their patience and are preparing for the final battle. . . .
> And Jacobo Árbenz and his ruffians will see that patriots know how to defend their ideal: GOD, COUNTRY, LIBERTY. . . .
> GUATEMALANS, THE HOUR IS NEAR. WE WILL KNOW HOW TO GIVE YOU THE WORD, BUT MEANWHILE, DON'T LET YOURSELVES BE FOOLED. THE COMMUNIST PULP WILL BE CRUSHED, AND WITH IT, ALL OF ITS HIRED GUNS. THE HOURS OF COMMUNISM ARE NUMBERED . . .[5]

A nice young North American man named Chuck taught the Guatemalans how to use the modern equipment. After each broadcast was recorded in Florida, the tapes were sent on Pan Am flights to Honduras, where the "liberationists" maintained their transmitter. The messages were beamed into Guatemala where, at night, behind closed doors, opponents of Jacobo Árbenz would pick up the signal.[6]

After some months in Florida, the two sisters returned to Central America to continue the radio broadcasts. First they operated from a farm just inside Nicaragua near the Honduran border where Castillo Armas and his men were preparing for the invasion of Guatemala. Trying to increase popular sentiment for an uprising, Sonia and Sara would falsely declare that they were brazenly broadcasting from a secret location within Guatemala.

> The VOICE OF NATIONAL LIBERATION, transmitter of the free people, initiated its work in spite of the government, which, trembling even more, has dispatched all of its dogs in order to locate it. The movement of Guatemalan resistance isn't weak any more. On the contrary, it's now a gigantic force which the red government fears and . . . trembles in terror.[7]

From Nicaragua the sisters returned to Honduras, to the farm of their maternal grandparents, where they continued their broadcasts while the "liberation army" completed its final phase of training. Critical to the strategy of the CIA was the demoralization of the Guatemalan army:

> With true stupor, we've been informed of the incident that occurred between the Defense Minister, Colonel José Ángel Sánchez, and one of the high-ranking commanders of the Air Force, when the latter returned to his home and found the DIGNIFIED MINISTER making love with his once honorable wife. . . .
>
> We in exile view the immorality that now reigns in some military commanders as a true threat to the dignity and security of the army since these acts of savagery denigrate the institution and upset the morale of the soldier. This is a fruit of Marxist doctrine, which favors free love.[8]

Sonia and Sara Orellana were the daughters of Manuel Orellana, an anti-Communist leader working in exile with Colonel Castillo Armas. The exiles in Honduras were not acting alone, but in concert with the anti-Communist organizations inside Guatemala organized and encouraged by the CIA.[9] "The basic key to all operational planning," explained one CIA memorandum at the time, "is the realization that the strength of our movement is going to be from *within* the target country rather than being in the nature of an 'invasion' from without."[10]

Consequently, the Catholic Church and the media were active in the campaign to oust Árbenz.[11] The Catholic clergy "worked like ants" to bring down the Árbenz government, and the stress caused stomach problems for Monsignor Mariano Rossell Arellano, the tall and distinguished archbishop.[12] Several right-wing, anti-government newspapers were in circulation, such as *La Opinión,* whose masthead read "Newspaper of the poor, and also of the rich."[13] And there were a number of fiercely anti-Communist journalists. But none of them was fiercer, tougher, more dogmatic and radical than a radio journalist named Oscar Conde.

Born of a union between a father of mixed Spanish blood and a mother who was part Mayan and part African, Conde was tall and dark, with wavy black hair and a black moustache. He was also quite thin, which sharpened his features and only added to his intensity. Conde was a leader of PUA, the Party of Anti-Communist Unity, and through his program called *Radio Sucesos* was by far the most widely listened to of the anti-Communist radio journalists of the Árbenz period.

Every day at lunchtime in this pretelevision era, families in thousands of homes around Guatemala City would cut short their conversation and tune in to Oscar Conde. Even his friends, who admired him, acknowledged that Conde was "violent, dogmatic, obnoxious if you will."[14] Conde could not stand anyone who bore the slightest taint of left-wingism, and he relentlessly criticized the Árbenz regime and its members.

The defection of army personnel was another key component of the CIA's strategy for overthrowing Árbenz. The agency had infiltrated the armed forces and by late May 1954 the CIA's station chief in Guatemala City was reporting that the Guatemalan army would not resist their "liberation":

> The army is reportedly divided into two groups: the older officers, and the younger officers. The older officers are determined to form a "junta" as soon as any action starts and then try to make a deal with Castillo Armas and the "Americans." The younger officers are reportedly decided not to fire a shot or else go over to Castillo Armas.[15]

In early June, officials at the Guatemalan Embassy in Tegucigalpa picked up rumors indicating that the attack was imminent:

> A group of exiles that eat in one of the downtown restaurants in Tegucigalpa came to eat supper on Sunday night after having a few drinks. Thus, it slipped out that THE FIFTEENTH OF THIS MONTH WILL BE the date of the invasion.[16]

But it would not be much of an invasion. CIA officials were aghast when Colonel Castillo Armas confessed that he only had one hundred and fifty men under his command. This news forced the agency to reevaluate its plans, but ultimately the agents in command decided to go forward. Castillo Armas's "movement" might become even weaker if they postponed the invasion, and the possibility of gathering sympathizers along the way kept the CIA's goal within reach.[17] The *Voice of Liberation* broadcast a series of warnings to the Guatemalan people. Everyone should withdraw money from their bank accounts, buy food and durable goods, try to get valuables out of the country. Don't support the "outlaw regime."[18] Fortuitously for Castillo Armas and the CIA, Guatemala's state-run radio required a new antenna in May. This problem knocked out power to the government's only broadcast medium for three weeks. So the largely illiterate populace turned to the *Voice of Liberation* for news, giving the liberationists a virtual propaganda monopoly.[19]

When they finally entered Guatemala on June 18, 1954, Castillo Armas and his soldiers carried with them the Radio of Liberation's transmitter, accompanied by the only two women in the invading force, the young sisters Sonia and Sara Orellana. Radio broadcasts might still be needed to swing the Guatemalan army over to Castillo Armas's side.[20] People came out into the streets of small towns to offer the liberators food and water. "It was a party," Sonia recalled many years later, "we weren't afraid."[21] They camped in the town of Esquipulas, home of Guatemala's patron saint, and there the two girls made their last clandestine radio broadcast, exhorting the population to join the uprising.[22]

GUATEMALA CITY

Thursday morning, July 23, 1992 In the back of the car, Maritza struggled to free herself but the men began to beat her. They covered her mouth with their hands and forced her head down between her legs until Maritza began to feel dizzy. When they put a sweater over her head, Maritza thought that she would suffocate. Finally, they've taken me. It's finally happened.

Then the men began to speak. "We know that you're 'Ruth.' You have to do what we tell you, or else you know what will happen to you." They spoke of Sebastián. "Your son is very cute. We've seen the two of you together. You have a good relationship with him."[23] Maritza began to feel even more terrified. What will they do to Sebastián?

The same voice spoke to her again. "Cooperate with us and nothing's going to happen to you. We know that you're Ruth." He seemed to be in charge. After fifteen or twenty minutes the car slowed and passed over some speed bumps. They passed through a wide gate and stopped in a large garage containing a red bus and many other vehicles. The men covered Maritza's face with a piece of newspaper.

They pulled Maritza into the bus's front seat and handcuffed her, taking care to put paper in the metal handcuffs and placing them over the sleeves of her sweater so as not to cut Maritza's wrists. The men took her keys and her watch, telling her they would return them later. Someone brought Maritza a pair of large tennis shoes and told her to put them on.

A group of men sat near Maritza in the red bus and began to interrogate her. "We know that you're Ruth. We want information. We have your letters."[24] They brought a packet of letters that Maritza had written to "Esteban," her ex-husband and Sebastián's father. The Organización had assigned Esteban to the "Ho Chi Minh front," in the mountains far to the north of Guatemala City. Maritza sent him letters via a secret mail system, but someone had intercepted her letters.

The fair-skinned man spoke to her. "We want you to be calm because we have your son. Did you listen to me when I spoke on the radio? They went to get your son at the school. *No problem.* Your son is fine. A special person is taking care of him. He's eating cookies. He's fine."[25] Maritza was crying, nearly going crazy with worry. "My son, my son," she kept repeating. "You're going to see your son again," replied the fair-skinned man. "*If* you cooperate with us."[26]

The men showed Maritza three letters she had written to Esteban. They showed her photos of Sebastián, photos Maritza had included with her letters, and Maritza began to feel sick.

In the months before her disappearance, Maritza had sent a total of four letters and an audiocassette to her ex-husband. This correspondence was captured when the army intercepted and killed the Organización's mail carrier. The letters described the road construction that occurred near Maritza's home during early 1992. Moreover, the cassette contained the sounds of jets taking off and landing at Guatemala's International Airport. So whoever intercepted the recording would know that the voice belonged to a woman who lived close to the airport.[27]

Maritza never used her true name in her letters to Esteban and always referred to Sebastián as "the dwarf" or "the little kid." Nevertheless, she made the mistake of remarking that she had enrolled Sebastián in "the school near the airport" that Maritza attended as a little girl. She also included photographs of Sebastián in some of the letters and mentioned that she walked him to school everyday. Maritza's captors probably identified Sebastián as he entered and left Walt Disney School and, through the boy, his mother.[28]

Her captors had other photographs as well. They showed Maritza photos of her brother, her mother, her brother-in-law, and her nephew. They had a photograph of Sebastián playing outside near Maritza's house. "Your son likes to play in the street in the afternoon. We've seen him."[29] There was a photo of Maritza's house and her car. "The car. Why isn't it registered in your name?" Maritza told them that her ex-husband had purchased the vehicle.

The men demanded Esteban's true name. The Organización had trained Maritza about interrogations and she knew that she had to tell them something. If you were captured, you should give a mixture of the truth and fiction. You have to confuse the enemy. Esteban was far away in the rugged mountains of El Quiché. So Maritza gave up his name: Carlos Barrientos Aragón. One of the men left the vehicle and returned a short time later with some paper in his hand.

They had a file on Esteban, but it contained only information through 1982, when Esteban was an EGP leader in Guatemala City. At that time, members of an army intelligence unit raided a house near Guatemala City where Esteban slept. Tipped off, Esteban fled the home ahead of his pursuers, but in his haste, he left photographs of himself and weapons behind. So the army opened a file on Esteban, but it had no new information about him for the last ten years. Now the men pushed Maritza harder. "Tell us about Esteban!" But she resisted.[30] She hadn't seen him in years.

Her captors explained that they were members of a very secret organization. They were not part of the army, but they pursued any person who endangered the security of the nation. They took action against subversives, drug traffickers, even against members of the armed forces if they posed a threat to Guatemala. If Maritza wanted to get her son back, she would have to tell them how to find Esteban.[31] Maritza stalled for time. Esteban had left her two and a half years ago. She didn't know how to contact him. Maritza explained that she sent Esteban letters via a woman named "Argelia," a name that she made up.

The men continued to press her. Her son was all right, but she had to give them information. If Maritza wanted to see her son again, she would have to give them something: a telephone number, an address, a contact person. They knew that Maritza had been involved with "subversive organizations." She would have to give them information if she wanted to free herself and reunite with her son. The men asked Maritza questions about her brother, Edmundo René, and her sister, Carolina, and showed her copies of her siblings' passports. After reading another of her letters, the men told Maritza that they were sure that she was involved in something subversive. No, she was a mother. Her only interest was her son.

The men forced Maritza to take a pill that made her feel drowsy. "I'm sleepy!" she cried. She was trembling and crying with fear. All Maritza could think about was her Sebastián. She wanted to return home and hug him and know that he was safe.

But the men would not let her rest. "We know you're not just anyone. Your husband is an important person. He's been involved in 'subversive organizations' since he was very young."[32] Maritza explained that she knew little of Esteban's political activity. They had met in a party in Mexico in 1986. They had a child together, but they had been separated for two and a half years. She didn't have any of the information that they wanted.

One of the men said that they had to make a phone call. They took Maritza out of the red bus and put her in another car. After driving a short distance within the installation, the men took her out of the car again. Maritza could see some olive green backpacks and some military weapons leaning against a wall, and she assumed that she was in an army compound.

The men told Maritza that she was going to call her family. She was going to tell her father to go and pick up Sebastián at his school. Perhaps they don't really have my little boy? Part of her life returned to Maritza. But she was also confused, afraid, and nervous. What mental game were they playing with her? She had left Sebastián safe in his school. But perhaps they *did* have Sebastián, only now they were trying to trick her into thinking he was safe.[33] These men are professionals. They know what they're doing.

The men brought Maritza to a bathroom. They told her to act like everything was fine when she spoke to her parents. Maritza should tell them she was with a friend. The men brought a telephone and called Maritza's family via a switchboard. When Maritza's mother, Pilar, answered the phone, Maritza used a tone of voice that was unusual for her. She sensed from the worried tone of Pilar's voice that her mother already knew something was wrong. Maritza told her mother that she was with her friend Sandra. "Don't worry. Could Papá please go and pick up Sebastián at school?"

After the call, Maritza fought back. "My family already knows!" she told them. "They're going to stir things up! And we have friends in the army."[34] Her captors were unimpressed. One of the men left the bathroom and returned a few moments later. Maritza would have to call Sandra and tell her to reassure Maritza's parents that Maritza was fine.

The men dialed the phone and Maritza asked Sandra to call her family and tell them that Maritza was with her. Sandra said that she would telephone, but Maritza's tone of voice worried her. "What's happening?" she asked.

"I'm fine," replied Maritza. "Please do me this favor."[35]

After the telephone calls, the interrogation began again inside the bathroom. In the past, Maritza had read a great deal about revolutionaries who were captured by *el enemigo*, about the methods of interrogation in countries like Argentina, Nicaragua, and El Salvador. Maritza's captors seemed to be fighting for time. Why? She was frightened, but Maritza knew she had to tell the men as little as possible. When the men let slip that they did not have Sebastián, they made an important tactical error. Maritza knew that if she could minimize the information she gave them, then perhaps only *her* life would be at stake.[36] Soon Maritza's *compañeros* in the Organización would begin to move to secure locations. She had to win time in order to protect her contacts, who were scattered around Guatemala City.[37] So Maritza spoke about her family, and about her distant relatives. And she tried to prepare herself for her last battle.

June 1954 Maritza's paternal grandmother, Ester de Urrutia, wife of a printer and mother of seven children, was the vice secretary general of the Guatemalan Women's Alliance (AFG), considered by many to be the women's branch of the Árbenz government and of PGT, the Guatemalan Communist Party.[38] The Women's Alliance fought hard for women's rights and especially to increase the participation of Guatemalan women in the country's public and political affairs.[39] At the time, it was the most important women's organization in the nation.[40]

And for revolutionary women like Ester de Urrutia, an early feminist who lived for politics, the Women's Alliance was also a social welfare organization that provided services to needy women and to Guatemala's poor.[41] Although she never studied beyond the third grade, Ester founded a number of literacy and civic education centers where adults and children came to learn to read and write. Most of these centers were established in the markets where groups of volunteers would come to educate the women vendors. But Ester even set one up in her family's home in zone eight of Guatemala City. With her daughter Julia, Ester also started cafeterias for children who had no place to eat.[42] Short and stocky, always simply dressed, with a streak of gray running down the middle of her dark hair, Doña Estercita, as she was known in her community, was a natural orator and politician, and during the early 1950s she traveled throughout Guatemala, to El Salvador, and to Eastern Europe on behalf of the Women's Alliance and the revolutionary government of president Jacobo Árbenz.[43]

In pursuit of his dream to transform Guatemala, Jacobo Árbenz implemented the first agrarian reform program in Guatemala since 1524, when the ruthless Pedro de Alvarado subjugated what is today Central America on behalf of the Spanish Crown. Guatemala's Mayan peoples were largely enslaved and exploited, their many cultures nearly destroyed during the five centuries that passed between the Spanish conquest and the October 1944 revolution. But during the early 1950s the reform-minded President Árbenz expropriated over a million acres of untilled land, which he redistributed to thousands of landless peasants, provided small farmers with access to credit, and began a literacy campaign in the predominantly Mayan communities in the countryside.[44]

President Árbenz's successful agrarian reform program was largely the "brainchild" of the Guatemalan Communist Party. During the Árbenz era, the springtime of Guatemala's revolution, Guatemalans on the left like young Roberto Paz y Paz wanted to transform the feudal economic structures in place in their society. "We were all 'Nerudanos,'" Roberto recalled four decades later, referring to the famed Chilean poet who wrote "Love Song for Stalingrad." "Romantics. And Communism seemed beautiful."[45]

Now with the Guatemalan Revolution facing the ominous threat of U.S. intervention, the Women's Alliance tried to defend its country. A number of the women received an emergency course in nursing, and some of them began to sleep in the hospitals. In case of bloodshed, they'd be there to assist the nurses on duty. Ester de Urrutia and a young colleague, Atala Valenzuela, read proclamations on all of the pro-government radio stations denouncing the imminent invasion and the danger facing the nation.[46]

Thousands of men, many of them organized by unions or political parties, offered to fight on behalf of the Árbenz government; but they needed weapons from the army, and the Guatemalan army had lost its nerve.[47] On June 25 the officer corps, convinced that their resistance would lead to an overwhelming U.S. invasion, called on Árbenz to resign. Finally, on the evening of June 27, 1954, an exhausted Árbenz resigned in order to eliminate the pretext for the U.S.-sponsored "invasion."

Within the diplomatic community, no one doubted that the United States would decide who would take the reins of power.[48] But the U.S. government faced an awkward choice. Apart from the persecutions carried out by the new regime, the Eisenhower administration knew that it might face repercussions throughout the Americas for installing a mercenary government in Guatemala. One high-ranking CIA operative was a bit defensive about the situation: "Instead of yelling about Yankee imperialism and invasion, the free world should be grateful that a handful of brave but maybe pathetically comical exiles got the pitch and decided to do something about it."[49]

On July 9 Castillo Armas, the United States' trusted friend, was proclaimed president of Guatemala's provisional junta.[50] Anti-Communist repression swept the country.[51] All political parties that had supported Árbenz, whether Communist or not, were banned.[52] Rumors circulated about bands of masked men who were killing the revolutionaries.[53] Indeed, the CIA had included the elimination of "top-flight Communists" in its Guatemala strategy since 1952 and had repeatedly discussed "disposal lists" of Árbenz sympathizers who warranted assassination or imprisonment.[54] Of course, the names of Ester de Urrutia and her colleagues in the Guatemalan Women's Alliance went directly into the military government's new Black Book.[55] According to the Law against Communism, imposed by Castillo Armas in August 1954, inclusion in this register created a "grave presumption of dangerousness" and authorized a suspect's indefinite imprisonment without charge or trial.

Soon the embassies of Mexico, Argentina, Chile, Ecuador, Brazil, Costa Rica, and El Salvador were full of Arbencistas seeking shelter from the terror. Julia Urrutia, Ester's oldest daughter, heard a radio broadcast reporting that Oscar Conde, the well-known anti-Communist radio journalist, was moving about Guatemala City with the police, singling out alleged Communists for arrest. "They're like rats!" said Conde of the fleeing Arbencistas.[56] Representatives of the new military regime announced that supporters of Árbenz would be arrested and—as punishment for being Communists—sent to the isolated province of El Petén.[57] This vast tropical region of sweltering, mosquito-infested jungles and swamps had few roads, towns, or modern facilities. If the heat and malaria did not kill the banished "Communists," the isolation would drive them mad.

Julia Urrutia knew that her aging mother would die in El Petén. So Julia took Ester and five of her brothers and sisters to the Argentine Embassy, where nearly two hundred people sought asylum and safe passage out of the country.

Then Julia went to find her father. Manuel was still at work at PGT's newspaper, *Octubre*, although soon the paper would be shut down. Tall, thin, and balding, with big ears and dark bags under his eyes, Manuel resisted the idea of going into exile. "I'm not involved in anything!"[58]

he protested to his daughter. But apart from his printing duties, Manuel also helped sell *Octubre* on the streets of Guatemala City, which publicly linked him with PGT. In the months leading up to Árbenz's resignation, right-wing activists painted the word "Communists" on the Urrutia family's house. Julia eventually convinced her father of the danger he was in and brought Manuel to the Argentine Embassy, where he joined his wife and most of his children.

All together, one hundred and eighty-eight persons took refuge within the small Argentine Embassy. There was Raul Sierra Franco, a former government minister, prominent congressmen, and PGT leaders like Víctor Manuel Gutiérrez, doctors, lawyers, union leaders, Communist Party members, and others linked to the party.[59] Ernesto "Che" Guevara was there; an unknown but aspiring young revolutionary who would later win fame during the Cuban revolution.[60] Che, an Argentinean, passed the time reading and playing chess, while Ester and Manuel cooked for the refugees.[61] Che needed a special diet. "I'm an asthmatic, señora," he explained to Ester, "so I only eat boiled vegetables."[62] So Ester prepared boiled vegetables especially for Che.

Some of the refugees in the Argentine Mission fought from within the embassy to keep the Guatemalan Revolution alive. "Take all measures to assure the maintenance of the union movement," instructed a note probably written by the PGT leader Gutiérrez to a colleague, "even in this period of repression unleashed by imperialism: you must not faint, since the consciousness created in ten years cannot be destroyed just like that."[63]

Family members of some refugees were appalled by their relatives' decision to go into exile and did what they could to prevent them from leaving Guatemala. "Mr. Ambassador," wrote an anguished father to Julio Leguizamon on August 5, 1954:

> Permit me to interrupt your busy affairs to consult you about the case of my son . . . who since the fall of Colonel Árbenz's regime has been sheltered in the embassy of which you are in charge.
>
> The case is, Mr. Ambassador, that I want my son . . . to leave the asylum that he has generously been given there. He is no more than a youngster without any experience in life. He's not a politician, nor a leader of any significance. I believe that he has not caused harm to anyone, nor ever performed a public function.
>
> I think that his asylum is due, more than anything, to advice of some colleagues and friends on the one hand, and to a certain panic, product of the natural nervousness produced by the fall of the prior regime, but I sincerely don't see the need that he receive asylum.[64]

Argentine Embassy officials apparently had a different opinion of the young man. The Argentines included him in their list of "Communist Party activists" who had sought asylum in their embassy.[65]

Another worried parent honestly explained to the ambassador her son's real motive for requesting asylum:

> I am the mother of . . . , sheltered in your embassy, for reasons unknown. He has never had political connections that I know of. The only thing that I imagine is that he wants to gain the opportunity to see another country. He believes that he will get the same attentions and favors in another country as he has received in the embassy.[66]

For three hot and humid months, the refugees became increasingly bored and desperate as they waited within the embassy grounds for safe passage to Argentina. They began to fight among themselves as tensions increased, and after the first month passed under these conditions, Julia Urrutia became concerned about her parents' health.

Julia had decided not to seek asylum. She was relatively apolitical, and she had a husband and three children of her own to care for. Naively, she decided to seek assistance from Adan Serrano, the interior minister for the new military regime. Julia pleaded with the minister not to arrest her parents if they left the embassy and quietly returned home, forsaking all further political activity.

"Forget it," responded Serrano, "if your family leaves the embassy, we'll arrest them and send them to El Petén."[67]

Thus admonished, Julia knew that her parents' only option was to remain inside the Argentine Embassy and hope for safe conduct out of the country. Adan Serrano had a son named Jorge who would be president of Guatemala in 1992, when Maritza disappeared in Guatemala City.

In a list of suspected Communists, written in English and most probably circulated by the U.S. Embassy to the diplomatic missions where the Arbencistas had taken refuge, Ester de Urrutia was described as "Secretary for Peasant Affairs AFG (Communist-front women's organization)."[68] CIA Director Allen Dulles wanted the embassies to turn the refugees over to the junta since their crimes allegedly included "murder, torture and thievery while in power." The Guatemalan courts should prosecute these criminals. Dulles recommended that the junta limit its arrests to "hard core commies and sympathizers against whom criminal charges can be legally and clearly drawn. Incidentally," Dulles noted, "such charges should be quickly formulated in [the] most important cases to provide [a] legal basis."[69]

Colonel Castillo Armas was no stranger to exile, and he once benefited from the Latin American custom that embassy asylum and safe conduct passes were fair resolutions to political conflicts. So he resisted the pressures from the U.S. government. Castillo Armas eventually granted safe conduct passes to several hundred Arbencistas, and after three months of waiting, the Argentines finally flew nearly two hundred Guatemalan refugees, including Ester de Urrutia, her husband, and five of their seven children, as well as spouses and grandchildren, twenty-two Urrutias in all, to Buenos Aires.[70] Che Guevara never went to Argentina. Instead he made his way to Mexico, where he befriended a Cuban exile named Fidel Castro.[71]

In their first months in Buenos Aires, the Urrutia family was well treated by Juan Perón's right-wing government. General Perón was fiercely nationalistic and adamantly opposed to the U.S. government's interventions in Latin America. So in spite of the leftist politics of many of the refugees, Perón welcomed the Guatemalans as victims of U.S. imperialism. Adjustment to life in exile, however, wasn't easy. "My very dear daughter," wrote Ester to Julia on November 11, 1954:

> I hope that when you receive this, you'll be in good health and in union
> with your husband, little daughters, and your brother. . . . Until now,
> we haven't suffered anything, thanks to the government of Mr. President
> Perón, which for the past four months has given us everything in its
> power. We're still in the Immigrants' Hotel. We knew that the time limit
> in the hotel was one month, but since they've seen that we haven't found
> a place to lodge us, they haven't told us to move out. What saved us are
> the children; Argentina is for children and for them they find everything
> and we've been able to obtain everything.

Nevertheless, Ester noted that not all of the Guatemalan refugees acknowledged their debt to the Argentines:

> But as always, some people are ingrates and unappreciative. Many of
> those who arrived on the first flight behaved very badly. They got drunk
> and committed abuses and censurable acts in order to spoil things for
> those of us who came with the intent of working in Argentina. Who knows
> if the government will throw them out of the country and we hope it does
> since without these people maybe we can regain the confidence of the
> authorities. Thus, we are suffering the consequences of their behavior
> (all members of PGT). You know that the just pay for the sinners.

In spite of the generosity of the Argentine government, money was tight for the Urrutia family. But they never lost their faith:

Everything is a question of money, which the working class like us has the least of. In the end, God is everywhere and He's closest to those who suffer, and that's why we're calm. You know that we'll never deny anything, nor will we regret what we do. Thanks to our parents, who formed our characters, we're determined, and that's how we want you to be in the struggle for life.

For the men of the family, there was an interminable search for regular employment:

With respect to work, the only one who's working is [your brother] Héctor. Maybe your father, Miguel, and Edmundo will work next week in a publishing house where the three of them have been promised work. But if not, they'll find something on their own; they'll work somewhere else. There's a lot of work, yes there is, as laborers, but they earn more than office workers. Almost all of the big shots who came with pretensions of being intellectuals are factory helpers, or hod carriers. Here you work; you don't make money easily. Before five in the morning the streets are full of people running to work, like an anthill. The trains, the underground, the trolley buses, the microbuses, the collectives (all big trucks) go loaded with people rushing to work. The truth is when you see this activity, it makes you want to work. . . . There's all kinds of work here for everyone. Only the depraved and the idle don't work.

Of course, when work was over for the day, the exiles thought of their family back home in Guatemala:

At night when your father takes me out for a walk, to window-shop, we think of you a lot. There are some shoes and handbags that are so pretty that you'd go crazy if you saw them. And there's fabrics, blouses and so much that I can't describe it to you. . . .

We never stop thinking of you, not for a moment, and we'd like to have you by our side in order to be complete. You're all part of our lives and we don't lose the hope of telling you [someday] that we have a place to welcome you. But if you have secure work and you're calm, protect it and defend it and economize as much as you can. Because the more you have, the more you're worth.[72]

In time the Urrutias found a more permanent place to live. All the relatives rented a large house together in Buenos Aires. On Sundays the family socialized with other Guatemalan exiles, cooked Guatemalan dishes, and tried to maintain some sense of community. The leaders of PGT were less fortunate. They were detained in Villa de Voto, an Argentine prison, and treated "a little worse than dogs."[73] Fairly soon, Ester began delivering bags of food, clothing, cigarettes, and sweets to her imprisoned compatriots.

But Guatemalans at home were being imprisoned as well. While her husband, Humberto, was in Argentina, Laura Aldana was arrested and jailed three times for allegedly being a Communist. On the third occasion, Laura was held for nearly a month in the women's penitentiary. The conditions in the jail were bad and Laura saw the poor self-esteem of many of the prisoners. The women were not taking care of themselves and their clothes were always dirty. So Laura, true to the spirit of the Women's Alliance, began to organize the other prisoners, encouraging the women to wash their clothes more often, to keep themselves cleaner, and maintain their self-respect. "Revolutionary politics is humanitarian," Laura later explained. Eventually her captors told Laura that "it's better that you go," and she was released.[74]

After Jacobo Árbenz resigned and Colonel Castillo Armas took power, the new dictator convoked a special assembly to "reform" the Guatemalan Constitution. Castillo Armas appointed the most important anti-Communist leaders as delegates to the assembly, including Manuel Orellana and Oscar Conde. Orellana's daughters, Sonia and Sara, attended the inauguration of the assembly, and from a balcony they perused the delegates below them. Sonia had always been an admirer of Conde, but she didn't know what he looked like. "Which one is Oscar Conde?" she asked her sister.

"That skinny black one!" said Sara, pointing to the dark-skinned Conde, as usual in conversation with a number of people. After the inauguration, there was an elegant reception at the National Palace, and Orellana escorted his two daughters and introduced them to Oscar Conde. "How are you?" Conde asked the excited young women. "How do you feel?" Eventually Conde began coming to the house to court Sonia.

Archbishop Mariano Rossell married the couple in Guatemala City's cathedral in August 1955. In December 1956 their first son, Manuel Conde Orellana, was born. When Maritza disappeared in 1992, Manuel Conde led the Guatemalan government's negotiating team engaged in peace talks with Maritza's revolutionary Organización.

Buenos Aires, 1956 Ester de Urrutia and her family had become obsessed by the possibility of returning to Guatemala.[75] Finally, after two years in exile, President Castillo Armas announced that the refugees could return home.

By that time, Guatemala's wealthy elite had reclaimed most of the land provided by the Árbenz government to five hundred thousand beneficiaries during the agrarian reform program. Ester and Manuel had to sell their house in order to pay their debts, so they bought a machine for making shoes. For a while they made and sold shoes, but that business failed. Then they sold fish, also without much success. And in the early 1960s they would start a brewery. But that business failed too.

In spite of the financial problems, or perhaps because of them, Ester never strayed from her love of politics and social causes. During the late 1950s Ester organized Guatemala City's market women into small cooperatives, promoting her revolutionary belief that women had to participate in Guatemala's development.[76] On November 24, 1958, another daughter was born to Ester's son Edmundo and his wife, Pilar. They named her Maritza. It was an auspicious moment to be born in Latin America. The next month, in late December 1958, Fidel Castro led his guerrilla army down from the Sierra Maestra, overthrew the corrupt Batista regime, and launched the Cuban revolution.

TWO

THURSDAY MORNING AND AFTERNOON

They took the newspaper mask off Maritza's face and she saw the fair-skinned man. "I don't care if you see me," he taunted. "You can't do anything."[1] A shorter man, his face covered, held a video camera and a camera for still photographs. Reinforcing their power and Maritza's impotence, he filmed Maritza for about fifteen minutes as the fair-skinned man interrogated her that Thursday morning. The men covered Maritza's face again with the mask and brought her back to the garage. Tell us more about your brother, Edmundo René. He's a leftist, the men insisted, a Communist. Maritza swore that it wasn't true.

How did you meet your ex-husband? Maritza concocted a story about meeting Esteban in Mexico City, at a party at the research institute where her brother worked. Later on, she and Esteban began living together. Well, yes, Esteban was involved in an "organization," but Maritza didn't know much about that.[2] Besides, she hadn't seen Esteban in years. Who was this woman Argelia? Argelia sent Maritza's letters to Esteban but that was all Maritza knew about her.

The fair-skinned man showed Maritza a series of horrible photographs of dead bodies, the cadavers tortured and mutilated, and warned: "Perhaps one day your ex-husband will appear in one of these photographs. And the same thing could happen to you if you don't cooperate with us. We could kill you and throw you into a volcano, or a ditch or into the ocean. *Your family would never find you.*"[3]

Maritza was now a guest at a prison and interrogation center operated by the G-2, one of the Guatemalan army's intelligence sections.[4] Called the Island (*la Isla*) by its employees in order to hide the true nature of the work performed within its walls, the secret prison lay in zone six of Guatemala City, on the grounds of the Military Police headquarters.[5] From the Island, military intelligence officers and their subordinates investigated suspected *guerrilleros* and "terrorists" and performed abductions or assassinations of their targets.[6]

The man in charge of the Island when Maritza arrived there in 1992 was the portly major "Don Gaspar," also known to his men as "the Fat Man." For security reasons, all the members of military intelligence used nicknames instead of their real identities. One of Don Gaspar's subordinates was the fair-skinned man interrogating Maritza: Don Chando, a young army captain from the eastern Guatemalan town of Zacapa. Always dressed in civilian clothes, tall and slim, with long arms, honey-colored eyes, and straight, light brown hair that he parted to one side, Don Chando was very sure of himself, aggressive, meticulous, and highly disciplined.[7] He didn't have to speak twice when giving orders to the army specialists who served under him.

Don Chando and his men had investigated Maritza for about a month before they "disappeared" her. Every morning at 6:00 A.M., small groups of men would leave the Island and head across the city to Maritza's home and Sebastián's nursery school, from where they could easily follow her movements and observe her contacts. Once they were sure of Maritza's daily routine, members of the technical intelligence unit became involved. These soldiers secretly photographed Maritza and her family outside their home, using vehicles or hot dog stands as cover. The telephone was tapped and the family's mail was probably intercepted since military intelligence also had its agents working in the general post office. All of the information was passed on to Don Chando for his analysis.[8]

Finally, it was time to strike. The day before Maritza's disappearance, on Wednesday, July 22, Don Chando called his team into the "War Room." This was a large room within the Island where operations were planned. The walls were covered with maps of Guatemala and in the center was a great, glass-topped table, big enough for twenty-five people to gather round. Don Chando stood at a blackboard and diagrammed the next day's mission while Don Gaspar observed.

"You, Chino, you're there. You"—Don Chando pointed to "Ganzo"— "you're here in the car. And be careful once you grab her," Don Chando cautioned his men. "We're not going to beat her." This woman was important. Don Chando was already hoping that Maritza might serve as a source of information for the intelligence service. Perhaps she would collaborate with them.

Not all of Don Chando's men were quite pleased at that moment. There were a few new men in the unit and their commander wanted to test their mettle with Maritza's disappearance. That meant that more seasoned veterans of the Island, like the twenty-one-year-old army specialist "Coroncho," was excluded from the work he enjoyed. By the time Maritza disappeared, Coroncho had served at the Island for nearly three years. Coroncho's disgruntlement was based on economics rather than any perceived threat to his professional status. When low-ranking specialists carried out an operation well, they usually received a cash bonus. Frustrated and anxious to receive a piece of the pie, Coroncho sat in the War Room and listened as Don Chando gave instructions to the other soldiers. "Isn't there a bone for me?" Coroncho asked his commander. But the kidnap team was already full.

So Coroncho, who had performed some of the surveillance on Maritza, was waiting in the Island on Thursday morning when a trembling Maritza arrived at about 9:00 A.M. "What happened?" Coroncho asked "Sompopon," one of the men who grabbed Maritza and threw her into the car. "She left a shoe lying [in the street]," Sompopon replied worriedly. "There may be a problem there."[9]

Don Chando began the interrogation in the garage, accompanied by Catrín and Chesperito, two office workers who took notes for the report that they would compile about Maritza. "*Mi hijo. Mi hijo,*" Maritza murmured.

Coroncho watched until about noon, when Don Chando called all of his men together. This woman was very intelligent and very important, he explained. In case she was released, Don Chando did not want Maritza to be able to say *where* she was or *who* had detained her. So they had to be very careful. They couldn't make any unnecessary noise or use any names or nicknames. She could cause them a lot of trouble later on if they didn't take these precautions.

So the men knew that Maritza was no ordinary *subversiva,* and that physical torture was out for now. To extract information from a captured *guerrillero,* Don Chando would normally beat him or give him a ride in "the chair"—first he would be doused with water, then forced to sit in a metal chair while Don Chando touched him here and there with an electric current—before he ordered one of his men to get rid of the prisoner.

At about 3:00 P.M., the men told Maritza that they were going to take her outside to make another telephone call. They pushed her into a vehicle and held her head down toward the seat. From a public telephone in zone eighteen, Maritza called her home again as the men recorded the conversation. "I'm fine, Mamá. I'll be home soon. Don't try to do *anything*. You don't want trouble." As Maritza spoke, Don Chando held her by the arm. The others stood close by, all with guns underneath their jackets.

After the telephone call, the men brought Maritza back to the Island. The green backpacks and the weapons were still stacked against a wall. They brought Maritza to a room with a metal bed, several cots piled in a corner, a table, and a large desk with mattresses on top of it. The men forced Maritza to sit on the bed and handcuffed her right wrist to the bedside. Once more they put the handcuff over her sweater so as not to cut the skin.[10]

The interrogation began anew. Don Chando wanted to know about Maritza's family and about Esteban and his work with the Organización: "Your father is a subversive and your brother Edmundo René as well."

"That's not true! The government of the United States gave my brother a scholarship to study in New Mexico. And once AID sent him on a trip around the U.S.A.!"

"The people in AID are Communists too."

Maritza acknowledged that Esteban was still "in the revolution." But she was dedicated to raising her son. *Mi hijito. Yo quiero mi hijito.* Besides, Esteban already had another woman in his life. Apart from the letters that she wrote to Esteban, the men seemed to know little about Maritza. So as the hours passed, Maritza tried to mix facts with fiction, all the time minimizing her own political activities. She spent her days caring for her son, watching soap operas and cartoons on television, and visiting friends.[11]

At about 7:00 P.M., the men announced that Maritza had to make another phone call. She had to tell her mother that she was all right, and that she was making plans to leave the Organización. Don Chando and four others surrounded Maritza in a large gray luxury car and took her again to a public telephone. Coroncho stood close by the phone as Don Chando wrapped his arm around Maritza while she called her parents. "I'm fine, Mamá. Don't worry, Mamá, I'm fine." But Maritza would be making a long trip so her family would not see her for a long time. She would not be calling back. Once more, under orders from Don Chando, Maritza told her parents not to do anything on her behalf.[12]

"But where are you?" asked Maritza's mother. "Do they want a ransom?"

"Hold on a minute," replied Maritza as she covered the phone and turned to Don Chando. "What should I tell her?"

"No. Tell her that you're fine," said the captain. "And you're with friends."

"I'm fine, Mamá. I'm with some friends."

Now her mother was crying. "But where are you, *mi hija*? Tell me where you are! Don't hang up! I want to talk to you!"[13] But Don Chando cut off the call.

The men brought Maritza back to her room and handcuffed her to the bed again. She tried to negotiate with them. Argelia was going to contact her on August 3. If they let her go, Maritza would arrange a meeting for them with Argelia.

Impossible, said Don Chando. They already had Maritza under their control. If they let her go, Maritza could betray them.

Don Chando questioned Maritza again about the same subjects. What was her ex-husband doing? What were the names of the people who worked with Esteban? The interrogation continued until 4:00 A.M. and Maritza was exhausted and terrified. She wanted to see her little boy. "*Mi hijito* . . . Are they going to take me to call?" she asked Coroncho. "I want to speak with my mother!" "Look, you can't call now," said Don Chando. "I'm going to take you to call tomorrow."[14]

When the questions finally stopped, the men continued to try to break her. They brought a portable radio into the room and left it blasting at full volume. The radio also kept Maritza from hearing the dogs barking next door in the Military Police headquarters and blocked the noises of persons coming and going through the main entrance to the Island, which was close to her room. With the radio blasting, the men left the light on as Maritza lay handcuffed to the bed.

During the remainder of the early morning Don Chando's office helpers, Catrín and Chesperito, repeatedly entered and exited the room. They stopped by her bedside and told Maritza that she had to cooperate with them. She had to give them some information. Maritza talked about her son. "*Mi hijito*. I want to see my little boy." The men told her that she would call tomorrow. But first she had to talk. Did she have any contacts with the guerrillas planned soon? Tell them!

After Catrín and Chesperito left Maritza alone for a few minutes, she began to doze. Suddenly, from deep inside Maritza, a voice began to call her: Ruth. The voice called her urgently: Ruth! Maritza had not used the pseudonym Ruth in her revolutionary life for nearly a year. More recently, she had taken up the name "Camila," and her numerous contacts in the

Organización knew her by that name. But Maritza had continued to sign her letters to her ex-husband with the name Ruth, so her captors believed it was Maritza's pseudonym. If the fair-skinned man learned she was Camila, he would realize Maritza had many more contacts, and much more responsibility, within the Organización. Now Maritza had to be Ruth, to protect herself and to protect her *compañeros*. She shook herself awake and began to review the story she had told her interrogators: all of the lies and the parts that were true. Drilling the "details" into her memory over and over and over again. She had to be Ruth.

What will happen now? Maritza asked herself. Will they torture me? Rape me? Kill me?[15] She felt like she was in a hole.

During the late 1950s and early 1960s when Maritza was a little girl, Guatemala's Communist Party, the PGT, survived only as a clandestine organization.[16] Maritza's grandmother Ester, then nearly seventy, would take two of her young grandsons out at night to post antigovernment propaganda around Guatemala City. Risking arrest, they secretly roamed around the old bus terminal in zone four, where there were few lights and fewer police, and hung posters bearing political slogans and the likeness of Fidel Castro.

Ester also carried PGT mail secretly to revolutionaries still in exile in Mexico. On one occasion, border officials searched her and found her secret mail and propaganda. Fortunately for Ester, although this offense might have cost her her life, the man who searched Ester knew her. And he told her: "Doña Estercita, don't do this. You're endangering your life. If someone else had searched you—*who knows what they'd do*. You're already old—don't mess with this."[17] But politics and the struggle itself, *la lucha*, gave life to Ester.

In 1961 the central committee of the PGT, inspired by Fidel Castro's successes in Cuba, issued a resolution that defined armed struggle as the "principal road" for the Guatemalan Revolution.[18] In December 1962 members of the PGT and a group of former army officers who had rebelled against the military regime formed the Fuerzas Armadas Rebeldes (forces of armed rebels), known as the FAR.[19]

Nostalgia for *la lucha* was in the air.[20] Like Ester, her son Edmundo (Maritza's father) could never completely divorce himself from the "lost revolution." So Edmundo joined the FAR, and from the time Maritza was four or five, strange "uncles" and "cousins" would periodically sleep in the Urrutias' house. Sometimes the men would play with Maritza and once, underneath a pillow, she found a pistol that one of these uncles had left behind. Maritza learned quickly not to talk about the visitors or their activities. And *la lucha* began to be vital for her as well.

The neighbors labeled the Urrutias "Reds" and one night during the mid-1960s, while he watched television with his son, Edmundo René, Edmundo Urrutia heard the unmistakable metallic sound of bullets being loaded into rifle chambers outside his front door. When young Edmundo René opened the door, the police rushed in and began searching the house.[21] Maritza's sister, Carolina, then about ten, sneaked into her father's darkroom to take down the photographs of Che Guevara and the Guatemalan revolutionary leaders Yon Sosa and Turcios, which hung there. But once immersed in the darkness, Carolina could not find them on the wall. The police officers entered the darkroom and turned on the light, but they didn't recognize the men in the photographs.[22]

In 1964 Ester de Urrutia fell ill with ovarian cancer. Even on her deathbed, Ester was still obsessed by politics, and her friends brought her packets of revolutionary propaganda to read. When Ester passed away, a number of PGT leaders left their hiding places in the middle of the night and came to her wake. Bernardo Alvarado Monzón was there, the former secretary general of the party who accompanied Ester to Czechoslovakia years earlier when Jacobo Árbenz was president. Mario Silva Jonama, another founding member of the PGT, came too. Both men would disappear in 1972 after the police raided a secret PGT meeting and abducted them.[23] After Ester's wake, hundreds of women—"blocks and blocks of women," wives, mothers, and children who had come to Ester for help over the years and had not forgotten her kindness— accompanied the casket to the cemetery.[24]

In 1966 Edmundo René, then a ripe old thirteen, joined the FAR. For the most part, he handed out flyers and leaflets on the streets and at his middle school. But in 1969 when he was sixteen and Maritza ten, Edmundo René left home and became a full time "professional" member of the FAR,[25] joining thousands of brave and idealistic young people who threw themselves into armed struggle in Latin America during the 1960s.

Together with his *compañeros* in the FAR, many of them not much older than himself, Edmundo René believed they would create a new society. With the coming of socialism, there would be no more suffering, no more conflicts, no more imperialism. They would accomplish in Guatemala what Fidel Castro and Che Guevara had achieved in Cuba. It was a passionate, messianic movement and all aspects of life unrelated to the revolution were pedestrian.[26]

Edmundo René's decision to take part in the armed struggle provoked a major family crisis amid concerns for his safety. Both of his parents opposed the idea, and Edmundo Urrutia wrote a letter to the commander of his son's guerrilla unit, asking that the young man be permitted to leave the Organización. The commander was unmoved: "We're going to make him into a good revolutionary."[27] So Edmundo René spent the next year as a full-time member of the FAR, performing surveillance, stealing cars, and supporting other revolutionary tasks. At the same time, emerging right-wing death squads dedicated themselves to eradicating anyone suspected of belonging to a revolutionary group.

One day in 1970, as a test of Edmundo Rene's revolutionary courage, his superior ordered him to kill a man suspected of collaborating with the army. Maritza's brother could not carry out the order. Perhaps someday *he* would be just as weak and vulnerable as the collaborator. Would anyone have pity for *him?* The deed was eventually done by a *compañero* who seemed nonplussed by his own homicidal behavior: "Red cells. White cells," the man remarked as he wiped blood off his hand with his handkerchief. "They're all the same!" Edmundo René decided that he wasn't cut out to be a revolutionary.

His *compañeros* spent three months trying to change Edmundo René's mind with revolutionary literature and discussions about Guatemala's poverty and oppression. But their efforts were no match for the deep well of his emotions, and so the guerrillas reluctantly let Edmundo René go. He was traumatized but fortunate to survive the armed conflict. Shortly after he left the FAR, his first girlfriend and a group of young *compañeros* blew themselves up as the police closed in on their safe house. One by one, the remainder of the guerrilla unit were captured and killed.[28]

After leaving the FAR, Edmundo René entered the National University of San Carlos (USAC). Edmundo René studied Marxist philosophy during the early 1970s, and he married for the first time in April 1975.

By mid-1980, as the university moved further to the left, Edmundo René was a Marxist professor in a university where virtually everyone, students and teachers, belonged to one revolutionary organization or another. One night in June Edmundo René's oldest friend came to his home at 11:00 P.M. "Edmundo," he warned, "you have to leave the country because you're gonna be killed." When Edmundo René's wife sought out the source of this message, she was informed that the army had already tried to kill her husband twice but had somehow failed each attempt. She returned home and said: "Edmundo, you *really* have to leave!"[29] So, at age twenty-six, more than two decades after living in Argentina with his parents and grandparents, Edmundo René went to Mexico and began his second period of exile.

After five difficult years in Mexico, Edmundo René and his wife divorced. His political views also underwent a transformation as he began to question his once dogmatic Marxist beliefs. Eventually he decided to renounce Marxism. After completing a master's degree in political science, Edmundo René returned to Guatemala in 1987 and began to teach once again at USAC.

In October 1988 the U.S. Agency for International Development offered Edmundo René a one-month tour of the United States. The former Marxist revolutionary traveled in AID-sponsored luxury from Miami to Washington, D.C., Chicago, Albuquerque, and San Francisco. When Edmundo René returned to Guatemala, he knew that he wanted to spend more time in the States. The opportunity came in 1989 with a Fulbright Scholarship to study political science at the University of New Mexico.

After three years in Albuquerque, Edmundo René and his North American fiancée, Katharine "Kappy" Riker, returned to Guatemala in 1992. Apart from some work with a research institute, Edmundo René returned to his first love: teaching at USAC. He and Kappy moved into a cute house in the quiet Colonia San Cristobal. Life was going well until the phone rang about 3:00 P.M. on July 23. It was Pilar, his mother: "You already know what happened?"

"No," he answered.

"We need your help."

The strain in Pilar's voice revealed the crisis: Maritza had been kidnapped or killed. Edmundo René hung up and turned to Kappy: "I have to go to my parents' house immediately. Something's happened to Maritza." He thought again. "Get a pencil," he said, "and write down everything I tell you."[30]

A number of people had witnessed Maritza's kidnapping that morning. One was a military policeman guarding a factory located near Walt Disney School. Then there was a maid who lived in a house close to the scene.[31] When Maritza was thrown into the car, leaving her shoe in the street, the witnesses all looked at each other as if to ask, *Should we tell someone or not?* The maid ran back home after the car drove away, but her employer ordered her not to say anything.

A few mothers taking their children to the nursery school also observed the crime. Diana passed Maritza on the sidewalk that morning as Diana walked her daughter to nursery school and Maritza was on her way home. Suddenly, another mother from Walt Disney School, looking very frightened, came running up with her son from behind Diana. "They grabbed a mother from the school!" she cried. "There were four men! They threw her in a car! She left a shoe lying in the street!" The two women ran to the nursery school, dragging their children behind them, to report the crime.[32]

Another mother who witnessed the kidnapping had recognized Maritza. She rushed back to Maritza's neighborhood and told one of the neighbors what she had seen. Maritza's father, Edmundo, was making breakfast when the neighbor knocked on his door: "Don 'Mundo, they just kidnapped Maritza!"[33]

Edmundo rushed to Walt Disney School to see if Sebastián was there. Perhaps he had been kidnapped too. Fortunately, his grandson was safe but the school was in an uproar. A group of six or seven women who witnessed the kidnapping had come running into the office. They thought the victim was a mother from the school, but they didn't know her name. All of the women recalled different details. One described Maritza being thrown into a car, another that Maritza had screamed, another that they grabbed Maritza by the hair. Several mothers mentioned that one of Maritza's shoes was knocked into the street.[34] Rumors began to circulate that one of the students had been kidnapped and some mothers pulled their children out of school.

Edmundo told the teachers to keep Sebastián inside, and then he followed Maritza's route back home, walking out to Fifth Avenue, where he found his daughter's shoe in the middle of the road.[35] Edmundo picked it up and brought it home.

In 1992 Gustavo Meoño commanded the EGP's urban division; he used the nom de guerre "Manolo." An hour or two after Maritza's kidnapping, her superior in the Organización informed Meoño that the army had taken Maritza.

Tall, thin, and charismatic, Meoño joined the revolutionary movement in 1967 when he was eighteen.[36] Meoño was one of the "uncles" and "cousins" who found shelter with the Urrutia family during Maritza's childhood. He first met Maritza when she was a little girl "in bobby socks." Meoño knew that when *guerrilleros* were disappeared, they were almost always tortured and killed.

But Meoño had little time to mourn for Maritza because his first responsibility as commander was to protect the other members of the Organización. Who else might be at risk? Meoño grilled his *compañeros*. Did Maritza carry a diary with names, addresses, and telephone numbers? Was she carrying documents with her that might implicate other *compañeros*? Did Maritza have files in her home that would have to be removed and destroyed? Maritza had many contacts scattered throughout Guatemala City. What could they do to prevent Maritza's disappearance from becoming the start of a chain of disappearances?

Reflexively, from years of experience as an urban guerrilla commander, Meoño started giving orders. Some safe houses had to be abandoned. "Don't be taken by surprise! Be alert! Don't have EGP papers or documents in your possession! Have a logical explanation for your activities in case you're questioned." The *compañeros* who had the most direct contact with Maritza would go into hiding.

In addition to his security concerns, Meoño also had to consider the EGP's political response. What could they do immediately to publicize Maritza's disappearance? After losing so many friends and *compañeros* over the years in similar operations, Meoño and his colleagues had no doubt that army intelligence was responsible. The EGP did not want this crime to remain in the shadows, where the army could continue to act with impunity. "The goal was to make them see that the political price they'd have to pay for the disappearance, kidnapping, and eventually the *murder* of Maritza would be very high. For the state in general and for the army in particular." And perhaps if the authorities realized how high the cost of Maritza's death might be, they would release her alive.

So the revolutionaries lobbied their contacts in USAC, in trade unions, and in the hundreds of small nongovernmental organizations scattered around Guatemala City to agitate on Maritza's behalf. Many Guatemalans who were not part of the insurgency, but who supported its ideals, understood that a fast reaction might be the difference between life and death. Soon the Guatemalan press began reporting about Maritza's disappearance, which encouraged Maritza's friends to redouble their efforts.

Meoño also communicated via radio and the media with other EGP leaders based in Mexico. His *compañeros* began to drum up international support for Maritza. Phone calls, faxes, and letters began to flood the Guatemalan government and its embassies abroad.[37]

Meoño and others spent all of Thursday and Thursday evening alerting Maritza's contacts and moving people out of their homes and workplaces into safe houses.[38] By 9:00 P.M. all of her contacts were secure.

Maritza's interrogators would break her, but she resisted long enough for her comrades to protect themselves.

When Edmundo Urrutia got back home on Thursday afternoon, his wife, Pilar, told him that Maritza had telephoned. *Now* what should they do? Should they call Edmundo René? At first, they couldn't bring themselves to call their son. Edmundo René had warned them repeatedly that something like this would happen to Maritza. His parents had ignored him and now they felt ashamed. Edmundo René had suffered so much during his brief participation in the revolution. *"Red cells. White cells. They're all the same!"* Now the army had taken his *hermanita*.

Then came Maritza's three o'clock phone call. Once again, she told her parents not to do anything but it was clear what had happened to her. Shortly after three, Maritza's anguished parents finally called Edmundo René.

"All I thought of was '*how* could I save her life?'"[39] As Edmundo René dictated, Kappy wrote down all of the friends and contacts that he would visit to publicize Maritza's disappearance: journalists, the U.S. Embassy, academic institutions, television stations. By Thursday evening, students and professors at USAC formed a commission to publicize Maritza's kidnapping. The members of the commission (some of them also members of insurgent groups) began organizing students and contacting the media. The following day the Guatemalan press would carry a detailed account of the kidnapping, describing Maritza as a former anthropology student at USAC, and calling on the national and international communities to support her prompt return.[40]

Shortly after 7:00 P.M. Maritza's parents received her third telephone call. Later that evening, two army officers from the president's high command arrived at the house. After attaching a special recording device to the family's phone, the officers counseled them not to publicize the kidnapping to avoid harming Maritza.[41] After the army officers left the house, two officials from the human rights ombudsman's office arrived to speak with Maritza's parents. The ombudsman is charged with protecting the rights of all Guatemalan citizens and has the obligation to investigate and denounce cases of human rights abuse. In July 1992 the ombudsman was Ramiro de León Carpio, an energetic attorney and politician. It was an open secret that de León Carpio hoped to use the ombudsman's office as a springboard to the National Palace.

Edmundo Urrutia was upset but very gentlemanly as always. He sat on Maritza's bed with one of the officials and talked about his daughter. She didn't have any political connections, Edmundo explained. Maritza dedicated herself to simple tasks and to her son. There was no reason for anyone to kidnap her. The army's tap on the telephone seemed to terrify Edmundo—suppose one of Maritza's *compañeros* were to call?

That same evening, Edmundo Urrutia and one of his nephews drove to one of Guatemala City's more affluent neighborhoods. The nephew belonged to the same Protestant church as Carlos Arana Osorio, a retired army general and dictator who first won a national reputation as the "butcher of Zacapa" and "the Jackal" during the brutal counterinsurgency campaigns of the 1960s. Given his own leftist politics, it had never occurred to Edmundo to contact General Arana. But when his nephew broached the idea, Edmundo understood that he had to do everything possible to try to save his daughter's life. He had to literally knock on the doors of power, and it was rumored that the aging Arana still asserted considerable influence within the armed forces.

General Arana, looking weak and ill, and Edmundo's nephew embraced like brothers when the general received them. Arana led them into an ostentatious living room where they sat among a collection of antique guns lining the walls. For a moment Edmundo, the old revolutionary, pondered the ruthless history of the old soldier facing him. The Jackal. But at the same time he thought of his daughter. He had to try to help Maritza.

Arana listened patiently as Edmundo and his nephew explained the reason for their visit. The general promised to do what he could on Maritza's behalf, and he made a phone call. "This is General Arana speaking." Edmundo had the impression that Arana was calling a military installation, and Arana became angry when the other party apparently did not recognize his name. "You don't realize that this is the ex-President?" It seemed that the person Arana wished to contact was not available and finally the general hung up. But he promised Edmundo that he would do everything he could to obtain information concerning Maritza.[42]

Later that Thursday evening Edmundo René and Kappy drove to the home of one of Edmundo René's childhood friends, the son of a very wealthy family. Edmundo René thought that this would be a safe place to stay because the family was part of Guatemala's conservative elite. But neither Edmundo René's friend nor his family was at home. Attempting to avoid surveillance and in need of a phone line that would not be tapped, Edmundo René and Kappy started sleeping in different locations, trying to protect themselves as they struggled to help Maritza.[43]

THREE

FRIDAY

July 24, 1992

In the morning the men brought Maritza a cold breakfast. They removed her handcuffs, brought her to a bathroom where she had a chance to bathe, and then handcuffed her to the bed again. The men alternated the wrist that bore the metal cuff. They told Maritza to keep the newspaper on her face at all times, even while she "slept."

The interrogation began again. The men wanted to know about Maritza's relationship with her ex-husband. Esteban was an important man. Maritza must have more information. No, she didn't have any more facts to give them.

The men started to get angry. If Maritza did not cooperate with them, they would kill her. They had Maritza under their control, and they could do what they wanted with her. It would be sad if her little boy grew up without a mother.[1]

Maritza began to tell the men more details, some true, others false, about her life with Esteban in Mexico. They met in Mexico in 1986 and started living together later that year. Esteban worked with the Organización, and Maritza worked with him. All she did was review the press for articles about Guatemala and pass them on to Esteban. That was all she did. She really only worked for the EGP because of her relationship with Esteban. As a matter of fact, Esteban's colleagues had criticized her for not getting more involved.[2]

Maritza's evasive responses began to anger her interrogators. "We've treated you well. We haven't hurt you," said the fair-skinned man, Don

Chando. "[But] when we need violence, we use it, and we can be very hard. I have a big heart and your tears move me, but I want you to know I can be hard. We can make sure you never see your son again."[3]

Maritza told them that she wanted to cooperate with them. There wasn't much that she could do to help them, but perhaps Maritza could arrange a meeting with Argelia. Although Argelia did not exist, Maritza told the men that her next contact with the woman would be on August 3, in the cafeteria of CEMACO, a large department store. If the men let her go, Maritza would keep the appointment and lead them to Argelia.[4] Maritza knew the men would not want to hold her for ten days until August 3 if there was a chance of catching a "bigger fish." Or if they did keep her until August 3, perhaps she would have a chance to flee inside the store. Even if they killed her there in public, at least people would know what happened to her. She would not just disappear.

The men wanted to know more about Argelia. Their meetings were very short, Maritza told them. They only met when Maritza gave Argelia letters for Esteban. Yes, Maritza knew that Argelia worked for the Organización, but she didn't know anything more about Argelia's role. Argelia had asked Maritza to work with her, but Maritza always told Argelia she didn't have time.[5]

The interrogation continued all day Friday. Around 5:00 P.M. the fair-skinned man told Maritza that they were going to bring in a new man and *he* would not treat her as kindly as they had. Maritza was exhausted, nervous, and shaking. "Please!" she shouted, "Don't bring the other man!"[6]

Maritza began to beg them not to hurt her. She would cooperate; she would do anything she could. Yes, she worked for the Organización, but now she wanted amnesty. Guatemalan law provided that members of insurgent organizations could receive "legal amnesty" from the government, vitiating their "criminal" participation in "subversive" activities, so that they could reincorporate into civil society.[7] Couldn't they give her amnesty? Maritza was desperately saying whatever came to her mind, imploring the men not to hurt her.

Now the fair-skinned man began to relax a bit. He told Maritza that perhaps she could receive amnesty. But they would have to make a deal. If the men arranged to get her amnesty, Maritza would have to denounce the EGP and work for the Independent Movement of the Masses, known as MAM. This was a government-sponsored organization for former insurgents who received amnesty. Maritza could work for MAM, suggested the fair-skinned man, and raise her voice against the subversives. She could go to Geneva, for example, in order to speak on the government's behalf at the United Nations Human Rights Commission.[8]

All these ideas made Maritza feel dazed. *I only want to be with my son. My sister and I were going to open a nursery school together . . .* The fair-skinned man assured Maritza that she could have Sebastián with her. She protested that this plan would not be good for her son. But the men reassured her. She could raise her little boy and maintain a quiet and peaceful life.

As the conversation continued within the room, a door opened in a passageway that connected the Island with the grounds of the Military Police headquarters. The door was supposed to be locked at all times, but the Island's switchboard operator had carelessly left it unlocked. Coroncho watched as one of the commanders of the Military Police, clad in his dress uniform and shiny, polished shoes, stepped through the door and into a corridor of the Island. Don Gaspar intercepted the officer in the hallway and led him into Maritza's room.[9]

The interrogators told Maritza that they were going to bring her a pencil and paper, and she would write down everything that she knew, including what she had told them about Esteban. The fair-skinned man left the room and then some other men entered. Although Maritza had the newspaper over her face, she could see a bit toward the floor, watching the feet of the people who entered the room. She saw the shoes and trousers of a man who apparently had not entered previously. His pants were khaki and his black shoes were polished shiny, lustrous. So Maritza knew that he was an army officer.[10]

On Friday morning Edmundo René continued to make inquires on Maritza's behalf all around Guatemala City. He had an old friend who worked for *El Grafico,* one of Guatemala's leading daily newspapers. Could the newspaper print a story about Maritza? The reporter was sympathetic, and an article and an editorial appeared the next day.[11]

Edmundo René had a short speech prepared, and after visiting *El Grafico* he gave interviews to Guatemala's other major papers, *La Prensa Libre* and *Siglo Veintiuno.* He spoke to members of the Guatemalan Congress, asking the politicians to do what they could on Maritza's behalf. Soon newspaper and television reporters began to arrive at his parents' house, and Edmundo René and his father gave repeated interviews.

One of their cousins was a tough army colonel who worked in the Defense Ministry in Guatemala City. Edmundo René visited his cousin on

Friday to see if he could do anything for Maritza, but the colonel cynically blamed the Guatemalan insurgent groups for Maritza's kidnapping.[12]

Carolina, Maritza's sister, also lobbied on behalf of her younger sibling. For years Carolina had taught at the Colegio Asunción, a private school serving a mixture of upper-class and military families. When the granddaughter of a powerful army colonel was in kindergarten several years before, Carolina was her teacher. A decade earlier the colonel had served on a military junta during part of the Guatemalan army's "scorched-earth" counterinsurgency campaign. But grandchildren can transcend politics, and the colonel and his wife had some affection for the Urrutia family.[13] Although retired, the colonel was still well connected within the armed forces, and Carolina asked for his help.[14]

Very few of the Urrutias were practicing Catholics, but Edmundo René left no stone unturned. On Friday afternoon he came to the Archdiocese of Guatemala's Human Rights Office, commonly referred to by its Spanish acronym, the ODHA. It was located in the archbishopric, a massive stone building built in the early nineteenth century, next to the cathedral and just across the plaza from the National Palace. The ODHA promoted greater respect for human rights in Guatemala and whenever possible assisted the victims of Guatemala's civil war. Edmundo René tried to speak with the director, Ronalth Ochaeta, but Ochaeta had another commitment. "Daniel, can you speak with this guy?" Ochaeta asked me. "He says that they kidnapped his sister."

I was the ODHA's "international presence," a young attorney from the United States who (the hope was) provided greater security for the exposed Guatemalan lawyers who worked in the office. Inexperienced, idealistic, and naive, I had only a superficial understanding of the brutal politics of Guatemala's civil war. Consequently, I was ill prepared to help liberate a disappeared *guerrillera*. I was swimming in waters too deep for my understanding or experience, a dynamic that could exacerbate the danger to Maritza and her family.

Speaking softly, Edmundo René explained the facts of Maritza's kidnapping the day before and described Maritza's telephone calls to her family. I tried to clarify *why* Maritza would be a target but Edmundo René's responses were vague. While living in Mexico during the 1980s, Maritza continued her anthropology studies, he explained. "There's no indication that she was *systematically* involved in political activities" during that time.[15]

What about after Maritza's return to Guatemala? She has been working for a psychologist giving aptitude tests and teaching in a primary school, Edmundo René explained. According to his parents, Maritza has been a "homebody" with her son. As far as they knew, Maritza had no ties with political organizations in Guatemala. Skeptical, I pressed Edmundo René for more details about Maritza's life. Was Maritza having problems with a jealous boyfriend? No, she didn't have these kinds of personal problems. Then *why* would she disappear? Edmundo René stuck to his version of his sister's life. He was not politically active at that time, Edmundo René explained, and he had the same perception regarding Maritza. But he gave me a funny look. "The family," he noted, "has historically been to the left."[16]

Two years later Edmundo René recalled why he lied to me when we met in the ODHA. "I needed someone to help me," he explained. "I was incredibly worried. I couldn't say clearly what I knew because the guerrillas' law is that these things happen if you're one of them—that is, *compañeros* are captured, tortured, and killed. And I was afraid that if I told you the truth, you wouldn't help me because of the degree of her involvement with the guerrillas. Or, if the information had filtered out [of the ODHA], it could affect her. The army might say: 'OK, we've confirmed that she's a *guerrillera*,' and they'd kill her."[17]

So Edmundo René was in a bind. "I had to communicate that it was a political problem—but I couldn't tell you everything. That's why I tried to say it in a subtle way. When you asked me about problems with boyfriends, I thought: 'God, they're gonna think this is a personal thing.' And I wanted you to know that she was kidnapped for political reasons."[18]

After Edmundo René left the ODHA, I prepared a writ of habeas corpus, which was filed by fax that afternoon at Guatemala's Supreme Court of Justice. The writ requested that the judicial system take all necessary steps to locate Maritza. It was a reasonable but uninspired effort, given the army's power and the legal system's weakness and the fact that few such writs produced any results. I also sent out an "Urgent Action" request to the ODHA's support network of international human rights organizations. After briefly describing Maritza, the details of the kidnapping, and her subsequent calls to her family, the Urgent Action asked the international community to pressure the Guatemalan authorities to investigate her kidnapping.[19] But it was now after 5:00 P.M. on the East Coast of the United States, where most of the ODHA's counterparts were located, and early Saturday morning in London.

After he left the ODHA, Edmundo René joined Kappy at his parents' house. Aware that the house phone was tapped, they went to GUATEL, the public telephone office in zone eight. They called Kappy's friend Susanne McShane, in Albuquerque, New Mexico. After explaining what had happened to Maritza, Edmundo René and Kappy asked Susanne to inform their mutual friend Bill Robinson. Robinson was another Albuquerque resident who had political connections as well as ties to international human rights groups and the media. Edmundo René was tense and paranoid, and he was convinced that the woman at the switchboard was eavesdropping on their conversation.[20]

In this conversation as well as in many others, Edmundo René would tell his contacts in the United States that Maritza was a "human rights activist" and an "anthropology student." "I didn't want to say that she was a *guerrillera*. I thought that it would be harder [for the Americans] to help her [if they knew that Maritza was a *guerrillera*]."[21]

Friday, 7 A.M. Far to the north of Guatemala City, in a region called the Ixil, the rugged mountains of the Sierra de las Cuchumatanes transverse the province of El Quiché. Wave after wave of steep green ridges rising three thousand meters above sea level crash into sheer valleys that fall to just five hundred meters and flow like a great sea toward the horizon. Cut by driving rivers and bordered by steaming jungles, the range forms an almost impenetrable wall that is perfect for guerrilla warfare. In 1992 this was EGP territory, and the army could enter it only at its peril. The terrain belonged to the fighters of the EGP's Ho Chi Minh front.

Carlos Barrientos Aragón, the father of Maritza's son, worked with the leadership of the Ho Chi Minh front on political and military issues. On Friday morning, in one of the EGP camps strategically placed to guard against army incursions, Barrientos borrowed a colleague's radio. He wanted to listen to the 7:00 A.M. news that the insurgents could pick up from Guatemala City. There was a garbled notice about the kidnapping of a university student. The announcer said the victim's name was "Maritza," but the woman's last names were reversed. So Barrientos wasn't sure if his former wife had disappeared or not.

Worried, Barrientos listened to the news broadcast at 12:00 P.M. as well. The newscaster referred to "Dr. Edmundo Urrutia, brother of the kidnapping victim" and confirmed Barrientos's fear that Maritza had been kidnapped.

But, Barrientos wondered, what about Sebastián? Barrientos had joined the EGP in 1980 and had survived the worst years of the army's counterinsurgency campaigns. He had lost many *compañeros* and was familiar with the methods used by the G-2, the army intelligence section, to extract information. Barrientos knew that the army would use children in order to pressure their parents for information. But the radio broadcast said nothing about his son.[22]

And what had they done to Maritza? Barrientos hoped that her body would show up soon. If it didn't, then Barrientos assumed that Maritza would be tortured for a long time and would simply disappear forever, leaving her relatives to wonder about her fate. Or perhaps her army captors would break Maritza and force her to work for them. And she would become one of the "living dead," condemned to serve the army forever as a spy and source of information about her revolutionary peers. If they killed Maritza soon, then neither she nor her loved ones would have to suffer as much.[23]

Friday, early evening The fair-skinned man, Don Chando, entered the room and sat down next to Maritza. Although her face was covered, Maritza recognized his voice as Don Chando began to tell Maritza about their plan. They were going to film a video. The video would show Maritza giving a declaration, which he would dictate to her.

Maritza's declaration would begin with a greeting and an expression of thanks to the many people who had been concerned about her, including retired General Carlos Arana, General José Domingo García, the defense minister, the retired colonel whose granddaughter had been a student of Carolina Urrutia, and others. Then Maritza would speak about her exile in Mexico and meeting her ex-husband there in 1986. She would say that her ex-husband was an EGP member and that Maritza also began to work for the EGP after they met. She would give the names of some of the people with whom she had worked in the Organización, including Esteban's true name.

Maritza, Don Chando continued, would express her regret for causing so much worry for her family, and state that she wanted to leave the EGP. She would say that she had left home for a while in order to "legalize" her situation. Maritza would ask forgiveness from the Organización but insist that she wanted to leave in order to end the battle that had caused so much damage to her country. She would also call on her *compañeros* to give up the armed struggle. At the end of the declaration, Maritza would ask the government for amnesty and protection.[24]

The men brought Maritza to the bathroom, gave her a comb, and told her to fix her hair and get ready to make the video. Then they brought her to another room with wooden chairs and a blackboard. The men wrote pieces of the declaration on the blackboard and began filming Maritza as she read from the board. There wasn't much space on the board, so the men had to write a few sentences, film Maritza as she spoke, then stop while they wrote a few more sentences. Finally, in frustration, the cameraman complained that it wasn't going to work; it was too slow to work like that.[25]

One of the men said that they were going to stop filming for now. Maritza had to make another telephone call. She was going to call her father and tell him that she was fine and was going to Mexico for four days to see Esteban. She was told to ask whether her parents could take care of Sebastián for her. Maritza was exhausted and asked what time it was. Someone responded that it was midnight. Then they put Maritza into a large gray car. In about fifteen minutes, the car stopped at a phone booth in zone eighteen. As in the earlier calls, the men stayed close to Maritza as she spoke, and she realized that there was no hope of escape. She called her father and told him what her captors had told her to say.[26]

When the men brought Maritza back to her bare room, Don Chando realized that the radio wasn't there. He yelled at those who had removed it: "The radio isn't for you guys; it's for her!" Don Chando made sure that someone returned the radio to Maritza's room, and that it played at full volume. The music was mainly *ranchera,* a style akin to Mexican country and western. The station periodically announced the time, so Maritza was conscious of the hours as the night passed. The noise from the radio prevented her from sleeping and kept her constantly nervous and trembling.[27]

Worse still, for the second night in a row, strange men entered and exited the room throughout the night. They burst into the room, came close to Maritza's bed, and leaned over her. With the newspaper over her head, Maritza saw only their feet. Are they going to attack me? And the radio blared at full volume.

ALBUQUERQUE, NEW MEXICO

Bill Robinson and Edmundo René Urrutia were old friends. The two met in Albuquerque in 1990 when Edmundo René was a Fulbright Scholar and Robinson was finishing his doctorate at the University of New Mexico and they lived in the same apartment complex. Robinson had had an unusual undergraduate career. He left the United States when he was eighteen and studied journalism in Africa, first in Kenya and later in Nigeria. Many of Robinson's student friends were participants in South Africa's African National Congress, as well as in Zimbabwe's liberation movement. African nations were still emerging from colonialism at that time and Robinson studied the histories and legacies of the colonial era. He came to understand third-world perspectives on international economics and politics, particularly issues of Europe and the United States' dominance over the third world.

Robinson finished his studies in Africa just as the struggle to overthrow the Somoza regime in Nicaragua was coming to a head in the late 1970s. After a brief period in Costa Rica studying Spanish, he arrived in Nicaragua shortly after the Sandinistas came to power and took a job as a journalist for the Nicaraguan News Agency. In 1987 the Sandinista government hired Robinson as an adviser on U.S. policy issues to the Nicaraguan Foreign Ministry. He worked out of the Nicaraguan Embassy in Washington, D.C. and also served as the Washington editor for the Nicaraguan News Agency.[28] Robinson loved the Central American region and was married to a Nicaraguan woman.

Robinson had met Maritza on a trip to Guatemala, and the two became friends. From his old days as a policy adviser and journalist, Robinson had sources in the State Department, the media, as well as in the community of nongovernmental organizations (NGOs) that focused on human rights issues. So apart from his personal ties to the Urrutia family, Robinson had the ability to mobilize support for Maritza from within the United States.[29]

After receiving the call from Susanne McShane on Friday night, Bill Robinson did not stop for two weeks. Working around the clock to create political support on Maritza's behalf, he would eventually contact dozens of NGOs, representatives of the U.S. State Department, the U.S. Congress, the Organization of American States, as well as Guatemalan government officials. The human rights NGOs were largely sympathetic to Robinson's pleas for assistance, in part because Maritza's phone calls to her family indicated that she might still be alive. There was a chance that something could be done to help her. Soon support for Maritza would pour out of many corners of the United States, the nation that had been Maritza's enemy since she joined the revolution in 1982.

Concurrently, Robinson used his contacts in Washington, D.C., to ascertain the important issues at the time for U.S.-Guatemalan diplomatic relations.[30] Within the first few days of Maritza's disappearance, Robinson learned that the two governments were involved in "quiet and delicate negotiations" concerning the future roles that the United States and Guatemala would play in the control of narcotics trafficking in Central America.[31] Maritza's disappearance, and the ensuing publicity and

political pressures brought by human rights activists on both governments, was particularly ill timed for U.S. and Guatemalan interests in
that regard.

With the assistance of William Stanley, one of Edmundo René's professors at the University of New Mexico, Robinson was able to obtain
a letter on Maritza's behalf from Richard Peck, the president of the university, to Guatemalan President Jorge Serrano. Moreover, Stanley asked
a colleague with connections within the Guatemalan military to make
inquiries about Maritza, hoping that even a "friendly inquiry" through
military channels might reinforce the message that Maritza should not
be harmed. Stanley's colleague eventually called a Guatemalan colonel,
who told him that there was absolutely no truth to the allegation that
Maritza had been kidnapped by the army. It seemed, rather, that she was
the victim of a personal dispute.[32]

Stanley spoke by telephone with either Edmundo René or Kappy during each day of Maritza's disappearance. For security reasons, since they
knew that the phones were probably tapped, they spoke in English and
edited their conversations. During one call, Kappy pointedly stated that
the family was not interested in learning *who* had detained Maritza, or in
making public statements; their only concern was Maritza's well-being.[33]
Even a telephone tap could be an avenue for negotiation, and for winning Maritza's release.

Phone calls from the University of New Mexico's Latin American Institute and from other faculty helped generate a letter from Congressman Bill Richardson, an Albuquerque representative, to Guatemala's
President Serrano.[34] Robinson also fed the story to all of the local and
national newspapers, desperately seeking to create enough publicity to
keep Maritza alive.[35]

Unlike her brother, Maritza joined the revolution relatively late in life.
She was a dedicated student in the Instituto Belén secondary school during the early 1970s and preferred playing with her friends to politics.
When Maritza passed notes to her friend "Patricia" in class, she adorned
them with flowers. In 1973, during their first year in the Belén, Maritza
and Patricia studied together and discussed boyfriends and other typical
subjects of adolescence. Although on occasion they rebelled a bit in school
by trying to escape the control of hall monitors, the two girls were the
most serious students in their class.

But during 1974, their second year at the Belén and an election year,
revolutionary politics began to separate the two girls. Propaganda ap-

peared around the school and students entering the library in the morning found guerrilla flyers bearing Che Guevara's likeness scattered on the chairs. At the same time Patricia, then thirteen, began to spend time with older students from other, more politicized schools. They encouraged Patricia to try to change the Council of Classes, the only student group at the Belén. Conditions at the school *must* be improved, the older students explained to her, and so the council would have to be politicized. That same year, under the guidance of these older youths, Patricia and another schoolmate clandestinely began to produce propaganda within the Belén. They left messages on blackboards, signs in the bathrooms, and flyers on students' desks. The Belén *must* have a student organization to address the problems of the school. Maritza continued to spend time with her group of friends and never joined Patricia in this rudimentary political work.

By the beginning of 1975, their third year of middle school, Patricia and her adolescent colleagues publicly founded the Student Association of the Instituto Belén. They held strikes and demonstrations, lobbying for better teachers, resources, and improvements in the curriculum. Patricia and her friends didn't really understand the political dialogue they expounded at the time. The discourse came from their outside "advisers," and they were just too young. "We repeated it without really understanding what it meant."[36] But the passion of their youth carried them forward. They were young teenagers, living their dreams, and they threw themselves completely into their political work.

And slowly the students became organized. What Patricia and her friends did not know at the time was that their extracurricular activities were actually coordinated by one of Guatemala's revolutionary organizations seeking to expand its base amongst the idealistic student population. When disputes occurred within or between student political groups, they often reflected developing divisions between the various insurgent factions that were manipulating them.

At the end of 1975, when Patricia was fourteen, her older advisers in the student political movement finally confided to her about their links with the insurgency and asked her if she wanted to join their revolutionary organization. Rather than feeling deceived, Patricia was proud that the *guerrilleros* expressed this level of trust in her. In the mid-1970s, a revolutionary bore the image of someone with exceptional human and personal qualities: a Che Guevara, an individual dedicated to the construction of a new society. It was a great honor for Patricia and her teenage friends to receive an invitation to join the revolution.

"You're losing your youth!" scolded some of her apolitical friends. But Patricia had begun to read the works of Che, to dream of his ideals, and she felt that her political work gave her a role in the revolutionary struggle to humanize Guatemala. Besides, the support of the revolutionaries helped them to grow, and with this support the student association became stronger and more effective.

In their last year of high school, Patricia thought that perhaps Maritza might join the student association. But Maritza still hung around with the same apolitical clique of girls, so Patricia assumed that Maritza was simply not interested. "I never thought that she'd get involved politically."[37]

In fact, politics were never far from Maritza's mind while she was growing up. Occasionally, while she studied at the Belén, Maritza participated in youth activities organized by the PGT or the FAR. There were cultural activities like revolutionary music, or occasional political struggles in school over shortages of resources or mistreatment by a teacher. At home she listened to Radio Havana and to her family's discussions of the liberation movements underway in Latin America as well as the former Soviet Union and other socialist countries. When Maritza and her friends exchanged letters about their dreams of the world, they wrote about Cuba and the hopes of the revolution.[38] At fifteen or sixteen, Maritza also began to read the works of Che Guevara. She admired this revolutionary asthmatic's capacity to suppress his own suffering in order to struggle for the people.

As the repression sharpened during the 1970s and Maritza began to mature politically, her father's political life declined as many of his friends and comrades fled into exile. In May 1976 Laura Aldana, a former colleague of Maritza's grandmother Ester, lost her second son to the revolution when Luis Arturo Pineda Aldana was disappeared. Laura's daughter, Rita Josefina, was disappeared in 1985, literally torn from her mother's arms on the street in Guatemala City.[39] Most of Maritza's relatives left the revolution out of fear and disillusion, but one handsome cousin, much loved by Maritza's family and involved in the struggle since adolescence, was determined to continue his work. He and his wife were kidnapped and never seen again.[40] Despite the dangers, Maritza's family never completely cut its political ties.

Political violence was not the only cause of tension in the Urrutia family. Maritza's father and mother battled constantly over money, among other issues, and Maritza tried to escape the pain of her parents' marriage by passing hours reading alone in her room. She buried herself in

The Count of Monte Cristo and *The Diary of Anne Frank* and lost herself in fantasy underneath the moon and stars on the open terrace of the house.[41] Maritza could transform pain into fantasy and fantasy into reality, psychological skills that she relied on twenty years later as she tried to confound her interrogators. "We know that you're Ruth. Give us a name, an address. Tell us something!"

Each year, as Maritza progressed through her high school studies and preparation for a teaching career, her mother took her to watch the annual Desfile de la Huelga de Dolores, a satirical parade staged by students at USAC. One year when Maritza was about sixteen, a handsome, bearded young man marched in the parade dressed as Che Guevara and carrying a cross. Shortly thereafter Maritza heard that the young man had been disappeared and killed. People talked about what a lovely person he was.

In January 1979 Maritza entered USAC with the intention of studying history, later switching to anthropology. Her classmates quickly nicknamed her *Colochita* (little curly), for her mass of curly brown hair. At times their student lives seemed surreal within the context of the violent repression directed at the university community. On a Friday night Maritza and her close friends might be dancing in El Cayuco, a bar with live music not far from the university, or celebrating a birthday. Two days later they would bury a fellow student or a professor. The next week they would celebrate another birthday.

Week after week, especially in the schools of law, medicine, and engineering, students and faculty were murdered for their real or imagined political affiliations. Patricia, Maritza's old friend from the Instituto Belén, was now studying at USAC. One day in March 1980 Patricia's older brother, by then a medical student and still active in student politics, was kidnapped in downtown Guatemala City. His mutilated body later appeared wrapped in barbed wire. After the wake, hundreds of students and political activists traveled by bus to the cemetery to attend the burial. As she walked grieving down the cemetery road to her brother's tomb, Patricia sensed that someone was walking beside her. It was Maritza, who silently accompanied her until Patricia's brother was buried.

In 1981 Maritza received an invitation to join a revolutionary organization. She no longer saw the relevance of her studies in the midst of the carnage, so she decided to join. Within two weeks, Maritza began her clandestine work.

Later that year Maritza left Guatemala for Mexico. Her brother, Edmundo René, was there, as were many friends now in exile. "The whole world was fleeing," and Maritza had felt lonely in Guatemala. But after just a month in Mexico City, she felt disillusioned. As reports of guerrilla safe houses and comrades falling in Guatemala City reached the exile community, Maritza watched her friends getting drunk and depressed, wallowing in guilt, and dreaming about Guatemala. In spite of the repression, Maritza decided to return home to take a more active role, reasoning that she was not yet marked as a revolutionary.

Shortly after her return, Maritza had a chance meeting with an old friend of the Urrutia family, a revolutionary who had spent years in *la lucha* and who at the time was a member of a different revolutionary group, the Ejército Guerrillero de los Pobres. Maritza was already attracted to this group. In January 1972 fifteen exiled dissidents secretly returned to Guatemala from Mexico and began to organize the Mayan farmers in the remote Ixcán jungle region.[42] For several years this group secretly built a social base in the Guatemalan highlands without engaging in military activities.[43] In 1975, in its first public action, this nucleus of the EGP killed a notoriously brutal landowner named Luis Arenas Barrera.

Moreover, the EGP's symbol and philosophical leader, even after his death, was Che Guevara, Maritza's hero. In December the family friend came to see Maritza at her parents' home. Would Maritza like to join the EGP? On New Years Day 1982 she said yes, and her life as a clandestine EGP militant began.

Maritza spent most of 1982 working for the EGP in the capital, primarily producing revolutionary propaganda. In September, after several *compañeros* were killed, Maritza received an order to leave the country, and she traveled to Nicaragua. After losing many members to the repression, in part because those who were captured knew details of the Organización that could be extracted under torture, the EGP tightened its discipline and security measures. Although Maritza was far from Guatemala, she lived in isolation and knew only three of the many EGP comrades in Nicaragua. This would ensure greater safety for her, and for the Organización, on her return.

In 1982 the four primary revolutionary organizations in Guatemala, the FAR, ORPA, the PGT, and the EGP, united under a joint command: the Guatemalan National Revolutionary Union or URNG (Unidad Revolucionaria Nacional Guatemalteca).[44] By means of a "popular revolutionary war," the guerrilla organizations planned to eventually take power and set up a revolutionary, democratic government.[45]

In early 1983 Maritza began a relationship with Carlos Barrientos Aragón, another member of the EGP who was also in exile in Managua.

In February, Maritza and Carlos returned to Guatemala as an EGP team. They tried to reconstruct the EGP's operations in the capital until August 1983, when a close *compañero* was kidnapped and disappeared. The Organización ordered Maritza and Carlos to leave the country immediately. On August 30, 1983, they went to Mexico, where Maritza would remain for five years.

Maritza passed these years in Mexico living and working within the closed, clandestine world of the EGP. After suffering serous losses during the counterinsurgency campaigns of the early 1980s, security was the paramount concern within the EGP, which developed a more rigid, compartmentalized, and hierarchical military structure.[46] In order to avoid "burning" herself and other members of the Organización, Maritza spent her years in Mexico City living with a small cell of disciplined EGP members, and the EGP became Maritza's family, her second mother.[47] She spent much of her time assisting in the production and distribution of a magazine that promoted the EGP's ideology and also reported the news of armed struggles in other parts of the world. The magazine promoted the EGP's internationalist philosophy, part of Che Guevara's legacy, which emphasized the value of uniting revolutionaries around the world. In order to sustain the morale of its members, the Organización would inform them of the revolutionary conflicts taking place in other regions so that the EGP comrades would know they were not fighting alone. Occasionally, Maritza also conducted classes in political development for groups of Guatemalan refugees.[48]

Although many of her university friends were also in exile at the same time, Maritza always avoided their parties and gatherings. Once or twice on the street by chance she ran into her old friend Julia, who had fled the violence of Guatemala for Mexico City after a close friend was killed in 1983. "Let's get together!" Julia would tell her. "I want to see you! I want to know how you are!"[49] They would set a date to meet for coffee at a certain time and place.

But Maritza would never show up. That was hard, but it was safer that way, and Maritza had her work and her dreams to dull her loneliness. After all, the revolution gave meaning to Maritza's life; the struggle transcended her.[50] In spite of the sacrifices, limitations and isolation that she endured, she was content. Everyone had a role in the revolution, no matter how simple, and Maritza was contributing to the transformation of Guatemala.

On occasion Maritza saw her brother, but political differences drove a wedge between the siblings. Edmundo René's views about socialism had changed, and when he began to criticize the Guatemalan revolutionary movement, the conversation between brother and sister descended into bitter ideological arguments.[51]

In 1987 Maritza gave birth to a son, and she and Carlos named him Fernando Sebastián. Concurrently, Maritza's professional skills for producing revolutionary propaganda had not gone unnoticed, and in 1988 the Organización ordered Maritza and Carlos to return to Guatemala. Now she would have more responsibility than in the past. Maritza, Carlos, and their infant child settled into her parents' house in zone eight.

The army's counterinsurgency pressures were still fierce and now Maritza was the mother of a baby boy. She knew that whatever happened to her would impact Sebastián as well, and the ominous presence of *el enemigo* made life much more stressful than her days in Mexico. For weeks she did not want to leave the house.

At long last Maritza and Carlos began their new duties. Maritza's new position in the EGP meant that now she would have many more contacts. Now responsible for the political formation of new EGP recruits as well as propaganda, Maritza taught revolutionary theory clandestinely to groups of young people. The experience was intimidating at first because Maritza's "students" often had more formal education than she did. But Maritza had years of practical experience working for the revolution, and under the EGP's strict discipline, she had spent much of her "free" time reading and discussing politics, philosophy, history, sociology, even psychology with her *compañeros*. Soon she realized that she could answer her students' theoretical questions about Marxism and socialism, often using examples of factory workers or peasant farmers.[52]

In early 1990 Carlos and Maritza separated and he took a new position at an EGP combat area, the Ho Chi Minh front. Maritza continued her work with the Organización, constantly seeking to win the hearts of others for the revolution.[53] But security concerns made the urban area a difficult place to work. Maritza had contact with dozens of people, any one of whom could make an error that would be detected by the army. In an effort to reduce the risk, she used various pseudonyms so that her contacts would never know her true name.

On a typical day Maritza would meet with her *compañeros* in the morning to discuss their activities. In the afternoon there might be an hour or two of political instruction and study with one of her groups, as well as short meetings with her contacts to exchange information or to plan events. Very public places, like the great cathedral in zone one, were common meeting points. For these short meetings Maritza carefully selected sites where neither she nor her contacts would stand out.

Sometimes she made quick trips to Mexico in order to bring people or documents across the border. In these dangerous excursions, it was important to gain an edge on *el enemigo*. Maritza would distract the customs men at the frontier by wearing clothes that emphasized her physical charms, and by flirting with the officers.

Edmundo René returned from his studies in the United States in early 1992. The ideological differences between brother and sister were now sharper than ever, and they had angry exchanges. "Do something that will prepare you for the future," he told her. "The struggle for the revolution is going to end!" Their quarrels became especially heated when Edmundo René criticized Maritza for putting members of their family at risk. "Maritza," he told her, "you're going to *fuck* me!"[54]

"I knew that sooner or later, she would be caught," recalled Edmundo René. "The urban guerrilla is so vulnerable for many reasons—and she would involve us in one way or another. And I was really worried especially because of my past and my family's past. I thought the whole family would be arrested or killed for the things she was doing."[55]

But Maritza was proud and happy in her work, and she refused to change her commitment. Finally, Edmundo René gave up and stopped challenging his *hermanita*. "She was *so happy* doing this. So I said to my mother: 'OK, let her do it.'"[56]

Apart from the tensions with her brother, Maritza felt fulfilled by her work. January 1992 marked her tenth anniversary as a member of the EGP, as well as the twentieth anniversary of the first EGP revolutionary activities in the Ixcán jungle. Maritza helped organize the anniversary celebrations, even producing EGP T-shirts bearing Che Guevara's likeness that were sent to the comrades at the front. Maritza was good at what she did, and by early 1992 she was responsible for propaganda in the capital, not only for the EGP, but for the entire URNG.[57]

FOUR

SATURDAY AND SUNDAY

July 25–26, 1992

On Saturday morning, Maritza's third day of captivity, one of her interrogators, a dark-skinned man, came into Maritza's room and handed her a pen and a piece of paper. Write down everything you know. Around 11:00 A.M. Don Chando entered the room. The video that they made last night had not turned out well. Did Maritza use makeup? Yes (she lied), she used a lot of makeup. Trying to undermine her captors' propaganda efforts, Maritza told Don Chando she used blue eye shadow and red lipstick, colors she never used on the rare occasions when she did wear cosmetics.

Don Chando left the room and was gone for about half an hour. While he was away, Maritza heard the voices of a group of men coming from the parking area; it sounded like they were washing cars. When the men returned, they took Maritza to the bathroom, handing her new makeup from a Mega 6 department store located near the Island along with soap, shampoo, and towels. After bathing, Maritza painted her face heavily. She hoped that friends or family, seeing her altered appearance in the video, would realize that Maritza was acting under duress.[1]

The men brought Maritza to the same room where they had filmed the night before. They had written every word of her new speech on large pieces of paper. The text was similar to what Maritza recited on Friday evening, but her captors had added an additional section wherein Maritza expressed her gratitude to the ODHA, as well as to the U.S. Embassy. Like an actress repeating her lines, Maritza used the repetitive amateur filming process to recall and memorize the mixture of fact and fiction she had fabricated under interrogation.[2]

They filmed a first take as Maritza read the declaration. Don Chando angrily berated her again, shouting that she looked too nervous; she didn't seem normal! Maritza must speak naturally in the recording, she must not appear to be reading. After filming, her interrogators brought Maritza back to her room, where she was again chained to the bed.

Don Chando came in a few hours later, in a fury. The video still wasn't any good, he berated Maritza. They would have to film again on Monday. He continued ranting. Maritza was being used, he maintained. "Your *compañeros* are trying to turn you into a martyr."[3] USAC's Association of University Students had made public statements about Maritza, indicating that she was connected to the university. Maritza tried to calm him down. Perhaps the group was issuing statements because her brother, Edmundo Rene, taught at USAC, and because Maritza studied there in the past.

After Don Chando finally left her, Maritza spent the remainder of Saturday handcuffed to the bed. Desperate to relax, she tried to do some exercises while lying on her back and on her side.[4] She tried to lose herself in fantasy, dreaming of her university days when Maritza and her favorite dance partner would dance the night away. And the radio played on.

Disappearance means an arbitrary or illegal detention that is denied by government authorities.[5] The victim, like Maritza, simply vanishes. Four decades ago, Guatemalan military and paramilitary forces began the practice of disappearances, and during the cold war Guatemala registered "the highest number of disappearances, abductions and missing in the Western Hemisphere."[6] Victims are taken to secret detention centers beyond the reach of court inspections and controls, where they are interrogated, tortured, and often executed.[7]

In many disappearances—including Maritza's case—the family and friends of the missing person also suffer mental torture, unsure whether their loved one is alive and, if so, where she is held, under what conditions, and in what state of health. At the same time they are aware that they are also under threat, that they might receive the same fate themselves, and that any search for their friend or relative also increases their personal danger and may imperil the victim.[8]

And what of the children of the disappeared such as Sebastián, Maritza's four-year-old son? Edmundo René and Kappy agreed that if Maritza did not survive, they would raise Sebastián. But determining the new caregivers of orphaned children is only one issue created by a disappearance. The day that Maritza disappeared, Sebastián was justifiably confused as to why his mother had failed to pick him up at school. He didn't want to go to sleep that night until Maritza came home. "Wasn't there a telephone where they could call her? Why doesn't she come home?"[9] Whenever the doorbell rang, Sebastián asked if it was his mamá. His relatives tried to shield Sebastián from the truth about Maritza's kidnapping. Nonetheless, Sebastián overheard the adults' conversations and the television news programs while pretending to be asleep in his grandparents' bedroom.[10] Then he stopped asking for his mamá.

When should adult relatives explain to a child that his mother, father, or both parents are not coming back? Is it best to tell a child that his parents are dead in order to spare him the anguish and uncertainty that normally accompanies a disappearance and allow him to begin to grieve? And would a four-year-old boy like Sebastián ever be able to forgive his mother for disappearing?[11]

Torture is often a component of the experience of disappearance.[12] The term includes any act by which severe pain or suffering, whether mental or physical, is intentionally inflicted on a person for such purposes as obtaining information or a confession, or punishing, coercing, or intimidating the person.[13] Consequently, torture entails purposeful, systematic activity. Although infliction of severe physical pain and/or mental suffering is integral to the process of torture, the purpose of torture is to break the will of the victim and ultimately to destroy his or her personality.[14]

All of the different methods used to systematically break Maritza's will—constant interrogation with threats of violence against herself and her family, especially her son; the forcible consumption of drugs; the forced viewing of photographs of mutilated bodies; sleep deprivation; constant light and the noise of the radio; and later, repeated recantations of her political life—all created severe psychological pain and eventually broke Maritza down.[15] Coroncho, well trained, understood the objective: "It was pressure so she would break and tell everything she knew."[16]

In their brutality, Maritza's captors stripped Maritza of her identity, her sense of personhood as a revolutionary, and threatened the most important person in her life, her son. Her feelings at night of being "in a hole" were apt: "It is the intense pain that destroys a person's self and world, a destruction experienced spatially as either the contraction of the universe down to the immediate vicinity of the body or as the body swelling to fill the entire universe. . . . World, self, and voice are lost, or nearly lost." Hers was an "unthinkable isolation."[17]

In a psychological sense, Maritza felt small, naked, and vulnerable while Don Chando's world grew ever larger.[18] "It is only the prisoner's steadily shrinking [psychological] ground that wins for the torturer his swelling sense of territory" and his sense of power.[19] As the writer Lawrence Weschler explains, "it is essential to the structure of torture that it take place in secret, in the dark, beyond consideration of shame or account. When the torturer assures his victim 'no one will ever know,' he is at once trying to break the victim's spirit and to bolster his own."[20]

Don Chando's boast to Maritza, "I don't care if you see me. You can't do anything," was just the beginning of this process. Psychologically, the men forced Maritza to submit to their will, invaded her, and used her. She became a mere instrument of her captors in their efforts to weaken the military and political capability of the URNG.[21] It was all part of the process of breaking Maritza down and establishing their control over her, and they were very good at their work. Coroncho recalled with some pride a few years later that he and his colleagues "brainwashed her well."[22] But on that point he was wrong.

WASHINGTON, D.C.

After Bill Robinson received the news about Maritza's disappearance, he called Frank LaRue in Washington, D.C. LaRue was a Guatemalan labor lawyer living in exile in the United States. For many years he had lobbied members of Congress on human rights issues, particularly cases involving Guatemalans. LaRue had recently founded the Center for Human Rights Legal Action, a nongovernmental organization dedicated to investigating human rights abuses in Guatemala and adjudicating these cases at the Inter-American Human Rights Commission in Washington and the Inter-American Court of Human Rights in San José, Costa Rica.

During the 1980s Bill Robinson was a Washington correspondent for Agencia Nueva Nicaragua, a Nicaragua-based international news agency. The population of Central American activists in the U.S. capitol was relatively small in those days. Both the Robinsons and the LaRues had young children, so the two families often socialized together and the two men shared a relationship of trust. "I want you to give me your advice," Robinson told LaRue after explaining the facts of Maritza's kidnapping. "What do you think we should do? Should we go public on this? Or should we be discreet and use quiet diplomacy?"[23]

Robinson's instinct was to publicize Maritza's disappearance, but when he had spoken earlier by phone with Edmundo René, Maritza's brother had not been entirely persuaded by the strategy of using public pressure to win Maritza's release. In her brief telephone calls, Maritza had told her family not to do anything. *Nothing was going to happen to her.* If they made a scandal about Maritza's disappearance, perhaps her captors, infuriated by the publicity, would kill her. But if they kept things quiet, they *still* might kill her. So perhaps if they created a lot of publicity, they might save her life. Edmundo René was torn as to what strategy to take.[24] Robinson wanted LaRue's opinion in order to convince Edmundo René of the necessity of using publicity to help Maritza.

LaRue had long, hard experience trying to help disappeared union members in Guatemala. He understood the necessity of making these cases public as soon as possible in order to save the victims' lives. In the first moments of a disappearance, the primary concern is that the victim will be killed that day, before any pressure can be brought to bear on her behalf. From the facts that Robinson described to LaRue, it was obvious that Maritza had been abducted. "Yes," he told Robinson. "I agree with you. We should go public. That's the best way to save her life."[25] Robinson called Edmundo René in Guatemala City, and a short time later he called LaRue again. "Edmundo says 'OK.' Let's go public."

Robinson asked LaRue to call his contacts in the U.S. Congress and to help coordinate a response from the human rights NGOs in Washington, D.C. What else could be done? The Center for Human Rights Legal Action sent out a press release about Maritza's case, and LaRue immediately called officials in the U.S. State Department. LaRue also spoke to members of the Inter-American Human Rights Commission and to Guatemalan solidarity groups based in Washington. By publicizing Maritza's case, the NGOs sent a message that people would not be silent about Maritza's disappearance. Tactically, the NGOs were trying to put political pressure on the Guatemalan government to release Maritza alive. Concurrently, they lobbied the U.S. government to act on Maritza's behalf. LaRue asked his congressional contacts to call the U.S. Embassy in Guatemala City as well as the State Department headquarters in Washington in order to "inquire" about Maritza's case.

Anne Manuel was at home on Saturday when Bill Robinson called her from Albuquerque. In 1992 Manuel was the associate director of Americas Watch, a division of Human Rights Watch, which conducts regular, systematic investigations of human rights abuses in seventy countries around the world.[26] Human Rights Watch publicizes human rights abuses committed by governments or by insurgent forces in order to stigmatize the perpetrators of these violations and thereby force them to change their conduct. Americas Watch was established in 1981 to monitor human rights in Latin America and the Caribbean.

After Robinson told her about Maritza's disappearance, Manuel drove to her office in Washington, D.C., to write a letter to the Guatemalan government. While she worked on the letter, Manuel received a fax from Heather Wiley containing more details about Maritza's case. An editor by profession, Wiley directed Amnesty International's Guatemala Coordination Group, members of Amnesty who focus exclusively on human rights abuses in Guatemala. Renowned for its work to free prisoners of conscience around the world, Amnesty concentrates its energies on research and publicity concerning human rights abuses. For many years, Wiley selflessly assisted Guatemalan citizens whose lives were in danger from military and paramilitary repression. From her home in the Boston area, she devoted the next few weeks of her life to Maritza's case.[27]

Wiley had received a call from Bill Robinson earlier that day, explaining Maritza's predicament. Later she spoke by telephone with Edmundo René Urrutia and then sent faxes to Guatemalan authorities on Maritza's behalf. On Monday, two days later, Amnesty issued an Urgent Action Appeal to its members around the world, asking them to communicate with the Guatemalan government and urge that Maritza be released.[28]

After receiving the information from Wiley, Manuel finished her letter and faxed it to officials of the Guatemalan government. Thereafter she was in almost constant contact with Wiley, Robinson, and Bonnie Tenneriello, a Guatemala specialist at the Washington Office on Latin America (WOLA). Founded in 1974 by a coalition of religious and civic leaders in response to the spread of military dictatorships throughout the Western Hemisphere, WOLA lobbies for United States and multilateral policies that advance human rights in Latin America. WOLA gained influence among policy makers on Capitol Hill during the 1970s and early 1980s by providing the most reliable data available on human rights abuses in Central and South America.[29] Years of excellent reporting on Guatemalan issues coupled with an unassuming lobbying style had won Tenneriello some close contacts on Capitol Hill.

In 1991 Senator James Jeffords, then a Republican from Vermont, had traveled to Guatemala with a delegation of congresspersons and aides to investigate human rights abuses committed by the Guatemalan security forces. Following the first reports of Maritza's disappearance, Bonnie Tenneriello spoke with Senator Jeffords's legislative aide, Laurie Schultz-Heim. Would the senator make some calls on Maritza's behalf? Moreover, Jeffords's counterpart from Vermont, Democratic Senator Patrick Leahy, was a member of the Senate Foreign Operations Subcommittee and respected as a man of principle.[30] A highly capable member of Leahy's staff, Tim Rieser, had also visited Guatemala. Tenneriello called Rieser to ask for his help.

Additionally, Tom Harkin, who as a congressman in the late 1970s had sponsored a bill that shut off U.S. economic assistance to governments with a record of gross human rights violations, was now a Democratic senator from Iowa and also a member of the Foreign Operations Subcommittee. Harkin's aide, the late Jim Sweeney, had traveled to Guatemala in 1991 on the same delegation with Senator Jeffords. Tenneriello called Sweeney, who agreed to speak with Senator Harkin about Maritza's case.

Moreover, both Rick Nuccio, a staff person for the House Committee on Western Hemisphere Affairs, and Alex Arriaga, an aide to the Congressional Human Rights Caucus, were interested in Central American issues. Would they make inquiries to the U.S. State Department and to the Guatemalan government regarding Maritza?

After speaking with Bill Robinson, Tenneriello realized that thanks to Edmundo René Urrutia's friends and academic contacts in Albuquerque, Maritza might have a special "state constituency" in New Mexico. So Tenneriello spoke with John Gerhart, an aide to New Mexico Democratic Senator Jeff Bingaman, and with Charlie Flickner, who worked for Republican Senator Pete Domenici. Robinson had already alerted some members of New Mexico's congressional delegation, and Bingaman and Domenici's aides also made inquiries to the U.S. State Department on Maritza's behalf.

Tenneriello asked the Senate aides if their bosses would be willing to sign a letter to Guatemalan President Jorge Serrano expressing their concern about Maritza's disappearance and urging Serrano to secure Maritza's immediate release. While the staff people consulted with their superiors, Tenneriello drafted the letter and faxed it to them. The final version, faxed to President Serrano on Tuesday, July 28, was signed by Senators Harkin, Leahy, Bingaman, and Domenici.[31]

Manuel, Wiley, and Tenneriello decided to put as much pressure as possible on the Guatemalan government to locate Maritza and secure her release. In addition to their own faxes and Amnesty International's Urgent Action requests, the three NGOs used their contacts in the U.S.

Congress and the State Department to impress upon President Serrano's administration the seriousness of Maritza's case.[32] They made a number of telephone calls to John Arndt, then the U.S. State Department's Guatemala desk officer. The desk officer is the Washington, D.C. focal point for any events in the country under his or her charge. Thus, any issue regarding Guatemala in 1992 came first to John Arndt, and from Arndt passed to his superiors in the State Department headquarters or to the U.S. Embassy in Guatemala City.[33]

In 1992 John Arndt's boss, Bernard Aronson, the U.S. assistant secretary of state for Inter-American Affairs, had an energetic "special assistant" named Mark Kirk. Kirk previously worked for the Appropriations Committee of the House of Representatives, "where the real power was in Congress." The State Department hired Kirk to help rebuild trust between the executive branch and Congress after the Iran-Contra debacle. And Kirk's contacts in the Appropriations Committee would be useful should the committee ever threaten to cut off funds for certain projects or aid to certain countries.[34]

Kirk understood the legislative process more than most foreign service officers, particularly those in far-away embassies "who didn't know about U.S. political architecture," so he tried to educate his State Department colleagues. Every night Kirk would draft a cable about upcoming important events in Congress and in the NGO community and send it to the different embassies and "country-teams" that comprised the Inter-American Bureau. Kirk understood that WOLA's Bonnie Tenneriello had good contacts with the Democrats on the Senate Foreign Operations Committee, as well as with Senator Christopher Dodd on the Western Hemisphere Committee. If Tenneriello called Kirk and explained that the human rights NGOs were working on an important case, Kirk would immediately cable the pertinent embassy:

> This human rights group is working on this case and I know you Foreign Service [guys] down there think that you're really important and elite, and you never listen to NGOs, but I gotta tell you: *this NGO has the ear of Senator Christopher Dodd, who is Chairman of the Western Hemisphere Committee, and if you want an amendment to a foreign aid bill rocketing right down your ambassador's throat, then *ignore the following information* . . . and to their credit, they got with the program.[35]

While Kirk believed that some members of the Foreign Service culture are elitist, he also understood that even elites respond to power: "So when it's explained to them that the NGO representatives are serious and not a bunch of hippies and have the eye and ear of Pat Leahy, Chairman of the Foreign Operations Committee—unless they were dumb—they'd start working on the case and developing information."[36]

President Jorge Serrano was a strong nationalist and jealous of his country's sovereignty. But in late 1992 Bernard Aronson told a Guatemalan government official, "Human rights [are] no longer the realm only of national governments."[37] The Guatemalan government could no longer credibly claim that cases of forced disappearance and other human rights abuses were purely "internal matters" and therefore outside the realm of foreign policy and international relations. Fifty years earlier, during the springtime of the Guatemalan revolution, Jacobo Árbenz dreamed of reducing U.S. power in Guatemala. But all of this feverish lobbying implied continued U.S. influence over Guatemalan affairs.[38] The URNG and other members of the Guatemalan left would have to swallow their anti-imperialist rhetoric if Maritza was to survive.

GUATEMALA CITY

Saturday, around 11 P.M. "Jones," a staff person in the U.S. Embassy in Guatemala, was not having a good night. People from the State Department's Operations Center in Washington had called the embassy's duty officer at 11:00 P.M. on Saturday evening. They were forwarding a message from Virginia White, an aide to New Mexico Senator Jeff Bingaman, expressing concern about the whereabouts and safety of Kappy Riker and her fiancé, Edmundo René. The embassy's duty officer called Jones, who had no idea where they were. The security of U.S. citizens overseas is a high priority for State Department officials, so Jones's response could not have pleased his superiors back in headquarters. Jones spent the next two hours on the telephone, trying to locate Kappy and Edmundo René and gather more information about the case.[39]

Eventually Jones called me at home, apologizing for the lateness of the hour. Did I know anything about the Maritza Urrutia case? The State Department and people from Albuquerque, New Mexico were calling him about it.[40] I told Jones that Maritza's brother had come to the ODHA the day before seeking assistance, but I didn't know Kappy Riker or whether she was in danger. Jones urgently wanted to speak with Edmundo René and Kappy to make sure that they were both safe. Did I know how to contact them? I recalled that my file in the ODHA contained the family's telephone numbers. "I'll go into the office on Sunday morning," I told Jones. "I'll call you at home when I find the numbers."

Sunday, July 26, 1992 The archbishopric, an old building made of wood and stone, was home to the archbishop, several ecclesiastic offices, and the ODHA as well. The building was normally closed on Sundays, but by ringing the doorbell long enough, I could summon one of the nuns who cared for the archbishop, or one of the guardians of the building, to open the door. I finally got into the ODHA at about 9:00 A.M. and pulled the new file on Maritza's case. Edmundo René had given me his parents' telephone number, but I hesitated before passing it on to Jones. Many Guatemalans bore a deep distrust of the U.S. Embassy, given the U.S. government's responsibility for so much suffering in the country. Maritza's parents might object to the Catholic Church releasing their telephone numbers to a U.S. Embassy official. Better to call her parents first and talk to them.

Maritza's father answered the phone and I explained the reason for my call. Did Edmundo have any news about Maritza? Always calm and polite, he explained that yes, Maritza had called again on Friday night. I jumped. My God, she might still be alive! I told Edmundo about Jones's concerns for Kappy and Edmundo René. Were they all right? They were fine, Edmundo assured me. He expected to see them later that day, and Edmundo gave me permission to pass his telephone number to Jones.

I didn't want to say too much over the phone. Could I come to his home, perhaps on Monday afternoon, to speak with him personally? "With pleasure, señor!" Edmundo answered.

After I called Jones and gave him the Urrutias' telephone number, Jones also telephoned Edmundo. Jones helped resolve many difficult cases during his tenure in Guatemala, at times risking his life to do so.[41] Jones was trying to obtain more information about Maritza and inform anyone eavesdropping (i.e., branches of the Guatemalan government and the armed forces) that the U.S. Embassy was now involved in Maritza's case. Whenever State Department personnel serve overseas, they assume that their telephones are tapped.

I reviewed the thin file on Maritza one more time. Her father's news about the second telephone call from Maritza had shaken me. In Guatemala, there were no political prisoners. People simply disappeared and were never seen again. But they were keeping Maritza alive. Why? There was something special about Maritza and I wanted to pursue her case. But if Maritza was part of the URNG, that would imply enormous risks for the ODHA and its staff, as the army could accuse the ODHA of assisting the insurgents. I would have to discuss the case with my boss, Ronalth Ochaeta, on Monday morning.

I was not the only Church representative preoccupied with Maritza that Sunday. In the afternoon Father Luis Pérez, one of two young priests assigned to the congregation of the great cathedral, visited Archbishop Próspero Penados in his quarters. The two men had known each other for years and had developed an unshakeable mutual trust. Many years before, when he was the bishop of the rural diocese of San Marcos, Penados befriended Luis's parents and became close to his entire family. Then in 1982 Penados helped Luis enter the seminary in Guatemala City. In April 1983, a period of extreme repression in San Marcos, Luis imprudently decided to visit his family. Luckily, he first arrived at Monsignor Penados's house and the bishop hid Luis in a bedroom and told him to stay there.

Shortly thereafter a group of soldiers knocked on the front door. Sister Tere Pineda, a tiny nun who was the bishop's housekeeper and cook, came out to greet them. "Is Luis Pérez here?" the soldiers asked. "No," replied Sister Tere, "he's not here. He doesn't live here." With the nun's word, the soldiers went away. After hiding Luis in his home for two days, Bishop Penados put Luis in his private car at two in the morning. The seminarian and the bishop drove all night, when there was less chance that soldiers would stop the car, through the mountains to Guatemala City. They arrived at the seminary at dawn, and Luis did not return to San Marcos for years.

After he was ordained in late 1990, Luis was assigned to the cathedral. On most Sundays the young priest visited his mentor in the archbishopric. That Sunday Monsignor Penados was worried about Maritza. He felt sad for the little boy that Maritza had left behind. The two men discussed how the Church might help Maritza and her family.

At the Urrutia home in zone eight, Don Edmundo's characteristic graciousness on the telephone masked his despair for Maritza and his anxiety for the safety of the rest of his family. Many friends came to the house to offer their assistance, their support, and their prayers for Maritza. The wife of a member of a former military junta came by, as did the wife of the interior minister. The wife of the former junta member brought her daughter and her son-in-law, who at the time was an army officer serving in the war-torn province of El Quiché, an area of regular EGP activity. The officer spoke softly to Maritza's sister: "Carolina, I'm sorry." Then all three guests knelt on the worn dark carpet in the Urrutia living room and prayed for Maritza.[42]

The Urrutias' neighbors, some of them Catholics and others evangelical Protestants, also came by to pray for Maritza. At Colegio Asunción as well, where Carolina was a teacher and her two children attended high school, they prayed for Maritza. They prayed for Maritza at Walt Disney Nursery School, and at USAC. Maritza's relatives living in Miami and Los Angeles set up a "prayer chain," and they too prayed every day for Maritza.[43]

Early Sunday morning Although never a devout Catholic in the past, Maritza was praying too. When she could not stop thinking about her son and her family, and she felt like she was going crazy, Maritza began to pray. On Sunday morning her interrogators did not come to question her and the installation seemed much more peaceful. From time to time Maritza heard the jingling bells of ice cream vendors passing on a nearby street, and the loud rumbling of city buses. She lay on the bed with her face covered by the newspaper, exhausted and afraid, reciting over and over the Our Father and the Hail Mary, pulling herself back from her madness.[44]

A man stood outside the door of Maritza's room. He repeatedly opened and closed the door, which made Maritza very nervous. Each time the door opened, Maritza smelled marijuana. Eventually the man entered the room and stopped very close to Maritza's bed. He shut off the radio and told Maritza to take the newspaper off of her head. She smelled the marijuana more strongly now and was very afraid. Maritza didn't want to take the mask off, but the man insisted. "Take it off and look at me!" Finally, she removed the newspaper.

The man was short and fat, with the copper-colored skin and black hair typical of Guatemala's Mayan population. His eyes were red and he reeked of marijuana. "Don't you remember me?" he asked. "You don't remember having seen me before?" No, Maritza responded. She had never seen him before. The man told her he had seen Maritza playing with her son. "I've seen you in front of your house many times."[45] Maritza remembered the photos of her home and Sebastián playing in the street and she realized that this man must have been part of the surveillance team that covertly photographed her for weeks leading up to her disappearance.

The man seemed nervous. He constantly went to the door and peered into the corridor to check whether anyone was coming. When he returned to Maritza's side, she feared that the man would rape her. He told her that she was pretty. *Mamita linda* he called her, and Maritza began to feel nauseated. "Your husband is the real guilty one," the man told her. "But you've also gotten involved in things you shouldn't have."

"Do you know where you are?" the man asked her. "Do you know what this place is?" No, Maritza replied. She didn't know where she was or who had kidnapped her. "You're with the army, of course," answered the man. "Where else could you be? You're detained by the army." From outside came the sound of a car in the parking area. Quickly the man left the room, and Maritza put the newspaper mask back onto her head.

A few minutes later the man came back into the room. "Take off the mask." When Maritza removed the newspaper, he asked her if she knew where they had intercepted her letters to Esteban. No, she didn't know. The letters were intercepted in Uspantán, in El Quiché, he told her, and she was a fool for having gotten involved in subversive activities.

"Would you like something to drink?" asked the fat man. No. Ignoring her response, the man left and Maritza heard the sound of a heavy gate opening. He returned in a few minutes and handed Maritza a plastic bag filled with Pepsi and a straw. As small shops in Guatemala typically sell individual portions of soft drinks in pint-sized plastic bags, and because the man left her room only briefly, Maritza concluded that he must have gone to a store close to her place of captivity.

The man kept talking to Maritza but he seemed very nervous. He constantly paced to the door and looked down the hall as if he was worried that someone might find him in Maritza's room. At the slightest noise from outside, he would scurry from the room, only to return a few minutes later. The man would stand by Maritza's bed, eyeing her lasciviously and calling her *mamita linda*. Since she was still handcuffed to the bed, Maritza's fear that he would try to rape her grew.

At about 6:30 P.M. the Mayan's shift ended, and another man came on duty, standing outside Maritza's door. The short, fat man had removed the radio from her room that morning, but the new guard brought it back and returned it to full volume. That night, despite her anxiety, Maritza managed to sleep a bit.[46]

FIVE

THE CATHOLIC CHURCH IN GUATEMALA

1524–1992

In 1954 the Catholic Church, led by the fiercely anti-Communist Archbishop Mariano Rossell, played a pivotal role in the downfall of Jacobo Árbenz's government, thereby sending Maritza's parents, grandparents, and siblings into exile. Now in 1992, the Urrutia family had come to the same Catholic Church, seeking help to save Maritza's life. But the Church was not the same. It had undergone its own transformation since 1954, and this metamorphosis would have a profound impact on Maritza.

In June 1524 Pedro de Alvarado became the governor of what is today Guatemala. He and his fellow Spaniards had come searching for two things: gold and souls to save on behalf of their Catholic sovereign, Carlos V.[1] Gold was scarce when the invaders arrived, but heathen souls were not, and the Europeans quickly turned to the task of religious conversion of the many Mayan ethnic groups native to Guatemala. While some indigenous people accepted the foreign values of their new masters, many were recalcitrant, and often those who resisted were put to the sword, chased off their lands, or enslaved to work the mines and rich haciendas established by the colonists.[2]

For the Catholic clergy who arrived with the conquering armies, conversion of Guatemala's Mayan population represented a daunting challenge. Indigenous communities were scattered throughout the rugged highlands, and there were few concentrated "towns" as Europeans knew them. Making communication harder still were the many difficult Mayan languages, each pertaining to a particular ethnic group, and usually without a written form. Furthermore, the Mayans already possessed a rich spirituality, a distinct "cosmovision" that cherished and worshiped the fundamental elements of Mayan life: the sun, the earth, corn, and rain. If the Spanish priests and friars were going to win true converts to the Gospel of Jesus Christ, first they would have to destroy the entire Mayan culture, which they nearly did.

According to a royal decree written in 1551,

> With much care and special attention, they have tried to impose the most convenient measures so that the indians can be instructed in the Holy Catholic Faith and the Gospel Laws. So that, forgetting the errors of their old rites and ceremonies, they will live in concert and order. In order to accomplish this most efficiently, the members of our Council of the Indias and other religious persons, as well as the prelates of New Spain, met several times in 1546 . . . and they resolved that the indians would be reduced to towns and would not live divided and separated by the mountains and forests where they are deprived of all spiritual and temporal benefits, without the assistance of our ministers.[3]

Consequently, many traditionally dispersed Mayan communities were forcibly concentrated into towns or *reducciones*, thereby permitting the Spaniards greater access to and control over their indigenous charges.[4] In 1631 Dominican Friar Francisco Moran described the method of capturing the natives:

> On Easter morning we [celebrated Mass] in their fields, which were well-tended, and we took advantage of the moment to grab them since that allowed us to relieve our necessity, leaving those who ran away with very little. We grabbed fourteen between children and adults, and the rest . . . ran away into the forest. . . . We burned the houses. . . . They're badly punished and they need to give themselves up peacefully. . . . And all of them are terrified. . . . Praise the Lord that we have overcome this difficulty.[5]

Although these harsh measures made it more difficult for Mayan farmers to tend to their communal lands and subsistence crops, their new masters now had a ready supply of labor and other forms of tribute for the construction of churches (often on sacred Mayan religious sites), roads, and other projects. And colonial practices enormously facilitated the work of spiritual conversion.[6] While Spanish clergy taught the Gospel to the indigenous population concentrated within *reducciones*, the practice of Mayan religious ceremonies, their festivals, rituals, and worshipping of idols, was forbidden, and violators were often severely punished or enslaved.[7]

The historian Julio Pinto Soria explains that the Spaniards did not impose their harsh policies simply to be barbaric, but rather for pragmatic reasons. They wanted to deny all aspects of the Mayan past in order to avoid the danger of its rebirth. Consequently, the colonists were quick to crush any indigenous efforts at cultural expression.[8]

More lasting forms of cultural resistance were often hidden, as many indigenous communities found surreptitious ways to mix some of their traditional religious rites into forced Catholic rituals, much to the frustration of evangelizing priests.[9] Some Mayan groups met clandestinely in isolated areas far from Spanish eyes to perform their ceremonies. "They've informed me that some eighty families haven't paid their taxes," wrote Friar Alonso de León, the parish priest of the mountainous community of San Mateo Ixtatán in 1687. This signified not only that "his Majesty loses much of his royal tribute," but also that "all of those hidden don't hear Mass, nor confess." And as for the children of these absconders and heretics, the parents "only teach them to work their fields and live all day like barbarians in the forest."[10]

Not all Spanish clergy accepted the cruel policies of their compatriots. For example, Bishop Francisco Marroquín, the first bishop of what is today Guatemala, fought hard to stop the worst abuses that resulted from the enslavement of indigenous people and lobbied the Spanish Crown to decree more humane forms of treatment of the Indians. But even Bishop Marroquín was a realist who understood that the colonists' new mining and agricultural economy required Indian labor. So he did not actually advocate an end to the forced labor of Mayans, but rather less cruel forms of servitude.[11] Today Guatemala's Mayan population remains largely impoverished and exploited, still fueling the country's great cotton, sugar, and coffee plantations, nearly five centuries after the Spanish conquest began.

Over time the ever-political Catholic Church acquired substantial wealth and power within Guatemalan society, becoming the greatest landowner in the country.[12] Besides the many great churches, usually built with Indian labor, were schools, hospitals, even Guatemala's first university, the San Carlos, all of them within the Church's orbit. The Spanish empire and the Church reinforced each other: the state defended ecclesiastical authority, while the Church supported the divine rights of kings.[13] Even after independence from Spain in 1823, the presence of scores of foreign-born priests and nuns ensured that Catholic doctrine governed Guatemala's social and moral life. The Church's brand of ruthless paternalism, especially in Mayan communities, guaranteed a permanent degree of dependence on the clergy that continues to this day.

Monsignor Mariano Rossell was named archbishop of Guatemala City in 1939. By the early 1950s, especially with gruesome stories of Soviet-inspired religious persecution behind the iron curtain, nothing could have been more threatening to Archbishop Rossell than the presence of unabashed Communists, not only in the Guatemalan Congress, but in President Árbenz's inner circle of advisors as well. Subsequently, Msgr. Rossell's rabidly anti-Communist diatribes played an important role in the United States' cold war plot to destroy Árbenz. After the murder of Carlos Castillo Armas in 1957, Msgr. Rossell wrote a passionate tribute to his friend: "Carlos Castillo Armas, may God keep you in his glory forever and may this country never forget you! May the liberty that you gave to your people be effective and ever lasting."[14]

By the time Msgr. Rossell died in 1964, Guatemala was again ruled by a military dictatorship and in the throes of civil war. Some years before he died, Rossell brought a trusted friend, Mario Casariego, from El Salvador to Guatemala to serve as his auxiliary bishop in Guatemala City. Several decades had passed since Casariego lived briefly in Guatemala as a boy. So he really didn't know the country, didn't know the local clergy, who were now *his* clergy, and it's doubtful whether Casariego had ever had any contact with Guatemala's impoverished Mayan population. "He fell from the sky."[15] Following Msgr. Rossell's death, Casariego succeeded him as the next archbishop of Guatemala.[16]

Msgr. Casariego was a deeply conservative man and he became archbishop of Guatemala at the beginning of an era of dramatic change within the Catholic Church. Up to the Second Vatican Council (better known as Vatican II), which convened in Rome during the early 1960s, the Catholic Church was rigidly hierarchical. The Church's government and society deliberately maintained its distance from secular "civilian" life. Catholic affairs were (and still are) the province of bishops and priests, with nuns remaining far below their male colleagues in status and importance. Lay Catholics were expected to attend Mass regularly but not play a prominent role in the daily life of the Church.

Traditional liturgy reflected these rigid formalities during Mass. Instead of speaking in the languages of their communities, priests celebrated the Eucharist in Latin, unintelligible to most participants. Priests kept their backs to their congregation as they celebrated Mass, thereby emphasizing the gulf between lay persons and the clergy. Rather than addressing social issues in their communities, many priests and nuns of that era focused instead on polishing their self-images of perfection and saintliness.[17]

All of this began to change with Vatican II. The Catholic Church would no longer be an insular world unto its own. Instead, it would be a more human church, a church of the people, and lay persons, not just priests and nuns, were encouraged to assume roles within the Church's daily life and work. Masses would no longer be celebrated in incomprehensible Latin but rather in native languages, and priests would no longer turn their backs on their congregations. Nuns could exchange their long habits for shorter, more casual dress.

Vatican II shook the Church like an earthquake and, unsurprisingly, these changes were difficult for the extremely traditional archbishop of Guatemala to accept. When more contemporary nuns from the United States arrived in Guatemala to begin their pastoral work, they would first present themselves to the cleric. "And your *habit?*" Casariego would ask them. "*Where's* your *habit?*"[18] Nevertheless, the edicts of Vatican II came with the blessings of Pope Paul VI, and so Msgr. Casariego was compelled to incorporate them, more or less, into the Guatemalan Church.

In 1968 a much deeper rift over Church policy opened in the Americas. That year Latin America's Catholic bishops met in the Colombian city of Medellín to discuss the implementation of Vatican II in their region. The bishops who gathered in Medellín were painfully aware of the bitter poverty that gripped most of Latin America's population. They were also cognizant of the grotesque and volatile disparities between rich and poor in most Latin American nations and believed that the Catholic Church could and should work to alleviate these conditions. "Peace is, first of all, the work of justice." Accordingly, the bishops declared that pastoral agents should denounce abuses resulting from the excessive inequalities between rich and poor, between powerful and weak.[19]

This "preferential option for the poor" became a cornerstone of the developing concepts of "liberation theology." After Medellín, Latin American Catholics were instructed to strive to end injustice as a means toward the liberation of the masses living in poverty. In other words, Medellín called on Catholics to lift up the poor, although this would mean a loss of power and privilege for the upper classes.

For Guatemala's Archbishop Casariego, who was named a cardinal in 1969, such ideas of liberation theology were akin to Communism, and he wanted no part of it. The moralistic cleric had a tendency to blame the problems of the poor on the poor themselves, and seemed indifferent, if not blind, to the plight of Guatemala's indigenous population. In his first pastoral letter as archbishop, Casariego observed:

It's not incumbent on the Church to get involved in technical aspects of social problems. Its mission is to direct consciences and to encourage them to do right toward others. . . . How often it's not low salaries that cause the ruin of most families, but rather moral disorder, the lack of ideals, and the rash use of money![20]

"The teachings of Medellín are not the Gospel," Casariego reminded his parishioners in 1971. And "for many reasons, not all of the recommendations of Medellín can be implemented soon."[21] During the remainder of Msgr. Casariego's lifetime, few of those social and ecclesiastic changes occurred in his archdiocese.

However, more broad-minded bishops working in the stark poverty of the predominantly Mayan highlands, such as Msgr. Juan Gerardi Conodera in the northern provinces of Alta and Baja Verapaz and Msgr. Próspero Penados in the western province of San Marcos, tried to instill the reforms of Medellín in their dioceses. These progressive bishops recognized the need for reforms in land ownership so that indigenous communities could win access to credit and other development resources.

Thus in rural dioceses of Guatemala, where only a tiny fraction of Mayan farmers possessed enough land to support their families, Catholic religious workers taught courses on the new progressive doctrines and discussed the role of social justice in the Gospel. They also encouraged more lay persons and catechists to take an active role in expanding the Church's presence in the countryside.

Predictably, the Church's new, more political tone was welcomed in some revolutionary circles. "We like your way of thinking, Monseñor," a group of ORPA *guerrilleros* once told Bishop Penados when they stopped him on a rural road in San Marcos. The insurgents had been listening to the bishop's weekly radio sermons. "We want your support." Penados politely demurred, explaining that the Church was opposed to the use of violence as a means toward social change.[22]

The levels of violence generated by Guatemala's expanding armed conflict began to increase during the 1970s. At the same time divisions widened between the Church hierarchy, as personified by Cardinal Casariego, and several more progressive bishops and the broader community of priests and nuns, many of them foreign born, working in the slums of Guatemala City and in the impoverished countryside. Msgr. Casariego maintained close relationships with the military dictators of that era and insisted that Catholics be obedient to government authority. "You have to obey all of them," the cardinal would say, sounding like a true descendant of the conquest, "the good and the bad."[23]

Msgr. Casariego may have felt that this strategy would protect his Church from the increasing violence and polarization that was engulfing Guatemala. Nevertheless, the cardinal's policy became increasingly difficult for many priests and nuns to stomach as government repression escalated. As it did, the Catholic clergy began to pay a price for siding with the oppressed. Father Hermógenes López was murdered in June 1978, the day after he published a letter calling for the dissolution of the army. Msgr. Casariego preached the sermon at his funeral and the cardinal essentially blamed the murdered priest for his own death. López had strayed from his mission, said Casariego, suggesting that he was the one at fault for becoming involved in politics.[24]

Priests like Jesuits Ricardo Falla and Juan Hernández Pico challenged the cardinal's views and attempted to explain their perspectives on conditions in Guatemala, but Casariego would not hear them. "Shut up!" he would scream. "Or I'll throw you out of here!"[25] Most priests did not dare to contradict their cardinal. But some priests and nuns simply decided to ignore Cardinal Casariego, as did some of the bishops, who discreetly tried to support the religious communities working in the countryside.

By 1979 armed conflict was engulfing the northwestern highlands, resulting in the death and disappearance of thousands of innocent civilians, most of them at the hands of the army. The priests and nuns ministering to the poor communities of this area struggled to find an appropriate pastoral response. Some provided medical attention to wounded *guerrilleros*. Others sent clandestine shipments of food and medicine to groups of displaced civilians driven from their homes into the mountains by army counterinsurgency campaigns.

The Catholic religious workers knew that some of these supplies would likely find the way to the insurgents. But they felt a duty to do what they could to prevent innocents from starving. "We felt that we couldn't make distinctions as to *who* got *what*," recalled one nun. "We knew that there were many women and children in these areas. So whenever we could get medicine to [them], we would do that."[26]

Perhaps no other diocese of Guatemala suffered so terribly during these years of violence as El Quiché, a poor region of rugged mountains and steaming jungle whose population was almost 100 percent Mayan. By the late 1970s, the Church was struggling against monstrous levels of poverty in El Quiché. Most of the population was illiterate and condemned to a life of miserable drudgery, working small plots of corn and beans or migrating for months at a time to large plantations on the sweltering Pacific coast to cut sugar cane or harvest coffee.

In communities like San Gaspar Chajul, babies would die and rot inside their mothers' wombs for lack of a hospital where a caesarian could be performed. Children who survived to be born would learn to carry firewood as soon as they could walk. And by two or three years old, they would spend their days trudging through mud and rain, stumbling after their parents and older siblings, bent over by the weight of the logs on their back. If these children had the good fortune to live in a village where there was a one-room school, there would rarely be a teacher.

Msgr. Juan Gerardi had moved from Las Verapaces to El Quiché in late 1974, and the bishop and his diocesan community of priests and nuns made great strides in promoting the Medellín principles. Groups of Catholic Action, lay persons and catechists committed to using the Gospel as a tool for social action, sprang up in many communities.

After the Latin American bishops' conference published the results of the Medellín principles, Bishop Gerardi carefully underlined his newly defined role: "The Bishop is 'Christ's witness before all men,' *and his essential task is to place his people in conditions of bearing live and active gospel witness*" [emphasis in original].[27]

The Church was often the only institution to speak out against the violence and injustices occurring in El Quiché, and it directly accused the army of responsibility for civilian massacres.[28] Progressive Catholics viewed Juan Gerardi and the Quiché Diocese as a model of "a prophetic church," meaning a church that truly taught and practiced the prophetic gospel of Christ.[29]

Although the members of the Quiché Diocese effectively promoted the new spiritual tenets of Medellín, they were powerless to create alternative structures that would implement social change. By promoting "the option for the poor," the Church adopted revolutionary ideologies identical to those of the insurgents. And with the support of a small number of priests, El Quiché was also quickly becoming a stronghold for the EGP.[30] A few priests, such as the Spanish Jesuit Fernando Hoyos, opted to join the armed struggle. Father Hoyos eventually became an EGP *comandante* and died in combat.[31]

Many peasants of El Quiché saw the insurgents as "the messianic response" to their hopes for liberation, and they channeled their aspirations to the rebels.[32] This was a fatal mistake because the EGP would be unable to protect the populace from the army's future terror campaigns. Large numbers of *campesinos,* trusting neither the insurgents nor the military, fled the volatile countryside. They sought more security in the larger towns, the southern coastal plantations, and the anonymity of the growing shantytowns of Guatemala City. Those who stayed, the Mayan farmers of the mountainous countryside, would reap the awful whirlwind of Guatemala's armed conflict.

Catholic activists in El Quiché soon became targets of the army's counterinsurgency strategy. By early 1980 hundreds of catechists had been killed or disappeared, and scores of innocent peasants fled the rampaging army into remote mountain areas. Many catechists and Catholic leaders were among these displaced communities, and several members of Bishop Gerardi's diocesan community approached him for advice. As priests and as pastoral agents, should they follow the people into the mountains?

"They're Christians. They're our parishioners," responded the bishop. "Just because they're persecuted doesn't mean that we can abandon our commitment to them." Msgr. Gerardi told his priests that they could go into the mountains to accompany the innocent victims of the war as a pastoral service, not as *guerrilleros* participating in the armed struggle. "So if some of you believe you have the charisma to go help these people in the mountains, then go!"[33]

The army accused the bishop of sending his priests off to join the insurgents. When Gerardi drove past the entrance to the military base outside the provincial capital of Santa Cruz del Quiché, the soldiers on guard would pointedly load their machine guns as he went by.[34]

On several occasions army officials called Gerardi to the military base to complain that the Church was not collaborating with them. The bishop remained firm: "It's *you* who are killing; *you* are the enemies of the people. We have to be *with* the people. Therefore, we're on the opposite side from you. While you don't change, there can be no dialogue. We can't create a bridge of communication, so there can be no agreement between us."[35]

On June 4, 1980, soldiers killed Father José María Gran, a Spanish priest who served the parish of Chajul in the rugged mountains of northern El Quiché. Domingo Batz, Father Gran's devout Mayan sacristan who accompanied the priest that day, died with him. On July 10 Father Faustino Villanueva, another Spaniard who worked in the poor Quiché community of Joyabaj, was shot to death in his office. The priests and nuns who served parishes close to those of Gran and Villanueva fled the area, leaving large parts of El Quiché without any pastoral presence. On Saturday July 19 Bishop Gerardi narrowly avoided an ambush set for him along the road to San Antonio Ilotenango.[36]

After his escape, Msgr. Gerardi called all the members of his community, the remaining priests and nuns in El Quiché, to an emergency meeting in the capital. Originally the bishop had fourteen priests in the diocese. But now two were dead, and others had fled for their lives. Only five priests remained in the entire rugged province of El Quiché. Thus, the diocese was already half-destroyed. If the remaining religious community pulled out, they would be accused of abandoning their people at their hour of greatest need. But if they stayed, they would die. The bishop and priests and nuns debated what to do.

A majority of those present finally reached a painful decision. Due to the overwhelming levels of violence, they would temporarily close the Quiché Diocese. They hoped the decision would relieve pressure on the many Catholics in El Quiché who had suffered threats and assassination attempts from roving death squads. It would provide Msgr. Gerardi and others with an opportunity to denounce the violence directed at innocent persons in El Quiché. Perhaps by bringing national and international attention to bear on the region they would force the government to change its tactics. Furthermore, they rationalized, they were only closing the diocese temporarily. Once the tensions subsided, the pastoral agents would soon return.[37]

Most of this thinking was naive. With the Church absent from the mountains, there would be no more witnesses who could denounce the army's repression and guerrillas' abuses to the outside world. Life in El Quiché would become much worse before it got better.

The decision to close the diocese was unprecedented in the history of the Catholic Church. Nearly five centuries earlier, the first Spanish friars arriving in El Quiché imposed the Christian religion on the Mayan population. Now the descendants of those missionaries were being driven out, victims of the legacy of injustice born from the conquest, and unable to protect those who had accepted their faith.

It was too much for one group of nuns who disagreed with the decision and insisted upon returning to El Quiché. The nuns changed their minds several days later when death threats forced them to retreat to Guatemala City.[38]

Some clerics, including Cardinal Casariego, were critical of Juan Gerardi's decision to shut the diocese. Bishop Gerardi had become involved in politics, suggested Casariego, and now he was paying the price.[39] "You guys are rebellious!" Msgr. Casariego lectured a group of priests from El Quiché. "Troublemakers! Your work is provoking these problems up there. You're a bunch of tools of the Communist cause!"[40]

Other clergy accused Msgr. Gerardi and his community of deserting their ministry, of disloyalty to the people, and of being afraid to cope

with the consequences of a difficult situation.[41] Juan Gerardi had endured
the slaughter of hundreds of his catechists, the murder of two of his
priests, an attempt on his own life, and the closing of his diocese. Now
he had to face the rejection of his peers.

"It was a time when the polarization within the Church was very
strong," recalled Gerardi years later. "Those of the right, went with the
army. Those of the left, went against the army."[42] It was a disillusioning
experience for Gerardi and the members of his diocese. They had expected
the episcopal conference to support them, to make a strong statement
condemning the situation in El Quiché. But the show of support never
came. The government later forced Msgr. Gerardi into exile in Costa Rica.

With a Church both persecuted and divided, peasants in the countryside could expect little pastoral support as the repression sharpened between 1980 and 1983, and the army wiped out whole villages with impunity.[43] During the genocide—"an explosion of deep-seated national
racism"—approximately twenty thousand Mayan civilians died, 440 villages were destroyed, and up to a million people (many of them newly
widowed and orphaned) were displaced.[44] Guerrillas committed abuses
as well, but on a far smaller scale than the government forces.[45]

In spite of the holocaust taking place around them, a number of courageous religious workers attempted to stay with their people. In El
Quiché, at least one priest who had gone underground made several clandestine trips to the dirt-poor, war-ravaged villages in the southern part
of the diocese, secretly celebrating Mass, marrying couples, baptizing in-
fants, trying to provide a sacramental presence to the people and to maintain their spirit.

After waiting fruitlessly for a show of support from the Church hierarchy, four priests from El Quiché, including Father Axel Mencos, openly
returned to the diocese in late 1980 and resumed their work in separate
parishes. When the four men gathered in the provincial capital for Christmas Mass on the evening of December 24, they were amazed to find the
town's cathedral and central park full of people. Thousands of faithful
risked their lives to worship at that Christmas service. In spite of the violence, the army had failed to destroy the Catholic Church in El Quiché.[46]

But the army wasn't finished yet. In February 1981 Father Juan Alonso
Hernández was murdered on the road between the northern El Quiché
towns of Cunén and Uspantán. The remaining priests met in the town
of Chichicastenango with Bishop Víctor Hugo Martínez, who was attempting to administer the diocese's affairs in Msgr. Gerardi's absence.
"Let's go," said most of the men. "We can't stay here anymore."

Msgr. Martínez proposed that Father Mencos move to the neighboring province of Huehuetenango, but Mencos resisted the idea. Mencos had grown up in the Quiché town of Joyabaj. He knew the region and its people were *his* people. If he stayed, perhaps the army would kill him, but if he went somewhere else, the army could still kill him. And if he stayed, he could try to help the people of El Quiché. Eventually Msgr. Martínez acquiesced. Father Mencos would remain and take over the parish of Santa Cruz del Quiché, the provincial capital. But he would restrict his work to celebrating Mass, baptizing babies, and nothing more. And under no circumstances would he travel out to smaller towns and villages where the armed conflict was most intense.[47]

Father Mencos's work during the next few years was difficult, to say the least. He was the only priest openly working in El Quiché and the army used various methods to try to drive him away. Soldiers would search houses belonging to the church, sticking their bayonets in cracks in the floor, trying to find the tunnels that the priests had allegedly constructed for hiding *guerrilleros*. Under these conditions, Father Mencos stuck to his promise not to travel out into the more volatile rural communities.

Then one day in the end of 1981 a group of four old men from the town of San Andrés came to see Father Mencos in his office. Due to the violence, no one had celebrated Mass in their community for years. Could Father Mencos please come and give communion and baptize the children? "No," the priest told them, sitting behind his desk. "The bishop prohibited me from leaving town."

"But the *children*, Father," implored the men. "*Please*. They need it."

Father Mencos remained firm. "I can't." The old men sat in his office for an hour, trying without success to convince Mencos to come to their community. At last the priest stepped out of the room for a few minutes. When he returned, the four old men were sitting there weeping. Father Mencos realized that he had to go, and shortly thereafter he drove out to San Andrés, risking his life, celebrated Mass, and baptized the children.[48]

The repression directed at the Catholic Church spurred the rise of evangelical Protestant churches throughout the rural highlands.[49] As the counterinsurgency campaigns sharpened in the late 1970s and early 1980s, religious conversion became a common tool for survival.[50] "We make no distinction," warned a military commander in El Quiché, "between the Catholics and the Communist subversives."[51] Many catechists, afraid they would be identified and persecuted, buried their Bibles.[52]

Fear of becoming an army target, consequently, compelled many Guatemalans to abandon their Catholic faith, with its focus on consciousness raising and social justice. Many turned to conservative Protestant sects, which drew more attention to the afterlife instead of the inequities of life on earth.[53] "The escape into passivity beckoned harder" as the violence increased.[54] Greg Grandin eloquently describes this process and the strategy behind it: "The key to counterinsurgent triumph lay in the creation of a new way of thinking. Terror trained citizens to turn their political passions inward, to receive sustenance from their families, to focus on personal pursuits, and to draw strength from faiths less concerned with history and politics."[55]

"The escape into passivity" received another boost in March 1982 when General Efraín Ríos Mont, a born-again Christian and member of the Church of the Word (a Protestant sect established in Guatemala by the California-based Gospel Outreach), ascended to the presidency after a military coup. Ríos Mont's public moralizing, his hostility to Catholicism, and his projected image as a protector of the Mayan population broadened the base of the Protestant churches.[56]

Ríos Mont's regime also brought a partial change in counterinsurgency tactics. With its "plan of development and national security," the new government began to replace the use of indiscriminate violence with arguably less brutal methods designed to separate the rural population from the guerrillas and establish political control over Mayan communities.[57] In the new "development poles"—four large areas in the western highlands from which guerrillas had been cleansed—the army constructed new "model villages" for the resettlement, concentration, and control of formerly displaced persons. Jennifer Schirmer describes the forced restructuring of Mayan life within the development poles as "the most significant reorganization of the indigenous population since the Conquest, when *pueblos de indios* were established."[58] Within the development poles, evangelical Protestant sects constituted a significant part of the "development"![59]

In 1983 Cardinal Casariego died, and Pope John Paul named Msgr. Próspero Penados, the bishop of San Marcos, to be the next archbishop of Guatemala. Apart from Msgr. Gerardi, Penados had been one of the few Catholic bishops to speak out publicly against human rights abuses. During the remainder of the 1980s, in the midst of continuing political violence, Church leaders searched for ways to provide more assistance to the innocent victims of the civil war. Archbishop Penados was able to forge a degree of unity among the members of the episcopal conference, which published several very strong and controversial pastoral letters condemning the massacres of civilians and the unjust system of land distribution in Guatemala.[60]

The bishops also discussed the possibility of establishing a human rights office as one measure of increasing solidarity with the suffering people. In Chile and in El Salvador, the Catholic Church had created institutions that provided legal assistance and other support to victims of repression. The idea was repeatedly shelved in Guatemala, however. Political tensions and continued suspicion of the Church as a left-wing bastion forced the Catholic hierarchy to maintain a strategy of pure self-conservation for many years. Personnel at the U.S. Embassy shared these suspicions, observing at the end of the decade the Church's "growing leftward lean" as well as a proportional growth in tension between the Church and the military.[61]

In spite of these obstacles, in 1989 Archbishop Penados decided that conditions permitted the Church to take stronger measures in response to the human rights abuses that still plagued Guatemala. He would establish a human rights office that could provide legal assistance to victims of political violence. The coordinator of the new agency, the person responsible for overall policy, would be Msgr. Juan Gerardi, the former bishop of El Quiché, who had returned from exile and was now the auxiliary bishop of Guatemala.

Yet many issues remained unresolved, including the question of *who* would direct the office's daily operations. Following the precepts of Vatican II and Medellín, Bishop Gerardi wanted the director to be a lay Catholic, not a priest. But this work had never been done before in Guatemala, and there were few people willing to take on such a dangerous task. So the position of director remained vacant until Msgr. Gerardo Flores, bishop of Las Verapaces, spoke to Archbishop Penados about a young lawyer named Ronalth Ochaeta.

A graduate of USAC's law school, and a Catholic, Ochaeta had been practicing law for several years in Guatemala City. When he wasn't attending to clients, he assisted groups of *campesinos* displaced by the civil war from areas near Ochaeta's native city of Cobán. Many of these persons lost their identity papers during the war, so Msgr. Flores would send them to Ochaeta, who would prepare their new documents without charge.

Ochaeta was also politically astute and a number of his friends sat on the board of directors of USAC's student association. In August and September 1989 ten members of the board were disappeared. They were tortured and killed at the Island, the same place where Maritza would be detained in 1992.[62] In the weeks that followed, the tortured bodies of five of the student leaders were found in Guatemala City. Gripped by fear that they would soon suffer the same fate, Ochaeta and several of his friends from the student association sought assistance from the U.S. Embassy. They were all given tourist visas to enter the United States. When the visas expired, suggested one embassy official, they should lose themselves there.

Ochaeta's friends fled to the United States, but he hesitated. He was a lawyer. He didn't want to spend the next few years in exile, washing dishes in Los Angeles or Miami. Instead he returned to his parents' home in Cobán. For three months Ochaeta never left the house, except to seek the advice of his mentor, Msgr. Flores. What should he do? Should he leave the country?

No, the bishop told him. Stay at home for a while and don't make a hasty decision. Stay if your conscience is clear. If you're not involved in anything, then you should not leave. If you leave, then the army will assume you *were* doing something wrong and *had* to leave. Msgr. Flores urged Ochaeta to remain in Guatemala to avoid this badge of guilt. So Ochaeta stayed in hiding at his parents' house. Shortly thereafter, Msgr. Flores heard that Archbishop Penados was looking for a lawyer to be the director of the archdiocese's new human rights office, known as the ODHA (Oficina de Derechos Humanos del Arzobispado). Msgr. Flores recommended Ochaeta for the job. In late 1989, just a few months after his friends were disappeared, Ochaeta left his refuge in Cobán and returned to Guatemala City to start the ODHA.

SIX

MONDAY AND TUESDAY

July 27–28, 1992

At 8:00 on Monday morning, they brought Maritza breakfast. At 9:00 A.M. Don Chando entered the room and told her that they had to re-film the video; they didn't like the previous version. The men took Maritza to a bathroom and told her to bathe and fix her makeup. Again Maritza piled on the cosmetics, trying to show whoever saw the video that she was not acting voluntarily.

The men brought Maritza to the same room where they had filmed on Saturday. The new speech that Maritza would read was printed on large sheets of paper attached to the headboard of a bed. The text was similar to the previous declarations, but this time Maritza acknowledged the help of Otto Peralta, the president of the University Students Association, and she omitted any expression of gratitude to military officers such as the retired dictator General Arana.

They spent the entire morning filming and then her captors brought Maritza lunch. While she ate, the men left to watch the new video. They returned in the afternoon and Don Chando was furious. *The film wasn't any good!* Maritza had to speak more slowly; she acted like she was reading the statement. And the other men had to be absolutely silent while they shot the video. Don Chando left the room and Maritza heard him order the people in the corridor to be silent while they filmed. When Don Chando returned to the room, he gave new instructions to the cameraman regarding the video. Maritza overheard the cameraman say: "I was a soldier too. I know something about military discipline too."[1] They continued to film the video until about 7:00 P.M., when her captors brought Maritza back to her room. Don Chando entered and told her that she had done a good job, and that they would film some more the following day. Maritza's mind was racing. She had done everything they asked. She had tried her best to record the video the way the men wanted it. She wanted them to let her go so that she could go home to her son. Maritza began to go crazy thinking about her little boy and how he would miss her. How he would be asking where she was.[2] Which, of course, was precisely what the men wanted her to do.

Monday, 7:30 A.M. On the way to his office downtown, an attorney from the human rights ombudsman's office stopped by the Urrutia home for the first of several visits, to offer help. Maritza's father, Edmundo, welcomed the attorney into the home, but he had little to say. Edmundo could not give any information as to why his daughter might have been kidnapped. He just knew that she was gone.

Edmundo had been awake for quite some time. Following Maritza's disappearance, the slight, silver-haired man anxiously arose every morning at five or six, when the sun began to rise, and went to the front door. Edmundo would stand in the doorway for a few minutes, looking up and down the street to see if Maritza was coming home.[3] Later on, around seven, the neighbors began to knock on the door to ask if Maritza had appeared.

Early Monday morning a piece of paper lay shoved under the ODHA's office door. Someone had scrawled "*Compañeros* of the Human Rights Office of the Archdiocese" across the top of the page. Below was a typed message describing how "heavily armed men carrying small radio communication devices" captured Maritza the previous Thursday morning. The vehicle that spirited Maritza away was a black, late-model Isuzu Trooper, with license plate number P4980. Another sentence was scrawled on the bottom of the page: "If possible, make a communiqué with this information."[4] Some men had come to the archbishopric late Sunday afternoon and asked the building's caretaker to deliver the message to the human rights office. They didn't say who they were or where they were from.

When Ronalth Ochaeta arrived at the ODHA, I briefed him about my phone conversations with Jones and Maritza's father over the weekend, and I showed him the anonymous message. I wanted to pursue this case. Ochaeta gave me his approval and said that he would try to trace the license plate to its owner.

Bonnie Tenneriello called from her office in WOLA in Washington, D.C. Tenneriello explained that she heard the news about Maritza's disappearance over the weekend. There was a possibility that some U.S. senators might sign a letter on Maritza's behalf. If so, WOLA would fax the letter rapidly to Guatemala.

"Juan" and "Pedro," two students from USAC's School of History, entered the ODHA. They explained that they were trying to help Maritza and asked what the Catholic Church could do for her. Juan and Pedro knew that the Church's involvement in Maritza's case would give more credibility to the campaign to save her life. Could we arrange a special mass for her? A public religious ceremony would demonstrate to the government how quickly the movement to save Maritza had grown. Perhaps we could invite the public to a mass for Maritza in the cathedral?

Pedro had already spoken with Father Sergio Orantes, one of the two priests who served the cathedral's congregation. Born into a middle-class family in Guatemala City, Father Sergio was the great-nephew of Msgr. Mariano Rossell, the anti-Communist archbishop of the 1940s and 1950s. Sergio's parents were deeply conservative Catholics, and when young Sergio graduated from high school in 1978, he considered joining the Jesuit Order, but his mother wouldn't let him. She thought that the Jesuits were too close to the Communists.

So Sergio enrolled in USAC, and for two and a half years studied electrical engineering and physics. He earned good grades, but Sergio felt that something was missing in his life. He decided to enter the seminary in Guatemala City and become a diocesan priest. He was ordained in late 1990, and in June 1992 Sergio became rector of Guatemala City's cathedral; the following month he was appointed director of the associated Catholic school known as the Colegio de Infantes. To an impressionable foreigner like myself, Father Sergio exuded vigor and idealism.

After Pedro explained the students' request for a mass for Maritza, Father Sergio seemed a bit suspicious: "And *why* are they doing this?" Father Sergio was well aware of the School of History's reputation as a center for Marxist students and faculty. Those who expounded these ideologies would likely be atheists, and Pedro sensed that Father Sergio was suspicious of their motives. *Why* would *these* students request the assistance of the Church?

So Pedro earnestly explained to the priest about his earlier university experience of the late 1970s and early 1980s, about the violence that devastated USAC. He talked about the fact that nearly all of Guatemalan society is Christian, and that in times like these they had to unify their efforts in order to save lives. The students did not want a repetition of the violence that occurred under the earlier military regimes.

Pedro explained that a general assembly of the School of History would convene later that evening to discuss Maritza's case, and they would ask all of the students to attend the mass. Besides, he reminded the priest, there were many Catholics in the university. By the time Pedro left Father Sergio's office, Father Sergio seemed convinced, even enthusiastic about celebrating the public mass for Maritza.

Father Sergio discussed the idea with his colleague Father Luis Pérez, and the two priests agreed that the mass should be a public expression of solidarity with Maritza's family and with the community. It would be a divine petition to God to protect Maritza's life.

But before committing themselves, Father Luis and Father Sergio wanted to consult their boss, Archbishop Penados. Father Luis called the archbishop and asked for his advice. Should we do the mass or not? Msgr. Penados was adamant: they *had* to celebrate the mass. But in order to reduce tensions, Father Luis or Father Sergio should do it, not the more visible and political archbishop. If Msgr. Penados celebrated the mass, the government might interpret it as a provocation or challenge, which was not the kind of message that would assist Maritza.[5] Eventually, it was agreed that Father Sergio would celebrate the mass on Tuesday afternoon at 5:30 P.M.

At 4:00 on Monday afternoon, Jones from the U.S. Embassy and two military officers from the U.S. Department of Defense in Washington, D.C., arrived at the ODHA for a meeting with Ochaeta and myself. We met in the ODHA's conference room, and the officers explained that in the near future, the Department of Defense would be sponsoring a five-day course in the United States concerning human rights and democracy. The course would be directed to Guatemalan military personnel with the rank of major and above, as well as members of other Guatemalan institutions that had ties to the Defense Ministry. Civilian and military students would be mixed together during the seminar, and the curriculum would emphasize the democratic principle that civilian institutions should control the armed forces.[6] Ochaeta and I listened politely.

When the meeting ended and we left the conference room, Edmundo René Urrutia and Kappy Riker were waiting to speak with Ochaeta and me. Before leaving the archbishopric, Jones stopped briefly to speak with Edmundo René and Kappy. Early on in their communications, Jones had made it clear that if Kappy chose to remain in Guatemala in order to help Maritza, that was her choice. But the embassy could not guarantee her safety. So Kappy's decision to stay in order to help Edmundo René and Maritza put Jones and his superiors at the embassy in a difficult position.

Since Sunday, Jones had been raising Maritza's disappearance with his superiors in the U.S. Embassy, hoping that higher-ranking officials would express their concerns to their counterparts in the Guatemalan government. Amongst themselves, embassy representatives debated whether Maritza had performed a "self-kidnapping," which was the explanation provided to the embassy military attaché by his contacts in the Guatemalan army.

After Jones and the U.S. military personnel left the ODHA, I showed Edmundo René the anonymous letter referring to the license plate that the ODHA received. Edmundo René handed the message back to me dismissively and told me to forget about it. I was shocked. *How could we forget about it?* But Edmundo René understood the tactics of the dirty war. He realized immediately that the message came from an EGP front group and that the story about the license plate was planted in order to link the Guatemalan government to Maritza's kidnapping. The URNG was trying to turn Maritza's disappearance to its own political advantage and was firing its own shots in the propaganda war to establish the "truth." "That's the problem with politics," Edmundo René remarked to me several years later. "It's theater. It's a game with masks."[7]

The afternoon newspaper *La Hora* contained two articles about Maritza. In a long report with photographs of Maritza's parents standing by prayer candles in their home, the story of the kidnapping was repeated, but this time it included the alleged license plate number. Edmundo and his wife continued to wear the masks of innocents, trying to sell this image to the government and to the public. As Edmundo had told the press that morning, he could not explain why his daughter was kidnapped, given that she never had any political ties or links to student groups. Pilar told the reporter that Maritza dedicated herself solely to caring for her son, who was now sad and calling all the time for his mother.[8] Sometime after 5:00 P.M. a colleague from the ODHA and I drove from the center of Guatemala City to the Urrutia home in zone eight. Some neighbors were leaving as we arrived, and Edmundo and Pilar received us warmly as we discussed Maritza over coffee and cake. After I explained who I was and the work of the ODHA, Edmundo was very calm and polite, but he could shed very little light on Maritza's disappearance. I did not understand that the family distrusted all of the individuals and institutions that had begun to investigate Maritza's disappearance. Who knew *which* organizations were infiltrated, and *which* were not?

And now I was asking a lot of questions. No, Edmundo explained, Maritza had not reported any problems to them in the recent past. She seemed fine. They had no idea why Maritza was kidnapped. Of course they would attend the mass for Maritza on Tuesday afternoon.

In the middle of the conversation Maritza's sister, Carolina, returned home with four-year-old Sebastián. His grandparents tried to play with Maritza's son as if they were happy and everything was normal. Finally I suggested to Edmundo that if Maritza was released, perhaps the ODHA could offer Maritza protection. Always gracious, Edmundo agreed to consider the idea, and thanked me for taking an interest in his daughter's case. After we left, Carolina cautioned her father: "Be careful, Papá. Don't tell them too much. We don't know where they're from." Then, as he had done every night since Maritza disappeared, Edmundo went to his room and cried.[9]

TUESDAY, JULY 28, 1992

On Tuesday morning, the men returned to Maritza's room and told her that they had to film the video again. There were mistakes in the version that they produced on Monday. Again Maritza was unnerved and she screamed at them that she wanted to return to her home. "You said that I could go home if I made the recording, and I obeyed you!"

"Calm down," Don Chando kept telling her. "You can't leave just yet. Calm down."[10]

Apart from her fear and exhaustion, there were other reasons for Maritza's outburst. She was afraid that eventually the men would capture one of her EGP *compañeros* who would inform them that Maritza had been lying about her role in the Organización, her fictitious comrades such as Argelia, and other parts of her story. Time was working against Maritza. And perhaps her captors were simply planning to kill her.[11]

Another man entered the room and asked Maritza questions about the declaration that she had written previously. He told her that he couldn't read her handwriting in certain sections. This man was very severe with his questioning and he asked about Argelia. "Where does she live?" Now from memory, Maritza answered many of the same questions over again.

Before the men took Maritza to start filming again, she went into the bathroom and put on a great deal of makeup. She pulled her hair back, arranging it in a style she had never used before.

There was a different man helping with the film that day. He was tall and dressed in black motorcycle clothing: leather jacket, gloves, et cetera. His entire body was covered; Maritza couldn't see a bit of his skin. This was "Caballo" (Horse), who outranked most of the other army specialists at the Island. Caballo had suffered an accident recently with an exploding gas canister, and he wanted to hide his burns from Maritza.[12] His face was covered, as were the faces of all the men who assisted in the recording.

Caballo took the job of changing the cards that Maritza read for the camera. He kept his gloves on, which made it difficult for him to change the cards quickly as Maritza spoke.

After they filmed Maritza's statement, the men brought a color television into the room in order to show Maritza the video. Don Chando was angry again. Maritza was blinking too much and she looked like she was reading. Her gestures seemed very nervous.

When the men left the room, they left Maritza alone with the escort who was guarding her that day. It was very hot and Maritza asked him if she could remove her mask. "Buche" said OK. He was a small Mayan man with very fine features who resembled a man from India. Buche worked with Don Chando in the office, compiling information for their intelligence reports.

The *guilty one* was her husband, the man said to Maritza. He had done bad things. But she had gotten involved in things she never should have done. Buche seemed to want to talk and Maritza began to ask him questions. "Have you ever kidnapped people?" That was his job, and he followed orders. "Have you ever killed anyone?" Yes. When they ordered him to kill someone, he did it. People like Maritza hurt the country. When people like her don't change their habits, sometimes they have to kill them.[13]

Buche kept talking: He knew Maritza had worked very hard on the video. Maritza told him she missed her son and wanted to see Sebastián so badly she could hardly stand it. "Are you married? Do you have children?" He had only recently been married. His bride was just nineteen.

After a while Buche told Maritza to put her mask back on, and he left the room. Soon the other men returned and started to film again. Her captors made some more changes in the text that Maritza had to read. There was more emphasis on Otto Peralta, the Students Association's leader, and on the School of History at USAC. The men had deleted part of the script, but they added a section in which Maritza called on her *compañeros* to abandon the armed struggle.

After they stopped filming, Don Chando said that Maritza was going to call her family and tell them that she was fine and that she'd be home tomorrow. He was moving very quickly; giving lots of orders concerning their preparations to leave the Island, and Maritza began to feel more afraid. *Are they taking me out to kill me?*[14] The fair-skinned man had spoken about amnesty, but Maritza had always been afraid to actually believe that they would free her. As the days passed, it seemed that the men were improvising; that events were not occurring according to their plan. Maritza knew that if she allowed her hopes to rise too high, she might be frustrated and then broken completely.[15]

What's happening? What does it all mean? The men had told Maritza that she would be freed after she made the video. But perhaps they actually planned to kill her and orchestrate her death as if the Organización was responsible. They could use the video to show that the EGP killed her in reprisal for making the statement. For treason to the revolution. The men brought her outside and put her in the cab of a truck. Maritza's mind continued to race: *Now are they going to kill me?*[16]

Don Chando sat in the driver's seat. "Don't make a lot of noise."[17] Maritza sat between Don Chando and another man. Previously, the men had carried pistols when they took Maritza outside the installation. But that evening they brought machine guns, and Maritza felt even more afraid. Every time the men changed a detail of the daily routine, Maritza's fear increased. *Perhaps they're using different weapons because they've decided to kill me.*

Once in the truck, the men permitted Maritza to remove her mask. For a long time they drove along the *periférico*, the semicircular highway that cuts around the interior of Guatemala City. Finally, they entered the parking lot of a shopping mall in zone seven. The men escorted Maritza to a public telephone where she called her father and told him she'd be back home the next day.

They returned to the truck and the men placed the newspaper back on Maritza's face and pushed her head down toward the seat. They drove for more than an hour and seemed to be leaving the city. Maritza assumed they were taking her to an isolated spot in order to kill her. Silently she began to recite the Our Father, trying to calm herself and prepare for her death.[18]

Eventually, Maritza was able to raise her head a bit and could see they were still in the capital. She began to relax. In a few more minutes, they arrived back at the Island. The men brought Maritza back to her room and handcuffed her to the bed.

For the first time, Maritza's captors turned the light off that night. But they left the radio on at full volume. It was tuned in to a Christian fundamentalist station. Maritza tried to calm herself and rest, but the events of the evening had shaken her terribly. The radio blared all night long. Maritza began to feel ill and she called out to her guard to take her to the bathroom. Her stomach was upset and she had diarrhea. "Look, I feel bad. Can you do me a favor?"

Coroncho was on duty that night, and he hesitated. Maritza had used the bathroom earlier, and their rules limited prisoners to one trip to the bathroom per day. But he saw Maritza's distress, so he spoke to his superior. "She says that she can't wait. She's sick to her stomach." So Coroncho unlocked Maritza's handcuffs and, keeping her face covered, led her to the bathroom.

As Maritza sat in the bathroom for a long time, Coroncho stood in the corridor with the door ajar, listening in case Maritza tried to do something out of the ordinary. Although his sympathy for Maritza prompted Coroncho to bend the rules that night, Coroncho usually followed his orders to the letter. Before Maritza's arrival, Coroncho had learned the art of assassination at the Island, killing several prisoners under orders, using his knife or strangling them. You could not refuse an order at the Island.[19] That would be to risk death.

After Maritza finished in the bathroom, Coroncho led her back to her room. She was grateful for his kindness. "I understand that you guys aren't in charge. But I needed to go to the bathroom."

"Don't worry," Coroncho told her. "I'm going to help you."

"Thanks."[20]

Before dawn Tuesday morning Father Sergio rose, as he did every morning, to pray, meditate, and prepare the masses he would celebrate that day. He selected the biblical sections and the prayers that he would use, trying to find passages that would be "illuminating" for Maritza's crisis. And he prepared a *strong* sermon, accusatory and confrontational, denouncing violations of human rights in Guatemala. After his morning run, Father Sergio celebrated early morning Mass in the cathedral and preached his tough sermon about Maritza's disappearance.

Next door inside the archbishopric, Ronalth Ochaeta had traced the license plate number of the mysterious Isuzu Trooper to a vehicle registered to President Serrano's office. When Bonnie Tenneriello from the Washington Office on Latin America called Ochaeta to ask for news regarding Maritza, Ochaeta explained that the license plate was registered to "the Presidential Guard."[21] Ochaeta urged Tenneriello to lobby interested members of the U.S. Congress. Ask them to act on Maritza's behalf as soon as possible, preferably that same day.

After Tenneriello conveyed this new information to her contacts on Capitol Hill, four U.S. senators co-signed a letter that day addressed to President Serrano.[22] The senators expressed their "serious concern" about Maritza's abduction and urged Serrano to do everything in his power to locate Maritza and secure her immediate release. The letter also noted that witnesses to the abduction indicated that a vehicle belonging to the "Presidential Guard" had participated in Maritza's disappearance.

Shortly after Ochaeta conveyed the news about the license plate to Washington, Edmundo René and Kappy arrived at the human rights office. As a young *guerrillero* during the late 1960s Edmundo René had seen his *compañeros*, even his lovers, die horrible deaths. The body of his first girlfriend appeared in a newspaper photograph shortly after Edmundo René left the FAR. She died when the police stormed a guerrilla safe house. Twenty years later those memories still haunted Edmundo René, still *taunted* him: "When the revolution comes, there will be no more conflict." "*Red cells. White cells. They're all the same!*" But after his *hermanita* disappeared, Edmundo René had to push these demons aside. So he held his fear and pain in check and tirelessly explored new channels of assistance for Maritza. He sent a letter that day to Msgr. Rodolfo Quezada, a Catholic bishop and leader of Guatemala's National Reconciliation Commission, asking him to act as an intermediary in order to obtain Maritza's release.[23] Msgr. Quezada served as the conciliator in ongoing peace negotiations between the Guatemalan government, the army, and the URNG. Edmundo René faxed newspaper articles concerning Maritza to Heather Wiley of Amnesty International and expressed his gratitude for anything that Wiley could do on behalf of his sister.[24]

When Edmundo René reached the ODHA that Tuesday morning, Ochaeta and I happily told him that we had traced the license plate to President Serrano's office, and that Ochaeta had provided this information to the NGOs in Washington. Edmundo René was appalled. He wanted to maintain a nonconfrontational strategy in order to save Maritza's life. Edmundo René wanted to send a very specific message to the army: "We are not your enemies. *Don't kill her.*"[25] Now the Catholic Church, working with good intentions but without all of the facts, was undermining his strategy. Coincidentally, a television news team arrived at the ODHA just moments after Edmundo René and Kappy did. Dumbfounded, I watched Edmundo René immediately approach the reporters.

Speaking before the cameras, Edmundo René explained that his family was not accusing the government, or any institution, of responsibility for Maritza's disappearance. Nor did they know anything about an Isuzu Trooper with license plate number P4980. They just wanted Maritza's safe return. Edmundo René would make the same statements to *La Hora* later that day, underscoring that he did not know the motive for Maritza's kidnapping.[26] But every human life was *precious,* Edmundo René emphasized to the press, and the Urrutia family was very humanistic. Using all his political skills and every cell of his brilliant mind, Edmundo René pushed the nonconfrontational line. Fighting, fighting, fighting to save his sister's life.

The mass for Maritza was scheduled to begin in the great eighteenth-century cathedral at 5:30 on Tuesday afternoon. The cathedral's cement facade was stained light brown by time and pollution. But the three pairs of old wooden doors with their circular brass plates retained their polished beauty. Cupolas constructed of ornate cement and glass tiles topped each of the two tall bell towers, and on each cupola stood a black iron cross that seemed to touch the sky. Soon the bells in the towers would call worshipers to mass.

Maritza's disappearance received a great deal of press attention that day as the battle for "the truth" intensified. The *Prensa Libre* reported that a delegation from USAC—including *el Rector Magnífico* of the university, the president of the students association, and students from the school of history—met with Vice President Gustavo Espina. The vice president acknowledged that he had received the university's request to locate Maritza. But he nimbly explained that "this doesn't imply that we had a direct participation in the kidnapping."[27] The human rights ombudsman, Ramiro de León Carpio, also met with the USAC delegation, and de León Carpio demanded that the government effect Maritza's prompt appearance.[28] Tuesday's *Siglo Veintiuno* contained three separate articles about Maritza and in one piece, the army's spokesperson denied any links between the armed forces and Maritza's disappearance.[29]

At 5:25 P.M. inside the cathedral, final preparations for Maritza's mass were under way. One by one, a sacristan lit the candles in the large silver candelabra standing at each corner of the marble altar. Father Sergio reviewed the text of his sermon and watched Maritza's family enter the church, embrace friends who had arrived, and take their seats in a front pew. Old friends of Maritza's parents, some they had not seen for thirty years, came to the mass to pray for Maritza. A large group of university students from the School of History, Juan and Pedro among them, sat in the back rows. Oblivious to the coming celebration for Maritza, a Mayan family, the mother wearing a brightly woven yellow blouse, knelt together in prayer at one of the smaller altars.

The air inside the great cathedral carried the musty smell of time and its worn, wooden pews were nearly full as Father Sergio began the mass. According to the afternoon *La Hora,* the celebration of the mass would be a prayer for Maritza's prompt and safe appearance.[30] But word had reached the ODHA about the strong sermon that Father Sergio had preached earlier that day about Maritza. I had explained to Father Sergio that it was important that he use a tone that was somewhat softer, one that would protect Maritza rather than provoke more confrontation with the authorities. So Father Sergio softened the tone of his sermon a little and made it a bit more conciliatory.[31] But not much.

Father Sergio spoke from a lectern on the large central altar below the cathedral's tall dome. A smaller dome of beautiful red and gray marble, topped by a golden cross and supported by four marble pillars, rested above the altar. Twelve crystal chandeliers hung from the tall ceiling over the center aisle.

"In the name of the Father, the Son, and the Holy Spirit, amen," Father Sergio intoned solemnly. "May the God of Hope . . . be always with you." He wore an emerald green velvet robe that sparkled down the middle.

> Good afternoon, brothers and sisters, I cannot say that it is with much happiness that I begin this Mass of the Eucharist, but it is a great honor. A great honor to be alive and to celebrate this mass of prayer for the appearance of Maritza Urrutia García. May the Lord move the human beings, *if that's what you can call them,* who kidnapped her, and not only those persons, but all those who kidnap in this country and in all of Latin America. . . . May the Lord move the hearts of those men so that we obtain the liberty of Maritza Urrutia, . . . and of all who suffer these abuses.[32]

A polished wooden crucifix glowed in the candlelight behind Father Sergio as he led the congregation in prayer. As he spoke, every bump or stumble against the wooden pews, every child's cry, every footstep on the floor of old, gray flagstones echoed throughout the great hall. The flagstones were unevenly worn by the feet of two centuries of worshipers, and at times one felt a bit off balance traversing the corridors. Two young women came to the microphone and offered special prayers, and then Father Sergio stepped to the microphone again to offer a homily.

"*Hallelujah, Hallelujah*, . . . The Lord is with you." Reading from the Gospel, Father Sergio described the prophets finding death in the countryside, as well as people dying of hunger in the cities. This passage, he observed, could well describe the present situation in Guatemala. Human rights are a positive expression of the Gospel and the Word of the Lord, explained Father Sergio. Nevertheless, "We have to recognize that at this moment, human rights are being violated in Guatemala; violations that make us remember the bloody repression of the military governments of 1978, and thereafter."[33]

Standing in the back of the cathedral, I was uncomfortably aware that this might not be the appropriate political tone for a mass requesting Maritza's deliverance. And in the front pew, poor Edmundo René went into shock.[34]

Father Sergio continued. "Disgracefully, although we have entered into a democracy, violence continues to operate in our country. . . . We have to change our hearts!" pleaded Father Sergio. "We're open to changing our society! It's time for men to assume power, and for the *gorillas* to go to jail!" *Gorillas* was student slang for members of the military.

"What the devil!" Juan sat in the students' pew in the back of the cathedral. "This priest has gone too far!"[35] The students knew that in these kinds of public events, army informants were often present, observing the people in attendance. Pedro noticed two suspicious-looking men, dressed in the cheap suits and ties typical of Guatemalan government bodyguards, leaning against the wall nearby. The men did not seem to be paying attention to the mass. So for their own security, the students tried to watch the people who were watching them.

"We have to transform ourselves in order to create a new system," continued Father Sergio. "We will transform [our country], and we will win respect for our fatherland. Let the Lord hear our prayers and let Maritza, and all persons who have been kidnapped, appear alive, healthy and well. And if not," Sergio continued fervently, "may the Lord take this blood into account, *and may this blood* (although we definitely hope not in the case of Maritza) transform and purify our Guatemala."[36] He was almost challenging Maritza's captors to kill her.

It was not exactly a conciliatory, apolitical sermon. As he left the cathedral, Edmundo René murmured to his sister Carolina: "I've never been to a mass like that."[37] I sat nervously in the back of the cathedral as Father Sergio recited his final prayers for the pope, the bishops of Guatemala, and for Maritza and her family. *If she was still alive, were we helping Maritza or hurting her?*

After the mass, Edmundo René and Kappy drove from downtown to his parents' home in zone eight. As they drove, they noticed three men in a vehicle in the lane next to them. The other vehicle would speed up and slow down whenever theirs did. The men followed Edmundo René and Kappy all the way to zone eight.[38]

SEVEN

WEDNESDAY

July 29, 1992

At 9:00 A.M. on Wednesday morning, the men brought Maritza to the bathroom. When she returned to her room, her breakfast was waiting for her, and that day, for the first time, they served her on china plates. All her previous meals had come on plastic dishes. Maritza's stomach was still upset, so she could not eat very much.

The dark-skinned man who had interrogated Maritza on Tuesday entered the room. He told Maritza to write more, to write down everything she knew about her ex-husband and about all of her friends. After Maritza had been writing for a while, Don Chando entered the room and told Maritza they were going to film again. They took Maritza to the bathroom so she could prepare herself. That morning her captors gave Maritza her own clothing, which they had taken the day of her kidnapping. They had washed her clothes. Maritza put her clothes on but, as before, applied a lot of makeup to her face.

They filmed all morning. At about 1:00 P.M. Don Chando came into Maritza's room and told her that soon she would be with her son. There were just some final changes in the video that they had to make. Don Chando said that they had to shorten Maritza's statement. They were deleting the section where Maritza requested amnesty from the government. Maritza objected, telling him that they *had* to preserve the part about her amnesty; that was an important part of her declaration. No, Don Chando told her, people would understand, based on everything that Maritza was saying, that she wanted amnesty.[1]

Don Chando left the room and then returned with two other men who he said were his superiors. One of them stood behind Maritza and rubbed her back, telling her that everyone knew how hard she had worked on the video. Soon they would permit Maritza to rejoin her son. She just had to try once more to make a good recording.

When that man left the room, the other began to speak to Maritza. She had to re-do the video, he told her. She had to do it convincingly. In the previous recordings, Maritza acted like she didn't want to pronounce the words she said. She had to do it in a way that seemed natural. It was just that she was incredibly tired, Maritza told him. She had gone almost seven days without sleeping; she was nervous and trembling from lack of rest. The man responded, "When you say in the video that now you don't want to be in the Organización, you have to say it like you really feel that way. It looks like it's painful for you to leave the Organización, like what you're saying is a lie."[2] Maritza told him that the only thing she wanted was to take care of her little boy.

At 5:00 P.M. they went back to work on the video's final version. The men told Maritza to smile when she spoke. Don Chando seemed to be in a big hurry. After they finished recording, he left the room. Returning fifteen minutes later, he told Maritza they had to make some telephone calls. Don Chando told Maritza she had to call the television news programs *Teleprensa* and *Notisiete,* telling them to broadcast a film that Maritza would send them.

Her captors handcuffed Maritza and briefly left her alone. She tried to understand what the men would do with the video, and what would happen to her after it was aired on television. Perhaps they planned to kill her, and then they would use the video as a pretext for blaming URNG guerrillas for her death. The video showed that Maritza was a traitor to the Organización, and the URNG would have a reason to seek vengeance against her.[3] Maritza lay there alone, waiting for what would happen next.

Don Chando returned to the room. Soon they would go to make the telephone calls. Don Chando told Maritza she was going to call her family and tell them that she would return home that night. Maritza said she would do it, but she didn't believe him. Maritza insisted that she wanted to legalize her situation. The men had forced her to say so much in the video, but now they had deleted the part where she requested amnesty. But as a protection for herself and for her family, Maritza wanted the Guatemalan government to take responsibility for her security. Once she formally received amnesty, President Serrano's government would lose face if anything happened to her.

"But what about my amnesty?" Maritza asked the fair-skinned man. "This isn't fair! You said you were going to arrange my amnesty! Are you going to call Acisclo Valladares to arrange it?"[4] Acisclo Valladares was Guatemala's attorney general. Don Chando thought for a moment and left the room.

When he returned ten minutes later, Don Chando said that they were going to call her family and the television stations. Now Maritza would tell her family she would return home on the following day, but they should watch the ten o'clock news that night on television. Maritza protested, "But you said that I would go home *tonight!*"

At about 7:00 P.M. they put Maritza in a large car with four men and drove to zone eighteen to make the telephone calls. When they arrived at a public telephone, Don Chando handed Maritza the telephone and told her to call *Teleprensa* first. Maritza called and told the station: "I'm Maritza Urrutia. Tonight on your program, I want you to broadcast the video that some friends of mine left you." Next she called *Notisiete* and gave them the same message. Finally, she called her family and spoke to her father. "Watch the news later tonight. I'll be coming home tomorrow."[5]

Don Chando brought Maritza back to the vehicle and fifteen minutes later they were back in the installation. Maritza was handcuffed to her bed again, and Don Chando sat by her side and told her that they were going to do some work.

He asked Maritza what she thought about the amnesty. Don Chando explained that he didn't have the power to grant it to her. He had already told her that his organization was not part of the government. But his organization was very patriotic and took action against any person who damaged the country, even if the person was part of the army or the government. "Don't you see how things are in Guatemala?" Don Chando asked her. "There are a lot of thieves and drug traffickers here." He then left the room to speak with someone.

A few minutes later Don Chando returned to the room. Did Maritza have any criminal record or any other kind of legal problem that could impede her amnesty? No, she told him. Don Chando left the room, returned, and told Maritza that the arrangements were being made. Try to sleep, he told her. Before leaving the room, he shut the light off. But he also turned the radio on to full volume.

Maritza couldn't sleep. The experience of the past seven days had broken her and she felt crazy with anxiety. Would they really let her go? Now they were saying she'd be free tomorrow. Maritza wanted to believe them, but she was afraid of having false hopes. Perhaps tomorrow they would decide it would be better to kill her.[6]

Early Wednesday morning I drove with a colleague to Walt Disney School to see if we could locate any witnesses to Maritza's kidnapping. We spoke with the school's director and with Sebastián's teacher. Could the director arrange a meeting with the witnesses for us? Could she give us their names? She hesitated, then asked us to wait while she tried to contact the mothers. After we waited in the reception area of the school for some time, the director finally returned and told us that the witnesses were not willing to speak to us. They were afraid. We drove on to Maritza's home.

Fear and paranoia were also building in the School of History at USAC. The previous day's letter from the four U.S. senators was causing an uproar from hard-line students on the left. "You guys!" they asked Juan and Pedro accusingly, "what do you have to do with the United States? You got us involved in this! You're going around involved with the gringos! With congressmen!" Juan and Pedro had become traitors.

At first Juan didn't know how to respond. "And in the ODHA," screamed his classmates, "there's lots of gringos! What are you doing there?" Juan finally explained that the results were the most important thing. They were trying to save Maritza's life, and they were getting results, such as all of the political pressure on the Guatemalan government. And besides, he reminded the students, "there are some democratic gringos too." That seemed to placate the opposition.

That same morning two investigators from the human rights ombudsman's office visited the Urrutia home in zone eight. When Maritza's father ushered them inside, they were surprised to find two higher-ranking officials from the ombudsman's office already in the house. One of the officials took the investigators aside and explained that Ramiro de León Carpio, the ombudsman, had put them in charge of the case. "Don't worry. We will keep the ombudsman informed of everything."[7]

Neither de León Carpio nor his staff were trying to obstruct progress in Maritza's case. But they had a problem: "Sanchez," the ombudsman's shadowy investigator. Sánchez was proud of his investigative skills but his colleagues believed that he could not be trusted. "Sánchez is a very mysterious person," observed one former high-ranking member of the ombudsman's office. "At the beginning I had a good relationship with Sánchez," recalled another former official, "but then, things began to happen. Other staff members, without saying it specifically, began to indicate that there was a problem with him."

Ramiro de León Carpio and his assistants had to trust each other completely in order to address "delicate" matters like Maritza's disappearance. If the army *was* involved, they would be risking their lives by trying to assist her. But one of their investigators, it was thought, was not trustworthy. So they would have to find ways to isolate Sánchez.

Ramiro de León Carpio had been following Maritza's case closely and wanted to do what he could to protect Maritza's life, and the lives of her family. It was imperative to avoid leaks of information and other security problems. So using one of his methods of working around his investigator, for the protection of everyone involved, de León Carpio delegated responsibility for Maritza's case to two of his trusted lieutenants, trying to keep the flow of information and events away from Sánchez and his associates.

When we arrived at Maritza's home, the representatives of the ombudsman's office had already left. I explained to Maritza's parents that, assuming Maritza was released, Msgr. Penados had given his permission for Maritza to stay in the archbishopric. There was a room in the back of the building where she could sleep. Edmundo suggested that perhaps Kappy and Edmundo René should stay there as well.

But what would happen then? Edmundo explained that the family had discussed the matter, and they all agreed that Maritza should leave the country. She wouldn't be safe in Guatemala. Kappy and Edmundo René had a large community of friends in Albuquerque, New Mexico, who could provide support to Maritza. They wanted her to go to the United States, but neither Maritza nor her son had U.S. entry visas. I mentioned that I had friends who worked in the U.S. Embassy. I would speak with them about obtaining visas for Maritza and Sebastián.

By the late 1980s the U.S. State Department, in large part freed from its holy war crusade against Communism and leftists of any stripe, had a new set of policy interests to pursue in Guatemala. Improving human rights was one of those interests, a daunting challenge since much of the country remained mired in poverty and polarized by the internal conflict.

Bernard Aronson, the assistant secretary of state for inter-American affairs, was the man responsible for State Department policy toward Latin America. "I wouldn't minimize how *little* influence we had with the Guatemalan army or government," Aronson recalled.[8] In contrast to the situations in Nicaragua and El Salvador, there were no titanic East-West conflicts being fought out in Guatemala during the early years of President George H. W. Bush's tenure. Substantial amounts of U.S. military assistance were cut during the 1970s by the Carter government, reducing the United State's ability to train and lead the Guatemalan armed forces,[9] "Guatemala was more of a longstanding festering problem, but it wasn't an immediate crisis for the U.S."[10]

Into that political vacuum in Guatemala stepped the United States' drug enforcement institutions: the CIA, the Drug Enforcement Administration (DEA), and the State Department's Bureau for International Narcotics Matters (INM). These agencies were eager to increase their antinarcotics activities, particularly as Guatemala became a major transshipment point for the Colombian cocaine cartels during the late 1980s. So the United States pursued a counternarcotics policy in Guatemala, promoted the ideals of human rights and democratization, and tried to nurture the nascent Guatemalan peace process.[11]

In mid-1989 the newly elected President George H. W. Bush appointed Thomas F. Stroock, Bush's baseball teammate from their undergraduate days at Yale, as U.S. ambassador to Guatemala.[12] Born in New York City, Stroock became a successful Wyoming oilman and banker after serving in the Marine Corps in the South Pacific theater during World War II. Stroock looked back on his Marine Corps years as one of the seminal experiences of his life, responsible for "teaching me respect and appreciation for others, the discipline to take on a job and see it through and whatever mental and physical toughness I have had to display in overcoming business, political and family difficulties."[13]

And while he served in the Marines, Stroock had to be very tough. As a young gunnery sergeant in an artillery regiment, Stroock saw combat during the 1944 invasions of the strategic Mariana Islands. The U.S. Army Air Forces had a new long-range bomber, the B-29, but it needed airfields within flying range of the Japanese homeland. The solution lay in the well-developed facilities of Saipan, Tinian, and Guam, but these islands were in the hands of determined Japanese soldiers and sailors who would bitterly resist the invasions of U.S. troops.[14]

"D-Day" for the Saipan invasion was June 15, 1944. Even after a naval bombardment that the Japanese defenders recalled as "too terrible for words," the U.S. forces suffered as many as two thousand dead and wounded on June 15 alone. For weeks thereafter the Japanese launched fearsome banzai counterattacks on the U.S. Marines advancing across the island, and Stroock's artillery regiment, the Tenth Marines, fought to beat back these assaults.[15] "I was not wounded," Stroock recalled five decades later, "but I was plenty scared."[16]

Stroock also learned an important lesson from his father that underlined his later commitment to public service: "After you drink from the well, never leave the bucket empty. Always put something back into the bucket."[17] Following the war Stroock settled in Wyoming and spent years as president of his local and state school board associations. In 1959 he helped a young man named Dick Cheney, then a Wyoming high school senior, obtain a scholarship to Yale.[18] Stroock put his Yale economics studies to good use, convincing his colleagues in the Wyoming legislature to raise the tax rates on oil and gas leases on state lands, a change that increased funding available to public schools. Stroock also created an audit program for mineral taxes that generated hundreds of millions of dollars for his adopted state.[19] As a member and vice president of the Wyoming State Senate, Stroock sponsored the Wyoming Air Quality Act, the Wyoming Water Quality Act, and the Wyoming Instream Flow Act, and was the floor manager in the Senate for the Wyoming Environmental Quality Act.[20] Broad-shouldered and aggressive, Stroock served twice as regional coordinator of George H. W. Bush's presidential campaigns.[21]

Tom Stroock "was an unlikely diplomat."[22] He was not a career foreign service officer, and his personal style was not "diplomatic" at all. "Stroock calls it as he sees it,"[23] remembered one former State Department colleague. In Guatemala, where personal communication is often highly circumlocutory and oblique, Stroock tended to be very blunt and direct. "Which was maybe not the worst thing for diplomacy," recalled David Todd, who in 1992 was the Guatemalan government's legal counsel and lobbyist in Washington, D.C. "But I'm not sure [that Stroock] ever fully came to terms with the nature of the society that he was accredited to."[24]

During the late 1980s and early 1990s the United States government had "four key areas of concern" in Guatemala: "human rights, drugs, democracy, and economic development."[25] Stroock was the first U.S. ambassador to Guatemala to call for greater respect for fundamental human rights and almost literally hit the ground running on the human rights issue when he took up his post.

Speaking to the press upon his arrival at Guatemala City's airport, Stroock stressed the importance that U.S. President George Bush attached to human rights. Moreover, Stroock and his staff met publicly with human rights activists and in private also urged high-ranking government officials to pursue the United States' human rights objectives.[26]

In early 1990 Stroock publicly rebuked the administration of then president Vinicio Cerezo for its lack of progress on the human rights front: "It
appears exceedingly strange to us that in none of these cases have the authorities been able to capture the vile and cowardly criminals. . . . It is impossible for the United States to maintain strong, stable and firm relations
with governments that violate or fail to effectively protect human rights."[27]

When he was informed of Stroock's remarks, "Cerezo exploded." The
president publicly said that Ambassador Stroock did not speak for the
U.S. government and privately hinted that Stroock would be expelled
from the country. In response, the State Department recalled Stroock "for
consultations" in Washington as well as a meeting with President Bush.
Stroock returned to Guatemala with a carefully worded letter, hand-
delivered to President Cerezo, in which the State Department made clear
that the U.S. Embassy's position was indeed the human rights policy of
the Bush administration. Subsequent embassy press statements reiterated
that the U.S. government would continue to take a high profile on human rights issues, and "that concern for human rights was an integral
part of the U.S. foreign policy towards the government of Guatemala."[28]
Tom Stroock was not going to be pushed around on this issue and he
was not shy about sticking his chin out when necessary to make a point.

Of course, the changing course of history also made it easier for
Stroock to be so outspoken about Guatemala's human rights problems.
By the late 1980s no one (except perhaps some myopic members of the
URNG)[29] believed that the Guatemalan insurgency would ever come to
power. So the URNG presented no national security dangers to the United
States. There were no cold war battles against Communists at stake, as
there were in Nicaragua and El Salvador. That made it much easier for
members of the U.S. government to criticize the Guatemalan government
about its human rights record.[30]

Tom Stroock was a "populist Republican," recalled a former official
at the U.S. Embassy in Guatemala. Stroock believed that the United States
was a different society "with higher ideals that should be spread to other
countries. This attitude was marked in Tom Stroock."[31] Stroock was a
conservative man, but he gave a very clear message to embassy staff: "You
don't sit still when people's human rights are being violated. It's not a
question of politics. It's a question of humanity."[32] Now, as the cold war
was ending, and after three decades of cruel armed conflict, the United
States ambassador, full of "American exceptionalism," was trying to bring
some humanitarian values to the hardened people of Guatemala. Not surprisingly, many Guatemalans were skeptical of his message.

But most of Tom Stroock's staff at the U.S. Embassy applauded his leadership. Sue Patterson, who as consul general was one of his closest advisers, "loved working for Ambassador Stroock." Career Foreign Service officers like Patterson often disliked working for political appointees who frequently struggled up a steep learning curve in the world of diplomacy, and who often brought grief to the junior officers with their mistakes. But Patterson believed that "the United States, as a nation, was very fortunate to have a man of that courage as Ambassador. Because [Stroock] was more forceful than most career officers would have been."[33] "Courageous" was also the description used by John Hamilton, who in 1992 directed the State Department's Office for Central America, Cuba, and the Caribbean. Stroock "makes the 'Marlboro man' look timid."[34]

Normally, policy instructions emanate from senior State Department officials working in Washington, D.C., to U.S. ambassadors in embassies around the world. But Tom Stroock was "a little bit more willing to jump the gates and get out in front of the Bureau" on some issues without clearing his actions with headquarters ahead of time.[35] "Unless you stop me," Stroock might tell Washington, "here's what I'm going to say in the next four hours."[36] Of course, that's not how the rigid, hierarchical State Department culture likes to do business. "How *dare* he?!" reacted some of Stroock's Foreign Service superiors back in Washington after the ambassador gave a speech criticizing human rights violations in Guatemala without first clearing it up the chain of command. "What's going on?! How could he give a major policy speech that the State Department has not even reviewed?!"[37]

But Assistant Secretary of State Aronson was also a political appointee rather than a career Foreign Service officer, and Aronson was more concerned about results than processes:

> It wasn't that I approved regardless of substance. If [Stroock] had given the same speech on something we diametrically disagreed with, it would not have been O.K. In this instance, being tough on human rights at a time when that was perfectly called for, the fact that he hadn't cleared it. . . . He had to learn that in general you can't have every Ambassador making up his policy regardless of the views of the President and the Secretary of State. I think that's important. You can't. But it was hard to be too harsh on somebody who saw gross abuses of human rights and stood up in public and said, "This is despicable and the U.S. rejects this," because that was the right message morally.[38]

Of course, this was also smart politics since the U.S. government had been criticized for years for its support for Latin American dictators.[39]

Stroock also enjoyed an important advantage over the typical career Foreign Service officers and State Department bureaucrats who tended to follow the normal chains of command: his long friendships with the president and the secretary of state:

> I tried to adapt as much as I could to the State Department's "culture" but I am sure that on several occasions I was a square peg in a round hole. On more than one occasion, I am sure to have caused heartburn on the sixth and seventh floors of the Department. The advantages of my personal relationship with President Bush and Secretary Baker were manifold. In the first place, I had a direct line to them should I ever want to use it, which I very rarely did. I was not interested in any "next posting" because I knew that when my tour of duty in Guatemala was over I was either going to go on to another job in the Bush second administration if there was one, or return to Wyoming—as I did—when he lost. I was not bound by any need to conform to bureaucratic practice, and my ability to make decisions and stay with them was unfettered by any need to conform to past practices.[40]

Of course, strong principles and forcefulness, even the ability to "get to Poppy right away,"[41] do not always guarantee success, particularly in a complicated business-like foreign policy, where so much depends on personal judgment. Indeed, the highest praise bestowed on a Foreign Service officer is "He has excellent judgment." Essentially that is how policy is made and courses of action defined. But sometimes Tom Stroock's strong principles and personality ran ahead of his judgment. The ambassador was "fair minded," recalled James Carroll, the embassy's public affairs officer from 1990–93. "But every once in a while we'd have to go into his office and shut the door and say: 'Goddamnit, Tom, you just stepped in something that you shouldn't have.'" Stroock could be blunt, at times mercurial, and tended to see things in black and white in a country where so much was a murky gray.[42]

One of the venues for ambassadorial judgments and decision making was the regular morning "country team meeting" in the embassy. Stroock would call together his senior staff, the heads of various sections, and discuss the latest directives from Washington and events in Guatemala that were likely to affect the operation of the embassy and U.S. interests. The ambassador would speak first, then the deputy chief of mission would present items from Washington. Then the discussion would move around the table, and each agency or section chief would tell Stroock "what he needed to know."[43]

James Carroll would often try to steer policy competitions on a more progressive course. Carroll believed that the rule of law would never exist in Guatemala until the armed forces underwent serious reforms such as downsizing and developing new missions and leadership. But he knew that members of the U.S. military, the CIA, and the DEA thought that Carroll lived in a dream world. These officers and agents believed that the Guatemalan army was the only effective institution in the country and argued that if the U.S. government was serious about stopping the cocaine cartels, "we had to get their cooperation." Counternarcotics activities were a major U.S. foreign policy priority in Guatemala, particularly given the Bush administration's heavy emphasis on drug interdiction before it reached the United States. Thus, a tense competition often developed between the CIA station chief, U.S. military officers, and other government representatives over the correct interpretation of information that reached the embassy, as well as appropriate strategies for achieving policy goals.[44]

Perhaps no topic better epitomized the internal policy conflicts in the U.S. Embassy during the early 1990s than the polemic produced by the murder of an American citizen named Michael DeVine. A group of Guatemalan soldiers killed DeVine in mid-1990, although it's not clear whether the killing was premeditated. U.S. officials eventually obtained information that high-ranking Guatemalan army officers were attempting to cover up the crime. The army's attitude infuriated Ambassador Stroock, and the successful prosecution of Michael DeVine's killers became the number one bilateral issue between the two countries.[45] At the time Stroock was unaware that Colonel Julio Alpírez, one of the officers implicated in the murder of Michael DeVine and the subsequent cover-up, was on the U.S. government's payroll as a CIA "asset."[46]

Stroock believed that if an institution was going to murder an American citizen and then cover up the crime, that institution did not deserve American assistance.[47] U.S. military aid to Guatemala was quite small at the time, a few million dollars a year in nonlethal aid such as trucks and barracks. But it was the only leverage the U.S. government had over the Guatemalan army. Assistant Secretary Bernard Aronson and his State Department colleagues wanted to use this leverage to send the army a clear message that their conduct was unacceptable.[48] Aronson believed that the U.S. government should suspend the nonlethal military aid to Guatemala until the Guatemalans made progress on the DeVine investigation. Ambassador Stroock agreed with Aronson and made the same recommendation to his old friend President George H. W. Bush.[49]

The issue of cutting off the remaining U.S. military assistance, however, provoked heated debates within the U.S. Embassy. The CIA station and U.S. military representatives were upset because the ambassador was taking on the Guatemalan army, and many of *their* sources and counterparts were in the army. Behind the scenes CIA agents unsuccessfully tried to perform "damage control" by urging Guatemalan army representatives to formally charge one of their officers implicated in DeVine's murder, "thereby polishing its human rights credentials."[50] If members of the army were responsible for DeVine's murder, the CIA and the U.S. military personnel argued, then they were "rogue elements" because the U.S. Department of Defense (DOD) was training and promoting a new kind of democratic military officer in Guatemala.[51] But others in the embassy did not buy this argument. In December 1990 the secretary of state finally confirmed the military assistance cutoff, just before Jorge Serrano Elías's election as president.[52]

The timing could not have been worse with respect to the relationship between the strong-willed ambassador and the egotistical, suspicious new president. "Why are they punishing the *next* government?" complained Serrano. "Even *before* it's taken office?"[53] Once in power, Serrano would have to contend with a resentful, fractious military that was not yet subordinate to civilian rule. He needed to appear strong, not weak and isolated by the superpowers. The new president—who already resented the U.S. ambassador because of perceived slights allegedly committed by Stroock during Serrano's election campaign[54]—assumed that Stroock was responsible for his predicament.[55]

"It was difficult to deal with Jorge," Stroock later reflected about Serrano:

> He suffered from a fatal flaw in a politician or statesman—he was a lousy listener. He never really "heard" what one was saying to him. You could tell by the look on his face and the glaze in his eyes that while you were talking he was putting together, in his own mind, what he was going to say to you when your lips stopped moving. He also suffered by surrounding himself with too many people who did not have first-rate abilities. He wanted to have "yes men" at his elbow and would not tolerate opinions contrary to his from his staffers—or from foreign Ambassadors, for that matter.[56]

In their first official meeting, even before Serrano formally assumed the presidency, Ambassador Stroock presented the new leader with an ultimatum regarding a number of notorious cases of human rights abuse. Stroock bluntly told Serrano, "You have to solve the 'Michael DeVine case,' the 'XX' case, etc."[57] The U.S. envoy insisted that there must be overall progress in the Guatemalan government's human rights performance.[58]

Baker
U S policy towards Guat

The nationalistic Serrano, of course, was offended—he felt that the U.S. ambassador was affronting Guatemala's sovereignty.[59] "He just about threw me out of his office!" Stroock later recalled with some satisfaction. "But we made an important point: We would not pursue the other important goals we have by ignoring human rights."[60] Maritza's case would put this principle to a difficult test.

State Department officials understood that Guatemala had few friends and a number of critics in the U.S. Congress, the source of foreign aid appropriations. Given these political realities in Washington, it would be very difficult to put the bilateral relationship, including interests in greater trade and stronger relationships with the Guatemalan military, "on an even keel" without significant progress on human rights.[61]

Consequently, when the United States government suspended its public military assistance to Guatemala in late 1990, it was already planning the renewal of this aid. In January 1991 Secretary of State James Baker instructed Ambassador Stroock to inform President Serrano of a series of U.S. government-designed "benchmarks" that would demonstrate a significant Guatemalan government policy change with respect to human rights. These targets included substantial progress in the investigation of the murder of Michael DeVine and other high-profile human rights cases, implementation of an agreement that would give the International Committee of the Red Cross access to police and military detention centers, and the development of an "outreach program" by the executive branch to meet periodically with national and international human rights groups. Progress on these benchmarks would be "essential to restore the military relationship."[62]

But that was only the beginning. Secretary of State Baker made it clear that further reforms in Guatemala were necessary to advance the interests of *both* countries. The State Department, Baker explained, "will, however, also be expecting the new government of Guatemala to make progress in other areas which seem to us critical to advance our and Serrano's agenda."[63]

The secretary of state outlined a series of additional, more fundamental reforms to be undertaken by the Guatemalan government over the longer term. Police should be held accountable for their excesses, and civilians, not military officers, should lead the police force. Reform of the criminal justice system, including changes in the judicial sector and the passage of a new criminal code, had to become a priority for the new Serrano administration. Most significantly for Maritza's case, President Serrano had to establish a monitoring system within the executive branch for cases of abuse where credible evidence existed of the armed forces' involvement. The achievement of these admirable goals would serve the political interests of both governments, and Secretary of State Baker assigned to Ambassador Stroock the task of pushing Guatemala's new president to meet them: "Embassy should encourage early action of the new administration and emphasize that these additional steps, together with [those outlined above] will constitute convincing evidence *both internally and externally* of real change in Guatemala. Department requests that the Embassy send bi-monthly reports on the development of these benchmarks" [emphasis added].[64]

And so, not surprisingly, shortly after Jorge Serrano took power, the president and the ambassador clashed again. Stroock requested a meeting and arrived at President Serrano's office bearing a letter. The United States government was pleased with the new Serrano administration's efforts up to that time on human rights cases, although the Bush administration considered that the Guatemalan government still needed to accomplish a, b, c, d, and so forth. Observing that Stroock was reading from a list of points in the letter, Serrano asked to see it.[65] When Serrano saw the letter, he read that, as a gesture of its goodwill, the United States government was going to release $100,000 of previously frozen military aid for Guatemala.[66]

"I believe that Stroock thought I was one of those donkeys that when you hold a carrot in front, the donkey would follow the carrot," explained Jorge Serrano when he recalled the meeting years later. Ambassador Stroock's attitude and letter infuriated the president. "I read the note and I couldn't believe it. It was something incredible! Inconceivable!"[67] *How could Tom Stroock treat his country like this?*

U.S. State Department officials were trying to increase their influence in Guatemala, particularly on the Guatemalan military. "We were trying to convince Guatemala to participate in a peace process that could only result in [the Armed Forces'] role being reduced," recalled Bernard Aronson; "the size of their forces being reduced, their budget being reduced, and some of their officers being drummed out for human rights abuses. So you have to send signals to elements in the military who are willing to cooperate [with U.S. policy] and want to see the army become a more progressive force . . . that the U.S. will be supportive and willing to work with them as they do make reforms."[68]

Worthy goals perhaps, but the State Department completely misread the likely reactions of President Serrano and his military commanders.

"You can talk 'state-to-state,'" explained Serrano, but he wasn't going to be bribed. "I felt horrible. They're going to give me $100,000. I keep doing what they want, and they give me another $100,000. It's a bribe! Blackmail!"[69]

The president "flew completely off the handle and began to rage and shout in anger" at Stroock.[70] Serrano ranted that the State Department's letter contained requirements, not requests. Rather than meekly meet the U.S. government's demands, Serrano preferred to forego the restoration of U.S. military aid. Stroock responded that the U.S. government would not force its assistance on anyone, and on that note the meeting ended.[71]

Serrano wasn't sure if Stroock understood what had happened, but he was determined to teach the ambassador a lesson. The president's first impulse was to declare Ambassador Stroock persona non grata and have Stroock removed. After Serrano discussed this option with his advisors, a high-ranking military officer told Serrano that Alfonso Sapia Bosch, then CIA station chief in Guatemala, wanted to speak with the president.

Serrano and Sapia Bosch had known each other since the 1980s when Sapia Bosch worked for the Reagan administration and Serrano studied in a Christian college in Texas. The two men had become good friends. In his position as station chief, Sapia Bosch would provide lists to Serrano of military personnel involved in drug trafficking, smuggling, and human rights abuses. But then Sapia Bosch would leave Serrano free to use the information as he pleased, which Serrano took as a demonstration of respect and sensitivity. "We're 'peripheral' and [the United States is] *metrópoli*," believed Serrano, "but . . . in dignity the two states are equal."[72]

Now with a storm brewing between the two governments, Sapia Bosch arrived at the president's home. "As your friend," he told Serrano, "I recommend that you let this go."[73] Sapia Bosch knew about the clash between Serrano and Ambassador Stroock and wanted to prevent the problem from growing larger. If President Serrano threw out the U.S. ambassador, there would be serious problems between the two countries. So Serrano reluctantly agreed to let the matter drop.

But Serrano was president of a country still embroiled in a brutal armed conflict, and he had to explain the matter to his armed forces. Thus in February 1991 Serrano spoke to a group of military commanders: "Look, gentlemen, this is a matter of national dignity."[74] Ambassador Stroock's message and delivery were insulting and insolent, he explained. If Serrano had accepted the United States' conditions, he would be nothing more than a puppet. The officers would have to tighten their belts, and the government would search elsewhere for military assistance that would be available without insulting conditions.[75]

CIA
covert $$

Many army commanders, angered by the U.S. government's recent cutoff of military aid to Guatemala, were inspired by Serrano's message. They were pleased that Serrano appeared to be taking a hard line with the U.S. government on the issues of human rights and what they perceived as interference in Guatemala's internal affairs. In their minds, the president had resisted pressures to accept unjust and rigid conditions set by the U.S. government, linking military aid with human rights reforms.[76] During Tom Stroock's tenure as U.S. ambassador to Guatemala, these issues would arise again and again.

Of course, it might have been easy for the army officers to applaud President Serrano's tough stance with the gringos because they really weren't suffering very much. The State Department publicly suspended nonlethal military aide to Guatemala in 1990 as a result of the army's failure to cooperate with the DeVine investigation, but the Central Intelligence Agency kept up its covert assistance to the G-2, the Guatemalan army's intelligence section. From 1990 to 1995, an estimated five to seven million dollars' worth of aid flowed in each year, lawfully but secretly.[77] This chain of events angered State Department officials, who threatened to raise the matter with their superiors in Washington: "It is totally inconsistent for U.S. to cut off all military aid, while maintaining [a] major . . . assistance program to an offending branch."[78]

This inconsistency was not lost on Guatemala's army officers, the recipients of the CIA's covert assistance: "You guys are crazy," officers told members of the Bush administration: "You shut us down in public, and then you give us stuff through the back door and everyone in the military knows it."[79]

In defense of its continued aid, the CIA argued that the U.S. government had already sent a strong message concerning the DeVine case to the Guatemalans.[80] The State Department's suspension of overt aid reduced U.S. military assistance to Guatemala by 50 percent. But its antinarcotics aid, much of it covertly channeled through the CIA, should continue. If we stop this aid too, argued the intelligence officers, we'll just alienate the hard-liners in the army more. Besides, U.S. intelligence officers should maintain their relationships with their counterparts in the G-2 so they can keep an eye on them and continue to push for a resolution to the Michael DeVine killing. This last argument was breathtakingly disingenuous given that, in the words of one scholar, "the CIA has been sanctioning the G-2's murderous impunity, and thus is itself deeply complicitous" in Guatemala's history of human rights abuses.[81] But if the United States cuts off *all* aid, the CIA contended, we lose

Drug War

influence with Guatemalan army intelligence, *and* we cut off our nose in the drug war.[82]

And the drug war was no small problem for the United States. By 1990 agents of the Drug Enforcement Administration detected so much cocaine in Guatemala that they began to call it *la bodega,* or the "warehouse."[83] The largest country in Central America, with poor roads, vast mountain and jungle regions, and very little radar, Guatemala was a mecca for pilots transporting cocaine. In 1991 traffickers used hundreds of uncontrolled landing strips in Guatemala to refuel aircraft or to off-load cocaine for transshipment from Colombia to the United States.[84] "So the U.S. had to draw a line in the sand and stop that from happening."[85]

The United States drew its line in Guatemala with OPERATION CADENCE (Central American drug enforcement). The U.S. and Guatemalan governments launched OPERATION CADENCE in 1991 to block the flow of drugs through the Central American region. Under CADENCE, various U.S. and Guatemalan government agencies coordinated their efforts to increase the scope and effectiveness of combined U.S. and Guatemalan cocaine interdiction efforts. The State Department's Bureau for International Narcotics Matters mandated that in 1993, "all drug enforcement activities must be coordinated with military intelligence . . . which actively collects intelligence against traffickers."[86] In addition to the CIA, the INM also continued to provide antinarcotics support that eventually reached the Guatemalan military. For example, INM funds were used to train Guatemalan air force pilots to fly the specially equipped helicopters used in aerial drug-eradication programs.[87]

Because the United States desperately wanted to stop the cocaine cartels, the Bush administration bet heavily on a policy of interdiction. But the antinarcotics policies obviously complicated the U.S. government's other efforts to "reform" Guatemala's abysmal human rights record and to "modernize" Guatemala's armed forces. As Ambassador Stroock recalled in 1995, "if you're going to interdict drugs, you have to use the agency involved in the country. Unfortunately, in Guatemala, that's the army. At the same time you're beating these people over the head because of human rights, you're using them to stop drugs. It's a dilemma."[88]

Within the embassy in Guatemala City, staff members debated whether the drug war could be fought without the armed forces. Representatives of the Defense Department, the CIA, and the DEA insisted that the only effective institution in the country was the army. So the United States had to have its cooperation. James Carroll disagreed. According to his sources in Guatemalan society, he argued, the army was the *problem,* not the solution. Probably there are corrupt *individuals* within the Guatemalan army, responded the DOD, the CIA, and the DEA, but the institution itself was not corrupt. "Unfortunately life is real. You have to work with the sons of bitches that you have . . . who can help us get the job done in the drug war."[89]

Thus the U.S. government was divided as to the best strategy for achieving its policy goals in Guatemala. Its agencies were working against each other, sometimes even against themselves, as they struggled to pursue their objectives.[90] And the Guatemalans skillfully manipulated these divisions.

Many army officers, resentful of declining U.S. military assistance, believed that the drug war was more important to the United States than it was to Guatemala.[91] Cocaine consumption, they believed, was a problem in the States, not in Guatemala.[92] "We were helping them to help ourselves," acknowledged John Arndt, the State Department's Guatemala desk officer in 1992. Consequently, Guatemalan negotiators tried to use the antinarcotics cooperation as leverage against the United States' human rights concerns and often pressed U.S. officials to reduce their criticism of Guatemala's human rights situation as a trade-off. "They would always want to link things together," Arndt recalled. The Guatemalans would tell State Department officials that "you've got to tone it [i.e., criticisms about human rights abuses] down, or we're gonna stop cooperating" with antinarcotics activities.[93] These arguments, of course, ran contrary to the United States' plan to achieve progress in its "human rights benchmarks" in Guatemala.

Wrapped within these tensions and contradictions, the relationship between President Serrano and Ambassador Stroock would not improve. "They could barely contain their [detestation] for each other," recalled Richard Nuccio, who would later facilitate peace negotiations between Serrano's government and URNG.[94] Serrano would bitterly resent Stroock's habit of sending him "written 'orders' on human rights and other subjects."[95] Stroock was not known for using subtleties and sometimes expressed his feelings to President Serrano without much finesse.[96] On occasion, the president would return from meetings with the ambassador, hysterical, furious. "This gringo son of a . . . " Serrano would say. "How *dare* he come and say these things!" Members of Serrano's government called Stroock the "Cowboy Ambassador," because of Stroock's strong personality and blunt manner of speech. "Here comes the cowboy, Tom Stroock, defender of human rights!" President Serrano would mockingly sneer while pointing his two index fingers into the air like two six-shooters. "Pow! Pow! Pow! Pow! Pow! Pow! Pow!"[97]

But President Jorge Serrano was no shrinking violet himself. Serrano's maternal grandparents had migrated to Guatemala from Lebanon. His paternal grandparents had come from Spain, but their ancestors were German Jewish.[98] Thus, Serrano was a volatile genetic cocktail of Arab, Jew, and Spaniard and manifested an extraordinary need to dominate and control situations. "He was very violent," recalled Haroldo Shetemul, then a journalist for the newsweekly *Crónica*. "He yelled at anyone he could, like he owned the country."[99] Serrano would regularly berate his staff and those who did not comply with his instructions "were fucked." He was tireless and stubborn, "sometimes like a mule." Guatemalans love to tell jokes about the idiosyncrasies of their heads of state. The joke about Jorge Serrano was that he was so difficult that no one joked about him.[100] Tom Stroock, indeed any ambassador, would have a very tough job maintaining a productive relationship with this man, and, indeed, by 1992 relations between them "had almost totally broken down."[101]

By Wednesday afternoon I had largely assumed responsibility for Maritza's case in the ODHA. Yet I was unaware of these different interests, pressures, and relationships. Soon I would begin to learn about them.

Early Wednesday evening Edmundo René and Kappy were feeling a little better. They knew from Maritza's phone call just a few hours before that she must still be alive. Perhaps she really would be released. They decided to drive back to San Cristobal to sleep in their own home. As they got ready for bed, they were feeling optimistic until they turned on the evening news at 10:00 P.M. There was Maritza on the television screen, all made up, talking about how her brother, Edmundo René, had introduced Maritza to her ex-husband, the leader of the Guerrilla Army of the Poor. Edmundo René and Kappy were terrified because Maritza implied in the video that Edmundo René had ties to the URNG. Panicked, Kappy called Jones at his home. She told Jones about the video, that she and Edmundo René were out in an isolated area, and that they were afraid for their lives. They wanted "embassy assistance in departing Guatemala immediately."[102] Jones's initial response was: "Well, *did he?*" (that is, did Edmundo René introduce Maritza to her ex-husband?) "*Was he a guerrillero?*"[103] "No, of course not," responded Kappy. Kappy told Jones that Maritza had obviously been forced to make her statement. Kappy explained that Maritza's hair and makeup were totally out of the ordinary and obviously something very peculiar was happening.

Jones told Kappy that he would call the U.S. Marine guards, and they would come out to San Cristobal. But in fact, Jones didn't call out the Marines. He did bring the burly embassy security officer and several armed Guatemalan policemen in a bulletproof embassy Suburban.[104] Jones was now risking his life for the Urrutia family, and he expected to find the house in San Cristobal under siege. But when his driver finally found the house, everything seemed quiet.

Jones and the security officer entered the home while the policemen stood in front of the house, holding their machine guns in a defensive stance.[105] The plan was to bring Kappy and Edmundo René to the embassy, where they would spend the night, then get them out of Guatemala the next day on the first available flight.[106]

Wednesday, 10:00 P.M. Edmundo René and Kappy were not the only ones thrown off balance by Maritza's video. Juan, the School of History student, was relaxing at home that evening with his girlfriend when the news came on. "Oh shit! Oh God!" cried Juan when the shock of Maritza's statement hit him. No, she had *not* been kidnapped. She just needed some time to arrange to leave the Organización. *What was happening?* Juan asked himself. *What was the game? Had they been duped?* Had he and Pedro exposed all of the students to danger for *nothing?* Now the students at the School of History would be cursing him, saying, "That son of a bitch got us into this mess!"

But as Juan and his girlfriend listened carefully to the full text of Maritza's presentation, they realized that something was awry. Maritza seemed to be reading, as if her speech was rehearsed. Then Maritza expressed her gratitude to all of the institutions that had demonstrated concern for her, including, she emphasized, "the History *Faculty.*" Once he heard the word "Faculty," Juan knew that Maritza was speaking under duress and that she was trying to convey that message to the public. No one who had ever attended USAC's *School* of History would refer to it as the "Faculty." (It would be analogous to a U.S. citizen's referring to the White House as the "President's House.") Only military personnel, Juan realized, with no experience at USAC, would have put the word "Faculty" in the text. And Maritza had made the most of this error in her video. Juan began to breathe easier. She was still alive, and their efforts had not been wasted.

Maritza's aunt Julia was watching the news at home with one of her daughters when Maritza appeared on the video. "Mamá!" cried Julia's daughter, "that dumb kid!" Julia thought it was all theater; it wasn't the Maritza they knew. Maritza never used all that makeup, and her voice was different. Julia thought of Father Luis Pellecer, a Jesuit priest who in 1981 had been disappeared by the army and forced to make a public "confession" of his ties to the EGP. She called Maritza's father. Edmundo was in shock. "Those bastards have her," Edmundo said.

In the rectory next door to the cathedral, Father Luis Pérez was watching the news. When Father Luis saw Maritza appear in the video and realized that she was alive, he began to relive a powerful experience from his own past. He had been a young seminarian in March 1983, when the army kidnapped his brother in the rural town of San Marcos. Luis's father spent months searching for him in military bases, detention centers, and morgues. Finally Luis and his family gave up hope that the young man would return alive.

But Próspero Penados, then the bishop of San Marcos, began knocking on doors in the government. He visited Ricardo Méndez Ruiz, then the interior minister, who had been a childhood schoolmate. With the papal nuncio, Penados spoke to the defense minister and asked him to intervene on behalf of Luis's brother. Another priest, whose brother-in-law was a colonel in the Guatemalan army, also made a special plea. Then, after more than six months of captivity and brutal torture, Luis's brother was released alive and returned to his family.

Now watching Maritza on television in July 1992, Father Luis felt the same powerful emotions he had experienced when his brother returned from the dead nine years earlier. There was joy because so few of the disappeared ever returned, but there was also concern about Maritza. *What would happen to her now,* the young priest wondered. And was the video authentic? Or had it been staged?

Gustavo Meoño, the EGP's *comandante* Manolo, was also watching Maritza's video that night. Meoño too had prior experience with persons who had been captured, mistreated, and later released by the Guatemalan army. Back in 1981 the army kidnapped an EGP member named Emilio Toj Medrano. At the time Meoño was the only high ranking member of the EGP in Guatemala City. Toj eventually made a very public reappearance and then escaped his army captors. Thus, it was Meoño's task to debrief him and determine whether Toj had really been forced to make statements under pain of torture or whether he had "turned" and become an army spy. This experience helped Meoño to evaluate Maritza's video.

Meoño understood that the army had forced Maritza to make her video statement. She expressed things in such a way that the viewer knew it was a farce. "Maritza had found a way to say things *without conviction,* and you *felt* that there wasn't conviction."[107]

But now the EGP faced the task of convincing their contacts and the public at large that the video was a farce. As a political-military strategy, Meoño was determined to undermine the army's charade. If the EGP failed, the army would continue to use the same tactics in the future, and would kidnap more *compañeros*. But if it succeeded, the army would be unlikely to try such a maneuver again. Meoño and his team began to alert their allies: "Don't believe what she's saying. It's not true."[108] And so the EGP and the Guatemalan Army began a new battle, the battle to capture the truth about Maritza.

Back at the Island, Don Chando and his men had gathered in their lounge, "the Casino," to watch the video on the nightly news. Everything seemed to be going well. Two women from Counterintelligence had delivered the video to the news stations without incident, and Maritza was still under their power. They had brainwashed her well, and she was going to cooperate with them. Don Chando's men were playing cards. Soon they would receive their bonuses for a job well done. "Hey, Beto!" Don Chando called out to the cook. "Bring me some food." As the video aired on the television, the cook brought Don Chando his supper: refried beans with sour cream, cheese, and the garlic bread he enjoyed so much.[109]

Edmundo René and Kappy hurriedly threw some clothes into their bags and got into a vehicle with Jones and the security officer. The policemen followed in a separate vehicle. It was now about 1:00 A.M. Edmundo René was beginning to waffle about his decision to leave the country, but Jones and the security officer convinced him that it was the right thing to do.[110] The U.S. officials insisted that Edmundo René and Kappy spend the night in the embassy. Edmundo René asked whether there were beds available there, because both he and Kappy were exhausted, and Jones of course took the question as a sign of ingratitude. They could sit on the sofas in the embassy reception area until morning, Jones said.

Kappy and Edmundo René suggested that a hotel would be a better alternative, and so the embassy officials brought them to the luxurious Camino Real, which had good security, and put them in a suite on the ninth floor. Jones would call at 7:20 A.M. to finalize their departure plans. After the embassy officials left the hotel, Kappy and Edmundo René sat quietly for a good while, trying to decide whether their room was bugged.[111] Eventually they tried to sleep.

EIGHT

THURSDAY

July 30, 1992

The telephone woke me up at six on Thursday morning. It was Edmundo René and he was in a panic. "Daniel, did you see the news last night?" No, I didn't own a television. "*Daniel!* Maritza was on the news! She gave a statement and said I introduced her to her ex-husband! Now I'm leaving the country! I have to leave!"

I struggled to calm Edmundo René down and eventually he told me that he and Kappy had spent the night at the Camino Real. "Give me twenty minutes," I told him, "and I'll be there."

Traffic was still light at that hour as I drove to the hotel. I stopped to buy the morning papers from a newspaper vendor and glanced at the headlines. "Maritza Urrutia: I Was Not Kidnapped," blared the headline of *El Grafico*. Its front-page story described Maritza's video, noting that she had actually sought the authorities' protection in order to leave the EGP. Maritza's brother had called the newspaper after Maritza's video aired. Edmundo René had emphatically rejected his sister's declarations. "The family would consider Maritza disappeared and kidnapped until she was restored to the bosom of her family." Additionally, Edmundo René told the press that his sister's claim that he introduced Maritza to her *guerrillero* ex-husband was not true. Edmundo was *never* involved in illegal activities. Instead, he had dedicated himself to his university studies, which included "a scholarship from the United States government."[1]

The defense minister, an army general, spoke to *El Grafico* later that day. "We are investigating," said the minister, referring to Maritza's videotaped statement: "What we want first, by God, is for her to appear. In her face, you don't see any pressure and you see that she's not in a kidnapped state. And the family has assured [authorities] that it has always had contact with her."[2]

When I arrived at the Camino Real, I found Edmundo René and Kappy's suite on the ninth floor. After I knocked, an eyeball peered out at me for a long moment through the glass peephole. Kappy and Edmundo René were exhausted and their clothes were strewn around the room. The hotel had a restaurant on the same floor, so Edmundo René and I walked there, sat down, and ordered coffee while Kappy finished dressing. Edmundo René looked at me with a grim smile. "I feel *fuck!*" he told me in English. For some reason I decided this was the moment to correct Edmundo René's grammar: "You mean 'you feel *fucked!*'"

"That's right, I feel *fucked!*" Edmundo René replied. "Because now I have to leave again! Now I have to leave my daughter and my books again!"[3] Edmundo René's daughter by his first marriage was then thirteen.

"Why?"

"Because Maritza said I introduced her to her ex-husband!"

"But that's not true! It's a lie!"

"But now everyone will be convinced that I am a *guerrillero*. Now I have to go into exile again. I'm *fucked!*"

I told Edmundo René that he should not leave the country. He had not done anything wrong. But if he left, people would *think* that he had done something wrong. And besides, we needed him to help get Maritza back. Edmundo René's powerful mind and political expertise had become more apparent to me with each passing day, and I knew I could not possibly navigate the maze of Guatemalan politics the way he did. If Kappy wanted to go back to the States, well, OK, but Edmundo René was indispensable. After more discussion, over rolls and coffee, I convinced Edmundo René and Kappy to stay, at least until Maritza reappeared.

Within the gray, fortress-like United States Embassy, a small group of people sat in front of a VCR inside the office of the deputy chief of mission. Besides Ambassador Tom Stroock, George Chester, head of the political section, was present.[4] So was the CIA's station chief at the embassy. His official title, "political officer," served as a diplomatic cover for his intelligence-gathering activities. The agency's focus in Guatemala at that time was exclusively counternarcotics. When particular human rights violations drew a great deal of public interest, the CIA station chief often limited his expressions of concern to diplomatic hints to his colleagues in Guatemalan army intelligence: "It would be good if you guys had information to give to the minister of defense or the president, that he could share with the ambassador." So it is possible that the station chief simply paid little attention to Maritza's case, except for its impact on his anti-drug work with the army.[5]

The military attaché, an army colonel, also attended the meeting. The military attaché knew more about the Guatemalan army than anyone in the embassy and, given the army's involvement in so many human rights abuses, he was a full player in the embassy's human rights activities.[6] A member of the consulate was present, as was Jones. James Carroll and Lee McClenny, from the Public Affairs office, also joined the group. Silently, they all sat watching a copy of Maritza's video, which had been broadcast on television the previous evening.

When the video ended, the room was quiet for a moment. Finally, someone asked: "Well, what do you think?"

"The tape's a fake," volunteered Jim Carroll. He noted that Maritza appeared to be looking for cues, and her body language seemed forced and rehearsed. Carroll believed that the tape was clearly some kind of military operation, clumsy and poorly conceived. Ambassador Stroock and Jones shared Carroll's viewpoint, as did another colleague: "Plus, the tape's not made in one cut. It's spliced together."[7]

But the CIA station chief took a different viewpoint. "We know of cases where guerrillas have left their organizations and tried to get free," he argued. "So the story itself may be true, regardless of the nature of the tape."[8]

The other officials present sat quietly, looking around the room. At least one of them thought that the station chief's comments were "laughable."[9] Nevertheless, whatever the CIA's interests and motives were, the CIA's ability to help Maritza should not be discounted. The station chief's most important intelligence sources were in the Guatemalan army. It's possible that he, or one of his colleagues, may have called members of Guatemala's army intelligence section during Maritza's captivity to say "If you did this, you'd better undo it!"[10] Which meant that this leftist guerrilla possibly owed her life, at least in part, to the CIA. Perhaps the cold war had really come to end, but the road ahead was not very clear. "I wonder how many times they made her do this," mused one embassy employee to another, "to get her statement out."[11]

On Thursday morning, the fair-skinned man came to Maritza's room and asked if she still had stomach problems. She felt a little better, Maritza replied, but she was still weak and nauseated. Could he get her some Lomotil? Don Chando left and returned at about 10:00 P.M. with the medicine. He also brought Maritza new clothes: underwear, black pants, and a blouse with blue and white stripes. He removed Maritza's handcuffs and told her to put on the new clothing.

Maritza dressed and noticed that the new clothes still had the price tags attached. They had purchased the articles in Paiz Mega 6, a large department store in zone six. Maritza toyed with the idea of hiding one of the price tags, but she was afraid that her captors would search her. After she finished putting on the new clothing, Don Chando returned to her room. He looked at Maritza and said that the clothes were not her type. He stalked out complaining, "You guys don't know how to do anything!" and ordered someone to go out and buy Maritza another blouse. In about twenty minutes Maritza had a different blouse to wear. It was black and white and also had a Mega 6 price tag.

Another man came in with Don Chando this time and handed Maritza her watch and house keys, which they had taken the day of her kidnapping. Maritza's brother had sought asylum in the U.S. Embassy, he told her. The people in the embassy would give Maritza money and offer her asylum in the United States. She was going to stay in Guatemala, Maritza replied. All she wanted was to be released and she would cooperate with them. She just wanted to be home with her son.

Don Chando gave Maritza detailed instructions concerning what she had to do after she was freed. She had to meet with the attorney general, Acisclo Valladares, and tell him that she wanted amnesty. She had to hold a press conference saying that she wanted the army's protection. Maritza should be sure that the defense minister and the army spokesman were present. Maritza must tell the defense minister that she wanted to cooperate with the army, that perhaps she could travel to Geneva and speak at the United Nations on the army's behalf.

Don Chando repeatedly threatened Maritza. Now she had to work with the army and if she refused, they would consider her a traitor to the nation. If she tried to betray them, they would make her pay. If Maritza tried to leave the country, she wouldn't be able to take all of her family with her. So if she left, the family members remaining in Guatemala would pay the price.[12] Maritza assured Don Chando that she would comply with all of their instructions.

They left Maritza alone in her room for a few hours, and Don Chando called his men together. They had done their job well. There would be no problem with Maritza. They were going to free her because she was going to collaborate with them. Some of the men were concerned. "But why did we trust her so much?" they asked Don Chando. "She saw some of our faces."

"No. There's no problem," replied the captain. "Everything's gone well. She's going to work with us."[13]

At about 2:00 P.M. Don Chando returned to Maritza's room and told her it was time to leave. They were going to leave Maritza at the attorney general's office. As they removed Maritza's handcuffs, Don Chando continued to threaten her. If Maritza didn't comply with their orders, they would seek revenge. He seemed worried that Maritza would try to do something. If anything happened to him, the fair-skinned man assured her, his colleagues would avenge him. His organization was very powerful and patriotic, with worldwide influence. Maritza would never be able to escape, and if she betrayed them, they would capture someone in her family or in her ex-husband's family. *That* person would pay for Maritza's actions.[14]

Her captors took Maritza outside and put her in a large luxury car. Coroncho sat next to Maritza in the backseat while Don Chando continued giving her instructions from the front. She was going to ask the attorney general for amnesty. Then Maritza would hold a press conference and confirm everything that she said in the video. Then she would return home to her parents. Maritza would also meet a contact on August 6, in El Tecolote, a restaurant located in zone seven. At that rendezvous someone would bring Maritza a letter with more instructions.

They drove to the attorney general's headquarters on busy Eighteenth Street in zone one. Don Chando indicated the building, saying that's where Maritza had to go. "Get out and walk to the office," said Don Chando. "We'll be watching you from here. There are others located in the area who will also be watching you closely, so do exactly what we have told you to do."[15]

Maritza got out of the car and walked into the attorney general's building. There was a policeman at the reception desk and he was reading that morning's *El Grafico,* with its front-page headlines about Maritza and her video.[16] Maritza told the policeman that she wanted to see Acisclo Valladares. Five minutes later the attorney general walked down the stairs. When Maritza saw him she said, "I'm Maritza Urrutia and I have to speak with you." "Of course," Valladares replied nonchalantly. "Come with me." And he took Maritza upstairs to a large conference room.

After I left the Camino Real, I drove to the Urrutia home in zone eight. As I sat in the living room, the doorbell rang. It was Sánchez, one of the ombudsman's investigators.

"According to my investigations," Sánchez assured us, "she's going to appear near one of the borders." We agreed that when Maritza appeared, she would be brought to the archbishopric for her own protection.

After Sánchez left, I raised the issue of U.S. visas for Maritza and Sebastián. We would need their passports. Did the family know where they were? I waited on the second floor while Maritza's sister Carolina searched for passports. Finally, Carolina came up the stairs holding the documents. "It's expired," she said. I began to feel sick. *What?* "Maritza's passport has *expired*."

At that time the Dickensian bureaucracy of Guatemala's Department of Immigration ensured that renewal of a passport could take months. There had to be another way. I took the passports from Carolina and told her that I would try to find a way to renew Maritza's travel document immediately.

In USAC's School of History that morning, some of the students who had worked to free Maritza were panicked by her video. "Did you see the news last night?! *Who are we defending?!*" they screamed at Juan and Pedro. "Now the repression's going to come! Now we're all going to get fucked!" Taken in by Maritza's video, the students thought that they had falsely accused the security forces of responsibility for Maritza's disappearance. They had been used irresponsibly, and now they feared reprisals from the army.[17]

As patiently as they could, Juan and Pedro explained the message that Maritza had sent by using the word "Faculty." She must have been speaking under duress. So she must have been kidnapped after all, and the students had to work even harder now so that Maritza would be freed.[18] Besides, the students were not alone in this. The ODHA was with them too. The Catholic Church was trying to get Maritza back. That seemed to calm the storm, at least momentarily.

In his camp at the EGP's Ho Chi Minh front, Carlos Barrientos had tried to stay close to the radio for the past week in order to pick up news about Maritza and his son. There was little that Barrientos could do to help them. It was a ten-day hike across rugged, dangerous terrain from his camp to the southern part of El Quiché, and the trip required the assistance of other EGP members along the way. Barrientos could not request permission to leave the front simply to go help his family.

And what if he had gone to Guatemala City? The army had apparently lost track of Barrientos for ten years after nearly capturing him in a raid in 1982. But the army had captured his papers with his photograph back then and now the G-2 had his ex-wife. They would be looking for him again. So Barrientos would have to stay hidden and he wouldn't be able to accomplish very much. If he was captured, many of his EGP colleagues would be at risk. Barrientos could easily fall into a trap by going to the capital to help Maritza and his son, and he would only create more security problems for the EGP.[19]

When a news report mentioned Maritza's telephone calls to her family, Barrientos's worst fears were realized. This was the beginning of an army intelligence operation. The army was holding Maritza in order to break her and extract information. They were going to break Maritza the way they had broken other EGP *compañeros*.

On Thursday morning Barrientos hiked to another EGP redoubt. There was a television at that camp, and one of Barrientos's *compañeros* told him about Maritza's video, which had been broadcast the previous evening and picked up on the insurgents' television. Barrientos knew the video was more army theater.[20] But there was nothing he could do.

Acisclo Valladares, the attorney general, was very polite to Maritza. Although a sign in the conference room said No Smoking, he acquiesced when Maritza asked him if she could have a cigarette. "Of course you can. *You deserve it.*" Maritza told Valladares that she was there to request amnesty. She told him that he should know about her situation. Maritza found it strange that Valladares did not ask her anything about where she had been during the past week, or if she had been detained against her will. Valladares never asked Maritza if she had come to see him voluntarily.[21]

Valladares told Maritza that he had been very worried about her, and that he wanted to help her, so Maritza asked permission to use the telephone to call her family. Valladares gave her the phone and Maritza called her parents. When Edmundo answered, Maritza told her father that she was in the attorney general's office and that she was coming home. Valladares took the telephone and said to Edmundo: "This is Acisclo Valladares speaking. Your daughter is here with me. You should come here as soon as possible." They were going to take Maritza to a local court, where she would receive amnesty. "Don't worry," Valladares reassured him, "she's protected by the laws of the state."[22]

After Valladares hung up the phone, he called Víctor Hugo Cano, his deputy, and asked Cano to come to the conference room immediately. Cano began to ask Maritza questions about the video and she told him that she wanted to confirm everything she had said in the recording. It was *all true.* Valladares responded that they should proceed to the court in order to arrange things so that Maritza could ask a judge for amnesty. Maritza felt that everything had been prearranged.[23]

Maritza was relieved to be partway out of her hole. Even so, she was aware that she was not free and that her captors would be watching her carefully. One wrong word, gesture, or action, and she would plunge again into the hole. Maritza had to remain as alert as she was in the Island. One wrong move could bring disaster for her and for her family.

As they drove the long city blocks to the court, both Valladares and Cano asked Maritza questions about her involvement with guerrilla organizations. What years was she active in the Organización? Maritza replied that she had been active until that year, 1992. This was going to be a problem, Valladares responded. He told Maritza that when she spoke with the judge, Maritza should tell the judge that she had left the Organización in 1988. Maritza reminded Valladares that in her video, she had said she was a member of the EGP until 1992 and she didn't want this to delay her reunion with her son. Valladares explained to her that Guatemala's amnesty law applied only to insurgent activities carried out through 1988, so Maritza could not tell the judge that she had been involved thereafter. "Don't worry," he told her. "This is going to be a *very fast transaction.* It's not going to take a lot of time. You'll be with your family very soon."[24]

When they arrived at the tall Torre de Tribunales building, everyone was very friendly toward Maritza. No one asked her where she had been or if she had been kidnapped. No one asked Maritza if she had been pressured to seek amnesty. No one mentioned her deteriorated physical and mental state after eight days in captivity.[25] Judge Leticia Secaira and Valladares talked about the funeral of a colleague scheduled for that day. Maritza felt that the entire scene was surreal, as if she had stopped by merely for a cup of coffee. The attorney general and Maritza chatted politely about children as they waited for the amnesty papers. But Valladares was less relaxed when Maritza asked to use the restroom. Valladares followed Maritza to the ladies room and remained outside, ensuring that Maritza remained close by.

When the amnesty documents were ready, Judge Secaira told Maritza to sign two copies of the documents. Cano reported that the press had located Maritza. Someone from *Teleprensa* was there in the building, and the reporters wanted to see her. Eventually, members of the press pool entered the judge's office. Maritza told them she was affirming everything she had said in the video.

If the attorney general had merely read his court file before arranging

Maritza's "amnesty," and if Judge Secaira had read the same file before granting it, they would have found a police report submitted by a detective the day after Maritza's disappearance. According to the detective's report, at about 8:30 A.M. on July 23, unknown men grabbed Maritza as she returned from Walt Disney School and forced her into a car. "At the scene of the incident, the victim left her shoe," which the police retained as evidence and turned over to the court.[26]

I joined Kappy, Edmundo René, and Edmundo Urrutia in the lobby of the attorney general's office. We all paced around nervously, awaiting Maritza's return from court. At last a few reporters wandered in, then several television camera crews, and soon the lobby was packed with members of the press. There were rumors that Valladares and Maritza had returned using a secret back entrance.

Sometime after 4:00 P.M. a man came partway down the stairs and called for Edmundo René and his father to come up to the conference room. Edmundo René tried to talk Maritza out of doing the press conference, but she insisted. It was part of the bargain she had struck with her kidnappers, and she was terrified that one of her relatives would suffer the penalty if she did not keep her word.[27] A short time later someone announced that Valladares would now meet the press in the conference room. As over forty journalists, all hungry for a story, surged up the stairs, I pushed my way toward the front of the pack.

Maritza sat on a couch next to the attorney general. Edmundo René sat facing them, expressionless. Maritza's face was pale and she looked tired. She wore a simple blouse with black and white stripes and black pants. Her curly hair was pulled back from her forehead.

Valladares spoke first. He explained how Maritza had presented herself at his office seeking amnesty and the judge had prepared the legal documents in which Maritza expressed her decision to give up her underground activities. Maritza had received amnesty. Reassuringly, the judge had forwarded the necessary papers to the state security forces so that they could provide the appropriate cooperation.

Valladares exhorted Maritza's *compañeros* to respect her decision to leave the Organización and resume her family life. He also urged the civilian and military authorities to respect Maritza's decision and the amnesty she had received. Finally, he opened the floor to questions.

In a soft voice, Maritza told the press that she had not been kidnapped. Instead, she had gone to the home of some friends in order to create "all of the conditions for getting myself back . . . into a legal life." "I was living in a difficult situation, in fear, outside the law," Maritza added. "So I decided to distance myself from that part of my life and that's why I'm here with all of you."

One of the reporters asked Maritza if it had been necessary to go to such great lengths and provoke a widespread protest by the general population against her supposed kidnapping. "What happens," she replied, "is that at times you lose control. One wants to do things maybe another way, but it doesn't work. That's why I thank you, and I also ask that you forgive me, because I know that all of you were worried about me, played a role in all of this, but it wasn't the way it was described."[28]

Back at the Island there was a miniature soccer court paved with cement where Don Chando's men usually played soccer in the afternoons. As secret intelligence operatives, they were not permitted to jog in the neighborhood streets, but their soccer games kept them physically and mentally fit for the daily grind of torture and assassination. For an entire week, in an attempt to reduce any noise that Maritza might hear while a captive at the Island, there had been no recreation. When he returned after leaving Maritza at the attorney general's office, Don Chando was jubilant. "Let's play ball!"[29] Soon the game was under way.

The next question at the press conference came from someone who knew the facts. "The day that you disappeared, one of your shoes was thrown into the street. Why?"

Maritza was very calm. "Sometimes life is like that. It was something unimportant, an accident."

Did Maritza have any intention of leaving the country?

"That's not my intention. On the contrary, I want to stay in Guatemala in order to enjoy my new legal situation. At this time, I'm going to be in my country."

Did she fear for her life?

"No. I have never feared for my life and even less now. I have guarantees that by accepting amnesty, my life will be more secure than before."[30]

It was an outstanding performance. Maritza spoke in a manner that was absolutely calm and sincere. There was just one incongruity: her eyes. Those enormous, terrible eyes. Maritza's eyes seemed to explode from her head.[31] They were huge white and brown saucers, and they told a very different story.[32]

When the press conference ended, I waited with Maritza, Edmundo René, their father, and Kappy for the reporters to troop downstairs. One of the news photographers snapped a picture of Maritza as she left the conference room. She beamed a radiant smile for the cameras. Outside, as the photographers continued to mill around, Edmundo René led his *hermanita* to his car.[33] Maritza sat between her father and brother in the front seat and Kappy sat behind. Finally, when the car doors were all shut, Maritza turned toward her father. "Papá!" she screamed. "They're going to kill us all!"[34]

Edmundo René became unglued as he drove his beat-up Datsun into the parking lot in front of the archbishopric. "Those sons of bitches said the door would be open! And the door is *closed!*" Soon I came out the front door to greet them.

Maritza was unaware of our plan to offer her refuge in the archbishopric, so when she left the attorney general's office, Maritza thought she was going to her parents' home in zone eight. After all, that was her agreement with her captors.[35] I led her through the massive wooden doors of the archbishopric, around the large stone patio, and into the archbishop's reception room.

Msgr. Penados, dressed in his black robes, silver crucifix hanging on his chest, took Maritza by the hand and they sat together on a worn couch covered in crimson velvet and satin. The couch matched the crimson chairs scattered around the room, the heavy crimson curtains, and the crimson carpet. To one side of the sofa was a polished wooden table with a crimson telephone. Three heavy crystal chandeliers, containing everyday light bulbs, lit up the room. The archbishop let Maritza cry on his shoulder for a few minutes and consoled her while the rest of the group sat quietly on the deep red chairs. "Calm down," Msgr. Penados told Maritza. "You'll be safe with us."[36]

The archbishop asked his cook and maid, Sister Tere Pineda, the tiny nun dressed in a blue habit, to prepare the back room for Maritza, Sebastián, Edmundo René, and Kappy. "They'll be here a few days. We have to help them while they arrange their trip."[37]

As Sister Tere prepared the room, I brought Maritza, Edmundo René, and Kappy to the archbishop's kitchen. Maritza began to speak, but her brother cut her off. "You're not going to say *anything!* The family has discussed this and you're not going to say *anything!*" But after a week in captivity, that was too much for Maritza. " 'Mundo, I need to speak!" she cried. "Let me speak!"[38]

So we sat around a small table, and Maritza began to tell her story.

For nearly an hour we sat transfixed as Maritza described her experience in captivity. At one point, I tried to take some notes but Edmundo René forbade it. "You're not going to write *anything!*" Maritza had clearly described her captors' threats against the family if she broke her vow of silence to them.

While we were talking, a group of men arrived at the archbishopric and announced that they were President Serrano's security detail. A party was scheduled for that evening in the elegant grand salon in honor of Msgr. Juan Gerardi, who was celebrating the twenty-fifth anniversary of his ordination as a bishop. The security men said that they needed to check the salon.

Claudia González, the ODHA's secretary, watched as the men went through the large salon and then walked across the stone patio and approached the polished wooden doors that opened to the corridor that led to the archbishop's kitchen. To Maritza.

González beat the men to the doors and refused to let them pass. That was the archbishop's private residence, she explained to them. They couldn't go through. The men protested. They needed to see if there were other exits to the building. Sorry, only the archbishop and his staff were permitted in the back of the building. The security detail retreated.[39]

Back in the kitchen, I tried to confirm that Maritza was in fact a member of the URNG. "*Bueno*, my husband, yes," she replied. "But not me." Maritza was free, but she was still under enormous pressure. In order to save her life, Maritza had given information about the Organización to her captors, a fact that now caused her tremendous pain and guilt. Although she had found a safe haven, the ODHA was not a revolutionary organization. Maritza could not explain to me or to my colleagues why she felt so guilty. Why she felt like such a traitor to the EGP. So she followed the same strategy she began when she was kidnapped: to say as little as possible and to mix fact with fiction.[40]

"Ay!" Maritza cried. "I feel like I'm not here!"[41] Psychologically, Maritza was still in the hands of her captors and she was having trouble accepting the fact of her release.[42] Kappy put her arm around Maritza and tried to console her. We discussed the possibility of arranging for Maritza to leave the country, and she agreed: "Oh yes, I'm leaving!"

After hearing about the threats made against his family, Edmundo René begged me not to divulge any information about what had really happened to Maritza. Fearing a security breach, Edmundo René asked me not to put the information in the ODHA's computer system. Later on

Edmundo René, his sister Carolina, and their parents made Maritza promise not to talk about what had happened to her.[43]

We heard noises from outside the kitchen. Maritza's mother, sister, and son had arrived at the archbishopric. We went out into the courtyard and Sebastián stepped forward with a bouquet of flowers for his mother. "Hola, Mamá." Maritza knelt down to embrace her little boy.[44]

Sister Tere had made up the beds and swept the floor in the back bedroom. The whole family trooped into the room to talk, and I took the opportunity to go to my office. Edmundo René gave orders to his relatives. "You're not going to say anything to anybody here! It might be infiltrated."[45]

From my office, I called Jones at the U.S. Embassy. Could we have a meeting to discuss U.S. visas for Maritza and her son? Jones said he would call me back the next day.

Edmundo René came into the office and asked permission to call Bill Robinson in Albuquerque in order to tell Robinson about Maritza's release. After they spoke for several minutes, Edmundo René passed the phone to me. Robinson explained that he was acting as the hub of communications between Guatemala and the human rights NGOs in the United States. We agreed that we would work together to try to get U.S. visas for Maritza and Sebastián. I told Robinson that I had already contacted the U.S. Embassy and was awaiting a response.

The soccer players at the Island were playing furiously when their commander, Don Gaspar, drove up and got out of his car. Don Chando stopped playing to speak with the major, and the other players overheard their conversation. "Man! Look at the problems we have!" scolded Don Gaspar. "Look at all the shit the boss gave me!"

"Yes, Major, I see—But I told you guys, I wanted to kill her. It would have been better to kill her."

The portly major was unmoved. "I've got to go to a meeting at 8:00 P.M. For sure they're going to talk to me about this. It's a foul-up!" The two officers stepped inside a room to continue their conversation in private. When they left the room, Don Chando was scratching his head. "Look at all the problems," he muttered. "With all of these organizations, you can't work like before."[46]

Darkness had fallen and a number of large, luxury automobiles were pulling up in front of the archbishopric and depositing well-dressed patrons at the door. They had come for the twenty-fifth anniversary celebration for Bishop Gerardi. Their bodyguards congregated outside the building, leaning against the wall and smoking. The festivities would take place only about thirty meters from the room where Maritza was now reunited with her family. President Serrano was there and when the president first arrived at the festivities, a reporter questioned him about Maritza's case. Serrano replied: "I can assure you that we had *nothing* to do with it."[47]

Members of President Serrano's cabinet were also in attendance, including the defense minister. Fortunately, a sturdy set of wooden doors separated the two sections of the archbishopric, one that held the celebration, and the other Maritza. "Keep those doors locked," I implored my colleagues. "And don't let anyone wander into the back of the building."

The celebration for Msgr. Gerardi began with a special mass in the cathedral. Ramiro de León Carpio, the human rights ombudsman and a devout Catholic, attended the mass. When the service was over, de León Carpio was passing through the atrium of the cathedral when his cellular phone rang. It was one of his assistants, speaking in code: "The person you want to speak with is closer than you can imagine. She's in the vicinity." Msgr. Penados stopped him and invited de León Carpio to the reception for Bishop Gerardi in the archbishopric's grand salon. "*But,*" the archbishop explained, "the invitation also has a political motive."[48]

Thus forewarned, de León Carpio passed through the great wooden doors of the archbishopric, turned left, crossed the lovely patio with its gurgling fountain, and entered the elegant salon. To his chagrin, he saw that President Serrano was present, accompanied by his crew of army bodyguards, as well as several members of the army high command in their smart dress uniforms. De León Carpio wanted to speak with Maritza discreetly, and he wondered *How are we going to do this?* But then the ombudsman saw an old friend, Msgr. Gerardo Flores, bishop of las Verapaces, and he quietly explained the problem to the cleric. The two men left the room, exchanging greetings with members of Serrano's security team, and went to find Maritza.[49]

Also in attendance at the party was Carmen Aída Ibarra, one of Guatemala's finest political reporters. She wrote for the daily newspaper *Siglo Veintiuno* at that time and had been covering the Congress and Guatemala's numerous political parties since 1985. Ibarra and Ronalth Ochaeta, director of the ODHA, had known each other for about a year and had collaborated on a number of issues. The ODHA needed press contacts to increase the scope of its work, and Ibarra wanted to use her role as a journalist to promote greater respect for human rights. Plus, she was raised a Catholic, so she tried to assist the Church whenever she could.

Initially, only *Siglo Veintiuno* had published the ODHA's press releases and criticisms. Other newspapers, with more conservative perspectives, viewed work on behalf of human rights, including the efforts of the Catholic Church, as being leftist and linked to the URNG. But gradually the ODHA began to take on an important political role as government critic and monitor of human rights violations. Eventually, other reporters lost their fear of covering human rights stories, and by 1992 the ODHA was a mandatory source of information for the Guatemalan media.

But Ibarra's relationship with Ochaeta and other members of the ODHA became more personal. She spoke with Ochaeta every day and they would exchange gossip about human rights, politics, legal cases, etc. Ochaeta would tell her: "This is for the public, and this is not. That's just for *your* consumption."[50] And Ibarra never published the confidential information, so there was a special relationship of trust between Ibarra, Ochaeta, and the rest of the ODHA staff.

Now as the white-jacketed waiters moved about the throng in the salon, serving hors d'oeuvres and glasses of whiskey and wine to the elegant guests, the short, roly-poly Ibarra observed the crowd. Never much of a drinker, Ibarra focused on the interesting people at the party, what gossip they discussed, and what bits of information she might pick up. Ibarra had not covered Maritza's disappearance, but she noticed Ramiro de León Carpio, the human rights ombudsman, deep in conversation with several bishops out by the fountain. Then suddenly, Ibarra watched the group go through a door and disappear. She wondered what the men were talking about.

Ibarra wanted to speak with Fernando Penados, the archbishop's nephew who worked at the ODHA, but she didn't see him at the party. So she wandered across the building toward the entrance to the ODHA to see if she could find him. Coincidentally, at that moment, Fernando Penados came through the doors from the street. He seemed very nervous, and he carried a load of baby clothes and bed sheets with little animals on them, such as a small child might use. Ibarra greeted Penados and tried to speak with him, but the young man brushed her off: "Look, excuse me, but I can't talk to you now because I have some things to do."[51] And then Penados hurried off into the back of the building. Ibarra felt that something strange was going on inside the archbishopric, but she didn't know what it was.

Carmen Aída Ibarra was not the only reporter busy that night. Juan Luis Font and his partner, Carmen Sofía Berganes, were hot on the trail of Maritza's story. They wrote for the weekly news magazine *Crónica* and usually had good sources in the ODHA. But in Maritza's case, the ODHA had suddenly shut them down. In five days Font and Berganes would have to file their next story. But now the Church became the most cautious and closed of their sources, forcing the young reporters to search for information elsewhere.[52]

Font and Berganes were good and they knew where to dig, and it did not take them very long to get their scoop. They shuttled from the office of one source to the home of another source, and then to the office of another source. Before the night was over, Font and Berganes knew that members of the army had disappeared Maritza and that the same unit continued to threaten Maritza and her son. They knew that Maritza had been pressured into making false statements and that her press conference at the attorney general's office was a farce. They worked until 1:30 in the morning, and they had Maritza's story.[53]

Msgr. Flores and de León Carpio entered the room where Maritza and her family were talking. Carolina was nearly hysterical. "We all have to leave the country!" she exclaimed to the ombudsman. He sat on a chair in front of Maritza, who looked exhausted. When de León Carpio asked where the family wanted to go, they explained that the best place for Maritza would be Albuquerque, New Mexico, in the United States. Edmundo René would be there. And he had a community of friends who could help Maritza.

De León Carpio offered to facilitate the process of obtaining U.S. visas for Maritza and Sebastián. He would speak with George Chester, the political counselor at the embassy. I explained that Maritza's passport had expired. Could de León Carpio also help us to expedite a renewal? De León Carpio agreed and I gave him Maritza's passport.

De León Carpio asked for a few minutes alone with Maritza, and the family paraded out to the patio. "Look," said de León Carpio to Maritza when they were alone, "I want to know. Did they kidnap you or not?" "Yes," she replied, "they kidnapped me."[54] To de León Carpio, Maritza seemed very scared and anguished. Maritza asked him to say nothing about what she told him, for fear of reprisals against herself and her family, because her captors had threatened to kill her and her young son if she talked. De León Carpio agreed, because he knew Maritza's life and the lives of her family were on the line. So Maritza told him the story of her disappearance, and de León Carpio could see Maritza's desperation to leave the country. He knew they could kill her at any moment.[55]

Back at the Island, the men watched the television news reports about Maritza. A more subdued Don Chando began to tell them about the problems that had arisen. Now this woman did not accept the conditions he had given her. Other persons, who were interested in accusing the army, were manipulating her. "Go talk to ——," said Don Chando, referring to the Island's paymaster, "they're going to give you something." Coroncho eventually received 150 quetzales (about $30) for his work on Maritza's case. Normally Don Chando did not smoke cigarettes, but that night he was smoking nervously and pacing back and forth.[56]

I stepped out of the archbishopric to buy some food for Sebastián. I was tense and it was a relief to be on the street and away from the emotional atmosphere inside. The magnitude of the decision to bring Maritza into the building was beginning to weigh upon me. If Maritza *was* a *guerrillera*, the ODHA was intentionally assisting a member of the URNG for the first time. Previously, perhaps naively, the ODHA adamantly maintained a position of humanitarian neutrality within the context of Guatemala's internal conflict. Now for the same humanitarian principles, the ODHA was crossing dangerous lines. Whatever Maritza's true status was, she was a prize in a fierce propaganda battle where the stakes were high for both belligerents. I had just put the staff of the archbishopric, more than a dozen people, at serious risk. And I had not thought it through.

1. Ester Castellanos de Urrutia, Maritza Urrutia's paternal grandmother, speaking in public in the early 1950s. She "lived for politics." (Courtesy of the Urrutia family archive.)

2. The Urrutia family, early 1950s. Ester Castellanos de Urrutia is seated next to her husband, Manuel Urrutia. Seated next to Ester is her daughter Julia. Standing, second from the right, is Edmundo Urrutia, Maritza's father. (Courtesy of the Urrutia family archive.)

RADIO LIBERACIÓN, 1/8/1954

3. Sisters Sonia and Sara Orellana, the voices of *Radio Liberación,* with members of Carlos Castillo Armas's "liberation army" in August 1954. The names "Sandra" and "Silvia" were pseudonyms used by the young women in their radio broadcasts. (Courtesy of the Conde family archive.)

4. Oscar Conde at *Radio Universal,* late 1950s—the fiercest, toughest, most dogmatic, and radical anti-Communist journalist. (Courtesy of the Conde family archive.)

5. Edmundo Urrutia and Pilar, his wife, seated, holding Maritza in 1961. Maritza's sister, Carolina, is standing to her right and Edmundo René, her brother, to her left. (Courtesy of the Urrutia family archive.)

6. In July 1992, Maritza's brother, Edmundo Rene Urrutia, speaks to the press about his sister's disappearance. "Every human life was precious." (Courtesy Tele Prensa.)

7. The *comandante:* Gustavo Meoño, the EGP leader in Guatemala City. "Who else might be at risk?" (Photo by Ricardo Ramirez Arriola.)

8. The activist: Bill Robinson. He did not stop for two weeks. (Photo by Esteban Pino Coviello.)

9. The bishop: Juan Gerardi Conedera. "It's *you* who are killing; *you* are the enemies of the people." (Courtesy Oficina de Derechos Humanos Arzobispado de Guatemala.)

10. The archbishop: Próspero Penados del Barrio. "The bishop took me out at night. *At night.*" (Courtesy Oficina de Derechos Humanos Arzobispado de Guatemala.)

11. Ronalth Ochaeta, director of the archbishop's Human Rights Office (ODHA). "And this is going to bring bloodshed and there could even be deaths! And it will be *your fault!*" (Courtesy Haroldo Shetemul, on behalf of *Crónica.*)

12. The priest: Father Sergio Orantes preaching his sermon for Maritza's deliverance, July 28, 1992. "It's time . . . for the *gorillas* to go to jail!" (Courtesy Sergio Valdez Pedroni.)

13. The ambassador: Thomas F. Stroock. He made "the 'Marlboro man' look timid." (Courtesy Patricia Goudvis.)

14. The president: Jorge Serrano Elías. "He yelled at anyone he could, like he owned the country." (Courtesy Haroldo Shetemul, on behalf of *Crónica*.)

15. Manuel Conde Orellana, center, president of the Guatemalan Peace Commission, speaking during negotiations with the URNG in Cuernevaca, Mexico, in 1992. He knew that Maritza's video would upset the URNG's high command. (Courtesy of the Public Relations Department of the Guatemalan Government/Conde family archive.)

16. The face of torture: Maritza Urrutia in her video broadcast on Guatemalan television on July 29, 1992. (Courtesy Notisiete/Canales 3 y 7.)

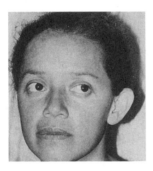

17. Maritza at her press conference in the attorney general's office, July 30, 1992. "An expression that shows fatigue and fear." (Courtesy Haroldo Shetemul, on behalf of *Crónica,* August 7, 1992.)

18. Maritza at her press conference. Sitting to Maritza's left is Attorney General Acisclo Valladares. (Courtesy Notisiete/Canales 3 y 7.)

19. Maritza and her mother embrace inside the archbishopric following Maritza's release, July 30, 1992. (Photo by author.)

20. The human rights ombudsman: Ramiro de León Carpio. "Did they kidnap you or not?" (Courtesy Haroldo Shetemul, on behalf of *Crónica*.)

21. The journalist: *Crónica*'s Juan Luis Font. "We repressed *ourselves*." (Photo by Moises Castillo.)

22. The journalist: *Siglo Veintiuno*'s Carmen Aída Ibarra. She kept the secret about Maritza. (Photo by María Antonieta Quiná; courtesy Carmen Aída Ibarra.)

23. The human rights professional: Carlos Salinas, speaking on behalf of Amnesty International at a 1995 conference on the CIA's role in Guatemala. "She might be dead on the tenth." (Courtesy Patricia Goudvis.)

PART II

THE VISA

There will always be the dark and tangled stretches in the decision-making process—mysterious even to those who may be most intimately involved.

John F. Kennedy, quoted in William I. Bacchus,
***Foreign Policy and the Bureaucratic Process* (1974)**

God save us always . . . from the innocent and the good.

Graham Greene, *The Quiet American* (1955)

NINE

FRIDAY

July 31, 1992

On Thursday night Maritza and Sebastián shared one of the single beds in the back room of the archbishopric and Edmundo René and Kappy crammed into the other. As they bedded down, Sebastián locked his hands around Maritza's neck. "You *left* me!" he scolded his mother. "*Why* did you *leave* me?"[1] During the frantic efforts to save Maritza's life, no one in the family had explained clearly to Sebastián why his mother was absent. She did not *want* to leave him, Maritza replied, but some men had taken her away against her will. Eventually her son fell asleep, and Maritza was able to pry his hands away from her throat. But during the night, nightmares interrupted her sleep.

On Friday morning the press was full of stories and commentary about Maritza's reappearance. "Was Mrs. Maritza Urrutia Kidnapped or Not?" headlined *El Grafico*. "There are contradictions. She was kidnapped," said Otto Peralta, president of USAC's Student Association: "It's a pity to know that again they try to fool us saying that it wasn't an act of kidnapping when there are real indications that yes it was. They've been doing these kinds of maneuvers for years."[2]

USAC's School of History issued another communiqué that morning. It announced that the government and its security forces would be held responsible for any attack against the university community, the student leadership, and the School of History.[3]

Maritza's brother, Edmundo René, was more diplomatic and concerned about his family's vulnerability: "Given the *very special* situation in which my sister spoke on television, what she said lacks credibility. We believe that it's very doubtful. I don't know the entirety of the statements that she made. We don't know their veracity or authenticity. . . . We hope to clarify her situation as well as our own."[4]

The president of Guatemala, Jorge Serrano, told the press that his only knowledge of Maritza's case came from what he saw in the press. Thus, he had requested some additional reports about the case so that he could be completely informed.[5]

The defense minister, an army general, was jubilant about Maritza's appearance. "You have to consider Maritza Urrutia's case *especially from the humane point of view,*" he explained. From his own perspective as a father, the general felt "delighted (as Maritza's father must feel), knowing that she was returning home." "It was a pleasure," he noted, "to see that Maritza was in good condition" [emphasis added].[6]

Furthermore, the general expressed his satisfaction for the sentiments expressed by Maritza in her public statements. She understood that participation in subversive activities was not the proper way to change Guatemala's social and economic situation. "We're looking for peace and reconciliation," the general emphasized. "That's why it's very important to take into account the profound message she sent to the populace."[7] The general assured the public that the army had the capacity and the obligation to guarantee Maritza's security as well as the safety of her family.

That Friday morning Maritza was obsessed with the need to see the newspapers. Shortly after my arrival, Archbishop Penados entered the ODHA. "Look, Maritza needs the newspapers from last week. She needs to see them. Can you get them for her?" Maritza seemed relieved when I handed her the editions that were published during the week she was in captivity. Maritza had been taken away from the world for a week, and, to reassure herself, she needed to regain the week that she had lost. And she wanted to find out if any of her comrades had been killed.[8]

A number of journalists were still pursuing Maritza's story. She had reappeared so mysteriously and then, after her press conference, disappeared again. No one knew where she was. So one curious reporter, Rony Véliz Samayoa, came to the ODHA to see if the staff could tell him anything.

Véliz was a writer and photographer working for Reuters news agency and the newspaper *El Grafico*. Like Carmen Aída Ibarra, Rony Véliz had a "special relationship" with the staff of the ODHA. He covered Ronalth Ochacta's press conferences and other office events and did his best to promote the ODHA's interests in the press. But that morning

Véliz was shut down. The Church could not give any statements about Maritza or say where she was.

Carmen Aída Ibarra, the reporter for *Siglo Veintiuno,* also had a busy morning. Thursday evening she had pondered the unexplained tensions she witnessed at Msgr. Gerardi's anniversary party. Checking with her sources on Friday morning, Ibarra learned that Maritza was inside the archbishopric, and that Ramiro de León Carpio, the human rights ombudsman, had spoken with her. So Ibarra tried to speak with her friends at the ODHA. Perhaps she could get an interview with Maritza to learn what *really* happened to her. But Ibarra too was rebuffed. Maritza would not be giving any interviews or statements. And the ODHA's staff made Ibarra promise not to tell anyone about Maritza's presence inside the archbishopric.

By noon on Friday many other members of the press were becoming frustrated about Maritza's case. They had gone to her parents' home in zone eight to try to speak with her, but Maritza was not there. Ibarra never told her colleagues where Maritza was; she knew that her discretion would help protect Maritza's security. Plus, she had promised her friends at the ODHA to say nothing.[9] The media's role in the case had turned upside down. For one week all the human rights NGOs had energetically used the press in order to win Maritza's release. Now, just as interest was snowballing, journalists had either been sworn to secrecy or denied information altogether. But it was all to protect Maritza.

On Friday morning Ramiro de León Carpio paid a visit to the U.S. Embassy. De León Carpio believed that the lives of Maritza and Sebastián were in imminent danger, so he wanted to get them out of Guatemala. He spoke with George Chester, the political counselor at the U.S. Embassy. Jones and Suzanne Patterson, the consul general, were probably present as well. De León Carpio explained that he had spoken to Maritza the previous evening inside the archbishopric. Although, at Maritza's request, he had sworn not to reveal the details of her kidnapping, de León Carpio told the embassy representatives that he believed that Maritza had been held for the past week by the army in an army installation.[10] The infamous video and press conference were a farce and Maritza had made her public comments only to save her life.[11] Two lives were at stake, de León Carpio explained. Could the United States grant political asylum to Maritza and her son?[12]

George Chester's response was "humanitarian, positive but reserved." He wasn't sure if the embassy could grant the ombudsman's wish, Chester explained. He had to consult with his superiors. "It was difficult." But de León Carpio had the impression that Chester was worried about avoiding problems with Jorge Serrano's government. In the past de León Carpio had worked on cases in which he obtained visas for Canada or the United States "in seconds!" Something about George Chester's response that morning suggested to de León Carpio that Maritza's case was not so simple. The ombudsman left the embassy feeling a bit disappointed.[13]

After his visit to the U.S. Embassy, de León Carpio came to the archbishopric to speak with Maritza. She and I stood in the large patio with him outside the bedroom as the ombudsman described his visit that morning to the U.S. Embassy. He had spoken with George Chester, the advisor for political affairs, regarding the possibility of obtaining entry visas for Maritza and Sebastian. "Frankly," he explained, "I'm not optimistic." I told de León Carpio that I had my own contact at the embassy: Jones. Would he have a problem if I approached Jones about the visas? De León Carpio encouraged me to do whatever I could to obtain the visas. He would work on renewing Maritza's passport while mother and son remained in the archbishopric. It seemed like an ideal place to protect their safety.[14] Arrangements were made for Jones and the consul general to speak with Maritza at the archbishopric that same afternoon.

At approximately 3:00 P.M. Jones arrived at the archbishopric with Sue Patterson, and I ushered them into the archbishop's dining room. The consul general had a well-deserved reputation as a professional, tough, and innovative administrator, a person who got things done.[15] Patterson started doing consular work in the U.S. Embassy in Tehran in 1974 when 150,000 Iraqi Kurds crossed the border into Iran and languished in refugee camps. Patterson admired the toughness of the Kurdish people and set up a program that eventually resettled 750 Kurdish families, many with ten or more children, in the United States. Some Kurds landed in Miami, where they learned Spanish instead of English, while the most successful group settled in North Dakota with the assistance of Patterson and the Lutheran Church. During the late 1970s—the era of the "boat people" desperately trying to leave Southeast Asia—Patterson worked on refugee issues at State Department headquarters in Washington, D.C. In cooperation with the UN's refugee agency, her program—known as the "Orderly Departure Program"—helped to resettle 120,000 Vietnamese refugees in the United States.[16]

Patterson's refugee work was rewarding, but early on she became aware of the difficult human complexities of her task. "I had this kind of romantic vision of helping out refugees," Patterson recalled. In the late 1970s Patterson went to Buenos Aires to set up a refugee program for dissidents held in jail by Argentina's military dictatorship. Under international pressure to free some of its political prisoners, the regime agreed to release them only if they would go directly from jail to a foreign country. With Patterson's help, three hundred Argentinean former prisoners came to the States and Patterson convinced her Episcopal church in Alexandria, Virginia, to sponsor one young man who had been imprisoned for three years. That's when things began to go wrong: "He was a very frustrating person for me to deal with. He wouldn't make a decision. He had no direction. . . . I couldn't motivate him. . . . I realized the difficulties of people going into exile, the language and cultural problems, the psychological scars."[17]

A break from consular work during the 1980s included a stint with the State Department's Bureau for International Narcotics Matters just as the United States' drug war in Latin America began to boil. Following Patterson's appointment as consul general to the U.S. Embassy in Guatemala in 1989, the experience helped her become an active member of the embassy's narcotics committee. In addition to control over visas, the embassy consul is responsible for all cases of American citizens who are victims of crimes within the country. After the 1990 murder of U.S. citizen Michael DeVine by Guatemalan soldiers, resolution of this killing became the number one bilateral issue between the two countries. Given her responsibility for the matter, Patterson often met directly with Guatemala's minister of defense and the foreign minister, an unusual situation for a consular officer.

Many Guatemalans thought, incorrectly, that visa matters made Patterson the most important person in the U.S. Embassy. But Patterson was a major player in the mission because of her skills and the nature of the cases and bilateral issues at the time. And she worked closely with Ambassador Stroock.[18]

That Friday afternoon I sat between Maritza and Edmundo René at Msgr. Penados's circular dining room table. An old tapestry of the Last Supper hung from one wall. Jones and Patterson sat down opposite us. They were frustrated by Edmundo René and Kappy's decision to remain in Guatemala. After all, the U.S. Embassy had rendered extraordinary assistance to Edmundo René and Kappy just two nights earlier because of what the couple *perceived* to be a life-threatening situation. Now the two of them had changed their minds. If something happened to Edmundo René and Kappy now, blame might be cast on Jones, Patterson, and their colleagues.

So at the archbishop's table, Patterson glared at Edmundo René and he glared back at her. "You have been manipulating us and abusing our generosity," hissed Patterson. Nor was Edmundo René in a chipper mood. "Look," he began to tell Patterson, "if you don't want to help us you can—" I grabbed his arm and shut him up, trying to prevent a battle. The issue before us was Maritza's need for a U.S. visa, not whatever had passed between Edmundo René, Kappy, and the embassy.

There was a brief silence and then Patterson began the interview. As she nervously smoked a cigarette, Maritza described her kidnapping, the treatment she received from her captors, her request for amnesty, and the making of the video. Maritza chose her words very carefully, but she implied that Guatemala's security forces were responsible for her disappearance.[19] Maritza recalled that there were at least two witnesses to her kidnapping: two women who had left their children at Walt Disney School on the same morning. Patterson and Jones were obviously moved by what they heard, and by Maritza's appearance. Maritza seemed very frail and shaken, and close to tears at several moments.

Patterson and Jones asked Maritza about her ex-husband and her life in Mexico. She had met Esteban in Mexico City where Esteban worked with student groups on projects repairing earthquake damage and did other odd jobs. What did Maritza do during all those years in Mexico? Oh, she worked at various places. She worked for a printer. What was the printer's name? "*Bueno,* I don't remember."

Maritza was unaware whether Esteban was involved with the URNG. Certainly *she* was not involved with the insurgency, nor had she ever been asked to join the guerrillas, or even do them a favor. She and Esteban had separated some years before. Maritza had lived a very peaceful life since returning to Guatemala, dedicated to raising her son. The two things she loved most, Maritza explained, were children and the movies.[20] It was a pretty good performance.

Maritza explained that she was afraid for her safety not only because she had been kidnapped, but because her captors were not finished with her. She was under instructions to appear at a certain time the following Thursday in a shopping mall in order "to receive further instructions." "How can I ever feel safe leaving my little boy at school under these conditions?" she asked Patterson and Jones.[21]

Patterson told us she would have to consult with the State Department in Washington, D.C., before making any decision about the visas. When would we know? Patterson couldn't say; that depended on Washington. But she would inform us as soon as possible. Both Patterson and

Jones were convinced that Maritza told them the truth: she was kidnapped and made her subsequent public statements only to save her life.[22]

Before they left, Jones spoke up. "Look, Dan, all of this pressure on the State Department and the embassy isn't helping things." He gave me a knowing look. "So turn off the pressure, Dan. It's not helping." I told Jones I couldn't control the outside pressure on the State Department, but I would see what I could do to help him.

After Jones and Patterson left the archbishopric, I phoned Bill Robinson. I relayed Jones's plea that the NGOs' pressure be turned off and naively suggested that we comply with Jones's request. He was my friend at the U.S. Embassy, and I wanted to trust him. Robinson hesitated when I described the request, but he agreed to pass my opinion along to the other individuals and institutions involved in the case.

Although I was unaware of it at the time, my suggestion to shut off the political pressure directed at the State Department Headquarters in Washington and the embassy in Guatemala from NGOs and sympathetic congressional staff generated a great controversy within the U.S. human rights community. Some argued that since I was the man on the ground in Guatemala responsible for Maritza, the NGOs should follow my advice. After all, I was the NGOs' contact in Guatemala.

Others, however, were disgusted by my naïveté in trusting the U.S. Embassy and wanted to disregard my suggestion. "We've been doing this for years. We don't need Dan Saxon to tell us what to do," was one rationale.[23] "If that's the advice of the embassy, then let's do exactly the opposite," argued Carlos Salinas of Amnesty International.[24] Salinas and his peers knew that I was misreading the situation and that, apparently aware of my naïveté, the U.S. Embassy was hoping to take advantage of it.[25]

Eventually Bill Robinson, "blowing his top," called Frank LaRue in Washington. "Look here," vented Robinson, "we're using the right strategy. The only strategy is keeping the case public and applying pressure. Now we're being asked by Dan Saxon to turn the pressure off! This can't be! We can't yield this way to pressure from the ODHA!"

LaRue sympathized with Robinson's sense of frustration. Once Maritza reappeared, the goals of the human rights NGOs had changed. First, they wanted to discredit the televised video as a farce, a charade, and a publicity ploy. But most important, they wanted to get Maritza out of Guatemala, both for her security and for other, more political reasons. Always the activist, LaRue wanted Maritza to publicly denounce the Guatemalan government for subjecting her to forced disappearance and torture: "We wanted her to leave because we wanted her to go up to the

Organization of American States [to testify about her experience]. So we were very much involved in getting her the visa. We wanted her to come to Washington. That's all we do."

From long experience assisting Guatemalan labor activists who were victims of state repression, LaRue knew that Robinson was correct to want to maintain the public pressure on the State Department. "Always go public. No matter what," he explained later. "Keep the pressure on, on any case—small or big. With one condition—you must be certain of the evidence and be able to defend it. If you have doubts, you don't go public." That way the NGOs protect their credibility, as well as the credibility of the victims. "As long as you're sure of what happened, go public. It's not always safe, but it helps."

"Bill, you're coordinating this process," LaRue told Robinson. "I'll defer to you."[26] Yet I was the link between the NGOs, Maritza, and the U.S. Embassy. Losing my cooperation would jeopardize all of the efforts to assist Maritza.[27] Robinson agreed with other members of the NGO community that people in Guatemala should make the final decision (although he disagreed with it). So my supporters won the argument, unfortunately, and the pressure was turned off.[28] And Maritza temporarily lost an "incredibly powerful machinery" that had been mobilized for the protection of her human rights.[29]

This phone call to Robinson probably marks the point when I adopted a guarded, cryptic style of speaking. And my unwillingness to convey much information further infuriated some members of the human rights NGOs who were working on Maritza's case from the United States. Robinson wanted to know if Maritza acknowledged that she was kidnapped, but I would not discuss the issue over the telephone: I had heard about the army's threats against Maritza's life and other family members' lives should she break her vows of silence. Nor would I respond to questions about Maritza's appearance, or whether she felt safe. Apparently I only acknowledged that Maritza was "in shock."[30]

In this pre-Internet era, Robinson and the NGO members knew that the ODHA's telephone lines were tapped.[31] Indeed, in early 1992 the U.S. State Department reported that the Guatemalan army routinely monitored private phone lines.[32] At the time, and especially after Maritza's relatives had begged me not to divulge any information about her disappearance, I worried that Robinson was putting the Urrutia family at risk by asking these questions. I did not consider, however, that the NGOs needed more information, in order to lobby more effectively from afar on Maritza's behalf. After all, if Maritza had never been kidnapped, why would she be in danger? Why would she need a U.S. visa?

"Look at all we've done for them!" complained one exasperated NGO representative in the United States. "Now they're not giving us anything!"[33] Two groups of actors who were struggling to help Maritza, one in Guatemala and the other in the United States, were not communicating very well and were beginning to antagonize each other.

TEN

SATURDAY

August 1, 1992

By Saturday morning, tensions were high between Maritza and Edmundo René. Maritza told her brother that she did not want to stay in the United States with him. She would remain an EGP activist even in exile and would continue the struggle with her comrades.[1]

Edmundo René was angry with Maritza because his own plans for resuming his life in Guatemala were falling apart. Now he had to leave the country again. Maritza's disappearance was such a dramatic event that it would be absurd for her to continue her life as an insurgent, he thought. Maritza should seize this opportunity to do something for herself and for her son outside of her life as a revolutionary. She and Sebastián could have a secure, peaceful (albeit dull) life in Albuquerque. "I was thinking of Maritza's needs in my own terms," Edmundo René acknowledged later.[2]

But Maritza totally rejected Edmundo René's suggestions. Maritza argued that her disappearance should have no effect on her; indeed her experience *confirmed* everything that she was doing as a revolutionary. So they fought. Edmundo René yelled at her and she was stubborn.

I was unaware of their quarrel when I arrived at the archbishopric on Saturday morning. Maritza and I talked and played with Sebastián as we waited for her father and a physician to arrive. After the doctor began his examination about noon, Ronalth Ochaeta returned from his conference in Costa Rica. "How are you?" I asked him. "Better than you," he replied. Ochaeta looked tanned and rested, and he infuriated his exhausted colleagues with tales of how the conference participants had spent the past few evenings drinking and carousing in the bars of San José. He wanted to know all about Maritza and when Maritza's medical examination ended, I introduced Ochaeta to her.

"There are people in Costa Rica who are concerned about you," Ochaeta explained when he was alone with Maritza, "and worried about your situation." Maritza knew that he was alluding to EGP members who were based in Costa Rica. She was smoking very nervously and she didn't want anyone else to hear their conversation.

"Relax," Ochaeta told her. "You're in the archbishop's home. Nothing's going to happen to you. Tell me what you can. I can suppose some things, but if you don't tell me, I'm not going to ask about them. Tell me what you want to tell me."[3] And so they spoke for a while about Maritza's kidnapping and her captivity.

At that time, little Sebastián had engaged the archbishop in a game of soccer out on the patio, using an orange for a ball. Msgr. Penados stopped playing momentarily in order to speak to his mother, Ochaeta, and myself. An enraged Sebastián, who by now had been locked within the building for nearly two days, promptly pelted the good archbishop in the chest with the orange. Maritza was horrified, but Penados laughed it off. "It's our fault, really," he explained. "We interrupted his game." So Msgr. Penados went back to play more soccer with Sebastián, and the boy calmed down.[4]

Conflicts were also brewing within the Organización. Gustavo Meoño, the EGP's urban *comandante*, wanted Maritza to feel supported, to understand that she wasn't alone, so that the army could not continue to pressure her. Meoño tried to place messages of support in the press where Maritza would see them so that she would dare to tell the truth about her experience.[5]

But Meoño faced dissent from within his own ranks. As Elaine Scarry observes in *The Body in Pain: The Making and Unmaking of the World*, "there is not only among torturers but even among people appalled by acts of torture and sympathetic to those hurt, a covert disdain for confession."[6]

Thus, other EGP members wanted to take a more hard-line approach toward Maritza's behavior. The hard-liners believed that Maritza should have died before agreeing to make propaganda statements or videos for her army captors, irrespective of the pressures and tortures that she suffered. They would not forgive Maritza's "sins" and believed that the EGP should punish her as a traitor.[7]

Meoño thought that the arguments of the EGP hard-liners were head-strong and shortsighted, but he had to address them. No one had the authority, he believed, to judge how someone in Maritza's position should have acted. "It's very difficult to put yourself in the shoes of someone who's been kidnapped, who's been tortured, and say: 'She should have endured. She should have resisted. The only things she should have done with her kidnappers and torturers was insult them and spit on them.'"[8]

Besides, Meoño told the hard-liners, think of the *political* gains for the EGP. The EGP stood to gain much more politically with Maritza *alive* and denouncing what had happened to her than by the EGP's killing her as a traitor. If Maritza publicly described her experience, it would be a great blow to the army and the government. It would show the world that they were still using the same barbaric methods. This would be a much better result for the URNG than the appearance of Maritza's body with a coup de grâce gunshot to the head. This was the argument that permitted Meoño to override the most radical, intransigent members of the Organización following Maritza's reappearance.[9]

Expressed in the oblique but potentially dangerous style of Guatemalan political activists, doubts and mistrust about Maritza lingered within the EGP. If she was cooperating with the army, Maritza would be a threat to the entire URNG.[10] Meoño knew that Maritza would have to speak out in order to avoid problems and accusations of treason. Ten years earlier, in 1982, two young EGP members were captured by the army and then escaped. When they made their way to Nicaragua, then an important base for the EGP, the national directorate decided that the young *guerrilleros* were part of an army trap. Over the objections of Meoño, they were adjudged "traitors" and shot. Now in 1992, Meoño wanted to avoid another "excessive act" by the EGP in Maritza's case.[11] Somehow, he had to let Maritza know that she was not alone, and that she had to speak out.

URNG leaders in Mexico City also focused on Maritza's case that weekend, albeit for different reasons. Miguel Ángel Sandoval, then in exile in Mexico, was one of the founders of the EGP as well as a member of the URNG's political and diplomatic commission, charged with assisting the rebel high command in ongoing peace negotiations with the Guatemalan government. Then forty-five, Sandoval had joined his first revolutionary organization, the youth wing of the Communist Party, at age fourteen. Shortly thereafter, Sandoval and his student *compañeros* graduated from political work to armed urban guerrilla action with the FAR, such as kidnapping the president of Guatemala's supreme court in May 1966.[12] Sandoval was a tough nut, but he was also an old friend of Maritza's father, Edmundo, and he had known Maritza since she was a little girl.

For a year, human rights was the topic on the agenda at the peace negotiations, and little, if any, progress had been made. Sandoval saw Maritza's video on cable television in Mexico. After concluding with his colleagues that the film was a charade by army intelligence, they asked each other, but a charade for what? With what objective?[13] Around the same period, the army presented other captured insurgents to the public as "repentant *guerrilleros*." Now with Maritza's amateurish video, it appeared that the army was mounting a special counterinsurgency campaign, and URNG wanted to stop it.

One fundamental norm of Guatemalan revolutionaries was that when a comrade was captured, he or she must be prepared for the worst. Historically, the URNG did not publicly intervene on behalf of captured insurgents, so as not to risk provoking more serious torture, or even death. The guerrilla leaders did not want to create more problems for their comrades' families either. In the past, gestures made on behalf of a detainee had brought their relatives swift retaliation. Now fear often kept families from taking any action to save a spouse, sibling, son, or daughter who had been disappeared. Hence the URNG used more discreet methods of channeling pressure through human rights organizations and other institutions to assist Maritza.[14]

Yet this case was different. Maritza had reappeared alive. On the following Monday, August 5, a new round of peace talks on the subject of human rights would begin in Mexico City. How could the URNG leadership negotiate about human rights while the Guatemalan army committed such abuses with the knowledge of the highest levels of the government and military and, furthermore, used the same violations for propaganda campaigns?[15] Even within the context of a savage armed conflict, it was just *too* duplicitous. So the URNG had to establish a precedent. If it remained silent about Maritza's case, it would appear to accept the army's brutality.[16]

Additionally, Maritza's case and others like it demonstrated that the Serrano administration was ineffective in defending and promoting human rights. On the contrary, her case showed that the government was using the same human rights violations to perpetuate its impunity. Acisclo Valladares, the attorney general, accepted Maritza's "amnesty" without any inquiry into the actual circumstances of her disappearance. The URNG leadership also wanted to respond to the army's manipulation of the media and its distortion of reality in order to set the record straight and demand protection and justice for Maritza. So just as a new round of peace talks was about to begin, the URNG issued a communiqué concerning Maritza to expose the incoherence of the government's policies.[17]

The authors of the URNG's communiqué knew that by publicly involving the Serrano government in Maritza's case, there could be serious repercussions for the army and the civilian administration if anything happened to Maritza or her family. However, once the insurgents seized the initiative in the media blitz surrounding Maritza's case, President Serrano was bound to take stronger measures in order to ensure that Maritza not leave the country and denounce her experience.[18] The last thing that Serrano and his advisors wanted was for Maritza's case to become "an enormous international incident."[19] Moreover, by proclaiming that Maritza was one of its members, the URNG gave the U.S. government a possible basis for denying her a visa. So although the communiqué served the URNG's political purposes, it did not help Maritza. Instead, it slowed the humanitarian efforts of the individuals and institutions struggling to help her flee Guatemala and enter the United States.

In July 1991, just seven months after it first imposed its ambitious benchmarks on President Serrano's government, the U.S. Embassy provided a very pessimistic report to Secretary of State Baker about the subject of human rights in Guatemala:

> The Serrano government is under increasing criticism for failing to stop violence and assaults on human rights. . . . Much of the political violence undoubtedly comes from elements within the army, an institution facing numerous and confusing decisions and pressures. We conclude that, so far, Serrano's administration seems no better at halting violence and punishing its authors than was Cerezo's.[20]

The ongoing peace negotiations between the government and the URNG and the uncertainty of the future role of the armed forces in a postwar state created "a great deal of unease in the nation's most powerful institution." Like chess players, the military and the insurgents jockeyed for stronger negotiating positions and for greater status after the signing of a final peace accord. "In Guatemala," Ambassador Stroock warned, "this sort of political maneuvering involves killing."[21]

Stroock noted that despite President Serrano's inaugural vow to assert total control over Guatemala's security forces, "he has a limited ability to probe the army on human rights issues."[22] "It became evident to us that [Serrano] could pull the lever of power, but it wasn't attached to anything,"[23] recalled Suzanne Patterson, the embassy's consul general. The U.S. Embassy knew that army personnel, "who have the means, the motives and the opportunities,"[24] committed a large share of Guatemala's serious human rights abuses, such as killings and disappearances.

Exactly four months later, however, the U.S. Embassy provided the secretary of state with a more upbeat perspective on human rights in Guatemala: "The government of Guatemala is close to meeting our list of specific benchmarks for resumption of military assistance." Ambassador Stroock noted that "the main benchmark," resolution of the notorious DeVine murder, "remains unmet." The U.S. government, however, had agreed to give the Guatemalan government a temporary "breather"[25] from public criticism about that case. More positively, the Serrano administration had met, or substantially met, the other specific U.S. benchmarks. The government had established a cabinet-level human rights commission within the executive branch to coordinate work on specific cases. There was greater access to persons detained by the security forces and President Serrano and his senior staff now regularly met with human rights activists.

In addition to the progress made on specific benchmarks, Stroock reported that the Guatemalan government "has made great strides in achieving our suggested general objectives." The director of the National Police had been replaced and the new director, a civilian rather than a military officer, had publicly pledged that his officers would respect human rights. Work was still unfinished on legislation to reform the criminal justice system. But the attorney general's Office, run by Acisclo Valladares, had "increased its budget and effectiveness."[26]

Such advances, of course, required a reward. Stroock explained: "We believe we should take a few 'small steps' to acknowledge this significant progress and to encourage more. One useful step would be to brief key U.S. Congressmen and staff informally about the progress that has been made and what we expect to happen soon. This would be done with an eye towards avoiding Congress completely eliminating our military aid carrot."[27]

Indeed, briefing Congress about this sudden "progress" in the human rights situation was a crucial part of the bilateral relationship between the United States and Guatemala. Two months before, in September 1991, President Serrano traveled to Washington to meet with U.S. President George H. W. Bush. Before their meeting, State Department officials advised President Bush to express U.S. concern "for the serious human rights abuses that still plague Guatemala." Progress on this issue, President Bush should explain, was closely linked to the economic relationship between the two countries: "Guatemala's dismal human rights record has made all forms of U.S. foreign assistance problematical. . . . Political killings have increased and while there is no concrete information to suggest the military or police are behind this, there is little evidence of a government will to correct them. *We have to fight a difficult rear-guard effort to keep Congress* from heavily conditioning most of Guatemala's economic assistance over human rights abuses this year" [emphasis added].[28]

The State Department's system of benchmarks, obviously, were central to the executive branch's "rear-guard effort" to prevent Congress from placing more severe restrictions on U.S. financial assistance to Guatemala, or, worse still, "completely eliminating our military aid carrot." The benchmarks were necessary to convince Congress that Guatemala was making real progress in human rights even as the country's human rights record remained "dismal" and, according to the U.S. Embassy, a large share of serious abuses were committed by army personnel.[29]

In addition to Congressional briefings about Guatemalan compliance with U.S. benchmarks, Ambassador Stroock suggested in November 1991 that the U.S. government provide some small "carrots" as a token of its appreciation. Previously embargoed nonlethal military aid, such as buses and prefabricated barracks, could be released to Guatemala and commercial licenses approved for the export of other goods to the armed forces. But the "stick" of reduced levels of military assistance must remain in place, and a "substantial thaw" in the military aid pipeline should not occur without a resolution of Michael DeVine's murder. The United States, Stroock advised, "should not move the goal posts."[30]

In February 1992, the State Department published its annual review for Congress on human rights practices of countries worldwide. The chapter on Guatemala's human rights situation during 1991 was highly critical of the Serrano government: "In 1991, the military, civil patrols, and the police continued to commit a majority of the major human rights abuses, including extrajudicial killings, torture, and disappearances of, among others, human rights activists, unionists, indigenous people, and street children. The motive behind many of the abuses appears to be the belief, whether factual or based on spurious information, that the victims were in some way supportive of or sympathetic to the guerrillas."[31]

When President Serrano saw the report, he blew up. He felt that the report should have cast his first year in office in a much more favorable light than it did. The Serrano administration eventually made diplomatic protests to the United States over the human rights report and threatened to find selected U.S. Embassy personnel persona non grata. Ambassador Stroock met with Serrano and told him that he was willing to discuss the report, but he strongly defended its contents.[32] Eventually Stroock agreed to issue an addendum to the report, should the Guatemalan government demonstrate that it contained serious substantive errors.[33] The report that Stroock defended described the possible fate of captured *guerrilleras* like Maritza: "Little information exists on the fate of many captured guerrillas. Information from previous years, however, leads to the conclusion that such persons often face torture and death at the hands of their military captors. There were some documented cases, however, of guerrillas who applied for and received amnesty and were well treated."[34]

Stroock continued to push the Guatemalan government to improve its human rights record, and on several occasions he courageously lent his personal support to Guatemalan activists working for justice and to victims of human rights violations. But Stroock also enjoyed close ties to the armed forces, the Guatemalan institution that the U.S. government considered responsible for many of the country's human rights abuses.

While Stroock spoke out aggressively regarding human rights reform, he also recognized the army as "the only institution that worked in Guatemala."[35] Thus, in 1992 Stroock explained how the U.S. Embassy had an antinarcotics liaison with G-2, the notorious intelligence branch of the Guatemalan army, the same section that maintained the Island and had disappeared and tortured Maritza. Stroock reassured his audience that "we're dealing with the *good guys* at G-2" [emphasis added].[36]

This attitude, so soon after the end of the cold war and after so much violence in Guatemala, did not inspire confidence within the human rights NGO community. It was very difficult for human rights NGOs, particularly Guatemalan NGOs, to place their trust in representatives of the U.S. government. James Carroll, Ambassador Stroock's public affairs officer in Guatemala, remembered how the U.S. Embassy's historical baggage affected its relationships: "You go to people—they think that the United States has supported those who hunted down, tortured and killed their friends—and you say to them: 'Trust me.'"[37]

Tom Stroock certainly wanted to be known as a human rights champion. In a long cable entitled "Guatemala: Thirty Months in the Human Rights Trenches," which he sent to Secretary of State Baker in March 1992, Ambassador Stroock discussed his embassy's contribution to improvements in Guatemala's human rights situation. "We have been essential," Stroock observed modestly, "in legitimizing human rights as a mainstream social and political concern." Stroock explained: "The U.S. Embassy in Guatemala *is widely seen as perhaps the only honest institution in the country.* Its pronouncements have tremendous credibility throughout Guatemalan society. Once we went public in a forceful way on human rights, it served as a green light for many others to do so. The thinking went something like this, 'the Gringos are not communists; they are for human rights; it must be O.K. to advocate human rights'" [emphasis added].[38]

This was nonsense. With the exception of the Guatemalan army, probably no institution in Guatemala was more despised, and more distrusted by all sides of the political spectrum in 1992, than the U.S. Embassy. A member of Ambassador Stroock's staff, a career foreign service officer and a keen observer of politics and society, later described how Guatemala "also suffers from psychological dependency on, and alienation from, the United States. Such an attitudinal complex runs throughout Guatemalan society, left and right. . . . The popular perception is that there are two great powers in Guatemala: the Guatemalan Army and the U.S. Embassy (acting as an extension of Washington)."[39]

Just eight months before Stroock sent his "Human Rights Trenches" cable, he acknowledged that one of these "two great powers," the army, had little trust in the U.S. government. Few military officers, Stroock explained to the secretary of state, accepted that the United States' recent suspension of military aid was a consequence of human rights abuses committed by members of the armed forces, in particular the unresolved murder of American citizen Michael DeVine:

> They prefer to see the suspension as part of our perceived effort to pressure the army into negotiating with the guerrillas, demilitarize the region, and turn its armies into U.S.-run anti-drug police forces—leaving the U.S. as the only military power on the block (or, some would say, in the world).
> We have already heard that in rural, conflictive parts of Quiché Department, army forces tell Indians reluctant to serve in the civil patrols "the Gringos won't save you. We don't have to listen to them anymore."[40]

By June 1992 the U.S. government was effectively buying the Guatemalan army's attention to human rights issues. The State Department negotiated a deal with the staff of the House Appropriations Committee. If the government of Guatemala agreed to permit U.S. army lawyers to conduct a weeklong human rights seminar in Guatemala, attended by military officers, government representatives, and members of human rights groups (at a cost of $30,000), the Foreign Operations Subcommittee would release another $70,000 earmarked for military training.[41] Preparations for this seminar began during the week that Maritza was disappeared.

A primary role of an ambassador is to observe the reality on the ground in the country where he is assigned and then accurately report these observations to the policy makers in Washington. For an intelligent man like Tom Stroock to paint such an unreal picture for the secretary of state—boasting of the U.S. Embassy's "tremendous credibility throughout Guatemalan society"—may indicate how badly the Wyoming oil man wanted to succeed as a diplomat as well as a human rights advocate. Stroock was in charge and in control. It was as if he could just say the right words and pull the right strings and Guatemalan society would respond accordingly. It was a very "American" attitude, brimming with "American exceptionalism." Can do. "A great deal of work needs to be done," Stroock noted: "But with a judicious combination of private and public diplomacy we are poised to help Guatemala and its well-meaning current government achieve much more in the area of respect for fundamental rights. The role played by the U.S. government in achieving progress in the human rights area in Guatemala is something in which all involved can feel a justifiable sense of pride."[42]

On Saturday night I was trying to rest at home. I realized that I had forgotten to discuss a matter with one of the ODHA's staff, so I called the archbishopric's antiquated telephone switchboard. For some reason the switchboard routed the call to the telephone in Maritza's room. I was astonished when she answered the phone—apparently Maritza had been sitting on the steps outside the room, above the large outdoor patio area—"How are you?" I asked.

"Fine. Have you seen the moon tonight?"

"Pardon?"

"Have you seen the moon?"

"Uh, no. I haven't seen it."

"Oh, you should go look at it. It's beautiful."

"All right. I'll look at it. Have a good night."

"Ciao."

I stared at my telephone for a few moments, and then I went out on the balcony. There was a bright yellow moon rising above Guatemala City.

ELEVEN

SUNDAY

August 2, 1992

I stopped at a newsstand on Sunday morning to glance at the morning papers. An enormous headline blared from the front page of *El Grafico:* "URNG: Maritza Urrutia Is an Active Militant." This was not what I wanted to see. I ran to the archbishopric.

Edmundo René lay in his bed in the back room with Kappy dozing by his side. Maritza's brother was partially sitting up, fully clothed, with a baseball cap on his head. *El Grafico* lay on the blanket in front of him. The article described a communiqué that the URNG's high command issued on July 31. Maritza was a member of one its organizations, they said, and the G-2, army intelligence, had kidnapped her.[1] Calling Maritza's case an "example of criminal cynicism," the URNG described Maritza's video declaration as "a maneuver of psychological warfare. These and other acts," it continued, were intended to "create a climate of mistrust and uncertainty" in order to justify the government's positions during the ongoing peace negotiations.[2] It's difficult to describe the expression on Edmundo René's face that Sunday morning. "I felt absolutely *used,*" he recalled later. "Because they [the URNG] did it to hurt the government politically." Maritza's family had a different interest: her well-being. "Our agenda was to save her life at whatever cost," explained Edmundo René. "We didn't care about the EGP. I didn't care if my actions affected the URNG. I just wanted to save her life. I didn't even care about human rights."[3]

The URNG made a strategic political-military response to Maritza's case rather than a humanitarian one. But the URNG was fighting a war, and Maritza was still part of that war, and she was still part of the URNG. Maritza had been part of the conflict for twelve years. Her brother, on the other hand, wanted Maritza out of the armed conflict and saw the crisis as an opportunity to get her out.[4]

On Sunday morning, Edmundo René was so furious that he could barely speak. Maritza was subdued. No, she told me, it wasn't true. She was not a member of the URNG. But whether true or false, the URNG's public statements would complicate Maritza's request for a U.S. visa.

Trying to provide damage control, I went to my office and called Jones at his home. He had already seen the newspapers, and *yes*, this news *was* going to complicate matters. The U.S. Embassy personnel would have to discuss the new development with the State Department in Washington. But she says it's not true, I protested. This was just URNG politics. "I don't know, Dan," replied Jones. "They say that her husband's a big-time G [i.e., *guerrillero*]." Jones promised to contact me as soon as they received a decision from the State Department.

After I hung up with Jones, I called Bill Robinson in Albuquerque. We discussed the problem and I sheepishly asked Robinson to request that the human rights NGOs restart the political pressure on the State Department. Robinson agreed.

While I was inside the archbishopric, Maritza's father arrived to visit his daughter. Shortly thereafter the doorbell rang, and the building's custodian, looking out through a small porthole in one of the massive wooden doors, found two men, dressed in civilian clothes, standing in front of the main entrance. The men did not identify themselves, but they said they had followed Edmundo Urrutia from his home to the archbishopric. They wanted to speak with him. The custodian shut the porthole and informed Edmundo and me of the "visitors." I unlocked a back door for Maritza's father, and he climbed over a fence and slipped away into the street behind the archbishopric.

The staff of the ODHA were not the only persons concerned about the URNG's communiqué that Sunday morning. The ten members of Guatemala's Peace Commission (COPAZ), a group of military officers and civilians charged by President Serrano with conducting the peace negotiations with the insurgency, had traveled to Mexico City that weekend to prepare for the session beginning on Monday, August 3. The two sides had been discussing the difficult topic of human rights for over a year, with very little progress, and the atmosphere of these talks would be quite tense. The negative publicity over Maritza's case would not make matters easier for the government's delegation, whose leader was a bright, ambitious young lawyer named Manuel Conde.

During the late 1950s, Manuel Conde's father, Oscar Conde, the anti-Communist radio journalist, and Manuel's maternal grandfather, Manuel Orellana, served in Guatemala's Congress. Oscar Conde continued his hard-hitting radio programs, while both he and Manuel Orellana maintained their anti-Communist activities. In late 1959 Conde ran for re-election outside his usual district against an army captain named Jorge Ponce. The popular radio-journalist won the election and late one night in January 1960, outside a Guatemala City restaurant an embittered Ponce shot Conde three times in the back, killing him instantly.[5] For several years, Conde's son Manuel, then just three, was told that his father had gone away on a trip.

In 1963, when Manuel Orellana served as the president of the Guatemalan Congress, Colonel Enrique Peralta Azurdia overthrew the civilian Ydigoras regime. The armed forces revoked the constitution, banned political parties, and shut down the Congress.[6] Former civilian political leaders like Orellana were a threat to the new military regime, and shortly after the coup the police entered Orellana's home, searched the house, and dragged him away. After two years of difficult exile in El Salvador, Orellana returned to his homeland in 1964.[7]

His political career now over, Orellana sold his house in Guatemala City and purchased a farm in the eastern province of Zacapa, the area where he first achieved success as a cigar manufacturer decades before. There was just one problem. By the mid 1960s the Fuerzas Armadas Rebeldes (FAR), a group of former army officers, had begun operations in Zacapa. FAR members killed a number of landowners in the area, and many other *finqueros* fled into exile or to the relative safety of Guatemala City. Some farmers who stayed paid a monthly quota to the insurgents as protection money, which meant they also financed the revolutionary movement. Sonia Orellana was worried about her father's safety and wanted to set up a similar arrangement for him.

"Look, Daddy," Sonia pleaded with Orellana, "I have the opportunity to speak with the guerrillas. And I'm going to ask them how much we can give them financially."

"No, daughter," replied her stubborn father. "I won't give them *water!* Not even *water!*"

"Well then, Daddy, why don't you leave Guatemala for a while? Leave me here to manage the farm."

"I'm not going! Because this is my heritage! And I have to take care of it for my children. They'll only take me out of here feet first!"[8] And so they did.

On the evening of August 13, 1966, Orellana, his wife, María, their daughter Alma América, an infant granddaughter, and a maid drove out of their farm in the direction of the town of Zacapa when they found the road blocked by a number of large stones. A group of men pulled Orellana out of the car and gagged him. Alma América, an epileptic, tried to intervene to help her father but the men clubbed her senseless with a gun butt. Then they dragged Orellana to a tree and shot him.[9] Two days later a photograph appeared on the front-page of *Impacto*, one of Guatemala City's newspapers. There was young Manuel Conde, at nine years old now the oldest man of the family, in a dark suit and tie, consoling his mother, Sonia, at his grandfather's funeral.

When he completed his law studies in the late 1970s, Conde worked as a court official and then practiced law in Guatemala City. In 1985 Guatemala held elections to determine the first civilian president in decades, and one of the candidates was a conservative Protestant engineer named Jorge Serrano, son of the interior minister who, after the fall of Árbenz in 1954, threatened to banish Maritza's grandparents to the jungles of El Petén. Serrano lost his first bid for the presidency, but he received a lot of support from middle-class women in the capital, thanks to the organizational skill of Sonia Orellana de Conde, Manuel Conde's mother.

In 1990 Serrano prepared to run for president again, and he asked Manuel Conde to work on his campaign. "Mamá, I had coffee with Jorge Serrano today," he explained to his mother. "And I like his vision for the country. I want to work on his election campaign, but first, I want your support."

Having already lost her husband as well as her father, Sonia Orellana was no novice to the cruelties of politics and she had some pointed advice for Conde. "If that's what you want to do, my son, it's fine. But be prepared for your friends to stab you in the back!"[10]

Manuel Conde became Jorge Serrano's campaign manager and did a superb job. This time Serrano's bid for the presidency was successful and after his inauguration, he rewarded Conde with the coveted job of presidential chief of staff.

More than anything else during his presidency, Jorge Serrano wanted to end the war between his government and the URNG.[11] Since 1987, Serrano had participated in unofficial talks with members of the insurgency, trying to find common ground for dialogue. Serrano had a huge ego, but he also had guts. Even before taking office, in January 1991, Serrano announced that his government would begin direct peace negotiations with the guerrillas.[12] This was a bold step since Serrano's predecessor, Vinicio Cerezo, suffered two coup attempts and nearly lost his presidency after sending some army officers to speak with URNG representatives in Madrid.[13] Serrano knew that he faced opposition from within his own armed forces, but he was determined to move the peace process forward.

Four years earlier, in August 1987, the five presidents of the Central American Republics met in Guatemala City and signed an agreement known as the Central American Peace Accords or Esquipulas II.[14] Esquipulas II was a broad blueprint for bringing peace to the war-torn Central American nations. The agreement effectively ended the Contra war in Nicaragua and established a structure for negotiated settlements in Guatemala and El Salvador.[15] The accord's requirement for the initiation of peace negotiations, however, was very specific. Governments facing internal conflicts could initiate dialogue only with those opposition groups who had already laid down their arms or had accepted an amnesty.

In 1991, when Jorge Serrano took office as president of Guatemala, the position of the army high command was clear: there could be no negotiation between the government and the guerrillas without compliance by the URNG with Esquipulas II.[16] Not surprisingly, the URNG had no intention of disarming, or of accepting amnesty for its members.

So in a courageous move, Jorge Serrano decided to ignore the preconditions of Esquipulas II and start direct negotiations with the insurgency. This was the *trago duro*, the moment of truth, the time to sit down and make agreements. One of Serrano's closest advisers, Amílcar Burgos, warned the president that the army would oppose direct negotiation with the URNG.[17] Many officers could not accept treating the insurgents as equals, particularly when the rebels were now so weak militarily.

"I've already made a decision," replied President Serrano.[18] He felt strongly that the time had come for the government and the insurgents to sit down together and make that *trago duro*.[19]

And so one morning in early 1991 Serrano, Burgos, and the defense minister, an army general, met in Serrano's office. The president told the minister that he wanted a list of army officers who could participate in a governmental commission that would negotiate with the guerrillas. "Mr. President," objected the defense minister, "I want to tell you, with much respect, that we shouldn't put ourselves in a position where they can trick us. And I think your decision is wrong."[20]

"I didn't ask for your *opinion*," snapped Serrano. "I asked you for a *list* by three o'clock this afternoon!"[21]

The general's face turned red, and President Serrano was livid. After the general left the room, Serrano began to worry whether his decision would provoke unrest within the ranks of the armed forces. He was going against the grain of the army's hard-line sector. But Serrano bet on the support of other officers who advised him that it was pointless to continue a war that was draining the country.[22] The insurgents were no longer a military threat, but the army could not destroy them completely. This group of more progressive officers agreed that negotiations were the best route for ending the war.[23] And at 3:00 P.M., the president had his list of officers.[24]

But the road to peace would not be easy, as both sides struggled with internal doubts and dissention. "We joined the Peace Commission because those were the orders of the president," recalled Julio Balconi Turcios, who as an army colonel became part of Jorge Serrano's negotiating team. "But if he had asked us, we would have said 'no.' No one thought that the talks would lead to anything positive."[25]

No one except the president and his advisers. They assumed, wrongly, that the peace negotiations would move along rapidly. Serrano was prepared, he announced optimistically in March 1991, to sign a final peace accord as soon as possible.[26] In April 1991 the Serrano administration and the high command of the URNG initiated direct peace negotiations. President Serrano appointed the young lawyer Manuel Conde to be the leader of the government's Peace Commission, composed of five army officers and five civilians, charged with representing the Guatemalan government at the talks. Msgr. Rodolfo Quezada, the respected Catholic bishop of Zacapa, would serve as conciliator of the discussions. "If you have to speak with the devil to achieve peace," Serrano instructed Conde, "speak with the devil!"[27]

One of the biggest "devils" impeding progress in the peace negotiations was the natural mistrust between the two enemies. The army officers knew the URNG and they understood that the talks were part of a broader insurgent strategy to gain political concessions from the government. The military assumed that the insurgents were negotiating only to gain time and wait for better conditions for a final settlement to the conflict. Concurrently, many in the URNG believed that the Guatemalan government lacked any serious desire to negotiate a just peace. Indeed, as Susanne Jonas explains, many of the Guatemalan government and international actors involved at the start of the formal peace process "thought of negotiations as a way to pressure the guerrillas politically into laying down their arms rather than addressing the root causes of the war."[28]

Internal divisions on both sides only made the process more complicated. Three of the five military officers assigned to COPAZ were General Mario René Enriquez and Colonels (later Generals) Julio Balconi and Marco Antonio Taracena, all hardened combat veterans of the toughest years of Guatemala's armed conflict and the army's counterinsurgency campaigns. These officers were *instituciónalistas,* adherents to a political-military strategy, the thesis of national stability, developed by former defense minister Héctor Gramajo. Gramajo's doctrine accepted the importance of democratic institutions in Guatemala, but it also sanctioned "necessary" violations of human rights in order to control "opponents" and maintain state security.[29] Somewhat ironically, Enriquez, Balconi, and like-minded colleagues were labeled "the doves," denoting the army faction that supported the peace talks with the guerrillas as an appropriate means to finally ending the war.

But in 1992 the doves had to watch their backs owing to opposition from "the falcons," the most hard-line members of the officer corps, who opposed any kind of negotiated peace with the insurgency. The falcons were veterans of the vicious and successful counterinsurgency campaign against the urban cells of the URNG during the late 1970s and early 1980s.[30] The falcons argued that the army had beaten the URNG militarily. Why should the rebels now receive political concessions from the Guatemalan government in the interests of some internationally sponsored "peace"? The army would lose in the political and international arenas what it had won on the battlefield.[31] Indeed, two of the military officers "representing" the government in 1991 were aligned with this hard-line sector of the army and opposed a negotiated settlement to the war.[32]

The URNG commanders also wanted to move very slowly during the talks because they needed time to convince their own hard-line elements of the validity of a negotiated peace.[33] Many midlevel insurgent leaders had been fighting in Guatemala's mountains and jungles for years. The armed struggle was their life and they resisted the idea of accepting anything short of their revolutionary goals.[34] It would not be easy for the aging URNG commanders in Mexico City to convince these combatants to eventually lay down their arms.[35]

No one expected the talks to provide solutions to Guatemala's problems. But the proponents of the negotiations hoped that the process would create conditions by which Guatemalans could solve their problems without killing one another.[36] Over time the negotiations paved the way for discussions about the future democratization of Guatemala, including issues that were literally explosive such as human rights, fiscal reform, the armed force's role in a postconflict society, and the rights of Guatemala's majority Mayan population.[37]

The two sides met regularly, usually in Mexico City or Cuernavaca, but progress was extremely slow, especially on the contentious topic of human rights. Adding further stress to the work of COPAZ was Jorge Serrano's overbearing, controlling style, as well as his obsession with a rapidly negotiated peace.[38] The president would always maintain a direct telephone line to his negotiating team, often clearing his calendar for several days and locking himself in his office close by the phone.[39]

At frequent breaks during the negotiations, Manuel Conde would call President Serrano in Guatemala City for instructions and, thus, had little room to act independently.[40] To be fair, the president *was* "totally committed to the peace process."[41] Nevertheless, the process was complicated and Serrano "wanted to maintain *total control* of the talks from Guatemala," remembered General Julio Balconi.[42] Sometimes the two sides would be close to agreement on a particular issue, then Jorge Serrano would call and tell his team to change their position: "No. No. It's not like that. Get back to the table!"[43] "This created obstacles for advancement in the negotiations, because we couldn't make any decisions [in Mexico] if we hadn't convinced the president that it was correct."[44]

Frequently the commission members would fax drafts of positions and agreements to President Serrano, only to have the drafts returned with many alterations. When Serrano's "improvements" were incorrect or liable to cause problems in the negotiations, the government representatives would have to call Serrano and implore him to change his mind.

At one point during the process, President Serrano made a decision that nearly brought the talks to a standstill. His COPAZ delegates believed that *their* position was correct and would encourage the URNG to take a more flexible approach to other issues. So first Manuel Conde called the president to ask him to change his mind:

"Jorge . . . "

"NO! You guys have to do what I say!"

A bit later, Amílcar Burgos called Serrano, and received the same response: "No!"

José Luis Asencio gave it a try: "No!"

Finally, General Mario Enriquez, who was a friend of Serrano, called the president and convinced Serrano to accede to the wishes of his negotiating team. But an entire day of valuable negotiating time had been lost. It was impossible for the government representatives to hide their problems with President Serrano from their URNG counterparts. Naturally, this dynamic "enormously effected the advance of the negotiations" and complicated the atmosphere of the talks.[45] On at least one occasion Manuel Conde, determined to push the peace process forward and risking his career and his relationship with the president, insisted that the members of COPAZ sign an important preagreement concerning human rights without consulting Serrano. Conde reasoned, correctly, that once Serrano understood the importance of the step forward in the talks, the president would swallow his ego and accept the decision of his subordinates.[46]

Not surprisingly, the United States government wanted to play a role in the peace process but, not surprisingly, President Serrano and the members of COPAZ resisted this idea. They felt that the U.S. government should not play a direct role in the peace talks because the North Americans were likely to promote their own geopolitical interests in the region, rather than the needs of Guatemala. Plus, the nationalistic Jorge Serrano and his colleagues opposed the idea of internationalizing the peace process, with or without the presence of the United States. Sensitive to imperialism from both the left and the right, as well as to competing pressures from many different sectors of Guatemalan society, they wanted the negotiations to occur between Guatemalan and Guatemalan in order to construct a Guatemalan peace, "not a United Nations peace, nor an international peace, nor a United States peace."[47] Of course, this strategy would isolate the URNG, which depended on international political support, and would thereby weaken the insurgents' bargaining position.

But even without a formal role in the early negotiations, United States influence nurtured the peace process. Early on, before formal "face-to-face" negotiations began, Ambassador Stroock helped convince leaders of Guatemala's business sector and political parties to participate in dialogues with members of the URNG, an effort that earned the appreciation of the usually prickly Serrano.[48] The State Department also set up an "underground conduit" for peace negotiations by facilitating talks between U.S. Representative Robert Torricelli, his aide Richard Nuccio, Guatemalan politicians and military leaders, and the URNG representative Dr. Luis Becker.

During Congress's Easter recess in 1992, Torricelli and Nuccio traveled to Guatemala to meet with President Serrano, and the president asked Torricelli to carry a message to the URNG: "I'm prepared to do what I need to do to reach an agreement with the guerrillas. But I need to know that if I take these risks, . . . they'll sign."[49]

Congressman Torricelli was an effective interlocutor and Richard Nuccio dedicated several years of his life to the Guatemalan peace process. "Nuccio killed himself trying to pull this thing off."[50] But the URNG delayed making its positions clear. The insurgents knew that once all their cards were on the table, they would have to sign an agreement, regardless of whether the conditions in Guatemala favored their interests.[51]

In October 1991, nine months before Maritza was disappeared, Manuel Conde and other members of COPAZ implored the State Department to ease up on its criticism of human rights abuses in Guatemala. Such comments, argued the Guatemalans, strengthened the hands of the insurgents in the ongoing peace talks. Conde explained to State Department officials that on more than one occasion when the two sides were discussing the complex issue of human rights: "The URNG would start by saying 'Even the United States has said . . . ' or 'Not even the United States believes that . . . '"[52]

These arguments drove the members of COPAZ crazy. The government representatives felt that the rebels ignored the Serrano administration's good faith attempts to improve the human rights situation in Guatemala. "You guys are fucking us! You're fucking us!" Conde and his colleagues would exclaim, "because you know what we're doing, but you never recognize what we're trying to do!"

"No," the insurgents would reply innocently. "We're just maintaining a political position."[53]

Commenting on the request from the members of COPAZ, Phillip Taylor, then the U.S. Embassy's deputy chief of mission in Guatemala, observed that "we have already agreed that both in private and public, the United States government would accentuate the positive efforts made by the government of Guatemala." Thus, even without a seat at the bargaining table, the United States could influence the course of the talks. But Taylor also urged the Guatemalans to make more progress toward resolving certain high profile cases of human right violations.

"We sympathize with the government of Guatemala team," Taylor noted:

They are nice guys. They are pro-American, and they have a very difficult
task negotiating an end to a bloody 30-year conflict. They are up against
some tough opponents. On the one hand they are trying to deal with the
guerrillas who are no friends of ours (the Guatemalan guerrillas are, after
all, the murderers of U.S. Ambassador John Gordon Mein). On the other,
they have to contend with a military establishment whose continued
unwillingness to permit its own people to be held accountable for their
actions undermines [President] Serrano's own sincere desire to change
the human rights situation in Guatemala for the better.[54]

Both parties to the peace talks tacitly agreed to a rule that forbade
discussion of particular cases of human rights abuse at the negotiating
table.[55] This prevented the process from breaking down into recrimina-
tion sessions concerning specific cases and permitted the two sides to focus on their negotiating agenda.[56] Specific problems or particular incidents resulting from the armed conflict were usually discussed away from
the table, in small groups over drinks or coffee.

Nevertheless, after Maritza disappeared and the international pressure concerning her case began to flood Guatemala, Manuel Conde grew
worried. Other human rights violations in Guatemala had received a great
deal of domestic and international publicity over the years, but all were
abuses that occurred during *earlier* regimes. This dynamic permitted President Serrano to disclaim responsibility for past crimes. But Maritza's
disappearance was the first highly publicized grave violation of human
rights and international humanitarian law (also known as "the laws and
customs of war") to occur on Jorge Serrano's watch. So it had the potential to cause serious damage to the government's reputation abroad.
The case had to be investigated and resolved quickly and internally in
order to head off this threat to President Serrano's prestige.[57]

Conde was at home on Wednesday evening, July 29, when Maritza's
video aired on the news, and the army's poor attempt at propaganda
only made him more pessimistic. It was obvious to Conde that Maritza's
speech was coerced, that she was overly made-up and nervous. In spite
of her statements, she was being held against her will. But Conde had a
new round of peace talks starting in five days, and the subject of human
rights remained on the agenda. So Conde knew that Maritza's video
would only upset the URNG's high command.[58]

Amílcar Burgos, another COPAZ member, worried that highly publicized cases like Maritza's disappearance would damage the negotiating environment.[59] Often the international community would pressure
President Serrano to resolve such cases, and Serrano in turn would vent

these demands on the Peace Commission members: "You guys have to figure out what happened and how we're gonna resolve this!"[60] Maritza's case would probably put more stress on the government negotiators, both from the URNG's commanders and from Jorge Serrano, who was so sensitive about his international reputation. The concerns of Conde and Burgos were prescient that weekend as they headed for Mexico City. That month the peace talks nearly collapsed entirely over the contentious issue of human rights.[61]

TWELVE

MONDAY

August 3, 1992

On Monday morning I found Maritza, dressed in her nightgown, sweeping the flagstones outside the back room. She looked upset and preoccupied, so I asked her what was the matter.

"Daniel, Edmundo René thinks that it's all my fault!"

"What do you mean?" Maritza was crying now, and I saw that her eyes were red and swollen.

"Edmundo René said that if I hadn't married Esteban this wouldn't have happened. That we wouldn't be in this mess and our lives torn apart."

Now she was sobbing. "But he doesn't understand that I was a victim too. I had a baby with Esteban because he loved me! He loved me! I couldn't make any other choice. I couldn't choose another man. My husband loved me! But Edmundo René thinks that it's all my fault!"

Tears fell down Maritza's cheeks as she sobbed and rested her head on my shoulder. "It's OK, Maritza. Edmundo was just tired. You *know* that this isn't your fault. You can't blame yourself for this. That's not fair."

Maritza cried silently. "I want to leave this place," she said. "I want to get out of here."

"Maritza, you have to endure. I know that you're strong. You have to endure a few days more."

"Ay." Maritza sighed and her entire body seemed to tremble. "I feel like I'm still in the hole."

At the Island the fair-skinned Don Chando was also upset that morning. Due to the pressures of Maritza's case, his superiors had decided to transfer the captain to another post. Coroncho noticed that Don Chando appeared distressed, so he asked his commander what was wrong.

"I'm not going to be here anymore. There are a lot of problems here!" Don Chando's world, once so large in Maritza's eyes, was shrinking. He began wearing a long-haired wig and dark glasses. Concerned that international human rights organizations might come to search the premises, the soldiers at the Island worked day and night to transform the facility. They changed the floors and turned Maritza's bathroom into another sleeping quarters. Old walls were knocked down and new ones were put up and painted different colors. Finally the Island that Maritza knew was unrecognizable.[1]

In Mexico City the new round of peace talks began that morning between COPAZ and URNG's high command. In spite of the efforts of Msgr. Rodolfo Quezada as conciliator and Dr. Frances Vendrell, a United Nations observer, the atmosphere was very tense. On the table was the gnarly subject of human rights, and specifically the status of the government's "civilian self-defense patrols," more commonly known as "civil patrols." The Guatemalan army organized these paramilitary groups, primarily in Mayan communities, and used them to carry out the army's counterinsurgency policies at the village level. The URNG wanted the civil patrols disbanded. The army, of course, wanted them to stay.

During a break from the negotiations, several representatives of the URNG approached Bishop Quezada and Dr. Vendrell to protest about Maritza's case: "Look, señores! What lack of political will! With these farces, we're not going to move an inch!"[2] Could Msgr. Quezada do anything to protect Maritza?

Trying to perform damage control and maintain the rapport between the two sides, Manuel Conde and other members of COPAZ promised that the government would do everything possible to discern what really happened to Maritza and to protect her life.[3] The insurgents acknowledged that Maritza was one of them, but they stressed that she had participated only in *political* activities. Maritza was never a *combatant*, so she posed no threat to the state.

"We've come to *negotiate*, to move the peace process forward," Msgr. Quezada reminded the *comandantes*. "We can't convert the negotiating table into an office for complaints."[4] So the matter of Maritza's disappearance and torture was pushed aside, away from the formal points for discussion. The two belligerents were negotiating over the topic of human rights, but the insurgents never considered using Maritza's disappearance and torture as an excuse to suspend the talks altogether.[5] Walking away from the peace talks would weaken the URNG's credibility in the eyes of the international community. The insurgents could not afford to lose ground on the battlefield of international politics.

At the negotiating table, as the haggling over the civil patrols continued, the conciliator grew increasingly worried. Msgr. Quezada wanted the process to advance quickly, but the discussions dragged on. The URNG insisted that the civil patrols were a form of forced labor as well as an instrument of repression. Therefore, they should be banned. The government's representatives argued that the army was incapable of addressing security needs throughout the country, so the civil patrols were necessary for the protection of rural communities.

The two groups struggled for an understanding that would be acceptable to both sides, but nothing satisfied the URNG delegates.[6] Aware that the talks were at a difficult impasse, Msgr. Quezada began to present different formulas to the parties, ideas not too far from the positions they had espoused; he was struggling to find some common ground.[7]

At the archbishopric that morning, there was no word from the U.S. Embassy. Maritza's head was spinning from all of her conflicting pressures. Don't say anything about what happened, insisted her family. Forget about the revolution. You're going to the States. And poor Edmundo René, Maritza's brother, had to leave Guatemala as well, *because of her.* But Maritza did not want to go to the U.S.A., and she didn't want to leave the revolution. It was her life. Maritza had spent a week in captivity lying about who she was, and now under the Church's protection, she went on lying about her participation in the URNG as if she were still a captive. Cooperate with us. We know that you're Ruth. I don't care if you see me. . . . No! Don't say anything!

Unaware of most of these conflicts and trying earnestly to do the right thing, I sat down with Maritza that morning and began to review other immigration options in case the United States refused to assist her. Canada might be another possibility. . . . And we have a good relationship with the Canadian Embassy; the Canadians will insist you remain there for at least a year. . . . Finally, Maritza thought that she was going to break down. She needed to speak with someone who would understand her, not just personally, but politically as well.[8] I was not the best choice. So Maritza asked for Ronalth Ochaeta to come speak with her.

Ochaeta was worried too as he walked through the archbishopric toward the back room. All morning different reporters and television crews had come to the ODHA, trying to verify rumors that Maritza was somewhere in the building. Eventually, after consulting with Archbishop Penados, Ochaeta decided to spread some disinformation in order to protect Maritza. "Yes," he began to tell the press. "We have her under the archbishop's protection. But [she's] not here."[9] Ochaeta explained that he could not disclose Maritza's true whereabouts.

"Look, Ronalth," Maritza began when Ochaeta reached the back room: "I haven't told you everything. There's something behind all of this. I need to speak with my people."[10]

Ochaeta suggested the possibility of arranging a meeting in Guatemala, but Maritza knew that her *compañeros* would have changed locations, so it would be impossible to contact them. She wanted to go to Mexico immediately, but Ochaeta pointed out that after so much publicity, the Mexican Embassy would probably not grant Maritza a tourist visa. And the political asylum process at the Mexican Embassy could take months.

Another option would be to send Maritza to Costa Rica first, and then try to fly to Mexico. But that left the same delay of several months before the Mexicans, with luck, granted Maritza a visa. Canada would be even further from Mexico.

But if Maritza could reach the United States, then she could travel to Mexico without any special visa.[11] Migration away from the United States was easier than migration toward it. And Edmundo René, Kappy, and the human rights NGOs in the United States were all pushing the importance of sending Maritza to the States. Several NGO representatives insisted that Maritza needed the specialized medical and psychiatric care that would be available to her there.[12]

But Maritza knew she needed a different kind of therapy. She needed to see her *compañeros* in Mexico and assure herself that no one had died as a consequence of her disappearance and interrogation. So Maritza and Ochaeta agreed that a visa to the United States was her best option, although Maritza had no intention of remaining in the U.S.[13]

Ochaeta had two priorities at that moment. First, he wanted to send Maritza out of Guatemala as soon as possible in order to improve her security. Once outside Guatemala, Maritza would be safer than she was inside the archbishopric. If she left the sanctuary, the army would probably detain her again because Maritza had begun to violate the conditions of her liberation. They might force her to give yet another press conference, denying once again that she was kidnapped, or slandering the Church representatives who tried to protect her.

Second, Ochaeta wanted to protect his colleagues in the ODHA. The entrances to the archbishopric were now under surveillance. The ODHA was in the "eye of the hurricane," and Ochaeta wanted to relieve the pressure on the Catholic Church.[14]

After interviewing Maritza the previous Friday, both Sue Patterson and Jones believed that Maritza was sincere about her reasons for wanting to go to the United States. But there were still nagging doubts about what had really happened to her. Maritza's televised video and press conference sharply contradicted her private testimony to the U.S. Embassy officials.

Nevertheless, for Patterson, the consul general and a veteran refugee coordinator, Maritza had said all the right things: she only wanted to go to the United States temporarily so that she and her son could recover. Then Maritza and Sebastián would leave. Maritza's statements enabled Patterson to consider issuing a tourist visa to Maritza, as opposed to refugee status. An application for refugee status is a much more cumbersome process and would have required the approval of the U.S. Immigration and Naturalization Service.

Patterson was worried about the pitfalls of winning INS approval for a refugee visa for Maritza. The INS, unlike the State Department, is a law enforcement agency, and its members might have given much more credence to Maritza's televised video statement and her comments during the press conference. Moreover, there were no INS representatives in Guatemala at the time, and INS personnel would have to fly in from Mexico. Patterson worried that the INS's lack of knowledge about Guatemala, coupled with Maritza's conflicting statements, would lead the INS to oppose refugee status for Maritza.[15]

Patterson had devoted most of her career to assisting persons caught up in armed conflicts, often in more difficult environments than Guatemala. She knew how to work the system to help people when they needed help and Patterson sensed that a simple tourist visa would be best for Maritza. The process would be much less bureaucratic because the embassy could issue the visa immediately. And the embassy could issue this visa in good conscience because of Maritza's plan to leave the United States instead of settling there permanently. So a tourist visa seemed to be the best option.[16]

"But it wasn't just a humanitarian decision," Patterson recalled years later. "It was a *political* decision because [President] Serrano called in the ambassador immediately."[17]

After my phone call to Bill Robinson on Sunday, the human rights NGOs once again targeted the U.S. State Department with repeated entreaties on Maritza's behalf. Before Maritza's reappearance, the NGOs had asked seven congressional offices to pressure President Serrano for Maritza's release. Now the NGOs asked the same politicians to call the State Department headquarters in Washington and the U.S. Embassy in Guatemala to lobby for the issuance of a visa to Maritza.[18]

But the congressional representatives raised new concerns. Maritza's story was confusing; there had been weird, surreal theatrics. If she was kidnapped, why didn't the army kill her? People didn't know what to believe. Maritza's video, of course, only added to the confusion. Maritza said on television that she was not kidnapped. State Department officials questioned Frank LaRue about Maritza's televised statements: "Do you believe the video is true?"[19] And the ODHA, although highly respected, was hesitant about divulging the facts.

Staff members of Amnesty International never doubted that Maritza had been kidnapped. "People wouldn't subject their family to this," reasoned Carlos Salinas. But Amnesty had to clarify this point in order to protect its own credibility. From Amnesty's perspective, it is better to be absolutely sure of the facts than to provide a weak link in a chain of information and political action. Any self-interested (and repressive) government would quickly disprove the inaccuracy and use it to damage the prisoner's interests, as well as Amnesty's reputation.[20] Members of Congress would not call the U.S. Embassy in Guatemala based on a *hunch*. And Salinas could not ask them to do so based on a hunch.[21]

Plus, there remained the touchy issue of whether Maritza was a *guerrillera*. The Berlin wall had fallen three years earlier, but the cold war was far from over on Capitol Hill. It was unusual to ask the United States Congress for assistance for a member of an insurgent organization, for a *leftist guerrillera*. There was implicit resistance: someone like Maritza "was not a *clean* victim."[22] After all, this is war.

The tenets of international humanitarian law oblige armed forces around the world to respect the fundamental rights of captured prisoners of war. Many U.S. politicians, however, did not understand these legal principles. So when U.S. government representatives learned that the subject of a human rights campaign was a member of an armed opposition group, they frequently declined to assist.[23] If the detained person was a civilian, recalled Mark Kirk, then working at the State Department's inter-American bureau, "we would kill ourselves, move heaven and earth" to save the prisoner's life. But if the victim was part of an insurgent group, the ability to protect them declined precipitously: "If they were an armed combatant, it was . . . we would definitely make the effort . . . but we felt that people who took up arms against the government of Guatemala were taking a big risk. But if we could pull it off, we'd make an effort to work on that person's behalf. . . . The attitude was 'Do what you can.'"[24]

Nor were the human rights NGOs united in their approach to this problem. When Maritza publicly accepted amnesty and confessed to being a *guerrillera,* some members of the NGO community refused to believe it. After all, "she'll say *anything* to get out of captivity."[25] Perhaps NGOs should use that response to queries from their congressional contacts. Bonnie Tenneriello at WOLA tried to use her persuasive skills and a different approach to gain continued support for Maritza on Capitol Hill. Tenneriello argued that even if Maritza *was* a *guerrillera,* the Geneva conventions, customary international law, and the Guatemalan Constitution clothed Maritza with rights that deserved protection, as well as the attention of the U.S. government.[26]

Given these murky facts and unusual politics, the human rights NGOs needed to establish that Maritza indeed had been kidnapped to make a compelling case to members of Congress that she was in danger and merited a U.S. visa. The NGOs argued that as long as Maritza acknowledged that she was kidnapped, then she was legally entitled to political asylum in the United States.[27] Their credibility was on the line. "We were pulling out 'our big guns,'" recalled Tenneriello, "our friends in the Senate. And we were asking them to put *their* credibility on the line."[28]

Anne Manuel from Americas Watch felt that the ODHA's original urgent action message contained enough facts to demonstrate that Maritza was kidnapped, but some of her peers disagreed.[29] Maritza's case "was a continuous shifting reality" for Amnesty International's Carlos Salinas. "We were never quite sure what had actually happened."[30] And they wanted more information. In my rigid concern for security, I failed to consider the political environment of the human rights NGOs. So I continued my cryptic form of communication. All of the human rights organizations were trying to help Maritza, but the ODHA was now out of sync with the group.

Maritza's father was at home on Monday when the telephone rang. It was Maritza's distant cousin, the army colonel. The colonel wanted Edmundo and his wife to come speak with him and with his superior officer. The colonel also asked Edmundo if he intended to send a letter to the press thanking the many institutions that had assisted Maritza. Edmundo would have none of it. "Look," he told his cousin, "stop screwing around! We share the same blood!"[31]

Eventually, Maritza's brother Edmundo René went to see this cousin at the Cuartel General, a large barracks in Guatemala City. When Edmundo René arrived, the colonel told him that the defense minister wanted to speak with Edmundo René. Edmundo René declined, reasoning that it would be much more difficult for him to say "no" to the minister than to his lower-ranking cousin.[32]

The colonel explained that the army wanted Maritza to live in an apartment in the Cuartel General. The army would protect Maritza and take care of her and guarantee her well-being. The armed forces did not want her to leave the country. Edmund René thought the idea was absurd and imagined his sister trapped and destroyed under the army's control. Maritza would never be free if she stayed in Guatemala. Edmundo René told his cousin he would try to stop Maritza from leaving, but that he couldn't make any guarantees. *That depends on her.* If Maritza left, her brother promised to try to convince her not to make any statements abroad. Maritza had a good laugh when Edmundo René subsequently told his *hermanita* about the army's "benevolent" offer of "shelter."[33]

The army also wanted more cooperation from Edmundo René. The colonel told Edmundo René that he should write a letter to the defense minister expressing his gratitude for the army's assistance in Maritza's case. When he relayed this "request" to his sister, Maritza told him that the decision to write the letter was his to make, but that this would be just one of many "favors" that the army would request.[34] Edmundo René never wrote the letter. Now he too had disobeyed the army.

At midafternoon Archbishop Penados stood by the archbishopric's switchboard, dressed in his black bishop's robe. Msgr. Quezada, the conciliator of the peace talks, was calling from Mexico City. During a break in the negotiations between the government and the URNG, Rodrigo Asturias, one of the insurgent leaders (better known by his nom de guerre, "Gaspar Ilom"), spoke to Msgr. Quezada and asked him if the Church was protecting Maritza. So Msgr. Quezada called Archbishop Penados in Guatemala and the two old bishops spoke in Latin because they knew that the telephone was tapped. Later Archbishop Penados, as excited as a child, told Maritza about the conversation. "Gaspar asked us to take care of her!"[35]

Later on Monday I spoke by telephone with Bill Robinson. Speaking slowly and carefully, Robinson explained that there was a very important point that the human rights NGOs needed me to verify. Could I confirm that during her interview with U.S. Embassy officials on the previous Friday, Maritza told the embassy personnel that she was abducted?

I hesitated because of the danger of speaking on the telephone, but I had heard the urgency in Robinson's voice.

"Yes. I can confirm that."[36]

I had just violated the Urrutia family's confidence and placed my colleagues in greater danger. Dan, did you just make a huge mistake?

Neither Bill Robinson nor his peers in the human rights community were insensitive to these pressures. Indeed, the NGO representatives assumed that my colleagues and I were under an inordinate amount of stress. Very few people had survived what Maritza had survived. She "was a 'crown jewel,' and her captors would not give her up easily."[37] But without the right information, the NGOs could not help her.

Edmundo René also spoke with Robinson. He and his *hermanita* were traumatized and near collapse. Edmundo René's voice had a new, desperate quality, and he told Robinson that he would not be able to endure the strain much longer. They would wait as long as possible to receive visas from the U.S. Embassy, but they would choose another country if the U.S. government denied Maritza's request.[38]

Following this telephone conversation, my confirmation of Maritza's statement about her kidnapping was communicated by fax to a number of human rights NGOs on Monday evening. Armed with this new information, the NGOs could again ask congressional representatives to pressure U.S. State Department headquarters and the U.S. Embassy in Guatemala to issue visas to Maritza and her son.[39]

"'Pressure' from the 'human rights industry' in the United States is often counterproductive and misguided," observed Ambassador Stroock years later: "In the Urrutia case, however, it was helpful. I was able to show our Guatemalan contacts the great interest and uproar that had been aroused in the United States on this matter and explain to them that the Embassy could not just ignore this kind of interest and the many expressions of concern."[40]

U.S. Embassy officials also tried to clarify the facts about Maritza. The Defense Department attachés, State Department political officers, CIA operatives, and DEA agents worked their contacts in the Guatemalan Defense Ministry. Not surprisingly, these inquiries shed little light on Maritza's experience. "We were certain that she had been 'handled' by the army," recalled Ambassador Stroock, "but exactly how, exactly in what manner and her exact relationship to the URNG was not something we were able to develop at the time. That came later. The contacts between our Defense Attaches were valuable, however, because through them we were able to explain to the Minister of Defense and the army chiefs what we were doing, how we were doing it and why we were doing it. They had trouble accepting what we were doing but they were in no doubt about our reasons."[41]

Shortly after nine P.M. on Monday evening Ambassador Stroock sent a terse cable to State Department headquarters in Washington, D.C.:

SUBJ: ADVISORY OPINION VISA FOR MARITZA URRUTIA

1. Summary: Kidnap victim Maritza Urrutia reappeared July 30, publicly confirmed statements made in her video that she had not been kidnapped, that she had been an Army of the Poor guerrilla for 6 years but sought GOG amnesty in order to resume a law-abiding life. Human rights ombudsman visited Embassy to say her public statements were made solely to save her life, that she was forcibly kidnapped and that she continues in danger. EMBOFFS interview Urrutia and come to same conclusion. Department's advisory opinion requested by COB August 3 *(sic)*. It is critical that this information be shared only RPT only with fully cleared personnel with a clear need to know. Any broader dissemination could jeopardize Urrutia's life as long as she remains in Guatemala. End summary.
. . .
4. On the morning of July 31, human rights ombudsman Ramiro de Leon Carpio called on ADCM, CG and . . . to request the USG to issue Maritza Urrutia and her 4-year-old son visas and assist them to leave the country immediately. He had just come from a private interview with Urrutia in the archbishop's palace, where her family had taken her for safety. *Although at her request he had sworn not to reveal details* of her kidnapping to anyone, de Leon stated that he believed she had been forcibly kidnapped by GOG security forces and only in order to save her life had she made the statements admitting and recanting guerrilla activities on the video and to the press. EMBOFFS said that before issuing her a visa, we would have to interview her and seek an advisory opinion from the department.
5. Later on July 31, CG and . . . visited Urrutia at the archbishop's palace and spoke with her for over one hour. She was accompanied by her brother Edmundo and by AMCIT lawyer Dan Saxon who works for the archbishop's human rights office.
6. Although she did not provide details about who her kidnappers were, she implied it was GOG security forces. She stated clearly that she had been forcibly kidnapped, and that there are at least two witnesses to the kidnapping, women who were near the school where she was dropping off her son. Following a day of questioning, when the kidnappers realized

that she was not involved with the guerrilla, knew nothing about their activities and had been separated from her common-law husband (who may have been and may still be active in EGP guerrilla) for 30 months, all concerned began looking for a safe way out of a life-threatening situation. Urrutia struck a deal with her captors; she would make the video they requested, she would not reveal to anyone what really had happened to her, she would not leave the country and they would release her. Her captors began filming the video on July 24, but not until July 30, after many attempts, were they satisfied with the results.

7. When she was released—believing that her safety was still not assured—her family took her directly to the archbishop's palace. There she broke one of her commitments, speaking in some detail alone to the human rights ombudsman about her captivity.

8. She told EMBOFFS she was not and never had been a guerrilla. That she had spent a lot of time in Mexico (her brother lived there 7 years, and she lived there at least one year during her pregnancy). She was there with legal visas, living an ordinary life with her husband, who worked for a printer. She said the statements on the video and to the press were made only to save her life and that of her son. She believes she must leave the country because the group that kidnapped her insists on having continued contact with her—their next meeting is to be August 7. She does not believe that either she or her son will be safe in Guatemala in the near term. She wishes to travel immediately to the US to stay with cousins in Los Angeles, and when things cool down here, return to resume her quiet life. She has no intention of speaking to the press or anyone else about her captivity or to seek publicity in any way.

9. Embassy is satisfied that Urrutia's intention is to return to Guatemala and is otherwise qualified for a NIV [a non-immigrant visa]. *However, we cannot overlook her public statement of being a guerrilla, and therefore ineligible under section 212(3)(b).** The Sunday August 2 editions of El Grafico and Prensa Libre newspapers and Teleprensa television news also reported that, according to an official URNG statement, Urrutia was an active guerrilla. The newspaper stories carried Mexico City datelines, but we do not know how the media received the statement. The statement could be genuine or propaganda from either the right or the left designed to exploit the situation for various purposes. No Embassy agency has a previous record of Urrutia's activities. She says she has been a grade-school teacher in Guatemala City for the last several years.

10. Based on the personal interview, however, both CG and . . . are convinced she is telling the truth; she was kidnapped and only made those statements to try to save her life. *Embassy's assessment is that—in spite of GOG's assurances of protection—Urrutia and her son are indeed in danger*

*Section 212(3)(b) of the Immigration and Naturalization Act made ineligible for U.S. entry visas all persons who were or had been members of a group that advocated the use of violence.

at this time in Guatemala. Urrutia does not plan to leave the archbishop's palace until she departs directly for the airport.

11. Action requested: the Ambassador requests department's advisory opinion by COB August 3 *(sic)* as to whether the Embassy can find Urrutia is not ineligible for a visa under 212(3)(b), as her statements to the effect that she was a guerrilla were made under force [emphasis added].

    Stroock[42]

In other words, "please acknowledge that we have the authority to issue a U.S. entry visa to Maritza, in spite of the fact that she is probably a leftist *guerrillera.*" It was a humanitarian request, reflecting the skill of Sue Patterson and the moral instincts of Tom Stroock. And it appeared that issuing the visa would not create significant political risks for the United States, since Maritza did not intend to create publicity about her disappearance. The request was also a tribute to the effective political pressures brought to bear on the U.S. Embassy by Bill Robinson and the human rights NGOs calling from the United States. But soon new pressures would fall upon the ambassador, pushing Tom Stroock in different directions, and making it more and more difficult for him to help Maritza.

THIRTEEN

TUESDAY

August 4, 1992

On Tuesday morning Maritza and her relatives began their fifth full day in the archbishopric. Nerves were raw. At breakfast in Sister Tere's kitchen, Kappy picked at the refried black beans that were standard breakfast fare in Guatemala: "There's nothing else to eat?" Kappy got up to buy a Coke and some donuts at a nearby store.

"Ah, Sister Tere," gushed Edmundo René to the tiny nun, "your beans are so *delicious!*" Edmundo René followed Kappy out of the room, screaming that she was being ungrateful: "Don't you *understand* what these people are doing for us?!"[1]

Rumors were circulating among the press that Maritza was inside the archbishopric, and soon she would be leaving the country. A steady stream of reporters, photographers, and television crewmen arrived at the ODHA to ask about Maritza, and many of them were genuinely concerned about her well-being. But Maritza also represented an issue of national security: a confrontation between the army and the insurgency.[2] In any matter of such compelling public interest, the investigative press would naturally want to get to the bottom of the story. In Maritza's case, this meant that members of the media had the uncomfortable job of probing into areas where they were not welcome.

Maritza was under the protection of the Catholic Church, acknowledged Ronalth Ochaeta. But he refused to discuss her whereabouts or her future plans. The ODHA considered some journalists to be "friendly," but others were army informants who received monthly payments to pass information on to the military.

Many members of the press were under a great deal of pressure to obtain information about Maritza, but the heaviest burden fell on the photographers. Dramatic photographs are vital to selling newspapers and magazines, and there is always intense competition for exclusive photos. That week the news photographers' priority was to get a photo of Maritza, and some did not care whether their efforts put her or others in danger. Groups of photographers began to take turns keeping watch at Guatemala's international airport, and also up the street from the vehicle entrance to the archbishopric. They were there twenty-four hours a day that week, waiting for Maritza to come by so that they could snap her picture.[3]

I tried to attend to business in the ODHA but Juan Luis Font from the weekly news magazine *Crónica* called to inquire about Maritza. "Where was she? Was she going to leave the country?" Normally the ODHA staff tried to maintain open relations with the press, but for security reasons, I refused to discuss Maritza. Font was insistent because *Crónica* intended to publish a story about Maritza in the next edition, and eventually, I simply hung up. Exasperated and tense, but not wanting to damage the ODHA's relationship with the media, I asked Ronalth Ochaeta to speak with Font in private and explain why I couldn't talk.

Inside his office at *Crónica,* Juan Luis Font was angry and frustrated. But his feelings were tempered by comprehension. Font understood that he was reporting a story in which many lives were at risk. The press knew that President Serrano did not have complete control over the armed forces, and the outcry generated by Maritza's case might provoke a reaction from the army.[4]

Early Tuesday morning The daily "country team" meeting at the U.S. Embassy got into "heated" discussions over the advisability of assisting Maritza. In Ambassador Stroock's recollection, Sue Patterson, the consul general, Jim Carroll, the embassy spokesman, and the defense attaché were all in favor of providing a visa to Maritza "for humanitarian reasons and because they placed great faith in the judgment and request of Ombudsman Ramiro de León Carpio."[5]

But the humanitarians met opposition from the proponents of realpolitik. Stroock recalled that the CIA station chief and the officer in charge of the Drug Enforcement Administration's Guatemala operations opposed the issuance of a visa to Maritza.[6] They argued that if the embassy issued a visa to Maritza, President Serrano would accuse the U.S. government of interfering with Guatemala's internal affairs and the Guatemalan army would curtail its cooperation with the United States' war against drug trafficking and close off the investigation into the killing of Michael DeVine.[7]

Stroock relayed President Serrano's entreaties that the U.S. government deny assistance to Maritza. Serrano knew that Maritza was inside the archbishopric and sought to leave the country. According to Patterson's recollection, Stroock explained that the peace negotiations were about to enter a "sensitive" stage concerning human rights and President Serrano felt very strongly that URNG was using Maritza in order to tarnish the image of the Guatemalan government.[8]

For Jorge Serrano, always careful of his international reputation, it would be a terribly embarrassing time for Maritza to leave the country and publicly denounce her disappearance and torture. Such a scandal, moreover, would not help the work of COPAZ, which had little progress to show after more than a year of tense discussions with URNG's high command. Guatemalan government representatives previously complained about U.S. criticism of human rights abuses because the comments allegedly provided ammunition to the insurgents at the negotiating table. Now what havoc might be wrought, both to the peace process and to that tangled web of interests politely referred to as the "bilateral relationship," if Maritza went to the United States?

Jorge Serrano recalled his communications with Tom Stroock very differently. According to the president, Maritza's case had "nothing, absolutely nothing" to do with the ongoing peace talks (which would drag on for another four years).[9] President Serrano wanted the Guatemalan legal system to establish what had happened to Maritza. Anxious to show the world that the rule of law functioned in *his* country, Serrano wanted to establish the facts and punish those responsible for Maritza's kidnapping, *if* she had been kidnapped. Desperate to protect his reputation, Serrano insisted that the embassy refrain from issuing a visa to Maritza until she provided testimony in a Guatemalan court about her experience. Serrano directed his foreign minister, Gonzalo Menéndez Park, to provide the same message to the U.S. Embassy.[10]

Tom Stroock's memories of these discussions and the Guatemalan government's objections differ slightly: "We were concerned about the possibility of being played 'for suckers' and about the official reactions of the Guatemalan government and the army. We were contacted—'strong-armed' might be a better word—by both President Serrano and [the] Defense Minister. . . . The army claimed they had nothing to do with her arrest and Serrano claimed that it was an attempt to 'set up' his government just at the time that the United Nations meeting in Geneva was considering whether or not to impose stricter supervision on Guatemalan human rights affairs."[11]

Whatever the arguments for denying or delaying the issuance of a visa, the ambassador was under great pressure from President Serrano, the foreign minister, and the defense minister. If the U.S. Embassy issued a visa to Maritza, effectively the U.S. government would be accepting *her* version of events over the assurances of the Guatemalan government.

President Serrano had personally authorized collaboration between his military intelligence section, the G-2, and the United States' Central Intelligence and Drug Enforcement Agencies to fight the drug war.[12] Making its way through the Guatemalan Congress in mid-1992 was a U.S. sponsored, comprehensive antinarcotics law. The new legislation targeted the increasing levels of money laundering by cocaine traffickers in Guatemala and provided for stiff penalties, including the death penalty, for convicted narcotics dealers.[13] Embassy officials worried that Jorge Serrano might limit Guatemala's role in the drug war in retaliation for their ignoring his entreaties and issuing a visa to Maritza.[14]

President Serrano's ire was not the ambassador's only concern. The embassy also had its very difficult relationship with the Guatemalan military to maintain and nurture. Now Maritza's case might create additional tensions with the Guatemalan army.[15]

Coincidentally, just days before Maritza's disappearance, Guatemalan military officers told the U.S. Embassy staff that the armed forces wanted a new bilateral agreement for the war on drugs. They wanted more money and training for their pilots, and a reliable share of assets seized in antinarcotics operations involving both countries.[16] As a bargaining chip in these very delicate negotiations, members of the armed forces demanded that the U.S. "lay off" on its criticism of the army's human rights record.[17] Now, by helping Maritza, the United States would place itself in a much more difficult bargaining position vis-à-vis the Guatemalan armed forces, which were critical to its goals of drug interdiction and intelligence. "We needed the military's cooperation on one of our four main issues in Guatemala: drugs," explained Patterson. "And Maritza's case might have damaged our relationship with the Guatemalan military even more. And hurt our drug policy."[18]

This policy was born in 1986, when President Ronald Reagan first declared that the international drug trade threatened the security of the

United States through its potential to destabilize democratic allies. The 1989 National Defense Authorization Act directed the U.S. armed forces to provide support to the counternarcotics mission, a role already played by the CIA.[19]

The last twenty years of the drug war have focused on "supply-side" attempts to lower the production of narcotics such as cocaine and heroin in source countries like Colombia, Peru, and Bolivia, and to interdict these drugs as traffickers moved them from the source countries to the United States. The underlying presumption driving these efforts is that a reduction in supply will raise prices, thereby reducing demand and driving the traffickers out of business.[20] To fight the drug war, the U.S. government now provides more than $1 billion annually in counternarcotics assistance to countries in Latin America and around the world.[21]

But all of these efforts and expenditures have had little impact on American streets where cocaine is sold and used. The fabulous profits of the "coke" trade trump the normal principles of supply and demand, since traffickers can absorb the losses caused by the capture and destruction of large quantities of their product. During both 1990 and 1991, for example, U.S. law enforcement authorities seized roughly one hundred and thirty tons of cocaine within the United States.[22] Hundreds of additional tons were seized around the world, including more than fifteen tons in Guatemala, the favored storage and transshipment point in Central America for cocaine originating in South America.[23] Yet prices for kilograms of cocaine *dropped* significantly in many major U.S. metropolitan areas during that time, while the average purity of the drug *increased,* suggesting that cocaine remained readily available there.[24]

In Guatemala, the lucrative narcotics trade easily corrupted officers in the armed forces, the United States' partner in the drug war. By 1992, the year that Maritza disappeared, a number of Guatemalan military officers were profiting from narcotics trafficking, and U.S. Embassy officials were aware of their activities.[25]

Even veterans of the State Department's antinarcotics efforts concluded long ago that this U.S. policy has failed miserably.[26] But in 1992 the U.S. Embassy dealt with the Guatemalan armed forces as part of the drug war, "especially the good members, who were rising in the ranks." Embassy representatives would cultivate their relationships in the army and try to influence the rising stars in positive ways. "We didn't want to damage our relationship with the Guatemalan military," recalled Patterson. "Because we need them too many times."[27]

If an embassy could express human emotion, its greatest fear would be that a particular act might upset the entire balance of bilateral relations between two governments. Maritza's case touched the nerve of sovereignty and President Serrano was fiercely nationalistic and famously impulsive. It was difficult to predict how Serrano, or his armed forces, might react if they believed that Ambassador Stroock was encroaching upon Guatemala's internal affairs.[28]

And was Maritza really worth all the trouble? Just an unknown woman, probably a leftist, *una písada* (a little shit), many Guatemalans would say. And if the various parties settled the civil war and won the drug war, two of the U.S. government's policy objectives in Guatemala, peace and macro improvements in human rights, might be within reach. Perhaps. But as Bill Robinson explains, "there has always been an enormous gap between intent and ability in U.S. foreign policy," as well as a divide "between intent and outcome."[29]

On Tuesday morning, given her conflicting statements, Ambassador Stroock wanted "a better feeling as to whether Maritza had been kidnapped or not." After Patterson and Jones conducted their initial interview, they believed that Maritza had told them the truth about being kidnapped, and that she had made false statements in public to the contrary in order to save her life. But no one else from the ambassador's senior staff—such as the political counselor, the military attaché, or CIA chief—had met with Maritza, and "we get lied to all the time."[30] "Played for suckers" by Guatemalans who, for different reasons, wish to enter the United States.

Ambassador Stroock decided to send an embassy official to cross-examine Maritza, "to do a more careful picking apart of her story, like a cross-examination lawyer." The ambassador asked Patterson and Greg Sears, an embassy security officer with a law enforcement background, to go back to the archbishopric and interview Maritza once more "to be sure which story was the true story."[31]

Midmorning Tuesday David Holliday arrived at the ODHA. Could he speak with Maritza? Holliday was the director of the Human Rights Watch/Americas office in San Salvador, and Anne Manuel had asked Holliday to drive up to Guatemala City and try to interview Maritza. Holliday and I were friends, but I refused to oblige him: "No. If I let you talk to her, I'll have to let everyone talk with her."

Maritza had now been inside the archbishopric for five days. So who should Maritza speak to? If Ramiro de Leon Carpio, the human rights ombudsman, was able to interview Maritza, then why not a representative of a prestigious human rights NGO like Human Rights Watch? Human Rights Watch was, and still is, one of the world's most respected and influential human rights organizations, and its members in Washington were lobbying hard to protect Maritza and win her a U.S. visa. If any organization could help Maritza, Human Rights Watch could, but it needed hard information.

What information should the Catholic Church divulge about Maritza? To whom? The Church had established the ODHA as part of its campaign to promote a "culture of human rights," to bear prophetic witness, and "to make its voice heard denouncing and condemning" situations of injustice and abuses of power.[32] Since its creation only three years earlier, the ODHA had earned a reputation as a credible source of information about human rights violations, *particularly* for the international media and human rights NGOs.[33] But was the ODHA's foremost role to denounce injustice? Or to protect lives?

The staff of the ODHA, still relatively young and inexperienced, never addressed these issues as a team as Maritza's case unfolded. The ODHA also ignored the institutional needs of professional NGOs like Human Rights Watch, whose existence depends on their abilities to obtain credible, firsthand information about human rights violations around the world. Their capacity to produce first-rate reports, and to raise funds for their own survival, relies on the work of talented researchers in the field such as David Holliday. If the staff of Human Rights Watch lost their access to eyewitnesses like Maritza, they could just as well cull their information from newspapers in the United States.[34]

After my rebuff, David Holliday complained to Ronalth Ochaeta: "Look, I can't do my job if I can't do this." But Ochaeta wouldn't budge. Holliday thought that the Catholic Church was behaving like a government with something to hide.[35]

Around midday on Tuesday The switchboard at the archbishopric routed a telephone call from Patterson at the U.S. Embassy to me. The State Department wanted the embassy to conduct a second interview with Maritza.[36] The department was concerned about the recent public statements by URNG claiming that Maritza was part of the insurgency, contradicting what she had told embassy officials. I was worried about Maritza's increasing exhaustion and trauma. Could Maritza hold up for another interview with the U.S. Embassy? The decision would have to be hers. Patterson and I tentatively scheduled the interview for that same afternoon at 4:00 P.M., but first I would speak with Maritza and Edmundo René.

I discussed the matter first with Maritza's brother, and Edmundo René agreed that Maritza should try to do the second interview with the U.S. Embassy. Maritza seemed to be in relatively good spirits as I explained about Patterson's telephone call. I told Maritza that I knew she was exhausted, but unless she did the second interview, the State Department would have a basis for rejecting her request for a visa. I would be with her, as would Edmundo René. And so Maritza agreed to speak with the embassy representatives once more.

Shortly after noon Sánchez, the shadowy associate of Ramiro de León Carpio at the human rights ombudsman's office, came to the ODHA. He had Maritza's renewed passport. Now she could travel! Sánchez, still wearing black leather, wanted to deliver the passport to Maritza himself, but I took it from him as we began to walk through the archbishopric. I had heard rumors that some persons did not trust Sánchez. When I passed through the locked door separating the office area from the archbishop's residence and Maritza's sanctuary, I slammed the door in his face and locked it. "Hey, Saxon!" Sánchez cried, pounding on the door.

Tuesday afternoon Heather Wiley from Amnesty International called me to inquire about Maritza's condition. I told her simply that Maritza was "traumatized." When Wiley started asking specific questions about how the ODHA intended to transport Maritza to the airport once visas were issued, I replied that I wasn't comfortable discussing this topic over the telephone. I was preoccupied with protecting Maritza and my colleagues, so Wiley's questions began to make me very afraid. Obviously, I did not want to divulge this information to the army over the telephone. But my attitude, of course, infuriated Wiley, whose work revolved around the exchange and strategic use of information.[37]

Shortly after 4:00 P.M. When Suzanne Patterson and Greg Sears, a huge mountain of a man, arrived at the archbishopric, I sat them at the archbishop's dining room table before bringing Maritza into the room. Kappy was going to mind Sebastián in the back room while Maritza was in the interview, but the recent stress and confusion were too much for the four-year-old. He didn't want his mother to leave again. As I led Maritza out of the room, he began to scream and cry: "Mamaaa! Mamaaa!"

"I'm coming, Sebastián. I'm coming—" Maritza's soft voice trailed away as Sebastián desperately tried to pull away from Kappy and follow his mother.

As the second interview began, Maritza sat between Edmundo René and myself. Patterson explained that in light of the recent press reports, they wanted to ask Maritza some more questions. Sears began to question Maritza about the details of her kidnapping. Obviously a trained investigator, his questions explored the minutiae of Maritza's disappearance. What did the first man who grabbed her look like? How tall was he? What was he wearing? What about the second man? What did *he* look like? And the driver of the car? Can you describe the car? How big was it? What kind of seats did it have? What color was the interior of the car?

I was bewildered by Sears's questions. If the U.S. Embassy's concern was whether Maritza was a member of URNG, then *why* was Sears questioning her about the particulars of her kidnapping? After more than an hour passed and Sears directed question after question at Maritza, I could see that she was tiring. The cross-examination put Maritza right back into her interrogation. Maritza repeatedly rubbed her face and furiously twisted a pen with her fingers. She puffed hard on a cigarette. Finally it seemed that the strain was overwhelming her, and I asked if we could take a break.

Sears and Patterson nodded their heads as Maritza rose and fumbled at the doorknob. I ran to help her as Maritza began to cry, and she stumbled out through the kitchen and into a corridor. Edmundo René followed me and I paused to speak with him: "Edmundo, I'm sorry she is suffering. But we have to finish the game."

"I know," he responded, and we passed into the corridor where Maritza was crying.

"Maritza," said Edmundo René softly, "you have to finish the interview."

She began to shake and sob. "No. No more. I can't take anymore." The kitchen door opened and Sister Tere announced that Edmundo René and I had a telephone call. Edmundo René went to take the call and I put my arm around Maritza.

Maritza cried and her body trembled violently. "No. No more. I can't take this anymore. I want to leave."

"No, Maritza. You have to finish. You have to endure. I *know* that you can endure another half hour. You *have* to finish."

"No. I can't endure anymore. I don't want to."

I was running out of arguments. "Maritza, look, I'm not doing this for *you*. I'm doing this for your *son* so that he will have a better future. Do you understand? You have to think that way as well. You have to endure for *Sebastián.*" Maritza did not have a handkerchief, so I lent her mine.

After a minute, Maritza stopped shaking and nodded her head. She took a long, deep breath: "I need my cigarettes." I held the lighter for her and then we walked back into the dining room.

Edmundo René was upset. Patterson and Sears were being too hard on Maritza. "Why all of these questions?" he asked.

"Well, we want the truth!" was Patterson's angry reply.

"But Maritza already told you about the kidnapping at the last interview," I reminded Patterson. Supposedly the second interview was necessary because of the embassy's concerns about whether Maritza was a member of the insurgency. But neither Patterson nor Sears had asked a single question about this issue.

There was a moment's silence as everyone calmed down. Sears began to ask more questions, but they were less detailed than his previous inquiries. Maritza again confirmed that she was never a member of the URNG. Finally, Patterson asked Maritza *who* she believed had kidnapped her. Maritza was silent for a long moment, then she looked at me. Her expression seemed to be asking: Should I trust them? Should I tell them? I nodded my head, but I wasn't sure if I really wanted this responsibility. "*Bueno,*" Maritza replied. "It was the army."[38]

Patterson explained that she would have to consult State Department headquarters in Washington once more. However, the embassy would try to give a response by the following day, Wednesday, August 5.

It was now early evening. After Patterson and Sears left the archbishopric, an exhausted Edmundo René used the phone to call Bill Stanley, his old professor at the University of New Mexico. Edmundo René reiterated that he and Maritza were on the verge of collapse; their parents were getting harassing postcards and telephone calls at their home. Edmundo René told Stanley that if the United States government did not grant the visas within the next twenty-four hours, Maritza and he would seek asylum in Costa Rica or Canada.[39]

I probably called Bill Robinson in Albuquerque that evening to tell him about the second interview, as well as Patterson's remark about an answer from the State Department by Wednesday. The NGOs would put as much pressure as possible on the State Department and the embassy.[40] "This was the command center!" Bill Robinson recalled, referring to the apartment in Albuquerque where he holed up for two weeks, working the telephone on Maritza's behalf. "People were calling here from all over, from Washington, from London, from Honduras and Nicaragua."[41]

Robinson had spent years working as an investigative journalist in Washington, D.C., so he understood that decisions on difficult political issues are normally made at the State Department headquarters in Washington, D.C., and then handed down to the local embassy. The embassies usually become mere transmission points for orders emanating from the State Department, so it was sound strategy to pressure the policy makers in Washington (which Robinson was trying to do), rather than negotiate with U.S. Embassy personnel in Guatemala (which I was trying to do).

But Ambassador Stroock, thanks to his close friendships with the president and the secretary of state, his ability to "get to Poppy right away" and make his own decisions, was much more than a mere conduit for orders from Washington.[42] "And nobody in Washington was gonna question him."[43] Now facing a difficult decision with respect to Maritza, Stroock and other State Department officials were becoming irritated and distracted by the constant pressure directed by international NGOs at the embassy, appealing for visas for Maritza and her son. "The NGOs should lay off," State Department desk officer John Arndt told Anne Manuel. The pressure was counterproductive.[44]

On Tuesday evening, Ambassador Stroock met with the foreign minister, Gonzalo Menéndez, who pressed his government's view that the U.S. Embassy should deny Maritza's request for a visa so that she would not leave Guatemala.[45] President Serrano and his advisors feared that Maritza's case would be "blown up" internationally if Maritza fled the country and spoke about her experience.[46] It was an internal Guatemalan matter, they argued, and the United States should not interfere with internal Guatemalan affairs.[47] Maritza should testify about her experience in a Guatemalan judicial proceeding so that Jorge Serrano could show the world that *his* government had the capacity to enforce the rule of law.

"Respect the internal law of Guatemala," implored Menéndez. "Investigate the case *inside* Guatemala." Granting a visa to Maritza would impede the government's ability to resolve the case.[48]

"It's not in our hands," replied the ambassador. The embassy had consulted with the State Department headquarters in Washington, and headquarters, the top of the Foreign Service's chain of command, would make the decision.[49] This was not quite the truth, as Stroock later recalled, "Washington had nothing to do with the decision—it was all ours—but I told him that to try and get him off my back."[50]

Tuesday evening Juan Luis Font and Carmen Sofía Berganes sat in their office and wove together their story about Maritza. The next issue of

Crónica would hit the streets on Thursday. They possessed all of the critical facts, but now they had to make hard decisions about important details: "What *can* we publish and what *can't* we publish?" The two journalists already had a tacit understanding that they would have to censor their own work. They could not cite their most important source, and the source had asked them not to publish the most sensitive material about the army's involvement in Maritza's disappearance. If *Crónica* revealed too much of the truth, the story might provoke reprisals against Maritza and her family, or against the press, against *them*.[51]

So on Tuesday Font and Berganes struggled over details and their own professional conflicts: "What is our true role as journalists? To inform? Or to protect? . . . We were sure about the torture that she received, [but] we couldn't write about it. . . . We knew that the entire press conference in the Attorney General's Office had been a farce. The video: a farce. But we couldn't write this."[52]

The story Font and Berganes passed to their editor omitted many of the details that might create more risk for Maritza and her family. "We repressed *ourselves*,"[53] Font recalled later. Such was the "free" press in Guatemala in 1992, but the journalists understood that their editorial decisions would help or hinder efforts to save Maritza's life.

Late Tuesday evening After Maritza's second interview with U.S. Embassy officials, Ambassador Stroock cabled a letter to four senators and a congressman: Patrick J. Leahy from Vermont, Tom Harkin from Iowa, and Peter Domenici, Jeff Bingaman, and Bill Richardson from New Mexico.[54] Twenty-four hours had passed since Stroock had sent his long cable to State Department headquarters, explaining why U.S. Embassy officials believed that Maritza was in danger, and requesting an advisory opinion concerning the legality of issuing her a visa to enter the United States. The Tuesday evening cable to the senators struck a different chord: "I am pleased to report that Maritza Urrutia is safe in Guatemala City." There was no mention of Maritza's request for a visa.[55]

FOURTEEN

WEDNESDAY

August 5, 1992

Just after six every morning, Archbishop Penados celebrated Mass in his private chapel, just a few steps from the back room where Maritza, Sebastián, Edmundo René, and Kappy slept each night. Sister Tere attended Mass in the chapel every morning, and since her arrival at the archbishopric, Maritza had come to Mass a few times. When they needed a place to talk quietly or simply escape the stress, Edmundo René and Kappy also retreated into the chapel. They slipped through the carved wooden doors to sit on the dark pews below a crystal chandelier.

On top of the massive golden altar that stood in front of the pews was a statue of the Virgin Mary. Her flowing golden robes were embroidered with red and green painted flowers. A gold sword pierced her heart, and painted tears fell from the Virgin's eyes and down her cheeks. With outstretched arms and hands uplifted, she turned her grief-stricken face skyward as if asking for mercy. Carved biblical scenes covered the rest of the altar. Above the Virgin, on the high ceiling, a dove of peace flew across a pale blue sky. A large vase sat on each side of the altar and it seemed to Edmundo René and Kappy that the vases would mysteriously move and vibrate from time to time.

On Wednesday morning *Siglo Veintiuno* ran a headline quoting Gonzalo Menéndez, Guatemala's minister of foreign relations: "Maritza Urrutia Has Not Requested Asylum in Embassies." I held my breath every time the phone rang in the ODHA, but there was no news from the U.S. mission. There was encouraging news, however, from Bill Robinson. He had spoken to John Arndt, the Guatemala desk officer at the State Department. According to Arndt, although a final decision about the visas had not yet been made, it looked like the decision would be positive, and it would come within two hours.[1] If visas were issued on Wednesday, we would try to put Maritza, Sebastián, Edmundo René, and Kappy on a flight to the U.S. that day.

Maritza was trying to keep up a brave front, but she was struggling. She had begun to hear the voices of her captors in her head. And Maritza's brother and his fiancée had undergone a role reversal. During the week of Maritza's disappearance, Edmundo René had been a tower of strength—struggling against his fear and paranoia and second-guessing every person he had dealt with—and performed brilliantly, while Kappy appeared periodically to be in shock. Now exhaustion and stress had taken a toll from Edmundo René, while Kappy began to play a stronger, more supportive role.

That Wednesday morning marked a bitter anniversary for me. Exactly one year earlier, on August 5, 1991, José Mérida Escobar, a police detective and an important witness in another highly publicized human rights case, was gunned down in front of dozens of people near the National Police headquarters in the middle of Guatemala City. At the time of the murder, the ODHA had begun the process of obtaining a visa so that Mérida could leave Guatemala. But we moved a bit too slowly: a fatal mistake.

Following their Tuesday afternoon interview with Maritza, Sue Patterson and Greg Sears reported to Ambassador Stroock that they believed Maritza had been kidnapped and that Maritza believed the army was responsible. The embassy was at an impasse, but a decision about Maritza's visa was needed quickly since the staff of the ODHA did not think Maritza could remain in the archbishopric for very long. Nor had the ambassador's superiors at State Department headquarters in Washington taken a position. "You're on the ground," headquarters told the embassy. "You've talked to her. You have the best information. So *you-all* make the decision."[2]

On Wednesday morning Stroock called together the embassy personnel who could provide some input. Patterson and Sears were present, as were Jones, George Chester, and the embassy's new deputy chief of mission who had arrived in Guatemala only days before. The chief of the embassy's CIA station was there, as was the military attaché. Both the military attaché and the CIA chief reported that they had been unable to obtain any information about Maritza's case from their intelligence sources in the Guatemalan military.[3] This was odd, given that one duty both of these men had was reporting back to the U.S. government on issues such as the size and structure of the Guatemalan armed forces, its doctrines, institutions, and officers, as well as "cocktail party" information, such as which officers were rising in the ranks or expected to retire.[4] After some discussion, Stroock asked: "How many of you think that the military kidnapped her?"

Everyone in the room responded Yes, except the CIA station chief. "How many feel that her life is in danger?" continued the ambassador. Everyone present believed that Maritza's life was in danger.[5]

"Well then," asked Stroock, "what would Mrs. Fogarty have us do?" Mrs. Fogarty was a widow and a junior high school teacher who had taught Tom Stroock's four girls when they were growing up in Casper, Wyoming. She paid her taxes—although she had a hard time making ends meet—and she believed in the U.S. government. When he was ambassador, Stroock invoked a metaphoric Mrs. Fogarty to bring his staff back to "heartland America" and its values. What would the U.S. taxpayer, who represents heartland American values, want her foreign service representatives to do in this situation?[6]

The consensus of those in the room was that Mrs. Fogarty would want the embassy to issue the visas to Maritza. And the ambassador agreed. It was the only time in Patterson's long career that she participated in a collective visa decision.[7]

"O.K." said Stroock. "I'm gonna have to see the president and tell him."[8]

Stroock did not have an easy relationship with President Serrano, but he enjoyed a very positive relationship with one of Serrano's closest advisers on the subject of human rights, Bernardo Neumann. Neumann was a dignified elderly gentleman from a wealthy Jewish family that owned a chain of department stores in Guatemala City. Neumann was the director of COPREDH, the president's human rights commission, which was established to fulfill one of the U.S. government's benchmarks laid down by Secretary of State Baker in January 1991. Many of the human rights NGOs did not take Neumann or COPREDH very seriously, viewing them as primarily dedicated to defending the Serrano government from attacks on its human rights record.

But Tom Stroock had great regard for Bernardo Neumann:

Bernardo Neumann was of great help in dealing with Serrano, not only regarding the Urrutia matter but on many other occasions. He understood the United States, he was a friend of mine and, as well, a true friend of

Serrano's. He had a calm demeanor and great good judgment. He was able to tell me how to approach Serrano: when I listened to his advice I was generally successful. I am sure he did the same thing in reverse and coached Serrano on how to deal with me. I had and retain an enormous respect for his abilities to understand, explain and meld differing points of view. I used to tease him and call him the American Desk Officer for the Guatemalan government. That is really what he became.[9]

Stroock had several telephone and personal conversations with Neumann during Maritza's case: "explaining what we were trying to do and how we were trying to do it. However, Serrano's hubris and anger on this matter was so great that I don't believe Bernardo was able to accomplish much with him."[10]

Shortly before noon on Wednesday, I spoke by telephone with Jones at the U.S. Embassy:

"Dan, we have to talk."

My patience had worn thin. "Look, are you going to give us the visas or not?"

Jones became quite excited. "Dan! Dan! You're fine! You're fine! I want to come to the archbishopric so that we can talk! When can I come down there?"

It sounded like we were going to get the visas, but the anxiety in Jones's voice confused me.

"Uh, anytime," I told him, "how about 12:30?"

"Fine! I'll be there at 12:30!"

"OK," I said, still confused by his tone of voice. Perhaps there was a problem. "Do you want me to do anything?"

"No! No! Don't do anything! I'll be there at 12:30!"

Still somewhat puzzled, but cheered by Jones's statement that everything was "fine!" I told Maritza and Ronalth Ochaeta about the phone call. It looked like Maritza would be able to travel that day.

At about 12:30 P.M. Jones arrived alone at the archbishopric. I took him into our conference room where we could speak in private, and we sat at the long wooden table. "OK, Dan," he said. "You're gonna get the visas. You're gonna get the visas today. Just give me their passports," Jones continued, "and I'll take them back to the embassy and have the visas stamped in them. You can come pick them up later this afternoon."

I began to feel very relieved. Jones just wanted to clarify a few things. "Turn off the pressure, Dan. Tell your friends in Washington and New Mexico to turn off the pressure."

194 / THE VISA

194 / THE VISA

It seemed like an appropriate request. If the visas were approved, the international pressure wasn't necessary anymore. I told Jones that I would do it.

"But don't tell them that you have the visas!" Jones warned me.

"Why not?"

"For security reasons. You don't want to say that over the phone."

Again Jones's point seemed to be correct. We might provoke a reaction from the army if we announced on the telephone that Maritza would receive a visa that day.[11]

I went to the back room where Maritza and Ochaeta were speaking. Maritza gave me her passport and her son's, and Ochaeta accompanied me back to the conference room. After I handed Jones the passports, we spent some minutes discussing how to ensure the Urrutias' security when we transported them to the airport. Jones explained that the U.S. Embassy had an armored van. He would check to see if we could use it. We agreed that I would come to the embassy that afternoon at 5:00 P.M. to pick up the passports with the visas. The Urrutias could travel to the States on a Thursday morning flight, and the embassy could provide security assistance.

While Jones was collecting Maritza and Sebastián's passports, Tom Stroock spoke with President Serrano. According to Jorge Serrano's recollection of their discussion, the president repeated his government's position: the U.S. Embassy should not give a visa to Maritza until she testified in court. The Guatemalan government, reaffirmed the president, wanted to begin a legal investigation in order to clarify what had happened to Maritza and, if she had been kidnapped, punish those responsible.[12] Serrano desperately wanted to demonstrate to the world that his government had the political will to resolve such matters.[13] Serrano argued that if the U.S. Embassy provided a visa to Maritza, or helped her leave the country, then the embassy would be obstructing justice.[14]

Furthermore, Serrano was concerned that URNG would manipulate Maritza's case for its own purposes during the upcoming meeting of the United Nations Human Rights Committee in Geneva.[15] The Guatemalan army wrote the reports presented at the biannual meetings of the human rights committee,[16] which had become another forum in the political war between the two belligerents.

So the president and the ambassador made a deal, a "handshake agreement" to delay the visa for forty-eight hours. Both men wanted the agreement kept in the strictest secrecy to protect their interests. Stroock agreed to the deal because in two days (he believed) the new report from the United Nations Human Rights Committee would become public and Serrano could not claim that the U.S. government had prejudiced Guatemala's position. Serrano agreed to the deal because he understood that if he rejected the agreement, Stroock would issue the visas to Maritza immediately.[17]

Later that day, Stroock spoke to his consul, Patterson. President Serrano was worried about the ongoing peace negotiations, Stroock explained. Serrano was concerned that URNG would use Maritza's case as a basis for pressuring the Guatemalan government during the talks.[18] So Stroock described how he had made an agreement with the president. The U.S. Embassy would delay issuance of a visa to Maritza for forty-eight hours, until the latest round of negotiations was over.[19]

Tom Stroock's memories of these discussions differ from those of Jorge Serrano and Sue Patterson. Stroock recalled that President Serrano never mentioned the ongoing peace talks in his several conversations with Stroock about Maritza's case.

But Stroock wasn't really worried about the peace negotiations or the Geneva meeting, and he did not intend to put Maritza at greater risk. Stroock was trying to calibrate two competing interests: Maritza's safety, and his desire to let tempers cool within the Guatemalan government in order to avoid problems in the bilateral relationship.[20] Put another way, Stroock wanted to provide the government of Guatemala with a way to save face *and* forestall any effort to prevent Maritza from leaving the country. At times Ambassador Stroock could be a rare breed of envoy. He had the courage and grit to challenge the Guatemalan government on fundamental humanitarian issues time and again. But now Stroock was trying to be, of all things, a diplomat.

"You don't want to have the president angry at you," recalled Sue Patterson: "And sticking a stick into the spokes on every other thing that you're trying to work out. And the important thing: we felt that she was safe. We felt that a . . . delay in her travel was not a significant price for mollifying the president."[21]

"We had no political agenda," insisted George Chester, who at the time was Ambassador Stroock's political counselor. "Our concern was for [Maritza's] safety."[22] But they *did* have a political agenda, as Ambassador Stroock later explained:

> My verbal agreement with President Serrano not to issue a visa to Maritza Urrutia until the weekend . . . was aimed at accomplishing the following: . . . to show our sensitivity to President Serrano and our desire to listen to his

urgent pleadings; to give our defense attachés time to find out more from
their colleagues in the Guatemalan army as to what really had transpired;
and to give all our Embassy officers time to visit with their opposite numbers in the Guatemalan government so that all our ongoing plans on drugs,
DeVine, democratic reform, economic development, pending treaties and
environmental cooperation were not stalled or derailed by the action we
had determined to take in granting Maritza Urrutia a visa.[23]

Such were the concerns of the U.S. ambassador when war and politics forced him to make a compromise about providing assistance to Maritza. Tom Stroock was walking his own tightrope with the Guatemalan
government and he felt terribly pressured by Maritza's case. There was
no perfect solution. Indeed from the perspective of the U.S. government,
every option it had vis-à-vis Maritza was a bad one. "The resolution of
the differences finally had to be made by the Ambassador," Stroock recalled, "and that is when I made the decision to grant the visa to Maritza Urrutia but to delay official notice of such a grant and her departure until after the United Nations' vote on Guatemala in Geneva."[24] But
to maintain the secrecy of his "handshake agreement," the members of
the embassy would have to tell a small "diplomatic fib."[25]

After Jones left the archbishopric, the ODHA began to make travel preparations for Maritza and her son as well as Edmundo René and Kappy. I
called Bill Robinson in Albuquerque. Everything was fine, I told him,
speaking in my usual cryptic style. They should turn the pressure off.
Everything was fine. Robinson was exasperated and told me that I would
soon have to level with the human rights NGOs as to what was going
on, that they could not operate this way. I told Robinson that I would
contact him later when we had more definite travel plans.

As the link between the NGOs and the ODHA, I was driving Robinson crazy. "It was like a well-oiled machine," Robinson recalled in 1995.
"All of the wheels turn together and each one knows what the other is
doing and if one turns here the other turns because the gears are all connected. And there was one which was out of sync with the entire operation."[26] Robinson and some of Maritza's other advocates in the U.S.
began to discuss ways of compelling me to be more open with them, as
well as possibilities of working around me in the ODHA.

After Robinson conveyed my second request to the human rights
NGOs to turn off the pressure on the State Department and the embassy,
there were more discussions as to whether it was the right decision. After all, Maritza wasn't out of Guatemala yet. But if the State Department

was granting the visas, it seemed rational. What would be the point of more pressure? So, on Wednesday afternoon, for the second time, the human rights NGOs suspended the pressure campaign on the U.S. government.[27]

The traffic was very heavy that afternoon as I drove across Guatemala City. So I arrived late at the U.S. Embassy. It was 5:30 P.M. before I reached the security guard at the main entrance to the building. The guard informed me that Jones was in a meeting, but he would be with me as soon as possible. I waited outside the front entrance until 6:00 P.M., when Jones emerged and brought me into the building. As we passed through the glass doors into the reception area, Jones said to me: "Dan, I have good news and I have bad news."

I assumed that Jones was joking. "What's the matter?" I asked, "did the Red Sox lose?"

"No, Dan. We're gonna give you the visas. But they're not gonna be ready until Saturday."[28]

My blood froze. "Why not?" I demanded.

"I can't tell you," Jones replied. "It's confidential." Now I was furious. "Why didn't you tell me this earlier in the archbishopric?"

"I didn't know," said Jones. "We've had a recent order from the State Department."

Bullshit! I thought. Jones is a very moral person and, thus, a very poor liar. Now the U.S. Embassy had control over Maritza's passport.

"And, Dan," said Jones, "Bernardo Neumann wants to speak with Maritza."

Now the game was getting rougher. "Look," I told him, "neither Bernardo Neumann nor anyone else from the [Guatemalan] government is going to speak with Maritza!"

Jones saw the anger on my face. "Dan," he implored urgently, "calm down."

My mind was racing. "I want to see the ambassador," I told him. "I want to see the ambassador *now*."

Jones was silent for a moment. Finally he said "OK. Have a seat." Jones entered the main office section of the embassy and I sat down in one of the chairs in the lobby. I removed my notebook from my briefcase and furiously began to write a summary of what had transpired between Jones and myself that day. After about five minutes, Jones returned to the lobby and brought me into the embassy. Without speaking, we rode up in the elevator to Ambassador Stroock's office.

Stroock had a large office with several paintings of scenes from the western United States on the walls. Stroock sat behind his desk, and Jones and I sat down in chairs facing him. There were two other men present I had never met before. One was the embassy's new deputy chief of mission. The other was the embassy's military attaché.

"Hello, Dan," said Stroock. "What can I do for you?"

I was shaken. "Mr. Stroock," I said, "I need those passports and visas for Maritza Urrutia and her son."

"I'm sorry, Dan," Stroock replied, "but those visas won't be ready until Saturday."

"That's not acceptable! This woman is suffering. She needs to leave the country now!"

Now Stroock got his back up. "Look, Dan," he said. "We've put a lot of work into this case. If you don't like the way we're treating you, you can ask for help somewhere else."

I wasn't going to let them off the hook that easily and my back was up as well: "We have no intention of seeking assistance elsewhere. Maritza needs to go the United States! And don't you complain about the work you've had to do. You receive a salary and you're paid to do this work. If you don't want to do it, you should go home and let someone else do it!"

I reiterated that Maritza was not going to speak with Bernardo Neumann of COPREDH or with any official of the Serrano government. I knew that could place Maritza in greater danger. But my mind was racing. *What was happening? Why were they doing this? What was the game?*

"Why were we promised the visas today," I asked, "and then suddenly told that they won't not be ready until Saturday?"

"We've had a recent decision of the State Department," Stroock replied. "I can't discuss the reason with you. It's confidential."[29]

"That's not acceptable," I responded. "We need those visas today."

"Why?" piped up the deputy chief of mission from his seat in the corner. "What's the problem? She's safe in the archbishopric."

"No, she's not!" I replied. "This woman is traumatized and she's suffering. She needs to get out of there now. And what you're doing is inhumane!"

There was a silence, and then I pressed them again: "Why didn't Jones tell us about this earlier when he took the passports at the archbishopric?"

Stroock responded in calm, measured tones: "Dan, because he didn't know."

I was furious and intent, and I directed my indignation at Jones:

"Well, if that's true, then I'm *ashamed* for you that your colleagues would use you in this way!" And then I trained my earnest guns on the ambassador. "And if it's *not* true, then I'm ashamed of all of you for the way you're handling this case!"

Stroock remained remarkably low key. "Well, Dan, I'm ashamed of *you.*"

Dumbfounded, I could only ask, "Why?"

"Because of the way you're acting," Stroock replied.

Stroock's remarks exasperated me, but my head was spinning in agony over the passports and the visas. If I demanded the passports back immediately without the visas, the embassy officials might oblige me and return them. But then they could assert that the Catholic Church had withdrawn its request and wash their hands of Maritza. But if the embassy held onto the passports, neither Maritza nor Sebastián could travel before Saturday. They were stuck in Guatemala. And they needed to go to the United States where they would have the best support system. *What was the game?* "Dan," a voice in my head repeated: "The visas. The visas."

"Look," I demanded, "when are we going to get the passports and the visas?"

"Saturday!" the deputy chief of mission piped up again, "at the airport."

I sensed that the embassy officials were trying to control the situation, and I struggled to regain a modicum of control.

"Why so late? Today Jones told us that we would get them back this afternoon at five o'clock so that Maritza could travel in the morning. Why can't we get them on Friday at 5:00 P.M.?"

There was silence, and for several seconds Stroock and Jones looked at each other without saying anything. Stroock's facial expression seemed to ask, Is that enough time? Jones nodded his head.

"All right," said Stroock, "then Friday at five o'clock. You have my word."

I wasn't feeling very trusting at that moment: "Can I have that in writing?"

"No, you cannot—" Stroock began to say. Suddenly the military attaché, who had sat quietly to my right throughout the discussion, rose up in his seat and turned toward me.

"That's an insult to an ambassador!" the military attaché yelled. "You can't talk to the ambassador like that! If I were the ambassador I'd punch you in the nose and throw you out of here! Now, I suggest that you shake hands and apologize!"

I stared at the military attaché in wonder for several seconds. But the same insistent voice began to drum again inside my head. Dan, the visas, the visas. I couldn't jeopardize Maritza's visa. I leaned forward across Stroock's desk and extended my hand. "I apologize," I said softly as we executed a perfunctory handshake.

Now Stroock followed his cue. "That's right. Now, up to now, Dan, I haven't gotten angry. But now I *am* angry. And I think it's terrible the way you're acting after all we've done on this case!" Stroock believed (in part correctly) that I "was a young whippersnapper who didn't understand the 'grays' of [Maritza's] case." I didn't understand *his* difficulties and was pressuring the embassy excessively.[30]

There was nothing more to discuss, and I got up to leave. "And, Dan," said Stroock, rising out of his chair and locking his eyes with mine: "If any word of this discussion gets back to your 'friends' in Washington, or if there is any more pressure from them, then no one from your office will ever get close to the U.S. Embassy again." I stared at Stroock, considering a response. Should I threaten to create a scandal? But I had already made a mess of things by turning over the passports, and I feared that I would only make things even worse. *The visas, Dan. The visas.* I turned and walked out of Stroock's office.

The deputy chief of mission beat me to the entranceway and shook my hand. "I hope we can still work together," he said earnestly. I stared at him in disbelief for a moment and kept walking.

Jones accompanied me in the elevator down to the lobby. I said nothing and stared at the elevator controls. Then Jones spoke up: "Well, I hope we're still friends." I stared at him. "Just get me out of here."

When I got out to the sidewalk, I leaned against some concrete abutments that stood in front of the embassy and wrote a summary of the meeting inside the ambassador's office. As I got into my vehicle for the drive back to the ODHA, I was nearly shaking with anger. It seemed to course through my veins, and on the drive through the darkened streets across the city, I pounded the steering wheel in frustration. I knew the embassy had made another deal, and I knew that I had failed, and now Maritza could not travel.

When I arrived back at the archbishopric, I wasn't prepared to tell Maritza what had happened at the embassy, so first I entered the ODHA to compose myself. Fernando López was there, and he saw how pale I was, and the worried look on my face. López listened in silence as I told him what happened at the embassy. He felt that all wasn't lost, but first he had to calm me down. "It's not your fault," López told me. Things had gotten out of my control. "We'll see what the embassy wants to do on Saturday." I was not relieved.

I picked up the phone and called Bill Robinson in Albuquerque. Humiliated, I briefly explained what had happened that day, and I asked him again to turn the pressure back on the State Department. Robinson was understandably exhausted and upset with me. The pressure had already been turned on and off twice, Robinson reminded me. The human rights NGOs could not continue to turn it on and off. If the pressure commenced again, it would not be shut off until Maritza had left Guatemala.

Finally I went to the back of the building to give the Urrutias the bad news. Maritza, Edmundo René, and Kappy were in the archbishop's kitchen. As calmly as I could, I told them that the embassy had the passports but they would not be returned until Friday, two days hence. And the visas would not be valid until Saturday.

Maritza was angry, but calm. Edmundo René, however, was overwhelmed by the turn of events. "Look, let's just go to any embassy and ask for political asylum!" he cried. I tried to explain to him why that wasn't a good solution. Maritza was safest within the archbishopric. It was a Church sanctuary that, as far as I knew, had never been violated. And besides, even if we brought Maritza and Sebastian to another embassy, they still had no passports.

By this time Ronalth Ochaeta had returned to the ODHA and Fernando López had explained the new predicament. "They didn't want to give the passports back to Daniel. *Los gringos* have the passports—they propose that they'll come get her on Saturday." Ochaeta didn't like what he heard. "Fuck!" he said. "We've got to fix this shit!"[31] Ochaeta and López agreed that the following day they would go to the U.S. Embassy and try to get the passports back. If they got them, they would send Maritza to Costa Rica.

When Ochaeta entered the kitchen, I briefly told him about the events at the embassy. Ochaeta's calmness was a contrast to my continued fury. "Sister Tere," I said, as the tiny nun scurried around serving us tea and coffee, "excuse my harsh language, but I'm really pissed off!" Sister Tere, as usual, simply smiled and went about her business.

"I don't understand the game," I told Ochaeta. "I don't understand why they're doing this."

We moved out onto the patio near the back room. Edmundo René was very nervous and upset: "Now the archbishopric isn't safe either!" he told Ochaeta. "Can't we go somewhere else?"

Ochaeta had another idea. He wanted Maritza to write a letter to Christian Tomuschat, a German law professor who served as the United Nations' special expert on human rights in Guatemala. If Tomuschat were aware of Maritza's predicament, he would ask the Guatemalan government to protect her security, as well as that of her family. That would get the United Nations involved. Plus, Tomuschat could raise the army's continued use of disappearances and torture with the Guatemalan government and in international bodies.

Edmundo René was now consumed by stress and fatigue, and his paranoia was beginning to overwhelm him. He was starting to distrust everyone, which was not irrational under the circumstances. "No!" he responded to Ochaeta's idea. "Yes!" replied Ochaeta. Maritza agreed to write the letter the following day.[32]

Maritza saw that I was still distraught, and pulled me aside: "Daniel, I want you to know that I am very grateful for everything you've done for me and I believe you are a marvelous person. Don't feel bad about what happened at the embassy. I have faith that everything's going to be OK. Don't worry."

Briefly, my head stopped spinning. Jesus, who *is* this woman? Now the victim was consoling her advocate. But at that moment, Maritza was stronger than I.

At 10:30 P.M. on Wednesday night, Heather Wiley received a call from Bill Robinson, who explained the latest denouement.[33] When Maritza first reappeared alive, the human rights NGO community was confident that Maritza would be able to leave Guatemala very quickly. After all, it was such a clear case of someone who needed protection. "Obviously the U.S. is gonna help," recalled Carlos Salinas from Amnesty International. "We assumed that because it was so unprecedented: somebody to reappear." But now as the process inexplicably began to break down, Maritza's supporters in the United States became very concerned that Maritza would have to spend the following weekend, August 8 and 9, in Guatemala. "We thought that if that were to happen, . . . she might be dead on the tenth."[34]

The human rights NGOs were surprised and frightened by the embassy's failure to keep its promise regarding the issuance of the visas, and by Maritza's new vulnerability. There were sectors of the army that the government could not control, groups that operated independently.[35] The longer Maritza remained in Guatemala, the more time her enemies would have to plan an attempt on her life. "Every second was working against her." And on the upcoming weekend, Congress would not be in session, and State Department personnel would be unavailable, except for the department's limited situation room. The NGO members would be away from their desks and telephones. Maritza was now more vulnerable, and a period of forty-eight hours was fast approaching when no one would be available to help her.[36]

In 1992, my next-door neighbors were Ana Pérez and Susan Parker, two North American journalists. When I arrived home on Wednesday evening, I saw that their kitchen light was on, and I still wasn't ready to be alone. So I knocked on their door and asked if I could come in for a while. Normally I didn't discuss my work with my friends because of its confidential nature, but that night I was upset and reaching out. They offered me some food but I wasn't hungry. I served myself a glass of Johnnie Walker and sat down at their table. Two years later, Ana Pérez recalled the conversation:

> [Dan's] face was flushed and covered with sweat. He was very serious, which is unusual because Dan tends to make jokes about anything to keep things light. He hardly ever talked about his work. So that night, I was surprised by his lack of appetite and by his somber mood.
>
> He started by saying that he felt like a fool. "I just got back from the Embassy. . . . I trusted them, I can't fucken [sic] believe it. I'm such a fool." Dan's voice was [so] full of emotion that at moments I thought he was going to cry. I couldn't figure out if it was out of anger or emotion but his voice sure was shakey [sic].
>
> At that point I had no idea what he was talking about. He kept his work to himself. But he said that he had been [working on] visas for Maritza Urrutia. Urrutia had been in the news for the last few weeks. Her case was being talked about everywhere. So, as soon as he said it I became intrigued by his [being] willing to talk.
>
>   . . .
>
> Dan exchanged some heavy words with Stroock. Stroock promised to have the passports no later than Saturday. "You have my word," said Stroock. "Can I have that in writing," was Dan's response. At that point one of the other men in the room reminded Dan that he was dealing with the U.S. ambassador.
>
> When Dan was telling us the story he kept on getting angrier at himself. "Shit, they can kill her in the next couple of days . . . " he said. Dan was feeling very responsible for [Maritza's] life. He went on to tell us how he had been negotiating a visa for someone else, I can't remember who, but the guy got knocked off before all the paperwork came through. So Dan clearly knew what was at stake.
>
> He went even further and talked about how since [the ODHA] had

gotten a "true" confession by Maritza, she was to sign it when she boarded the plane to leave (I'm not quite sure on this part) the Guatemalan government surely did not want that to come out and wanted her dead.

Dan was pissed at himself for being so naive and trusting this guy. He kept on saying "if he had been straight with me and told me that they would not grant the visa I could have gone to another embassy. Now they have our passports and they (the Guatemalan government) are now just buying time."

Dan also said that he trusted the guy at the embassy because . . . "they speak your language, they have similar experiences that you do, so I guess I forgot which sides we are on. I should never have trusted them."

I was shocked to hear the story. Again not only for the story itself but because Dan was telling us details about his work, that [he] had never done before. Dan seemed broken that night. He had bags under his eyes, his shoulders were down, and his tone was full of disappointment.

He also talked about leaving Guatemala. I think that this experience was the final straw. He was sure that Maritza would get killed and that it was going to be his fault for trusting the Embassy.

I guess the other surprising thing for me was that night alone Dan dropped his usual sarcasm. He was talking straight. He was talking slowly most of the time. Except for when he would burst into angry fits.[37]

Eventually, I wandered over to my own apartment, but I was unable to sleep. I tossed and turned, and I felt something running hard through my veins. When the morning came, I was still angry.

FIFTEEN

THURSDAY

August 6, 1992

Thursday morning's *El Grafico* devoted an entire page to Maritza's case. "Maritza Leaves the Country Today," read one headline. "Her Brother Is Going As Well,"[1] reported another. According to this account, Maritza's first stop would be Mexico, but her final destination was unknown. One of Rony Véliz's drinking partners in the ODHA had carelessly given the *Grafico*/Reuters journalist this "tip" on Wednesday afternoon. But the information was overtaken by Ambassador's Stroock's decision to delay the issuance of the visa. Unaware of this latest turn of events, *Siglo Veintiuno* immediately dispatched a photographer to the airport on Thursday morning to wait for Maritza to board a flight.[2]

This new publicity did not increase Maritza's security or the safety of the ODHA's staff. "What's our line with the press regarding Maritza?" Fernando López asked Ronalth Ochaeta. "The same," Ochaeta replied. "Keep a low profile." The ODHA would deny that Maritza was in the archbishopric and would deny any knowledge of her location. Moments later Fernando Penados, trying hard to keep Sebastián entertained, brought the four-year-old into the office so that he could play on the computer. Coincidentally, at that moment Rony Véliz happened to wander into the office. Véliz looked at the little boy as I curtly told him to leave. Véliz complied, but my attitude made him angry. Fernando López and Fernando Penados followed Véliz out into the patio to try to explain the situation.

"You know who the boy is?" López asked him.

"Yes, he's the son of Maritza Urrutia," Véliz replied.

"How long have you known that she was here?" López asked.

"Well, I suspected that she was here . . . "

"Yes, she's here," López told him. "I'm telling you because we trust you. She's in the back."

Véliz asked for an opportunity to take some photographs of Maritza when she left the country. López was unsure, as always thinking about Maritza's security. "I'll have to check. That will be difficult."[3] Fernando López pleaded with Véliz to keep this information confidential. Everyone in the archbishopric was now in danger, he explained, not just Maritza. The government wanted to speak with her too and the situation was very tense.

Other members of the press telephoned López throughout the morning. Where was Maritza? "We don't know," he lied. "We don't know where she is."[4] Olga Pérez and a group of students from the School of History arrived, hoping for a chance to see Maritza before she left the country. Edmundo René had not been in touch with the students for a week, and the members of the ODHA were equally noncommunicative. She wasn't there. They didn't know anything.[5] So Pérez and her friends stood around the entrance to the archbishopric. Perhaps they could give Maritza moral support before she left.

The press reports also increased tensions at the U.S. Embassy. Jones had told political counselor George Chester that in the interest of protecting Maritza, neither side would share any information with the press. Chester and his colleagues believed that someone at the ODHA had deliberately called the press to the airport or leaked the information about Maritza's travel plans, to envelop her departure in publicity and thereby promote *its* political agenda.[6]

The representatives of the Church, of course, felt the same way about the U.S. Embassy. Both institutions that morning had fallen into their usual stereotypes about the other. The embassy saw the ODHA acting like a front for a leftist Church.[7] The ODHA perceived the embassy to be, once again, undermining the struggle for human rights in Guatemala.

I received an early telephone call from Jones. "Dan," he told me, "the ambassador asked me to tell you that he's not happy about the publicity that the case is receiving this morning."

I was still angry, and still very earnest. "And I would like *you* to tell the ambassador that I am *still ashamed* of how all of you are acting in this case!"

Ochaeta was watching me closely. He did not understand English, but he understood the tone of my voice. "I want to talk to him," he whispered.

Ochaeta was calmer and more diplomatic. He asked Jones if he could come to the embassy and speak with him. Jones agreed. He was concerned and there were some things that needed to be discussed. But Ochaeta should not worry; they were going to supply the documents. "We shouldn't speak about this over the phone," cautioned Ochaeta. Come to the embassy, Jones told him. Plus, there had been an incident with Dan Saxon, and they wanted to talk to Ochaeta about that as well. Ochaeta told him that he would be there later during the morning.

Ochaeta explained to Maritza that he was going to go the U.S. Embassy to try to resolve the situation. Maritza was in tears. She was afraid and very worried about her son and the rest of her family. But in spite of the army's threats and her family's pressure, Maritza had decided that she would have to speak out about her experience, whether inside or outside Guatemala. If she was not allowed to leave, Maritza was determined to tell everything that had happened to her. She would hold another press conference and say that her "amnesty" was a farce. And Maritza would not allow the army to capture her again.

"Don't worry," Ochaeta reassured her. "If they won't give us the visas today, I'll take the passports back now, and we'll send you to Costa Rica tonight." Ochaeta worried that the U.S. Embassy's delay in providing the visas could result in the government of Guatemala's forcing Maritza to testify again under a procedure called an *arraigo*.[8] Under Guatemalan law, an *arraigo* was an order issued by a judge prohibiting a person from leaving the country before providing court testimony. Usually twenty-four to forty-eight hours were required to implement an *arraigo* request. Once it was in place, Maritza would not be able to leave Guatemala.[9]

And that would put Maritza into a terrible box. If she told the truth about her experience, then her original amnesty procedure would be called into question, because the government could say that Maritza had lied. The authorities would have an excuse to detain her as an insurgent and Maritza would become a political prisoner. Furthermore, exposing the truth at that time might bring army reprisal against Maritza or members of her family. Or even an attack from hard-line members of URNG who wanted to punish the "traitor" and cause an even greater scandal for the government.[10]

But if Maritza *lied* again—if she said that she was neither kidnapped nor detained against her will—any subsequent truthful testimony would have no credibility. There would be no defensible reason for Maritza to remain inside the archbishopric, or to leave the country. She would be, to use a Guatemalan expression, "between God and the Devil."[11]

Shortly afterward, around 10:00 A.M., Ochaeta and Fernando López drove to the U.S. Embassy, pointing out the pretty girls along Avenida Reforma. "Look at that one! *¡Qué culito!* That one's really nice!"

Jones received the two men in the embassy lobby. While they walked through a corridor toward an office, Jones remarked that I had been very hard on him in Ambassador Stroock's office the night before. He seemed quite hurt. "Last night Daniel told me strong words," said Jones in poor Spanish. Jones explained that he felt very bad about Daniel because they had promised to issue the visas on Wednesday. But some bureaucratic concerns had arisen that prevented their immediate issuance. But the embassy definitely intended to issue the visas. Could you please reduce the pressure from your "friends in Washington"?[12] Now López could feel the tension in the air between Ochaeta and Jones.

"But," said Ochaeta, "it was our understanding that the State Department [in Washington] has requested that you deliver the visas."

"Yes," Jones replied. "But there have been some bureaucratic concerns within the embassy." Ochaeta had his doubts. He knew from personal experience that it took only about four hours for the embassy to issue a U.S. entry visa.

"What do you think of the case?" Jones asked him.

"I don't doubt that Maritza was kidnapped by the army," Ochaeta replied. He explained why he believed that Maritza had been detained in zone six of the capital, on the grounds of the Military Police.

"Do you think that she's a *guerrillera*?" Jones asked. Ochaeta responded that he didn't think so. He was worried that the conversation was being recorded.

Jones and Ochaeta spent some time carefully discussing the details of transporting Maritza and her family members to the airport on Saturday morning. They discussed how Jones would bring the embassy's armored van to the archbishopric, the proper street entrance, the time and the route to the airport, and so forth. After an hour López, who remained silent, was mystified. *Why is Ronalth playing with this little gringo?* he thought.

Finally Ochaeta seemed satisfied with the travel plans for Saturday morning. "And when are you going to give us the visas?" he asked Jones.

"The ambassador told Daniel that we'd give you the visas soon," Jones replied.

"Well then," announced Ochaeta, "you know what? We urgently need to get her out of the country. Give us the visas or give us the passports. But I've come here for the passports with or without the visas. Because she's leaving the country today." Ochaeta explained that he wanted to send Maritza to Costa Rica immediately. "I want the passports now."

At this point, Jones began to appear nervous. "No. No. No," he protested. "We're going to give you the passports. *Understand*," he pleaded. "Why do you want to send her to Costa Rica?"

For security reasons, Ochaeta explained. There was a lot of pressure on Maritza and she needed to leave the country as soon as possible. "But if you're not going to give us the visas, then give us the passports! You don't have the right to keep the passports!"

"Well," Jones replied hesitantly. "In the afternoon. In the afternoon—" The passports were locked up in the consulate, Jones explained. He did not have access to them. The ambassador had told Daniel that the visas would be delivered soon, Jones reminded them. But the embassy staff was very upset because Daniel had been disrespectful toward the ambassador.

"Daniel is a U.S. citizen," Ochaeta responded. "And so he has the right to say to a United States ambassador what he has to say. Which I can't do. But he's a U.S. citizen and he said what he was thinking."

But Daniel had not maintained his diplomatic distance with the ambassador, countered Jones. "I hope that this will not damage the relationship between the ambassador and [the ODHA]."

Ochaeta tried to respond diplomatically. He lamented my conduct the previous evening in the ambassador's office. But it was understandable. Ochaeta did not excuse Daniel, but since Daniel was a North American citizen, he had the right to say what he said.

The two Guatemalans maintained their pressure. "You don't have the right to keep the passports!" Ochaeta reminded Jones. "I want the passports today! Bring us the passports!"[13] "We want to have the passports today," affirmed López, following Ochaeta's lead. "Because if she can't go to the United States, she could go to another country with the passports." Both men were fairly sure that the army knew that Maritza was still inside the archbishopric. And they knew from hard experience that it was dangerous to give the security forces time. The more time passed, the greater the risk that the army would kill Maritza. They had to stay firm.

Jones tried to explain his helplessness in Maritza's case. He was only following orders. "Please understand!" Jones implored. He did not have power at the embassy. He was only a low-level employee. Jones could not do anything because he "had orders from *above*, from Washington."

This explanation simply made Ochaeta press Jones harder. Maritza had the right to travel wherever she wanted. She no longer wanted to stay hidden in the archbishopric, "but the problem is, if they grab her again, Maritza is going to hold another press conference and she's going to tell the truth! And this is going to bring bloodshed and there could even be deaths! And it will be *your fault.*"

Ochaeta was visibly angry now. "And if they grab her and later there are consequences, we're going to make a scandal! And we're going to hold you guys responsible because you delayed the visas without right, and you had no right to hold onto the passports!"[14]

The last point was not necessarily true. The evening before I had never specifically requested that the passports be returned. But given that lives were at stake, Ochaeta could be forgiven if he was a bit too categorical. "We want the passports *now!*"

"Calm down," urged Fernando López.

For about ten minutes the three men sat silently, Ochaeta and López staring at Jones. At first Jones kept his face cold and impassive, but after some minutes he began to appear worried. He repositioned himself, crossing and recrossing his legs and shifting forward and backward in his chair. He tried to avoid the stares of the two Guatemalans sitting in front of him. Watching him, López began to feel sorry for Jones, who had already risked his life in this case. Jones seemed very conflicted and López sympathized with Jones's sense of being a passive conduit for orders.

Eventually Jones got up and walked around his office. He made one more weak effort. No, the embassy could not give the passports until Friday. "Not Friday," said López, "We need the passports now." Ochaeta remained silent, staring at Jones.

Jones was quiet for several moments and then said, "I'm going to ask," and left the office. López suggested to Ochaeta that perhaps they should compromise a bit. The embassy had the passports, but the Church had Maritza. Perhaps they could receive the passports later. "No! No! No!" responded Ochaeta. "We have to insist on this. They have to give us the passports." It was very risky to give the security forces any more time.

After about fifteen minutes Jones came back. He looked very relieved, as if a large weight had been lifted from him: "Everything's arranged, and we'll give you the passports at 5:00 P.M."

"No," insisted Ochaeta. "We want the passports now."

"Sincerely, Ronalth," said Jones. "This is the most I can do."[15] Ochaeta and López accepted this arrangement and agreed that they would communicate with Jones in the afternoon.

Many Guatemalans viewed the United States Embassy with a mixture of fear and respect, as a symbol of international power. But Ochaeta and López enjoyed one great tactical advantage over Jones and the rest of the U.S. Embassy staff: the Guatemalans were playing on their own turf.[16] "You're a son of a bitch," López told Ochaeta, laughing, as they left the embassy.[17]

Ochaeta and López next drove to Guatemala City's central court building. They checked in all the pertinent tribunals to see if Maritza was named as a party or a witness in any legal proceeding. They found nothing and returned to the ODHA.

On Thursday morning in the United States, there was confusion and panic amongst the human rights NGOs. For about twenty-four hours, State Department officials had not returned their phone calls. Up to that point, four to six people had been in constant communication with several officials in the Inter-American Bureau. Suddenly, the officials stopped returning all phone calls, even when Maritza's advocates called the State Department every three minutes for three to five hours.[18]

Now thrown off balance, the NGO members discussed the possibility of accessing "backdoor" (i.e., unofficial) channels of communications with the State Department. Analyzing the situation and possible scenarios to explain the government's silence, the NGO representatives realized that Maritza's case had become a very delicate matter for the State Department. Perhaps there was a problem between the U.S. and Guatemalan governments, or a conflict between different branches of the U.S. government regarding the proper treatment of the case, or perhaps both suppositions were correct. In any event, it appeared to them that State Department underlings had instructions not to communicate with the NGOs.[19]

Then, at 9:15 A.M. on Thursday, State Department desk officer John Arndt informed the groups working on Maritza's behalf that the visas had been issued. But several hours later, the NGOs received an urgent fax containing a summary of my experience at the U.S. Embassy in Guatemala City the previous evening, which told them that the visas had *not* been issued.[20] Instead, they would be issued on Friday and would be valid for travel on Saturday.

Before Bonnie Tenneriello heard about the new delay, John Arndt told her, "We've cleared it. She should have the visa."[21] The new delay prompted Tenneriello to call Arndt again.[22] Arndt seemed surprised. He told Tenneriello that the State Department had approved the visas. There was no reason why the embassy couldn't grant the visas. They (i.e., personnel at State Department headquarters in Washington) "didn't understand why it wasn't granted."[23]

Overwhelmed, John Arndt even stopped returning telephone calls from the congressional staffers involved in Maritza's case. This was a cardinal sin in Washington and it "pissed them off tremendously," recalled Carlos Salinas. The State Department's delays and lack of communication "got people infuriated, got people scared. They hit all of the panic buttons they possibly could." And so the congressional staffers, many of whom had never been involved in human rights issues before, began to "push and push and push" at the Department of State.[24]

Arndt was helpless before the "barrage of calls" flooding his office. Each NGO and congressional staffer, of course, wanted his or her telephone call returned, but they "were likely unaware of how well the call campaign succeeded."[25] Arndt's silence offended the staffers' pride as members of the congressional branch of government. How *dare* this executive branch civil servant treat them like that! Who leads here? And it raised suspicions on Capitol Hill about what the State Department was up to. "Perhaps there were in fact hidden agendas being played out. And that, of course, infuriated people." It made the congressional staffers believe in Maritza's case even more. "It made 'em work twice as hard" to pressure the State Department and the embassy over Maritza's visa.[26] And so began a blizzard of phone calls and faxes between the human rights NGOS, Congress, State Department headquarters, and the U.S. Embassy in Guatemala.

At Ambassador Stroock's large, elegant residence, the U.S. Embassy was serving lunch that day in honor of the new deputy chief of mission. The ambassador had invited a number of high-ranking Guatemalan officials, including Gonzalo Menéndez, the foreign minister, and Ernesto Viteri, a prominent attorney and one of President Serrano's closest advisers.

While the guests sipped drinks before lunch, Menéndez, Viteri, and George Chester, the ambassador's political counselor, discussed Maritza's case. According to Chester, the foreign minister "was all over" him, demanding to know why the U.S. Embassy was considering issuing a visa to Maritza. Chester responded that embassy representatives were persuaded that Maritza genuinely believed that her life was in danger, and that it was appropriate, "on human rights grounds," to grant her a visa.[27]

Menéndez's memory of the cocktail conversation differs. According to the foreign minister, Chester told Ernesto Viteri that Chester had information indicating that Guatemalan security forces were responsible for Maritza's abduction.[28]

Chester later denied making this remark (although the content was true!).[29] But for the foreign minister, the damage was done. This was a serious charge because it implied that as commander in chief of the armed forces, President Serrano would have known about Maritza's disappearance. When lunch was over, Menéndez went back to the National Palace and told the president about Chester's alleged gaffe. Predictably, the president blew up. The president would not permit anyone to slander his government! "Talk to Ambassador Stroock," Serrano told Menéndez. President Serrano demanded that George Chester retract his comment or provide his information to the Guatemalan government so that it could investigate properly.[30]

When John Arndt learned that the issuance of Maritza's visa was delayed once again, his reaction was disbelief: "What do you mean? Our credibility, our legal responsibility is on the line."[31]

After hearing the news from Bonnie Tenneriello, Arndt and his supervisors at the Office for Central American Affairs in Washington, D.C., issued a sharp rebuke to Ambassador Stroock in Guatemala City:

> We didn't feel there needed to be a delay, and we told the Embassy that in the strongest possible terms. There was no reason to delay the issuance of the visa. It had to be issued as soon as possible. This was conveyed directly to Ambassador Stroock.
>
> We told them that if the person was qualified then they should issue the visa as extraordinarily expeditiously as possible when there is a concern for the person's safety. Our feeling was that delaying it was tantamount to denying it.[32]

Ever tenacious, Stroock argued to the State Department that because of "certain sensitivities," the visas should not be issued immediately. The Guatemalan government would be unhappy if Maritza was issued a visa and the ambassador was concerned about how President Serrano would react, particularly if Maritza went to the United States, became a cause célèbre, and spoke out against the Serrano government.[33]

John Arndt, who was privy to all communications concerning Maritza's case except completely personal telephone conversations, disagreed with Ambassador Stroock. Arndt was merely a lowly desk officer, but he spoke to John Maisto, the deputy assistant secretary of state responsible for Central America and the Caribbean. The embassy was wrong, Arndt argued, and Maritza's visa should be issued *immediately*. Shortly thereafter, Maisto ordered Ambassador Stroock to issue Maritza's visa without further delay.[34]

"There was some tension there," agreed John Hamilton, who was director of the State Department's Office for Central American Affairs in 1992. Hamilton recalled the conversations that took place between his office and the U.S. Embassy in Guatemala: "It's important when you come into conflict with a government on one issue that it doesn't spill over and damage relationships and interests on other issues. With the U.S. and Latin America, there's always a great danger of that."

"It was a question of timing and Tom Stroock wasn't quite ready" to issue the visa, Hamilton remembered. But the State Department was now feeling the heat from the human rights NGOs and from members of Congress. "And we were saying: 'Oh, for God's sake, just go ahead and do it!'"[35]

Unaware of events within the State Department, the human rights NGOs planned a major press conference in Washington for Thursday afternoon at the office of the U.S. Committee for Refugees. There, the NGOs planned to denounce the State Department for violating Maritza's rights under United States and international law.[36]

On Thursday afternoon Bernardo Neumann, the president of CO-PREDH, President Serrano's human rights commission, and Juan Daniel Alemán, the government's secretary for political matters, arrived at the archbishopric to see Ochaeta and Archbishop Penados. They wanted to speak with Maritza.[37]

After Maritza's disappearance, as the faxes and other forms of international pressure had begun to rain down upon the government, President Serrano ordered his ministers, including the minister of defense, to conduct an investigation of the incident.[38] But Serrano was often a bit credulous about information he received from the armed forces and he placed a great deal of trust in certain members of the army's intelligence section, the same section that disappeared Maritza.[39] So the high command eventually gave the president its version of events: According to G-2's investigation, Maritza was an important *guerrillera* who had had some differences with the Organización. So the Organización had kidnapped her. The army had nothing to do with it.[40]

But once the infamous video aired on television and Maritza had reappeared, security forces insisted that all investigations cease. She was alive, they argued, the problem was over, and the case was resolved. So Bernardo Neumann and his COPREDH staff were left with the task of responding to all the international organizations that now clamored for a full accounting of Maritza's disappearance. Neumann, who harbored his own doubts about the validity of Maritza's video and her subsequent public statements, told President Serrano that the government's position was untenable. It was obvious from witness testimony, from Maritza's fallen shoe, from the amateurish video, that a crime *had* occurred. So Maritza's reappearance had not solved the problem. The case might be "closed" in Guatemala, but all of the evidence made it impossible to "close" the case internationally. The government's international credibility was at risk, Neumann argued, if it failed to fully investigate Maritza's case.[41] Thus warned, Serrano ordered Neumann to try to speak with Maritza.

As "proof" of the government's "good will," Neumann and Alemán left a formal, written request with the archbishop for the opportunity to interview Maritza directly and offer her, on behalf of the government, the protection that she needed. Maritza, however, declined the opportunity to speak with the officials.[42]

That left only one option for the Guatemalan government to "save face" and avoid damage to its reputation. Maritza must be "questioned by a judge in a court," responded President Serrano when he heard that Maritza refused to speak with his representatives. Clearly the Church was obstructing his efforts to learn the truth about Maritza's case. "Our only resort is a court that will interrogate her in order to learn *who* kidnapped her, *if* she had been kidnapped."[43]

Bill Robinson called me early on Thursday afternoon. After speaking with the human rights NGOs and congressional aides, he wanted to suggest a plan. By coincidence, Dr. Robert Kirschner, a highly respected forensic pathologist and member of the American Academy for the Advancement of Science and the NGO Physicians for Human Rights, was in Guatemala City. For years Dr. Kirschner had spent his free time traveling the world performing autopsies and medical examinations of victims of torture and human rights abuse. He was giving a seminar that day on forensic investigations in a hotel in zone ten. Perhaps Dr. Kirschner could examine Maritza and write a statement about her mental health.

At the same time the human rights NGOs would issue a parallel statement saying that there were eight hundred slots left that year for Guatemalan refugees: *Why can't this woman get a visa?* Amnesty International, the largest of the groups, would release a similar statement in conjunction with the other NGOs.[44]

Later that afternoon Dr. Kirschner met with Maritza at the archbishopric. Dr. Kirschner did not speak Spanish, and Maritza spoke no English, so I translated as they talked while sitting at the archbishop's dining room table. As Maritza described her experience, Dr. Kirschner noted that even one week after her release, she was still extremely agitated, very fearful, and under a great deal of stress.[45]

On Thursday afternoon a secretary walked into Ambassador Stroock's office with an "order" from State Department headquarters in Washington to issue Maritza's visa immediately. The order from the deputy assistant secretary was actually sent at Stroock's request "to provide paper backup" to Stroock's story to the foreign minister that the decision to grant a visa to Maritza would be made at State Department headquarters.[46] Stroock had already made up his mind to issue the visa.

When the order arrived, Stroock told Jones to call me at the archbishopric. "Tell him that we're going to give the visas now." Jones finally vented his frustration at his boss: "Look, I've been burned on this already! Who's gonna trust me there?!" Stroock apologized to Jones for placing him in a difficult position.[47]

Inside the archbishopric, shortly after Dr. Kirschner began to speak with Maritza, Ronalth Ochaeta received a phone call from Jones. They could come to the embassy and pick up the passports. Ochaeta still did not know if the embassy would issue the U.S. entry visas or not. He returned to the embassy at about 3:30 P.M. and was ushered into Ambassador Stroock's office.

Stroock had the passports sitting on top of his desk, and he handed them to Ochaeta. Stamped inside were U.S. visas valid for that day. Stroock spoke for some time. There had been a collaboration, the ambassador explained, but there had been misunderstandings owing to so much pressure. The embassy had been very concerned about this case. And Stroock was very angry with Daniel Saxon for the lack of respect that Saxon had shown him. Never in his life had anyone spoken to him like Dan. A smart politician, Ochaeta "apologized" on my behalf.

"Give my regards to the archbishop," Stroock told them as they left. "We've been very worried about this case. There's been a lot of confusion."[48]

Dr. Kirschner was still interviewing Maritza shortly before 5:00 P.M. when Ochaeta returned triumphantly to the archbishopric with the precious passports. Now Maritza and Sebastián could travel. Ochaeta's threat, the pressure from the human rights NGOs, and the State Department's own cumbersome bureaucracy had finally won Maritza her U.S. visa.

Acisclo Valladares, Guatemala's attorney general, was also a busy man that Thursday afternoon. Now, coincidentally, he wanted to get the facts about Maritza's "dark and mysterious case." To do so, Maritza would have to testify in a court proceeding regarding her disappearance. Of course, if Maritza left the country, she could not testify. So on Wednesday or Thursday, Valladares requested that a court issue an *arraigo* for Maritza. It would block her exit from Guatemala.[49]

Late on Thursday afternoon Valladares appeared at the home of Maritza's parents in zone eight. Valladares delivered a subpoena to Edmundo and Pilar and explained that Maritza had to testify in court the next day at 10:00 A.M.[50] Strange that the attorney general himself would be out in the gritty streets of Guatemala City issuing summons. Maritza's father politely told the attorney general that Maritza was not there, and he did not know where she was.

Francisco Perdomo, the interior minister, was informed on Thursday that a judge had issued an order summoning Maritza to testify on the following day. Perdomo immediately contacted the officials responsible for serving citations and asked them to speed up the process. Maritza had to be served with her subpoena immediately.[51]

Ramiro de León Carpio, the human rights ombudsman, understood how dangerous the game was: "We knew that they could have killed her within hours of leaving the court, either one of the two groups. Anything could have happened to Maritza. By the government or other groups who wanted. . . . So it was extremely dangerous for Maritza. Very dangerous."[52]

At about 5:00 P.M. a representative from one of Guatemala City's courts arrived at the archbishopric with a subpoena addressed to the archbishop and calling Maritza to testify the next day in court. Archbishop Penados came to Ronalth Ochaeta and Fernando López in the ODHA. *What should he say?* "Tell him that Maritza isn't here." So the archbishop told the man that Maritza wasn't there, and he left without delivering her subpoena.[53]

It was late in the afternoon. Ochaeta was tired and he wanted to go home. But first, before he could leave, Ochaeta had to speak with Maritza about a flight to the United States on Friday morning. But Maritza was busy with Dr. Kirschner, so Ochaeta wandered into the custodian's tiny bed-

room to watch the 6:00 P.M. news. As Ochaeta lay down on the custodian's bed, the newscaster announced that Acisclo Valladares, the attorney general, was about to launch an investigation into the case of Maritza Urrutia. Ochaeta exploded off of the bed. There it was. They were
about to put an *arraigo* in place.

Ochaeta ran to the back room to find Maritza. On his way through
the corridors he saw Dr. Kirschner and me. "Come here! Come here!"
he cried.

I followed Ochaeta into the back room. He explained the television
news report to Maritza and Edmundo René. The government would probably have the *arraigo* in place at all border controls by the morning. Maritza had to leave Guatemala that night. There was only one possible
flight, an American Airlines plane to Miami that left at 1:20 A.M. They
had to get on that plane.

Ochaeta sent a staff member to a trusted travel agent to see if tickets
could be purchased on the Miami flight. "See if they can make the reservations under false names." That would prevent Maritza's name from
appearing on the airline flight computer system, which was allegedly monitored by army intelligence. So on Thursday evening, the travel agent
stayed late at the office until all of his colleagues had gone home for the
day. By hand he wrote the correct names of Maritza, Sebastián, Edmundo
René, and Kappy on their tickets but then entered fictitious names into
the computer system for the same ticket numbers. Perhaps this would
provide Maritza with enough room to escape.

At the archbishopric, other preparations were made. Dr. Kirschner
agreed to accompany Maritza to the airport for added security. Msgr.
Penados also offered to go, but Ochaeta was worried that the archbishop's presence in the airport would attract attention. Shortly thereafter Father Sergio Orantes received a phone call at the rectory. He and
Father Luis were urgently needed in the archbishopric. Perhaps the two
priests could come discreetly? Sergio and Luis walked across the interior
of the great cathedral and stopped in front of an old wooden door that
was locked from the inside. Within a few minutes Archbishop Penados
opened the door and ushered the two young clerics into the archbishopric.

Informed of the plan to send Maritza out of the country that night,
Father Sergio and Father Luis said that they would go to the airport in
place of Msgr. Penados. At this point the Catholic Church had no desire
for more "assistance" from the U.S. Embassy, but security for Maritza
was still a serious concern. I tried without success to reach Ramiro de
León Carpio, the human rights ombudsman, as well as my contact at the

Canadian Embassy. We would have to do this ourselves. Ochaeta sent a staff member to pick up his pregnant wife and take her home from the university. "Don't worry," the employee explained. "Ronnie's going to come home late."[54]

At about 7:00 P.M. the journalist Carmen Aída Ibarra called the ODHA. Since the press reports that morning on Maritza's pending departure, rumors had circulated that Maritza would leave the country later that afternoon. Ibarra's newspaper, *Siglo Veintiuno,* had stationed one of its photographers at the airport to wait for Maritza, to no avail. For nearly a week, Ibarra had kept the secret about Maritza's presence in the archbishopric. Now Ibarra wanted to speak with Ochaeta to confirm that Maritza was still going to leave that day. But Ochaeta wouldn't talk to her; instead Fernando López came to the phone.

They spoke very carefully over the telephone and Ibarra never mentioned Maritza's name. "I don't want to know much," Ibarra explained to López. "I just want to know if I should keep my photographer in the airport." Ibarra wanted her paper to publish a photograph of Maritza fleeing the country. In addition to selling more newspapers, this would help sensitize the public to the suffering of victims like Maritza who had been subject to so much torture and abuse.

"No," López responded. "It's not worth it. Pull out your photographer. Nothing's going to happen."[55] So Ibarra called the photographer at the airport and told him to go home.

Edmundo René and Kappy were not sure they wanted to try to leave that night. "They told us from Washington that we should try to leave only in an armored car," Kappy argued. She still wanted the U.S. Embassy to help them leave the country. But Ochaeta would have none of it and he gave Edmundo René and Kappy an ultimatum: "You go, or you're not going!"[56] Edmundo René calmed Kappy down and convinced her that they had to leave immediately. But he wanted to call Ramiro de León Carpio. "*He* can protect us." This infuriated Ochaeta. "If you don't have confidence in us," he asked Edmundo René, "what the fuck are we doing here?!"[57] Maritza was very tense, but she took Ochaeta aside and told him that she would do what Ochaeta said rather than listen to her brother.

I was relieved that we now had the visas, but still smarting from the "loss" of the passports to the embassy the night before. I didn't want to take any more risks with Maritza's security. The plan required me to accompany the Urrutias until they passed through the airport's immigration checkpoint, but I worried that this was not secure enough. Maritza would still have to walk down a fifty-meter corridor to get to the gate and the airplane. She would be unprotected during those fifty meters. That risk was too great.[58] So Ochaeta and I changed the plan. I would use my credit card at the airport to purchase a seat on the flight. That way I could accompany the group through the airport and all the way to Miami.

Originally the group had planned to fly without their cumbersome luggage. I argued against that; it might attract attention both at the airport in Guatemala and at customs in Miami. Who travels from Latin America to the U.S.A. without any luggage? We have to appear *normal*. Eventually we agreed that the Urrutias should take a portion of their belongings.

As her little boy fell asleep, Maritza sat down and wrote a letter to Archbishop Penados:

> Monsignor: I have read the letter that Messrs. Bernardo Neumann and Juan Daniel Alemán delivered today. In response, I wish to tell you that I am unwilling to undergo any type of interview in order to discuss my case with authorities of the government, or with the media. I also wish to tell you that I intend to leave the country and hope to continue my life at my son's side. Given what we have discussed, you will understand that my safety and that of my son are not secure enough at the moment for us to continue living here.
>
> I would request only that you ask the authorities of the government for the protection that my family members need in order to develop their lives in peace and tranquility. . . .
>
> I wish to say good-bye, with respect and gratitude for the moral and humane support that you have given me.[59]

It was dark, and the upper stories of the southeastern tower of the National Palace loomed above the archbishopric. All the lights on the patio were turned off so that soldiers in the palace could not monitor movements within the archbishopric. Ochaeta told Fernando Penados and Edmundo René, who were smoking furiously, to put out their cigarettes. The glow from the cigarettes might attract attention.

Guatemalan army intelligence had a computer system that reportedly monitored arrivals and departures of airline passengers. Seven hours before each flight, the system presumably generated a list of passenger reservations so that the security forces would know *who* was traveling.[60] But the authorities could rest easy that evening. Maritza's name was not on the passenger list for the early morning flight to Miami.

During the evening Sister Tere told me that there was a phone call from Bill Robinson. He insisted on speaking with me. I knew that the call was about the visas, and I was exasperated and stressed. I had to tell Robinson something, but I didn't want to divulge our plans, and I couldn't stand the thought of more questions over the phone. "Yes! We have them!" I yelled into the telephone, and then I hung up.

Carlos Salinas was also on the phone that evening in his office at Amnesty International in Washington. He had something to tell Adina Siegel, a staffer from Representative Arthur Ravinel's office, who had worked very hard to generate congressional support on Maritza's behalf:

"Adina, I've got something that's a bit of a monkey wrench."

"What is it?"

"I think she might be linked to the guerrillas."

"Uhhhhuhhh." Siegel's disappointment was palpable and Salinas sensed that part of her disappointment was directed at him. After all, Salinas had led Siegel down a long political path, and Siegel had led Congressman Ravinel down the same path. "She's put herself out. He's put himself out! And then I say: 'Guess what? She's a commie-pinko.' That doesn't fly well in Charleston, South Carolina."[61]

Salinas knew that this information might complicate the situation on Capitol Hill tremendously. Many congressional staffers had worked beyond the call of duty in order to win a visa for Maritza. Her status as a member of the insurgency was irrelevant to Amnesty International, but it *was* relevant to the United States Congress. Had this news surfaced later on Capitol Hill, the human rights NGOs would have lost a great deal of credibility. So Salinas had to disappoint his allies on the Hill in order to maintain their trust for the next human rights battle.[62]

Late in the evening Maritza and Father Sergio sat together on the steps outside the back room. The great glass and cement dome of the cathedral loomed like a shadow in the darkness above the archbishopric. And above the building, on the opposite side, Maritza and Father Sergio could see a light glowing in the southeastern tower of the palace. Others were also working late that evening. It seemed to Maritza that the hours were not passing; it would be an eternity before it was time to leave.

Maritza and Father Sergio talked about the mass he had celebrated for her the week before, and Father Sergio proudly told her about the sermon he had preached on her behalf. The television news came on, and the newscaster was talking about "the *guerrillera* Maritza Urrutia." "No," insisted Maritza. "That's not true."

Later Archbishop Penados came to bid Maritza good-bye. "Don't worry," he reassured her. Everything was going to be fine. And if Maritza was not allowed to leave, they would bring her to a place that was even *more* secure. Then the archbishop blessed Maritza and told her that he would pray for her. Sister Tere also came to say good-bye. She had felt bad when she saw Maritza crying, so she presented Maritza with a gift-wrapped package of handkerchiefs.

Shortly after midnight, I pulled up to the doors of the departure terminal at Guatemala's airport and Kappy and I unloaded the suitcases and duffel bags. I went first to the American Airlines counter and purchased a ticket for the early morning flight to Miami. Then we pushed all the luggage up to the counter, and Kappy presented the tickets and passports for herself, Edmundo René, Maritza, and Sebastián.

Maritza and her brother were still sitting on the steps with the rest of the group overlooking the archbishop's patio. They laughed and joked and told stories until someone said: "It's time."[63] Suddenly the laughter stopped. They brought out the remaining bags and Edmundo René picked up a well-bundled Sebastián, who had fallen asleep.

Ochaeta and Fernando Penados carried flashlights to lead the group single file through a dark and narrow corridor along the back side of the archbishopric and through a set of wooden doors. At the end of another long corridor an old wooden door took them into the main hall of the great cathedral where Father Sergio had celebrated a mass for Maritza the week before. Candles burning at several altars provided some dim light, and Sergio had left a few lights on inside the cavernous building to guard against thieves. No one spoke.

As the group crossed the large altar, they passed a statute of Christ on the Cross, and Ochaeta knelt and prayed before moving on.[64] A moment later, they slipped quietly past the white marble tomb of Archbishop Rossell, Father Sergio's great-uncle and the anti-Communist cleric who helped bring down the Árbenz government in 1954. At the Sagrária, where the priests changed into their robes before Mass, they passed down the stairs into an unlit parking area where two vehicles awaited them.

Edmundo René and Dr. Kirschner got into the front seat of the first vehicle. Maritza, holding Sebastián on her lap, sat in the back between the two young priests, who linked their arms with hers. Fernando Penados, always so conscientious and considerate of others, made sure that everyone was seated before he slipped into the driver's seat and turned the ignition key.

But the engine would not start. Frantically Penados worked the ignition, the gas pedal, and the clutch. "Ah, fuck this shit!" But his sweating palms and his trembling legs impaired his efforts. "Fuck!" said Edmundo René, "this is all we need."[65] Ochaeta and López got out of their own vehicle and pushed the car down a slight embankment so that Penados could jump-start it. Finally the engine came to life and Penados steered the vehicle into the street without lights and headed up Eighth Avenue. "Keep accelerating," Father Sergio advised him from the backseat. "Don't slow down too much or it might stall again."[66]

Ochaeta and López followed in the second vehicle but they had trouble staying close because Penados was driving quite fast. Always sociable, Father Sergio tried to joke with Penados about his driving in order to calm him down. It was a very dark night, and Penados drove without lights down the empty streets until they reached Sixth Avenue.[67] A car trailed them for several blocks, and they held their breath until it turned west, up Eighteenth Street. It was a taxi.

Maritza knew she was beginning a long exile. "Perhaps this is the last time I'll pass through these streets," she thought. "*My* streets." They were hot inside the crowded car. Father Luis Pérez felt his palm sweating together with Maritza's as she squeezed his hand hard. The opportunity to support Maritza during the ride gave Luis special satisfaction. He remembered how in 1983, during another difficult time when he was a young seminarian, Próspero Penados, then the bishop of San Marcos, put Luis in his car and drove him all night through the mountains to the relative safety of Guatemala City. "The bishop took me out at night. *At night.*"[68] Both Father Luis and Father Sergio tried to keep Maritza's spirits up. "You'll be all right," they said. "You'll see!"

The two vehicles eventually pulled into a deserted parking area below the main airport lobby. Fernando López's assignment was to see if security men guarded the exit through the immigration checkpoint. Initially the way seemed to be clear, but López must have looked out of place at that hour of the morning. Suddenly two plainclothes police accosted him. "You! Where are you going?" They flashed antinarcotics squad badges at him. "Nowhere," responded López. "I just came to see if a friend was here."

When the policemen demanded some identification, Lopez showed them his passport. "Ah, so you have a visa to go the United States." "That's right," López replied, trying to sound secure and in control, "and check it out! So you'll see it's not false!"[69] The policemen returned his passport and moved on. They seemed to be looking for drug smugglers, not for Maritza, and López did not want to create more tension. So when he got back to the car he told no one about the police.

At the American Airlines counter, there was a delay. As planned, the names on the tickets did not match the names on the computer for the corresponding ticket numbers. Kappy stood impassively at the counter for what seemed like hours as one of the agents, a young woman new at the job, scratched her head and tried to figure out what to do. I stood nearby and eventually saw Ochaeta and Edmundo René wander in. Edmundo René spoke briefly with Kappy and then walked away. Ochaeta stood across the hall, making a telephone call at a row of pay phones. Christ, I thought, who the hell is he calling? Actually Ochaeta wasn't calling anyone. He was a public figure, and he wanted to keep the phone in front of his face so that no one would recognize him.

The occupants of the vehicle in the parking lot below grew increasingly nervous as time passed. The plane was scheduled to leave soon. *Why didn't they return?*

As the tension grew in front of the ticket counter, Father Sergio, who has a special aptitude for computers and electronic equipment, tried to encourage the flustered ticket agent. "The computer won't change the names," she explained to him. And she wasn't sure if the particular seats were still vacant or not. Father Sergio tried to calm the woman down, and he suggested that she call the other agent who might have more experience. Finally, the woman's colleague came over to the computer terminal and was able to change the names on the reservations to match the tickets.[70]

After the agents returned the tickets and passports to Kappy, we moved downstairs to immigration control. "Remember," Ochaeta hissed at me, "make sure she writes a letter to Tomuschat on the plane." Maritza still had not written her statement to the United Nations special expert.

Edmundo René and Kappy presented their passports to the immigration agents who reviewed them, stamped them, and passed them back. Maritza and Sebastián walked past me and Maritza presented their passports to the immigration agent. The agent looked at the passports, and then he paused. My heart stopped. The agent stood up, left his little booth, and showed the passports to his colleague in the second booth. The problem was not with Maritza's documents; it concerned Sebastián. The name on Sebastián's passport had only his mother's last name: Urrutia. This was unusual because most people in Latin America put their father's and their mother's last names on their identity documents. And in Guatemala, by law, children had to have the permission of both parents named on their passports in order to travel abroad.

Sebastián's father, however, was a member of URNG. He could not easily leave the war and come down from the rugged mountains to give his permission when Sebastián needed to leave the country. So Maritza placed only her last name on her son's passport to facilitate Sebastián's ability to travel.

I approached the two men as they discussed the documents. Just as I arrived at the booth, the first agent took the passports back to his booth, stamped them, and handed them to Maritza, who showed no emotion.

I passed through the immigration checkpoint and followed Maritza and Sebastián down the long corridor of duty-free shops to the gate. There was another security check, and Maritza presented her documents to the young American Airlines flight attendant. The woman looked at Maritza, looked at her passport, and laughed as she handed it back. "I already recognized you," she said. Maritza smiled weakly. After so many years of life underground, she was no longer anonymous.

Finally, we were called to board. Down yet another long corridor with an ugly red carpet and lovely Guatemalan travel posters of Tikal, Antigua, and Chichicastenango on the walls. Out again into the night and across the tarmac to the steps leading up to the door of the jet. There were only a few other passengers besides ourselves, so we sat together in a row in the back of the airplane. We began to breathe again as the plane streaked down the runway, and we were away.

Maritza and I sat next to each other and talked for a while as Sebastián slept with his head in her lap. For a moment Maritza worried about the man sitting in front of us. He was obviously Guatemalan. *Was he from the army?*[71] At last I urged Maritza to begin her letter to Professor Tomuschat, and she borrowed my pen and some of my paper and began to write. She wrote several pages and put them in an envelope I had brought for her letter.

When the plane landed in Miami and arrived at the gate, Edmundo René turned wryly to Maritza: "Welcome," he said, "to your country of liberation!" Maritza gave him an angry look and led a sleepy Sebastián— the fourth generation of the Urrutia family to flee into exile since the Árbenz era—off the plane.

Guatemala City was very quiet on Friday morning as the sun rose over the corner of the archbishopric containing Maritza's former bedroom. A bird sang to the brightening sky. Sister Tere and another nun knelt in prayer in the front pew of the archbishop's chapel, in their blue and white habits, white veils covering most of their heads. Sister Tere's chin rested on her hands as she prayed for Maritza. After a few minutes she stood up and lit the candles on the table where Msgr. Penados would give the sacraments. As Sister Tere sat down, the archbishop brought the wine and host to the table, his shoes squeaking on the floor. Finally he faced the pews, a large silver wine goblet on the table in front of him.

> In the name of the Father, the Son, and the Holy Spirit, amen. God all powerful, have mercy on us. . . .
> The Lord is my God and my savior. . . . With Him, I am secure and I fear nothing. The Lord is my protector and my strength, and has been my salvation. Give thanks to the Lord and invoke His name! . . . Because the God of Israel has been great with us![72]

Sunlight streamed through a window into the chapel, illuminating the altar and the Virgin Mary behind Archbishop Penados. The two nuns rose and approached the table to receive communion.

At 7:00 A.M. Msgr. Penados received an urgent telephone call from Acisclo Valladares. "Please have Maritza Urrutia at the court between eight-thirty and nine o'clock," instructed the attorney general. "She left!" replied the archbishop. "She's not here." By 9:00 A.M. Bernardo Neumann and Juan Daniel Alemán were present at the archbishopric to confirm that Msgr. Penados was telling the truth. Hearing that Maritza had boarded a flight for Miami, Neumann and Alemán assumed that her destination was Washington, D.C.,[73] home to many of the human rights NGOs.

Edmundo René and Kappy stood in a long line at a ticket counter while Maritza, Sebastián, and I watched the luggage. Finally they returned. There was a flight to Albuquerque within the next hour. They would have to hurry across the gigantic Miami airport to make it. We quickly said good-bye. Edmundo René and I embraced.

"I hope that this friendship lasts forever," he said to me. "I hope so," I responded.

I turned to Maritza. "Well, good luck in the future," I said.

"Thank you for everything, Daniel," she replied. They disappeared into the crowd. *Well,* I thought, *I'll never see her again.*

THE AFTERMATH

On Friday morning the Guatemala City newspapers were full of news about Maritza. "Maritza Urrutia Called to Court," blared the headline on the front page of *Prensa Libre*. "She must say whether she was kidnapped or detained," read the subhead. The article explained that Attorney General Acisclo Valladares had begun legal proceedings so that Maritza could resolve all of the doubts about her situation. In the event that Maritza *had* been coerced into requesting amnesty, Valladares explained, she will have to explain why she failed to make "the pertinent accusation" when she appeared before a judge in order to obtain amnesty.[1] "I don't discard any hypothesis," said Valladares. "Nor can the attorney general discard the possibility of a simulated crime, which is also punishable by law."[2] The state of Guatemala, Valladares observed, "is jealous of its prestige."[3]

The attorney general embodied many of the difficult contradictions in Maritza's case. As the channel for her "legal amnesty," Valladares provided a face-saving way for Maritza's captors to free her alive. But the political theater he staged to save Maritza's life came at a cost: continued impunity for her torturers. "This case was in the world of shadows," Valladares told me in 1996. "I belong to the world of light, the world of law and clarity."[4]

Rony Véliz's friends in the ODHA wanted to express their gratitude to the photojournalist. Véliz knew about Maritza's presence in the archbishopric but had not published the secret. So on Friday morning members of the ODHA gave Véliz the negative of a photograph supposedly taken when Maritza left the country so *El Grafico* and Reuters could publish it. Véliz developed the negative and transmitted the dramatic photo of a tearful Maritza embracing her mother worldwide via Reuters's satellite. Later Véliz generously provided copies of the same photograph to *Siglo Veintiuno* and other Guatemalan newspapers. "I took the photograph at the airport," Véliz explained. He arrived there just by coincidence when Maritza was leaving.[5]

Siglo Veintiuno reporter Carmen Aída Ibarra gratefully thanked Véliz for sharing his photograph, but she was angry because she suspected that *her friends* in the ODHA had placed more trust in Rony Véliz than in her. Why were they hiding things *from me?*[6] Early Friday evening, as Ibarra and her staff prepared the next day's edition, they noticed that in the photograph Maritza wore the same clothing as on the day of her release the previous week. Strange. But they sent the photograph to press anyway, and it would cover most of *Siglo Veintiuno's* front page the following morning.

That night Ibarra met a group of her friends, including Ronalth Ochaeta, at El Toboso, a popular bar in the center of Guatemala City. "Fuck! You didn't trust me!" Ibarra scolded Ochaeta, "You trusted someone else more than *me!*" During their conversation, Ochaeta explained to Ibarra that the photograph of Maritza hugging her mother was not taken at the airport, but a week earlier in the archbishopric just after Maritza's release. For security reasons, the ODHA did not want to have the press at the airport. Ibarra was not impressed. "So *on top* of everything else, we're going to publish photographs that don't correspond to reality!"[7]

Ibarra completely disagreed with the Catholic Church's decision to shield Maritza's departure from the media. Ibarra believed that the Guatemalan people had the right to know what was happening in their country. Full publicity of Maritza's departure would have demonstrated what victims of torture must endure even *after* the torture is over. By keeping things quiet, by concealing events, the people "are never sensitized to human rights abuses." Nor did Ibarra accept Ochaeta's concerns about Maritza's security. The army had lost control of the case, she reasoned, and politically, its hands were tied. *What more could the military do to Maritza?*[8]

That same Friday evening in Albuquerque Maritza could not stop crying. Finally her brother couldn't stand it any longer and handed Maritza a scrap of paper containing the telephone number of a mutual friend in Mexico City. Maritza called the friend and asked her to contact Maritza's EGP colleagues. A couple of days passed before a member of the EGP called Maritza in Albuquerque to say that her *compañeros* planned to fly to New Mexico. Soon they called again with a problem. The U.S. Embassy in Mexico City would not issue them visas.[9] Maritza would have to come to Mexico.

Heather Wiley from Amnesty International flew out from Boston and interviewed Maritza about her experience. Wiley encouraged her to seek psychiatric treatment, but Maritza declined. Her priority was to reach her colleagues in Mexico. Bill Robinson also tried to convince Maritza to remain in the States. She could make contacts there and report on her disappearance and torture, thereby serving the interests of the human rights NGO community as well as the URNG. But Maritza was adamant. She had to get to Mexico.[10] So after eight days in the United States, Maritza and Sebastián flew to Mexico City.

EGP leaders Miguel Ángel Sandoval and Gustavo Meoño met Maritza at the airport. The first words out of Sandoval's mouth were "Look! You have to denounce this! Now!"

Both Sandoval and Meoño had known Maritza since she was a little girl and the men were young urban *guerrilleros* who could find a meal and a place to sleep in the Urrutia home. Now it was their turn to help the Urrutia family. They brought Maritza to a safe house where they hid and protected her for a month while Meoño debriefed her and *made sure* that Maritza had not betrayed the EGP. Once Meoño and Sandoval were convinced that Maritza was telling the truth, they spoke with Rolando Morán, the EGP's highest *comandante,* and convinced Morán to support Maritza in a campaign to speak out about her experience. By the autumn Maritza would testify publicly in Washington, D.C., and in Europe.

Meoño and Sandoval were the only high-ranking members of the EGP to support her when she arrived in Mexico City. But because she had *el comandante's* support, she might have a chance to vindicate herself with the Organización.

Apart from the well-being of her son, justice and vindication were foremost on Maritza's mind. No one was captured or killed after Maritza broke under torture, gave up her ex-husband's name, and recorded the video. Nevertheless, Maritza had violated the cardinal rule of the dogmatic, highly disciplined EGP: *you do not give information to the enemy.* Consequently, several insurgents left the movement, reasoning that

it was pointless to fight in an army whose leaders would "betray them."
A number of Maritza's revolutionary colleagues, immersed in the EGP's
rigid doctrine, also believed that Maritza had betrayed them and their
trust in her.[11] They refused to speak with Maritza or even acknowledge
her presence when they saw her in the street.

Feelings of depression are common in survivors of torture, and the
scornful, guilt-inducing rejection by these former friends devastated
Maritza.[12] "The doubt of other persons . . . amplifies the suffering of
those already in pain." Thus torture, once begun, may take on a life of its
own.[13] The contempt of some of Maritza's *compañeros* underscored her
captors' efforts to destroy her personality, and the brutality of the
Guatemalan army found an unlikely ally in members of the Guerrilla
Army of the Poor. To regain her world, Maritza would have to speak
out.

The Guatemalan Episcopal Conference had a meeting scheduled during
the week following Maritza's flight to the United States. One of the invited guests was President Jorge Serrano, who was furious about the
Church's conduct in Maritza's case. The president gave the dignified bishops a good scolding: The ODHA had obstructed justice! It had prevented
an investigation. It was helping the insurgency! The president had intended to find the truth, but the Church had impeded his efforts. "This
is a mockery of authority! A mockery!"[14]

"You had her *hidden* there," accused Serrano, "and she's a *guerrillera*."

"Hidden, *no*," responded the archbishop. "She requested the Church's
protection, and everyone knew she was there, and your guys knew it too.
She wasn't hidden. And she didn't want to talk to anyone."

Serrano didn't buy it: "The Catholic Church has struck a blow against
justice in Guatemala!"[15]

"But, Mr. President, you knew she was there. When you asked to speak
with her, she didn't want to. And later she left [the country] by air, by a
normal route."

"That can't be," replied Serrano, "because we have a computer here
[in the National Palace] and seven hours before someone is going to leave
or going to arrive, we know who is going to travel in Guatemala. There's
a list of people. And the computer didn't say anything. So she didn't leave
by a legal route."

The bishops tried to explain. "But she left on an airline. And she
checked her baggage normally."

"It's not possible," insisted the president. "Because the computer knows who's going to leave. There's a list of who's coming and going. And she didn't appear there."

Serrano seemed determined to flush out the truth. "And what *time* did she leave?"

"At one in the morning," replied the archbishop.

"And why at *that* time?"

"Because *that's* the time the plane took off."[16]

One of the lessons I learned while working amidst Guatemala's "dirty war" was that the most ordinary of people often perform extraordinary acts when difficult circumstances push them beyond themselves. Acts that create the polar opposite of the world-shattering impact of torture, they expand the actors' universe and their ability to see themselves in that universe. Only the rarest of individuals can sustain their newfound dimensions for long periods.

During those frantic two weeks in the summer of 1992, dozens of people, including some employees of the U.S. State Department, used their skills and courage to assist Maritza and her family. But the temporal demands of contradictory United States policies hung like a stone on the U.S. Embassy, impeding the efforts of foreign service officers to act quickly and decisively. The inconsistent policies—punish the Guatemalan army for its human rights violations; reward the Guatemalan army for its antidrug work—became the subject of confusion, distrust, and ridicule.[17]

After Maritza fled Guatemala, U.S. Embassy representatives tried to cool President Serrano's anger over the issuance of the visa to Maritza. Further complicating matters were the allegations that political counselor George Chester had accused the Guatemalan security forces of responsibility for Maritza's disappearance.[18] Serrano wanted Chester out of Guatemala. State Department representatives in Washington and Guatemala City worked hard to resolve the "misunderstanding" and avoid further damage to relations between the two countries.[19] To make matters "right" with the president, embassy officials were prepared to categorically deny that the U.S. government had information indicating that Guatemalan security forces had abducted Maritza.[20]

But this still wasn't enough for Jorge Serrano, who was desperate to ensure that Maritza's case not damage his reputation, nor that of his armed forces.[21] The president wanted a retraction and an apology in writing from George Chester.[22] Without it, he would declare Chester persona non grata and expel him from Guatemala. Juan Luis Font recalled how furious the president became over the Chester affair. "It was unacceptable, intolerable," declared Serrano, that a U.S. diplomat had intervened in a national matter:[23] "Why did they [the Catholic Church and the U.S. Embassy] impede us? Why did they impede the presidency and the executive from hearing from her mouth what had happened? . . . They knew that I'd take this case to the ultimate consequences, so they obstructed me! . . . The intention of the president was to arrive at the truth. . . . This is a mockery of the authority of the country! A mockery! And that's why systems of impunity exist in our countries."[24]

Font thought that Serrano's behavior was absurd. "He wanted to deny reality."[25] The president wanted to deny at all costs that in the country *he* governed incidents such as Maritza's disappearance occurred. In order to sustain *his* reality, Serrano attacked the U.S. government and the Catholic Church, which only weakened him politically and supported Guatemala's culture of impunity.[26]

Trying to calm the waters, the U.S. Embassy's new deputy chief of mission and Gonzalo Menéndez, Guatemala's foreign minister, worked out the text of a letter that would be acceptable to both governments.[27] On August 20, George Chester sent the following letter to Menéndez:

Dear Mr. Minister:

With reference to our conversation of August 6, I assure you without any reservation or qualification that I had no information that any entity of the Guatemalan government was involved in actions against Maritza Urrutia. It was not my intention to imply anything to the contrary.[28]

The new deputy chief of mission, writing the next day to his superiors in Washington, D.C., was oddly vague about the likely identity of Maritza's kidnappers, particularly given the amount of information available to U.S. Embassy officials: "our best guess is that her captors were right-wing elements seeking information about her common-law husband, who is a guerrilla leader."[29]

Now the reputation of Jorge Serrano's government was secure, but at a cost to Guatemala and, in the long run, to the United States as well. In spite of their public commitments to improving human rights and establishing democracy, U.S. Embassy officials chose not to confront the Guatemalan government and, in particular, the Guatemalan army, over Maritza's case: "Obviously we cannot acquiesce in the [government of Guatemala's] refusing to deal with our political counselor. *We have gone out of our way to protect them from themselves*, in view of the firestorm of criticism against the government of Guatemala which would have ensued had we made the Urrutia matter public in the United States" (emphasis added).[30]

Years later, when asked to explain the "protect them from themselves" language in this memorandum, George Chester stated:

> Since we (the U.S. government) refused to accept their request that I be withdrawn, they could only have made it stick by declaring me persona non grata. This would have resulted in a firestorm of criticism internationally against the Guatemalan Government and only confirmed in people's minds that the kidnapping was real, and was carried out by the Guatemalan army, and make a mockery of their claims to be trying to improve the human rights situation in the country. Moreover, we would undoubtedly have expelled one of their diplomats in retaliation, and our relations, already strained by Ambassador Stroock's aggressive stance on human rights, would have worsened. Thus in insisting they withdraw their demand, we were "protecting them from themselves," i.e. from making a major blunder which would only have embarrassed the Guatemalan Government.[31]

One wonders whether the U.S. government's decision to "protect them from themselves" rather than to criticize the Guatemalan army for disappearing and torturing a dissident also "makes a mockery" of U.S. government policies dedicated to the improvement of human rights. The late historian Barbara Tuchman described "folly" as "the pursuit of policy contrary to the self-interest of the constituency or state involved."[32] All this hand-wringing, placating, and obfuscating would only increase the sense of impunity felt by Guatemala's armed forces, diminish the military's respect for U.S. government entreaties to treat human rights more seriously, and augment Jorge Serrano's sense of his own omnipotence. And for victims, something deeply dehumanizing occurs when perpetrators of human rights abuse and the governments responsible for them are "protected" in order to sustain political interests.

If only it were all so simple. There was a valid humanitarian reason for the U.S. government not to publicize all of its information about Maritza's experience: her captors had threatened to harm her family if Maritza broke the "agreement" made at the time of her release. It was reasonable, therefore, *not* to speak out in order to protect the security of Maritza's family.[33]

That rationale ended, however, about a week after the U.S. Embassy sent the "protect them from themselves" memorandum to State Department headquarters. In late September Maritza appeared before the Inter-American Human Rights Commission in Washington, D.C., and provided public testimony about her disappearance and torture. The event was widely covered in the Guatemalan media, and Ambassador Stroock was asked to comment about it. It was an internal matter for Guatemala, Stroock reportedly observed, so he shouldn't give an opinion.[34] Stroock believed that the U.S. Embassy's "actions spoke louder than any words and further quotations from me would only annoy Serrano, Menéndez and many others in the Guatemalan government."[35] Gone was the lofty rhetoric about capturing "the vile and cowardly criminals"[36] that had set the tone for the early part of his tenure.

But no individual or institution could effectively claim the moral high ground in Maritza's case. The Catholic Church, with all of its liberation theology rhetoric about "speaking truth to power" and providing a voice to those who have no voice, never publicly denounced the Guatemalan army for its conduct. The ODHA was concerned about the security of its staff and, understandably, chose not to provoke the army. Church workers did not want to tell the full story of Maritza's experience, "and in fact," Juan Luis Font observed, "they *never* finished telling the story."[37] Nor do I reveal all of the available details in this book since the individuals responsible for Maritza's disappearance and torture are still at large.

This silence in the face of cruelty and injustice, even when born from benevolent intentions, exacts a toll on the victims and their society. Without an acknowledgement of the truth of the victim's experience, the world of the victim can never be completely restored. Without punishment of perpetrators, the universe of the torturers remains powerful and immune. Primo Levi described this pain-inducing silence in the context of Nazi Germany in his classic work *The Drowned and the Saved:*

> The ocean of pain, past and present, surrounded us, and its level rose from year to year until it almost submerged us. It was useless to close one's eyes or turn one's back to it because it was all around, in every direction, all the way to the horizon. . . . Never again could it be cleansed; it would prove that man, the human species—we, in short—had the potential to construct an infinite enormity of pain, and that pain is the only force created from nothing, without cost and without effort. It is enough not to see, not to listen, not to act.[38]

In late October 1992 the Guatemalan government reportedly formed a secret "security council" tasked with neutralizing perceived enemies on human rights issues.[39] It included the defense minister, the ministers of interior and foreign relations, as well as the director of Jorge Serrano's Presidential Human Rights Commission, Bernardo Neumann. This new body planned to develop a global strategy for restraining critics of the Guatemalan government.

Serrano later bitterly complained to U.S. State Department representatives that "a few unscrupulous human rights activists" were orchestrating a campaign to denigrate his government and the Guatemalan army with "falsehoods and exaggerations." Serrano's government, he explained, as well as the army, had made great strides in ending impunity and instilling respect for human rights. It was outrageous that people would hurl unfounded charges against the army without taking responsibility for their actions. The army was a proud institution, Serrano insisted, and as president, he could no longer permit such "malicious conduct" to go unchallenged. "I can't let them continue to batter the military incessantly with these lies! I have to hit back and I'm going to do it!"[40]

On November 11 Serrano hit back. The defense minister publicly accused Ronalth Ochaeta, the ODHA, and several other Guatemalan human rights activists of working in tandem with URNG.[41] No accusation was more dangerous in Guatemala, and for Ochaeta, who had labored long and hard to shield himself and the ODHA from these kinds of threats, it was a personal failure. He sank into depression. Now he too would have to leave Guatemala.

That same month senior Guatemalan army officers informed the Central Intelligence Agency that relations between Guatemala and the United States were at their lowest point in ten years as a consequence of the U.S. government's issuance of a tourist visa to Maritza.[42] Subsequently, in early March 1993, the United States government sponsored a "crisis management" course in a large hotel in Houston, Texas. Students came from all over Latin America. Francisco Perdomo, Guatemala's interior minister attended, as did a number of high-ranking Guatemalan army officers. A majority of the lectures addressed how to deal with kidnappings.[43]

In May President Jorge Serrano was forced from office and into exile. Nearly drowning under the weight of his own hubris and corruption within his government, Serrano had attempted to dissolve the constitution, Congress, and the supreme court and impose authoritarian powers. Member states of the international community, particularly the United States government, forcefully opposed Serrano's attempted coup as a grave threat to Guatemala's democracy, and to business. As Bernard Aronson, who was responsible for State Department policy toward Latin America, noted, "We convinced the business community in Guatemala that they'd suffer seriously if the coup went forward. Not only would all aid be suspended, but [also] trading privileges into the U.S. market, which was important to them."[44]

Thus forewarned, Guatemala's economic elite refused to support Serrano's actions. U.S. government representatives also warned the Guatemalan military that the armed forces would be totally isolated if they supported the coup.[45] Consequently, many army officers also opposed Serrano's power grab and insisted that Serrano resign and Guatemala's constitutional court form a new, democratic government.[46] Serrano fled to Panama, and the Congress elected Ramiro de León Carpio, the human rights ombudsman, as Guatemala's new president.

Maritza lived in exile in Mexico City until early 1997 while Guatemala's armed conflict sputtered to an end as the government and URNG edged closer to a final peace agreement. But the conditions of poverty and misery that catalyzed the early reforms of the Guatemalan Revolution and provoked the armed conflict remained essentially the same. In areas like El Quiché, where Maritza's revolutionary organization began its work during the early 1970s, and where the Catholic Church introduced liberation theology during the same period, many Mayan peasants still lived in feudal circumstances. Health care was inaccessible to the majority of the population, malnutrition was rampant, and illiteracy was the norm. In some areas, nearly 90 percent of women could not read or write.

Of course, these communities were the fortunate ones. They had survived the cold war holocaust that swept over them during the 1970s and 1980s, taking so many of their husbands, wives, children, and siblings. Indeed, the Urrutia family was also relatively lucky since Maritza survived her ordeal.

Nearly three years after Maritza disappeared, U.S. Defense Department representatives reported that "human rights violations continue, indicating that the military still acts with impunity and is 'above the law.'"[47] In 1995 the U.S. government acknowledged that Colonel Julio Alpírez, an army officer accused of complicity in the murder of U.S. citizen Michael DeVine, as well as a captured rebel *comandante,* was actually on the CIA's payroll.[48] The resulting scandal precipitated a series of U.S. government actions, from a governmentwide review of existing intelligence bearing on the torture, disappearance, or death of U.S. citizens in Guatemala, to the declassification of government documents pertaining to Guatemala.[49] John Deutch, then the director of the CIA, disciplined a number of officers for shielding suspect agents and stifling reports of human rights abuses in Guatemala.[50]

Media coverage of the "American connection" to the Alpirez affair broke the silence about impunity in Guatemala. But there's the rub. The publicity shows another dehumanizing aspect of torture in the modern world. Torture provokes a scandal in the American media when the torturers are citizens or agents of Western, developed nations such as the United States.[51] The long-standing use of torture by Guatemalans, Egyptians, Pakistanis, or other distant peoples is somehow more "normal," more "acceptable," less appalling, and easier to ignore. But American exceptionalism implodes when *we* are the perpetrators, as the recent publicity about torture of prisoners in Guantánamo Bay, Afghanistan, and Iraq's Abu Ghraib prison illustrates.[52] The war against international terrorism has unleashed another form of terror: government policies that encourage and condone the kinds of torture used against Maritza.[53] Each of our worlds, all of our humanity, is diminished.

I continue to wish for a day when there is no more painful silence; when no government sanctions the use of torture or disappearance. Perhaps this too is a bit naive. But Maritza is alive, and I can still dream.

EPILOGUE

In March 2005 Donald Rumsfeld, the U.S. secretary of defense, announced that the United States would lift its ban on military assistance to Guatemala following efforts by the government of Guatemala to reform its armed forces.[1] In November 2005 U.S. Drug Enforcement Agency agents lured the chief of the Guatemalan government's Anti-Narcotics Analysis and Information Service (Guatemala's top antidrug officer) and two of his closest subordinates to Virginia, where the three antinarcotics officials were arrested and charged with crimes related to drug trafficking.[2]

Ambassador Tom Stroock left Guatemala in late 1992 and returned to his Wyoming oil business. Mentally and emotionally drained by his experience in Guatemala, Stroock decided to refocus his public service activities only on local and state affairs.[3] The University of Wyoming appointed Stroock Professor of Public Diplomacy. Stroock chaired the university's International Fellowship Scholarship and Exchange Program and Wyoming's Health Reform Commission, and he became a trustee of the Nature Conservancy. Stroock also served five years a member of the advisory board of the U.S. Commission on Civil Rights and supervised the construction of a $50-million addition to the public hospital in Casper, Wyoming.

Dispirited by budget cuts and falling morale within the State Department, Sue Patterson retired in 1997 after twenty three years in the foreign service. Today Patterson lives in Guatemala, where she administers reproductive health programs for poor communities.

Ronalth Ochaeta spent eighteen months studying in the United States before returning to Guatemala in 1994. Threats against his family forced Ochaeta into exile once again in 1999. Today he works for the Organization of American States in Peru. Fernando López is currently the legal director of the Center for Human Rights Legal Action in Guatemala City.

Edmundo René Urrutia spent several years in the United States, where he and Kappy Riker married and had a daughter. But the couple divorced in 1995, when Edmundo René returned to Guatemala. Today he serves as Guatemala's ambassador to the United Kingdom.

Jacobo Árbenz also came home in 1995. The remains of the deposed president were returned to Guatemala for burial with honors on October 20, the anniversary of the 1944 revolution. Followed by hundreds of students from USAC, a horse-drawn carriage bearing Árbenz's casket passed from the airport, down the broad Avenida Reforma, to the National Palace. "Murderers!" shouted the students as the procession passed the U.S. Embassy. "Assassins!"[4]

After Jorge Serrano was forced to step down as president of Guatemala, the Congress selected Ramiro de León Carpio to finish Serrano's term of office. De León Carpio served as president of Guatemala until early 1996. He died in Miami, Florida, in 2002 at the age of sixty.

Manuel Conde served for five months in the new administration of de León Carpio. When he left the government, Conde became the president of the Peace Commission of the Central American Parliament. For several years, he worked as an advisor to the government of Colombia on the peace process in that country and later founded the Central American Forum for Political Dialogue.[5] Conde ran unsuccessfully for president of Guatemala in 2003. Currently the secretary general of the Democratic Union Party, he will probably run for president again in 2007.

Neither the efforts of the participants in the peace process, nor the many progressive articles in the peace accords themselves could heal the polarization of Guatemalan society after three decades of war. To this day Manuel Conde's mother, Sonia Orellana, keeps a tall bust of her hero and liberator, Colonel Carlos Castillo Armas, in her dining room. "It wasn't a misguided cause. . . . If we hadn't rescued the country from the Árbenz regime, here we'd be like Cuba. The same or worse."[6] On the other side of Guatemala City Maritza's father, Edmundo, keeps a photo of *his* hero, President Jacobo Árbenz, taped on the wall by his bed.

Disgraced and exiled after his coup failed in 1993, Jorge Serrano began to develop the Hacienda Country Club, a new resort for wealthy Panamanians. Serrano lived with his wife, mother, and five children in a spacious and luxurious hilltop apartment with a gorgeous view of Panama City below. On evenings with good weather Serrano would sit on the balcony with his family and friends, sipping drinks and smoking cigars, and dominating discussions about Guatemalan politics and social affairs: tax reform, land reform, violence, and crime. In 1998, six years after the events, Serrano still became exercised about Maritza's case: "Why did they give us guarantees that she wasn't going to speak in the United States, and the first thing that she does is *speak!?* Why did they come and say, 'She's not going to speak. This case is already clarified. Here nothing happened. Nothing happened. Nothing happened.' Pah! And the first thing they do is make a big scandal outside the country!"

"In Guatemala, perception is the important thing, not reality," Serrano explained to me. "In my time there was no violence. There were no kidnappings."[7]

Msgr. Juan Gerardi, the auxiliary bishop of Guatemala and the ODHA's coordinator, tried to break through Guatemala's wall of silence and misperception. In April 1998 he presented a comprehensive study of human rights violations committed during Guatemala's long civil war.[8] The report was the result of nearly six thousand interviews with victims and perpetrators of the violence. The majority of the cases were attributed to the Guatemalan army, and the report, for the first time, published the names of many individuals responsible for war crimes.

Two days after Bishop Gerardi introduced the study, someone beat him to death inside his parish home, just a few blocks from the archbishopric where Maritza sought shelter in 1992.[9] The killer or killers (still unknown) used a cement block to smash every bone in Gerardi's face. Juan Gerardi gave more than fifty years of his life and eventually his life itself, trying to reduce human suffering and end the silence in Guatemala.

In 2001 a court convicted three members of the Guatemalan army—two active and one retired—as well as a Catholic priest (the brother of Father Sergio Orantes) for complicity in Msgr. Gerardi's murder. At the trial of the accused, another bishop reflected on the impact of the killing: "Just when we thought we'd recovered an environment that made it possible to live in peace, they answered: Here, take your dead man, who tried to discover the truth."[10]

Saddened and in failing health after the death of his close friend Juan Gerardi, Msgr. Próspero Penados retired as archbishop of Guatemala in 2001. He died in May 2005 at the age of seventy-nine. Father Sergio Orantes became the rector of the archdiocese's Colegio de los Infantes in 1992. Orantes left that post, and Guatemala, four years later after allegations of his financial and sexual misconduct at the school arose.[11]

Bill Robinson now teaches sociology at the University of California at Santa Barbara. Today Carlos Salinas is self-employed and spends a lot of time with his two small children. Salinas is a vocalist in a punk rock band and is making a film about pedophilia. Bonnie Tenneriello left WOLA to study law at the University of Michigan. Eventually moving to Massachusetts, Tenneriello now does civil rights litigation on behalf of prisoners. She and her husband adopted a baby boy from Guatemala.

After fleeing Guatemala in 1992, Maritza Urrutia and her son lived in exile in Mexico City for four years. The government and URNG signed a final peace agreement in late 1996, permitting Maritza and Sebastián to return to Guatemala in 1997. When she wasn't raising her son, Maritza organized women's groups in the grimy shantytowns that line the ravines on the outskirts of Guatemala City. After Maritza suggested that we become romantically involved, I reacted in my typical, earnest way. That would be highly improper, I insisted, and a violation of my professional ethical obligations in attorney-client relationships. "Plus, you were a *guerrillera*." Fortunately, Maritza fought as hard for love as she did for life, and we were married in 1999.

In 2003, after many years of litigation, the Inter-American Court of Human Rights ruled that the state of Guatemala had violated Maritza's rights to liberty, personal integrity, and judicial protection when members of the army disappeared her in 1992.[12]

The street known as La Castellana where the Urrutias lived during the 1940s and 1950s is still unpaved, rutted, and muddy during the rainy Guatemalan winter. It was a mostly middle-class neighborhood in 1944 when the revolution began, but the last few decades have brought waves of poor Mayan families to the area, fleeing the violence and misery in the countryside. Now a crowded shantytown of simple tin-roofed shacks covers the field below the old Urrutia house, sheltering the next generation of desperate and dispossessed. As bronze-skinned children play soccer in the street in front of the house, you can smell the smoke from the wood fires rising from the hovels below. For years gang graffiti have covered the wall where right-wing activists painted "Communists" in 1954.

One day in 1996 I sat down on a park bench in Guatemala City with Laura Aldana de Pineda, Ester de Urrutia's old colleague from their days in the Guatemalan Women's Alliance. Laura was nearly eighty-eight and very thin, with her white hair pulled back into a bun. She spent most of her days at a municipal center for senior citizens and, true to form, had all of the retirees organized. Her bright blue eyes were still sharp as she told me about Maritza's grandmother: "She was a revolutionary!" And Laura talked about how she and Ester used to work together promoting the rights of women in Guatemala, and how Laura tried to continue their revolutionary work after the fall of Jacobo Árbenz in 1954. She spoke about the many friends who did not survive the years of violence and counterinsurgency. "You see how many people were disappeared! Tons! All of the members of PGT were disappeared."

Just before our conversation ended, Laura described how three of her six children *are* disappeared": her oldest son, José Humberto, since 1966, Luis Arturo since 1976, and her daughter Rita since 1985. Laura very carefully used the present tense because she was not sure what happened to them. I asked her how she had survived so much trauma. She answered calmly, without a tear or a trace of grief or bitterness on her face: "Because I began to think that they had disappeared for their revolutionary struggle, and not because they were outlaws."[13]

While doing research for this book in the archives of the Argentine Embassy in Guatemala City in March 1996, I discovered the letter that Maritza's grandmother Ester sent from Buenos Aires to her daughter Julia in 1954. When I explained to Jorge Taiana, then the Argentine ambassador to Guatemala, that I knew the intended recipient of the letter and that Julia still lived in Guatemala City, Taiana graciously agreed to meet with Julia so that she could finally receive her mother's correspondence.

Several weeks later Julia and I sat in Taiana's office in the embassy. As his secretary retrieved the old file, Julia explained to the ambassador that back in 1954, everyone in her family was a revolutionary. She told him about the fall of Árbenz, when she brought food every morning from the market to the refugees in the embassy, and how her mother, Ester, cooked vegetables specially for a young man they called Che.

Now, more than four decades later, Julia was over seventy. When the ambassador's secretary returned with the file, Julia needed her thick glasses to see her mother's signature below the last few lines of her letter:

> Your father sends Oscar [Julia's brother] much love and regards, with the recommendation that he behave himself and work tenaciously. And that he try not to drink since it hurts him so much and doesn't allow his stomach

ulcer to heal. We congratulate him on the birth of his little girl and take good care of her so that she gets big and healthy.

So my daughter, receive the kisses and blessings of your mother, who loves you a lot and who never forgets you.

Ester[14]

Acknowledgments

The views expressed in this book are my own and do not necessarily reflect the opinion of my employer, the United Nations.

Many friends and colleagues provided support and advice during the years that I spent researching and writing this book. Gil Loescher at the University of Notre Dame and Richard Siegel at the University of Nevada encouraged me to turn my ideas into a written work. Wise teachers, and wiser friends, Gil and Richard pushed me to continue my work during the difficult, early days when producing a book seemed like an impossible task. The late Bill Lewers and Garth Meintjes at the Center for Civil and Human Rights at the University of Notre Dame also provided invaluable kindness and support. Other members of academia—William Robinson at the University of California in Santa Barbara, Beatriz Manz, Eric Stover and Patrick Ball at UC Berkeley, William Stanley at the University of New Mexico, Jennifer Schirmer at Harvard, and Julio Pinto Soria in Guatemala—gave me insights and inspiration. Research for this book was supported by generous grants from the University of Notre Dame and the Open Society Institute.

The staff at the National Archives in Maryland and the Library of Congress in Washington, D.C., assisted me with access to U.S. government documents concerning the overthrow of Jacobo Árbenz in 1954. The personnel at the Freedom of Information Reading Room at the U.S. State

Department headquarters facilitated my research into more recent U.S. policy toward Guatemala.

Representatives of international human rights organizations who labored long and hard to save Maritza Urrutia's life described their work to me and provided valuable perspectives. Anne Manuel and David Holliday from Human Rights Watch/Americas (formerly Americas Watch), Carlos Salinas and Tracy Ulltveit-Moe from Amnesty International, Bonnie Tenneriello and Rachel Garst from the Washington Office for Latin America, Frank LaRue, Anna Gallagher, and Wallie Mason from the Center for Human Rights Legal Action, and the late Dr. Robert Kirschner from Physicians for Human Rights were particularly generous with their time and expertise. Kate Doyle's outstanding work at the National Security Archive made possible the declassification and review of U.S. State Department cables concerning human rights abuses in Guatemala during the 1980s and 1990s. Tim Rieser, from the staff of Senator Patrick Leahy, was instrumental in the declassification of documents pertaining to Maritza Urrutia's case.

In Guatemala, my former colleagues at the Archbishop of Guatemala's Human Rights Office provided me with important insights about Maritza's disappearance: Ronalth Ochaeta, the late Msgr. Próspero Penados del Barrio, Fernando López, Fernando Penados, Claudia González, and Sister Tere Pineda Albizures. The late Msgr. Juan Gerardi Conodera, Father Luis Pérez, Father Sergio Orantes, Father Juan Hernández Pico, Father Axel Mencos, the late Sister Barbara Ford, Sister Raquel Saravia Valdés, and Sister Ana Evelyn Vásquez all described important parts of the Catholic Church's checkered history in Guatemala. Argentina's ambassador to Guatemala in 1995, Jorge Taiana, provided me with access to the Argentine Embassy's archive from the postcoup period in 1954.

A number of U.S. State Department officials shared their recollections and perspectives about Maritza's case and the making of U.S. policy in Guatemala: John Arndt, Bernard Aronson, Robert Blaud, George Chester, James Carroll, Ambassador John Hamilton, Donald Knight, Leonard Kusnitz, Suzanne Patterson, Ambassador Thomas F. Stroock, and Peg Willingham. Mark Kirk, Richard Nuccio, and David Todd also provided important insights about how U.S. foreign policy is made (and unmade) in Washington, D.C., as well as about the Guatemalan peace process.

Two former presidents of Guatemala, Jorge Serrano Elías and the late Ramiro de León Carpio were generous with their time and insights about U.S.-Guatemalan relations. Several former officials from the Serrano administration also granted me interviews: Acisclo Valladares, Francisco

Perdomo, Gonzalo Menéndez Park, and Juan Daniel Alemán. Manuel Conde Orellana, Amilcar Burgos, and Héctor Rosada shared their recollections of the Guatemalan peace process, as did Generals Julio Balconi Turcios and Otto Pérez Molina. From the other side of Guatemala's armed conflict, URNG leaders Miguel Ángel Sandoval, Gustavo Meoño, and Olga Pérez as well as other URNG members provided their perspectives about Maritza's disappearance and their efforts to free her.

A number of Guatemalan journalists had important roles in the events of this book and I am grateful to Juan Luis Font, Haroldo Shetemul, Iduvina Hernández, Carmen Aída Ibarra, and Rony Véliz Samayoa for sharing their experiences with me. Congressman Edmundo Mulet, Judge Leticia Secaira, and former adjunct human rights ombudsperson María Eugenia de Sierra were also very helpful.

I am indebted to all the members of the Urrutia family, particularly Edmundo and Pilar, Julia and Ester, Edmundo René and Kappy Riker, who shared their memories of life in Guatemala and in exile from 1944–92, as well as their efforts to assist Maritza. Sonia Orellana viuda de Conde and her sons Manuel and Carlos generously shared their personal files and recollections from the same period. Atala Valenzuela, Concha Deras, the late Laura Aldana, Carlos González, and the late Roberto Paz y Paz described the difficult days before and after the overthrow of Jacobo Árbenz. Julia González and "Patricia" shared their memories of Maritza's youth and early political activities.

Naomi Schneider at UC Press in Berkeley has been patient with me as I struggled to complete this book. Edith Gladstone, Dore Brown, and Chalon Emmons provided valuable editorial assistance. I was very fortunate to receive the support of friends like Frank Smyth in Washington, D.C., Peggy and Carter Twedt, Peter Smith, Patty Cooper Smith, and Harriet Cummings in Carson City, Nevada, Mike Martino, Sheila Leslie, Bob and Emma Fulkerson in Reno, as well as Ana Pérez and Bob Blauner in Berkeley. This is a better book thanks to the critical eyes and reflections of Klara Starr, Susie Kemp, Moya Magilligan, and Carol Buck in The Hague.

Finally, there are no words sufficient to express my gratitude to Maritza and Fernando Sebastián, whose love, patience, and encouragement flow through the pages of this book.

Notes

PREFACE

1. "Día Glorioso del Pueblo," *El Imparcial,* October 21, 1944, 3. All translations from Spanish to English are mine.

2. Edmundo Urrutia, interview by author, July 28, 1996. Except as otherwise noted, interviews took place in Guatemala City. For the vast majority of interviews, I have both tape recordings and handwritten notes.

3. Oscar Urrutia, interview by author, February 26, 1998.

4. "Madrugada de la Libertad," *El Imparcial,* October 21, 1944, 3.

5. Ester Urrutia (Ester de Urrutia's daughter), interview by author, July 28, 1996.

6. "Día Glorioso del Pueblo," 3.

7. Julia Urrutia [de Castellanos], interview by author, August 4, 1996.

8. Edmundo Urrutia, interview, July 31, 1996.

9. Julia Urrutia, interview.

10. Ester de Urrutia, letter to her daughter Julia Urrutia, November 11, 1954, Argentine Embassy file (copy in author's files).

11. My thanks to Carlos Flores for this insight.

CHAPTER 1

Part epigraph: from "The Guatemalan Military: What the United States Files Reveal," a report compiled by the National Security Archive, released in Guatemala City, Guatemala, June 1, 2000, vol. 2, doc. 34, par. 6.

1. Diana, interview by author, July 28, 1996.

2. Maritza Urrutia, declaration submitted to the Inter-American Human Rights Commission, Washington, D.C., February 24, 1993 (hereafter cited as declaration), 2.

3. Sonia Orellana viuda de Conde, interview by author, August 3, 1996.

4. Ibid. The CIA agent in charge of logistics for the operation was Robert K. "Bob" Davis. As the CIA station chief in Guatemala during 1960–61, Davis organized the training of Cuban exiles who participated in the ill-fated Bay of Pigs invasion in April 1961. Peter Wyden, *Bay of Pigs: The Untold Story* (New York: Simon and Schuster, 1979), 34–35, 37, 38, 51–53. The CIA operation's base was in Opa Locka, Florida. United Nations Office for Project Services (UNOPS), *Guatemala: Memória del Silencio,* Informe de la Comisión para el Esclarecimiento Histórico (Guatemala City, 1999), chap. 1, par. 306.

5. Radio script for Sonia Orellana and Enrique Coronado, early 1954, Conde family archive (copy in author's files).

6. Telegram to the Secretario General de la Presidencia, Secretario Privado de la Presidencia, by Eugénio Girón, José Ignacio Salán, Alfredo Arana, Rubén Castellanos Fuentes, San Marcos, May 3, 1954, Guatemalan Transcripts s.s., Support of Guatemala Government, box 5, Manuscript Division, Library of Congress; also see UNOPS, *Guatemala: Memória del Silencio,* chap. 1, par. 308.

7. Radio script, Orellana and Coronado.

8. Ibid.

9. Headquarters Operation Success, secret cables to Director CIA, 0337Z, April 6, and 0227Z, May 11, 1954; secret cable to Acting Chief of Station, Guatemala City, May 26, 1954, Studies and Other Records Relating to the Activities of the Central Intelligence Agency in Guatemala, 1952–1954, reference set, declassified NND974350, RG#263 (hereafter cited as CIA in Guatemala, 1952–54), National Archives (copy in author's files).

10. CIA memorandum, February 10, 1954, box 1, CIA in Guatemala, 1952–54.

11. "In Guatemala as Well, the Church Is a Bastion against Marxism," read a February 1952 headline in the Church's bimonthly newspaper (*Verbum,* February 24, 1952, no. 455). That same year, Archbishop Rossell publicly singled out Ester de Urrutia's Guatemalan Women's Alliance as he called on all Catholics "to reject as totally Communist, atheist, anticatholic and at least anti-Guatemalan, all the forms in which the Communist, pseudo-Communist, and philo-Communist organizations, such as the *Alianza Feminina Guatemalteca,* et cetera, use the Holy Father's words in support of the 'Pro Soviet Peace' political campaign." Msgr. Mariano Rossell Arellano, *Declaraciones al Pueblo Católico,* Guatemala de la Asunción, May 23, 1952, Conde family archive (copy in author's files).

12. Concha Deras, interview by author, June 15, 1996; and relative of Msgr. Mariano Rossell (name withheld at source's request), interview by author, August 11, 1996.

13. *La Opinión,* November 22, 1952, no. 8.

14. "La Muerte de Oscar Conde," *La Hora Dominical,* January 31, 1960, 13, 20.

15. CIA memorandum, February 10, 1954, box 1; secret CIA memorandum for the record, September 8, 1953, box 1; and Chief of Station, Guatemala, secret report to Headquarters Operation Success, May 28, 1954, box 2, CIA in Guatemala, 1952–54.

16. Guatemalan Embassy in Tegucigalpa, confidential memorandum to Guillermo Toriello, Minister of Foreign Relations, June 9, 1954, p. 3, Guatemalan Transcripts s.s., box 1, Manuscript Division, Library of Congress.

17. Top secret CIA report, RYBAT PBSUCCESS, pp. 10–11, box 1, CIA in Guatemala, 1952–54.

18. Headquarters Operation Success, secret cable to CIA Director, 2134Z, June 14, 1954, box 2, CIA in Guatemala, 1952–54.

19. Nicholas Cullather, *Operation PBSUCCESS: The United States and Guatemala, 1952–1954* (Washington, D.C.: History Staff, Center for the Study of Intelligence, CIA, 1994), 57.

20. Headquarters Operation Success, secret cables 1957Z and 1625Z, June 18, 1954, box 2, CIA in Guatemala, 1952–54.

21. Sonia Orellana v. de Conde, interview, August 9, 1996. "The moment of decision is here. Fight today, or you will weep tomorrow for having missed the opportunity to fight for your country" (June 18, 1954, cassette 170, Sherwood Tapes, PBSUCCESS, box 2, CIA in Guatemala, 1952–54).

22. The *Voice of Liberation* continued to broadcast propaganda until early July 1954. Secret CIA classified messages, 0551Z, 22 June and 2251Z, 23 June 1954, box 2, CIA in Guatemala, 1952–54. And see Cullather, *Operation PBSUCCESS,* 103.

23. Maritza Urrutia, declaration, 2.

24. Ibid., 3.

25. Ibid., 4.

26. Coroncho, former specialist, Guatemalan army intelligence, interview by author, June 13, 1996.

27. Maritza Urrutia, interview by author, June 26, 1995, Mexico City.

28. Ibid.

29. Maritza Urrutia, declaration, 4.

30. Maritza Urrutia, interview, June 26, 1995.

31. Maritza Urrutia, declaration, 4.

32. Ibid., 5.

33. Ibid., 6.

34. Maritza Urrutia, interview, January 12, 1995.

35. Ibid.; Maritza Urrutia, declaration, 6.

36. Maritza Urrutia, interview, January 12, 1995.

37. Ibid.

38. *The Black Book of Communism in Guatemala* (Mexico City: Permanent Commission of the First Congress against Soviet Intervention in Latin America, 1954), 22; Julia Urrutia [de Castellanos], interview by author, August 14, 1995.

39. Atala Valenzuela [de Marroquín], interview by author, June 19, 1996.

40. Carlos González Orellana, interview by author, August 1, 1996.

41. Edmundo Urrutia, interview by author, July 1, 1995.

42. Julia Urrutia, interview, August 14, 1995.

43. Ibid.; Edmundo René Urrutia, interview by author, December 20, 1994, Cleveland, OH; Maritza Urrutia, interview, January 10, 1995; Edmundo Urrutia, interview.

44. For a thorough discussion of Árbenz's agrarian reform efforts, see Piero Gleijes, *Shattered Hope: The Guatemalan Revolution and the United States, 1944–1954* (Princeton: Princeton University Press, 1991).

45. Roberto Paz y Paz, interview by author, June 14, 1996.

46. Atala Valenzuela, interview.

47. Moisés Hernández of Villa Canales and Secretary General of CGTG in Guatemala, exchange of telegrams, June 20 and 21, 1954, Guatemalan Transcripts s.s., Support of Guatemalan Government, box 5, Manuscript Division, Library of Congress.

48. Carlos Torres Gigena, Argentine Embassy Trade Officer, Guatemala, memorandum to Dr. Jerónimo Remorino, Buenos Aires, July 6, 1954, pp. 7–8, Argentine Embassy file, Guatemala City (copy in author's files).

49. Frank G. Wisner, Deputy Director, Planning, secret cable to Director CIA, 2251Z, June 27, 1954, box 1, CIA in Guatemala, 1952–54.

50. "Texto del Acta Levantada por la Junta al Ser Elegido el Coronel Castillo Armas," *Nuestro Diario,* July 9, 1954. Earlier, on June 28, the *Voice of Liberation* had called for "justice, justice, justice, and punishment as well" (June 28, 1954, cassette 241, Sherwood Tapes, box 2, CIA in Guatemala, 1952–54).

51. "Afectos al Regimen Pasado Se Asilan en las Legaciones," *El Imparcial,* June 30, 1954, 1.

52. José de Atitlán, *Guatemala: Junio de 1954, Relato de la Invasión, de la Caída de Árbenz y de la Resistencia Popular* (Buenos Aires: Editorial Fundamento, 1955), 44.

53. Edmundo Urrutia, interview.

54. Secret CIA cable WASH 24629, from OPC/OSO, 1938Z, January 26, 1952; secret CIA memorandum for the record, September 8, 1953; CIA memorandum, March 31, 1954, To: All Staff Officers, from C/[ ], "Selection of Individuals for Disposal by Junta Group," box 1, CIA in Guatemala, 1952–54.

55. *Black Book of Communism,* 22–23.

56. Sonia Orellana v. de Conde, interview, August 9, 1996.

57. Julia Urrutia, interview, December 9, 1995.

58. Ibid.

59. Carlos Torres Gigena, cable to Jerónimo Remorino, 4.

60. Maritza Urrutia, interview, January 10, 1995; Gleijes, *Shattered Hope,* 372.

61. Edmundo Urrutia, interview.

62. Julia Urrutia, interview, March 19, 1996.

63. Víctor Manuel Gutiérrez and Max González, letter to José Luis del Cid, Argentine Embassy file (copy in author's files).

64. Víctor Manuel Valdés Díaz, letter to the Ambassador of the Republic of Argentina in Guatemala, August 5, 1954, Argentine Embassy file (copy in author's files).

65. "Activistas del Partido Comunista," list on file in Argentine Embassy (copy in author's files).

66. María Isabel Grijalba viuda de Alvarado, letter to the Honorable Ambassador of the Republic of Argentina, August 18, 1954, Argentine Embassy file (copy in author's files).

67. Julia Urrutia, interview, March 19, 1996.

68. Argentine Embassy file (copy in author's files).

69. Director CIA, secret cables to unknown, 1942Z, July 9, Dir 0891 and 0010Z, July 20, 1954, Dir 09574, p. 2; and Director CIA, secret cable to Chief of Station, Guatemala, 2330Z, July 9, 1954, Dir 08428, box 2, CIA in Guatemala, 1952–54.

70. List of refugees in Argentine Embassy and family members, Argentine Embassy file (copy in author's files).

71. Stephen Schlesinger and Stephen Kinzer, *Bitter Fruit: The Untold Story of the American Coup in Guatemala* (New York: Anchor Books, 1990), 184.

72. Letter from Ester de Urrutia to her daughter, Julia Urrutia, November 11, 1954, Argentine Embassy file (copy in author's files).

73. Roberto Paz y Paz, interview.

74. Laura Aldana [de Pineda], interview by author, June 1, 1996.

75. Edmundo Urrutia, interview.

76. Julia Urrutia, interviews, August 14, 1995, and December 9, 1995.

CHAPTER 2

1. Maritza Urrutia, declaration submitted to the Inter-American Human Rights Commission, Washington, D.C., February 24 (hereafter cited as declaration), 1993, 6.

2. Ibid., 7.

3. Ibid.

4. The G-2 is also known as the D-2. For a review of the intelligence services that operated in Guatemala during the armed conflict, see Oficina de Derechos Humanos del Arzobispado de Guatemala (ODHA), *Los Mecanismos del Horror*, vol. 2 of *Guatemala: Nunca Más*, Informe Proyecto Interdiocesano de Recuperación de la Memória Histórica (Guatemala City, 1998), 65–111; and United Nations Office for Project Services (UNOPS), *Guatemala: Memória del Silencio*, Informe de la Comisión para el Esclarecimiento Histórico (Guatemala City, 1999), chap. 2, pars. 945–1157. Maritza Urrutia's disappearance, detention, and torture in the Island are described in chap. 2, pars. 1009 and 1115–26, and in the UN report's vol. 6, Annex 1, "Casos Illustrativos," no. 33, 245–50.

5. ODHA, *Mecanismos del Horror*, 72, 89.

6. Coroncho, former specialist, Guatemalan army intelligence, interview by author, June 13, 1996; "Egidio," former member, Guatemalan army intelligence, interview by author, December 20, 1998.

7. Egidio, interview.

8. Coroncho, interview.

9. Ibid.

10. Maritza Urrutia, declaration, 8.

11. Maritza Urrutia, interview by author, January 12, 1995, Mexico City.

12. Maritza Urrutia, declaration, 8; Edmundo René Urrutia, interview by author, July 24, 1992, ODHA.

13. Coroncho, interview.

14. Ibid.

15. Maritza Urrutia, interview, January 13, 1995; declaration, 9.

16. Piero Gleijes, *Shattered Hope: The Guatemalan Revolution and the United States, 1944–1954* (Princeton: Princeton University Press, 1991), 388–89.

17. Julia Urrutia [de Castellanos], interview by author, December 9, 1995.

18. See Régis Debray, *The Revolution on Trial* (Harmondsworth: Penguin Books, 1974), 299; George Black, *Garrison Guatemala* (New York: Monthly Review Press, 1984), 66–67; Concerned Guatemala Scholars, *Guatemala: Dare to Struggle, Dare to Win* (Brooklyn, 1982), 40 (copy in author's files).

19. "Fechas Importantes del Enfrentamiento Armado Guatemalteco," *Infopress Centroamericana,* no. 1169, March 28, 1996, 2.

20. Edmundo René Urrutia, interview by author, December 20, 1994, Cleveland.

21. Edmundo Urrutia, interview by author, July 1, 1995.

22. Carolina Urrutia, interview by author, July 1, 1995.

23. Julia Urrutia, interview; Gleijes, *Shattered Hope,* 388.

24. Ester Urrutia (Ester de Urrutia's daughter), interview by author, July 21, 1996.

25. Edmundo René Urrutia, interview.

26. Ibid.

27. Ibid.

28. Ibid. For a description of one such urban counterinsurgency operation, see CIA secret report, "Guatemalan Security Forces Kill Four," February 1968, in "The Guatemalan Military: What the United States Files Reveal," a report compiled by the National Security Archive, released in Guatemala City, Guatemala, June 1, 2000, vol. 2, doc. 7.

29. Edmundo René Urrutia, interview.

30. Ibid.; Katharine Riker, interview by author, December 21, 1994, Cleveland, OH.

31. Informe GUA-168–92/P, Human Rights Ombudsman's file (copy in author's files).

32. Diana, interview by author, July 28, 1996.

33. Edmundo Urrutia, interview, January 28, 1996.

34. Employee of Walt Disney Nursery School (name withheld by request), interview by author, July 23, 1996.

35. Edmundo Urrutia, interview, January 28, 1996.

36. See Julio César Macías, "Los Crater," in *Mi Camino: La Guerrilla* (Mexico City: Editorial Planeta Mexicana, 1998), 161–63.

37. Gustavo Meoño, interview by author, April 13, 1998.

38. Ibid., and Maritza Urrutia, interview, January 11, 1995.

39. Edmundo René Urrutia, interview.

40. "Hombres Fuertamente Armados Secuestran a Dama de 33 Años," *La Hora,* July 24, 1992, 2.

41. Edmundo Urrutia, interview, May 11, 1996.

42. Ibid.
43. Katharine Riker, interview.

CHAPTER 3

1. Maritza Urrutia, declaration submitted to the Inter-American Human Rights Commission, Washington, D.C., February 24, 1993, 9.
2. Ibid.
3. Ibid, 10.
4. Ibid.
5. Ibid.
6. Ibid.
7. Decreto 38–88 del Congreso de la República de Guatemala.
8. Maritza Urrutia, declaration, 11.
9. Coroncho, former specialist, Guatemalan army intelligence, interview by author, June 15, 1996.
10. Maritza Urrutia, declaration, 11.
11. Edmundo René Urrutia, interview by author, December 20, 1994, Cleveland.
12. Ibid.
13. Carolina Urrutia, interview by author, July 1, 1995.
14. Maritza Urrutia, interview by author, January 12, 1995, Mexico City.
15. Notes from author's interview with Edmundo René Urrutia, July 24, 1992, ODHA file (copy in author's files).
16. Ibid.
17. Edmundo René Urrutia, interview, December 20, 1994.
18. Ibid.
19. "Acción Urgente," July 24, 1992, ODHA file (copy in author's files).
20. Edmundo René Urrutia, interview, December 20, 1994; Katharine Riker, interview by author, December 21, 1994.
21. Edmundo René Urrutia, interview, December 20, 1994.
22. Carlos Barrientos Aragón, interview by author, February 20, 1998.
23. Ibid.
24. Maritza Urrutia, declaration, 12.
25. Ibid.
26. Ibid., 13.
27. Ibid.
28. William Robinson, telephone interview by author, January 23, 2005.
29. William Robinson, telephone interview, December 30, 1994.
30. Ibid.
31. William Robinson, interview, May 30, 1995, Albuquerque, NM.
32. E-mail messages from William D. Stanley to author, March 1 and 5, 1995.
33. Ibid., March 5, 1995.
34. Ibid.
35. William Robinson, telephone interview, December 30, 1994.

36. Patricia, interview by author, June 9, 1996.

37. Ibid.

38. Maritza Urrutia, interview, January 10, 1995.

39. Laura Aldana [de Pineda], interview by author, July 18, 1996. In March 1966 Laura Aldana's oldest son, Humberto Pineda Aldana, then a PGT leader, was part of a group of twenty-eight captured and disappeared by the Guatemalan security forces. The victims were reportedly executed and their bodies dropped into the Pacific Ocean. Greg Grandin, *The Last Colonial Massacre: Latin America in the Cold War* (Chicago: University of Chicago Press, 2004), 47–48; Miguel Ángel Sandoval, *Los Años de la Resistencia: Relatos Sobre las Guerrillas Urbanas de los Años 60* (Guatemala City: Editorial Óscar de León Palacios, 1998), 27–28, 50, 172–74. In a desperate plan to win the release of their comrades, members of the FAR subsequently kidnapped the president of Guatemala's Supreme Court, the president of Congress, and the private secretary of the president of the republic, in the hope of exchanging these figures for twenty-eight disappeared. The plan failed after the president of Congress managed to escape and a commander of the urban guerrillas was captured by the authorities. Ibid., 27–50; see also Julio César Macías, *Mi Camino: La Guerrilla* (Mexico City: Editorial Planeta Mexicana, 1998), 120–22.

40. Maritza Urrutia, interview, January 10, 1995.

41. Ibid.

42. Susanne Jonas, *The Battle for Guatemala: Rebels, Death Squads and U.S. Power* (Boulder: Westview Press, 1991), 137; Michael McClintock, *The American Connection: State Terror and Popular Resistance in Guatemala* (London: Zed Books, 1987), 153.

43. Jonas, *Battle for Guatemala*, 137.

44. McClintock, *American Connection*, 153.

45. Unidad Revolucionaria Nacional Guatemalteca (URNG), *Guatemala: The People Unite! Unitary Statement from the Guatemalan National Revolutionary Unity* (San Francisco: Solidarity Publications, January 1982), 3.

46. Anna Vinegrad, "From Guerrillas to Politicians: The Transition of the Guatemalan Revolutionary Movement in Historical and Comparative Perspective," in *Guatemala After the Peace Accords*, ed. Rachel Sieder (London: Institute of Latin American Studies, 1998), 217–18.

47. Sandoval, *Años de la Resistencia*, 74.

48. Maritza Urrutia, interview, June 26, 1995.

49. Julia González, interview by author, May 31, 1996.

50. Maritza Urrutia, interview, January 10, 1995.

51. "Maritza never changed politically." Edmundo René Urrutia, interview, December 20, 1994.

52. Maritza Urrutia, interview, January 10, 1995.

53. According to the EGP's philosophy and strategy, "Hay que ganarle el corazón para la revolución." Ibid.

54. Edmundo René Urrutia, interview, December 20, 1994.

55. Ibid.

56. Ibid.

57. Maritza Urrutia, interview, January 10, 1995.

CHAPTER 4

1. Maritza Urrutia, declaration submitted to the Inter-American Human Rights Commission, Washington, D.C, February 24, 1993 (hereafter cited as declaration), 99.

2. Maritza Urrutia, interview by author, January 12, 1995, Mexico City.

3. Ibid.

4. Ibid.

5. "Disappeared in Guatemala: The Case of Efraín Bámaca Vélasquez," *Human Rights Watch/Americas* 7, no. 1 (March 1995): 2.

6. CIA secret report, "Guatemala's Disappeared 1977–86," March 28, 1986, 4, reprinted in "The Guatemalan Military: What the United States Files Reveal," a report compiled by the National Security Archive, released in Guatemala City, Guatemala, June 1, 2000, vol. 2, doc. 30.

7. "Case of Efraín Bámaca Vélasquez."

8. Edmundo Urrutia, interview by author, July 28, 1996; United Nations Centre for Human Rights, *Enforced or Involuntary Disappearance,* Human Rights Fact Sheet, no. 6 (Geneva, 1989), 3.

9. Gabriela Escobar Urrutia, interview by author, May 1, 1996.

10. Carolina Urrutia, interview by author, August 1996.

11. Thanks to Demetria Martínez, author of *Mother Tongue* (New York: One World, 1996), for this insight.

12. ODHA, *Los Mecanismos del Horror,* vol. 2 of *Guatemala: Nunca Más, Informe Proyecto Interdiocesano de Recuperación de la Memória Histórica* (Guatemala City, 1998), 186, 196.

13. "Convention against Torture and Other Cruel, Inhuman or Degrading Treatment or Punishment," Article I, UN General Assembly Resolution 39/46, New York, December 10, 1984.

14. Eric Stover and Elena O. Nightingale, MD, eds., *The Breaking of Bodies and Minds: Torture, Psychiatric Abuse, and the Health Professions* (New York: W. H. Freeman, 1985), 5.

15. Robert Kirschner, MD, director of international programs for Physicians for Human Rights, interview by author, February 27, 1995, South Bend, IN.

16. Coroncho, former specialist, Guatemalan army intelligence, interview by author, June 15, 1996.

17. Elaine Scarry, *The Body in Pain: The Making and Unmaking of the World* (Oxford: Oxford University Press, 1985), 35, 50.

18. Robert Kirschner, interview.

19. Scarry, *Body in Pain,* 36.

20. Lawrence Weschler, *A Miracle, a Universe: Settling Accounts with Torturers* (Chicago: University of Chicago Press, 1990), 246.

21. Egidio, former member, Guatemalan army intelligence, interview by author, December 30, 1998.

22. Coroncho, interview, June 13, 1996.

23. Frank LaRue, interview by author, March 19, 1996.

24. Edmundo René Urrutia, interview by author, May 11, 1996.

25. Frank LaRue, interview.

26. Her office is presently called Human Rights Watch/Americas. Anne Manuel, interview by author, January 26, 1995, Washington, D.C.

27. Ibid.; Bonnie Tenneriello, interview by author, February 11, 1995, Ann Arbor.

28. Fax from Heather Wiley, July 25, 1992, WOLA file (copy in author's files).

29. Lars Schoultz, *Human Rights and United States Policy toward Latin America* (Princeton: Princeton University Press, 1981), 78–79.

30. Bonnie Tenneriello, interview.

31. Copy of letter dated July 28, 1992, addressed to President Jorge Serrano, signed by Senators Harkin, Leahy, Bingaman, and Domenici, WOLA file (copy in author's files).

32. Anne Manuel, interview; Bonnie Tenneriello, interview.

33. Peg Willingham, interview by author, January 26, 1995, Department of State headquarters, Washington, D.C.

34. Mark Kirk, former Special Assistant to Assistant Secretary of State for Inter-American Affairs, interview by author, March 23, 1998, Washington, D.C.

35. Ibid.

36. Ibid.

37. Secretary of State, cable to U.S. Embassy in Guatemala, 481625, December 13, 1992, Department of State, Washington, D.C. (copy in author's files). Nearly all the State Department material I cite subsequently—cables, letters, telegrams—comes from this depository.

38. See Jorge G. Castañeda, *Utopia Unarmed: The Latin American Left after the Cold War* (New York: Vintage Books, 1994), 311.

39. Ambassador Thomas F. Stroock, cable to Secretary of State, GUATEM 07935, July 30, 1992, "Safety of AMCIT Katharine Riker," 0017–18 (copy in author's files).

40. Ambassador Stroock, cable letter reply to Senator Patrick Leahy, GUATEM 08131, August 4, 1992, WOLA file (copy in author's files).

41. Mario René Cifuentes, interview by author, December 13, 1995.

42. Maritza Urrutia, interview, January 12, 1995.

43. Ibid.

44. Maritza Urrutia, declaration, 15; and interview, November 11, 1999, The Hague.

45. Maritza Urrutia, declaration, 16.

46. Ibid.

CHAPTER 5

1. For a summary of the Spanish conquest of what is today Central America, see Julio Pinto Soria, ed., *Historia General de Centroamérica: El Régimen Colonial (1524–1750)* (San José: Flacso, 1994), 22–40.

2. Edward O'Flaherty, S. J., *Iglesia y Sociedad en Guatemala (1524–1563): Análisis de un Proceso Cultural* (Seville: Publicaciones de la Universidad de Sevilla, 1984), 89.

3. *Recopilación de las Leyes de los Reynos de las Indias,* quoted in W. George Lovell, *Conquista y Cambio Cultural: La Sierra de los Cuchumatanes de Guatemala, 1500–1821* (Antigua Guatemala: Centro de Investigaciones Regionales de Mesoamérica, 1990), 78.

4. Julio Pinto Soria, "El Indígena Guatemalteco y Su Lucha de Resistencia Durante la Colonia: La Religión, la Familia y el Idioma," Centro de Estudios Urbanos y Regionales, Universidad de San Carlos de Guatemala, no. 27, September 1995, 4–5.

5. Martin Alfonso, *Relación Histórica Descriptiva de las Provincias de la Verapaz y de la del Manche, escrita por el Capitan . . . Año de 1635* (Guatemala City: Editorial Universitaria, 1960), 165–66, and as quoted in Pinto Soria, "Indígena Guatemalteco," 4.

6. Letter from Bishop Marroquín to the king, January 20, 1539, quoted in O'Flaherty, *Iglesia y Sociedad en Guatemala,* 96.

7. Pinto Soria, "Indígena Guatemalteca," 10–11, 18–19.

8. Ibid., 5.

9. Ibid., 11–13.

10. From "Testimonio de los autos hechos sobre la perdición general de los indios de estas provincias y frangentes continuos que amenaza su libertad" (1687), quoted in Lovell, *Conquista y Cambio Cultural,* 90.

11. O'Flaherty, *Iglesia y Sociedad en Guatemala,* 95.

12. Luis Samandu, Hans Siebers, and Oscar Sierra, *Guatemala: Retos de la Iglesia Católica en una Sociedad en Crisis* (San José: Editorial DEI, 1990), 19.

13. Pinto Soria, *Régimen Colonial,* 170.

14. Manuel Orellena, *Libro de Primer Aniversario de la Muerte de Carlos Castillo Armas,* July 26, 1958, 3 (Conde family archive).

15. Father Juan Hernández Pico, interview by author, August 15, 1996.

16. José Luis Chea, *Guatemala: La Cruz Fragmentada,* 2nd ed. (San José: Editorial DEI, 1989), 156n1.

17. Sister Raquel Saravia Valdés, interview by author, July 26, 1996.

18. Sister Ana Evelyn Vázquez, interview by author, April 7, 1996, Chajul, El Quiché.

19. Consejo Episcopal Latinoamericano (CELAM), *La Iglesia en la Actual Transformación de América Latina a la Luz del Concilio II,* 2nd ed. (Bogotá, 1969), 70, 75.

20. Mario Casariego, first pastoral letter, "En la Caridad Será el Consuelo para Todos" [March 3, 1965], quoted in Chea, *Cruz Fragmentada,* 157–58.

21. Mario Casariego, "Resumen de las Palabras de Saludo al Clero de la Arquidiócesis, en el retiro mensual del 19 de enero de 1971," quoted in Chea, *Cruz Fragmentada,* 171.

22. Msgr. Próspero Penados del Barrio, interview by author, February 26, 1996.

23. Msgr. Juan Gerardi Conedera, interview by author, August 5, 1996.

24. Sister Ana Evelyn Vázquez, interview.

25. Sister Raquel Saravia Valdés, interview.

26. Sister Barbara Ford, interview by author, February 24, 1996.

27. Underlined in the late Msgr. Juan Gerardi's copy of *La Iglesia en la Actual Transformación,* 222 (see note 19).

28. Diocese of El Quiché, "Comunicado de la Diócesis del Quiché al Pueblo de Dios y a Todos los Hombres de Buena Voluntad del Departamento" [October 1, 1979], and "Comunicado de la Diócesis del Quiché Sobre los Acontecimientos de Nebaj" [March 1980], in *El Quiché: El Pueblo y Su Iglesia, 1960–1980* (Santa Cruz del Quiché, 1994).

29. Msgr. Juan Gerardi, interview, May 2, 1996.

30. David Stoll, *Between Two Armies in the Ixil Towns of Guatemala* (New York: Columbia University Press, 1993), 88, 170.

31. Yvon Le Bot, *La Guerra en Tierras Mayas: Comunidad, Violencia y Modernidad en Guatemala (1970–1992)* (Mexico City: Fondo de Cultura Económica, 1995), 149–52. Priests and nuns working in other Guatemalan provinces—such as Americans Thomas Melville and Marian Peter, representatives of the Maryknoll Order in Huehuetenango—also became aligned with revolutionary organizations in spite of their reservations about armed struggle as a vehicle for change. See Julio César Macías, "Los Maryknoll," in *Mi Camino: La Guerrilla* (Mexico City: Editorial Planeta Mexicana, 1998), 159–61. Some *guerrilleros* found shelter from the security forces in Catholic schools.

32. Msgr. Juan Gerardi, interview, May 2, 1996.

33. Ibid.

34. Ibid.

35. Diocese of El Quiché, *El Pueblo y Su Iglesia,* 153.

36. ODHA, *El Entorno Histórico,* vol. 3 of *Guatemala: Nunca Más,* Informe Proyecto Interdiocesano de Recuperación de la Memória Histórica (Guatemala City, 1998), 136.

37. Diocese of El Quiché, *El Pueblo y Su Iglesia,* 155–57.

38. Msgr. Juan Gerardi, interview, May 2, 1996.

39. Ibid.; Msgr. Próspero Penados, interview.

40. Father Axel Mencos Méndez, interview by author, July 29, 1996, Chichicastenango.

41. Sister Barbara Ford, interview; Msgr. Juan Gerardi Conedera, interview, August 5, 1996.

42. Msgr. Juan Gerardi, interview, August 5, 1996.

43. ODHA, *Entorno Histórico,* 111–95; United Nations Office for Project Services, *Guatemala: Memória del Silencio,* Informe de la Comisión para el Esclarecimiento Histórico (Guatemala City, 1999), chap. 1, par. 586; Ricardo Falla, *Masacres de la Selva: Ixcán, Guatemala (1975–1982)* (Guatemala City: Editorial Universitaria, 1992).

44. Richard Wilson, *Maya Resurgence in Guatemala: Q'eqchi' Experiences* (Norman: University of Oklahoma Press, 1995), 217. But twenty thousand dead reflects a conservative figure. Other estimates range from twenty-five thousand to one hundred and fifty thousand. Jennifer Schirmer, *The Guatemalan Military Project: A Violence Called Democracy* (Philadelphia: University of Pennsylvania, 1998), 54–57. On the total of dead, see also *História General de Centroamérica: História Inmediata* (San José: Flacso, 1994), 185–86.

45. ODHA, *Impactos de la Violencia,* vol. 1 of *Guatemala: Nunca Más,* 255–57.

46. Father Axel Mencos Méndez, interview.

47. Ibid.

48. Ibid.

49. After a devastating earthquake killed thousands of Guatemalan *campesinos* in 1976, the resources offered by foreign Protestant denominations to assist in the rebuilding, as well as apocalyptic visions of further disasters, led many Catholics to embrace Protestantism. George Black, *Garrison Guatemala* (New York: Monthly Review Press, 1984), 133.

50. Le Bot, *Guerra en Tierras Mayas,* 219.

51. Black, *Garrison Guatemala,* 132.

52. ODHA, *Entorno Histórico,* 139.

53. Ibid., 113, 142.

54. Black, *Garrison Guatemala,* 133.

55. Greg Grandin, *The Last Colonial Massacre: Latin America in the Cold War* (Chicago: University of Chicago Press, 2004), 197.

56. Le Bot, *Guerra en Tierras Mayas,* 218–19, 226–27; UNOPS, *Memória del Silencio,* chap. 1, par. 629–33.

57. Le Bot, *Guerra en Tierras Mayas,* 212–13. The military adopted the concept of "minimum force" to further three strategic objectives: "bring the population down from the mountains, . . . recuperate those who have been indoctrinated with foreign ideas, and . . . neutralize the armed insurgents." Schirmer, *Guatemalan Military Project,* 103–4.

58. Schirmer, *Guatemalan Military Project,* 69–71, 73.

59. Le Bot, *Guerra en Tierras Mayas,* 218–19.

60. Conferencia Episcopal Guatemalteca (Guatemalan bishops' conference), pastoral letters, *Clamor Para la Tierra* (Guatemala City, 1988).

61. Ambassador Thomas F. Stroock, cable to Secretary of State, Washington, D.C., GUATEM 13999, November 21, 1989, "The Catholic Church and the Military: Systematic Repression of the Church? No Evidence So Far" (copy in author's files).

62. Coroncho, former specialist, Guatemalan army intelligence, interview by author, June 13, 1996.

CHAPTER 6

1. Maritza Urrutia, declaration submitted to the Inter-American Human Rights Commission, Washington, D.C., February 24, 1993, 18.

2. Ibid.

3. Pilar de Urrutia, interview by author, May 1, 1996.

4. Message received at the archbishopric, July 26, 1992, ODHA file (copy in author's files).

5. Father Luis Pérez, interview by author, May 24, 1996.

6. Notes from meeting in ODHA, July 27, 1992 (copy in author's files).

7. Edmundo René Urrutia, interview by author, December 20, 1994, Cleveland.

8. "Familia Clama: 'Que Aparezca Maritza,'" *La Hora,* July 27, 1992, 4.

9. Carolina Urrutia, interview by author, July 1, 1995; Pilar de Urrutia, interview.

10. Maritza Urrutia, declaration, 19.

11. Maritza Urrutia, interview by author, January 12, 1995, Mexico City.

12. Coroncho, former specialist, Guatemalan army intelligence, interview by author, June 15, 1996.

13. Maritza Urrutia, declaration, 20.

14. Ibid., 21.

15. Maritza Urrutia, interview, January 12, 1995.

16. Maritza Urrutia, declaration, 21.

17. "No hagamos mucha bulla." Ibid.

18. Ibid.

19. Ibid., 22; Coroncho, interview, June 13, 1996.

20. Ibid.

21. Fax from Bonnie Tenneriello to congressional staff, July 28, 1992, WOLA file (copy in author's files).

22. The four signatories were Senators Tom Harkin (D-IA), Patrick Leahy (D-VT), Jeff Bingaman (D-NM), and Peter Dominici (D-NM). Copies of the letter were faxed to Ambassador Thomas Stroock at the U.S. Embassy; General José García Samayoa, minister of defense; Licenciado José María Meléndez, director of the National Police; Ingeniero Bernardo Neumann, director of President Serrano's Human Rights Commission; Ramiro de León Carpio, then Guatemala's human rights ombudsman; Acisclo Valladares, the attorney general; Juan José Rodil Peralta, president of the Supreme Court; and Ambassador Juan José Caso Franjul at the Guatemalan Embassy in Washington, D.C.

23. Letter to Msgr. Rodolfo Quezada Toruño, July 28, 1992, WOLA file (copy in author's files).

24. Fax from Edmundo René Urrutia to Heather Wiley, July 28, 1992, WOLA file.

25. Edmundo René Urrutia, interview.

26. "Maritza Urrutia Ha Hablado Cuatro Veces con Su Familia," La Hora, July 28, 1992.

27. "USAC Exige Libertad de Maritza Urrutia," Prensa Libre, July 28, 1992, 68.

28. "Tienen Pistas Para Aclarar Secuestro de Ex-Universitaria," Prensa Libre, July 28, 1992, 8.

29. "Ejército Niega Vinculación con Secuestro de una Universitaria," Siglo Veintiuno, July 28, 1992, 2.

30. "Maritza Urrutia Ha Hablado Cuatro Veces con Su Familia," La Hora, July 28, 1992, 4.

31. Father Sergio Orantes, interview by author, August 5, 1996.

32. Video of mass for Maritza Urrutia, July 28, 1992, Guatemala City, in author's possession.

33. Ibid.

34. Carolina Urrutia, interview.

35. "Este cura se le fué la barra." Juan, interview by author, January 27, 1996.

36. Video of mass for Maritza Urrutia.

37. Carolina Urrutia, interview.

38. Katharine Riker, interview by author, December 21, 1994, Cleveland.

CHAPTER 7

1. Maritza Urrutia, declaration submitted to the Inter-American Human Rights Commission, Washington, D.C., February 24, 1993, 23.

2. Ibid.

3. Ibid.

4. Maritza Urrutia, interview by author, August 21, 1996, Mexico City.

5. Maritza Urrutia, declaration, 24.

6. Ibid., 25.

7. Transcript of recorded notes, Informe GUA-168–92/P, 11–12, Human Rights Ombudsman's file (copy in author's files).

8. Bernard Aronson, interview by author, July 20, 1998, Washington, D.C.

9. After the reduction in U.S. military aid, the Guatemalan army turned to governments like Argentina, Uruguay, and Colombia for support. Jennifer Schirmer, *The Guatemalan Military Project: A Violence Called Democracy* (Philadelphia: University of Pennsylvania Press, 1998), 37, 161.

10. Bernard Aronson, interview.

11. Ibid.; Mark Kirk, former Special Assistant to Assistant Secretary of State for Inter-American Affairs, interview by author, March 23, 1998, Washington, D.C.

12. "Appointments," *State: United States State Department*, August–September 1989, 14.

13. Ibid.; *Who's Who in American Politics, 1995–96*, vol. 2, *Nebraska–Virgin Islands*, 15th ed. (New Providence: R. R. Bowker), 3032.

14. See H. I. Shaw, Jr., B. C. Nalty, and E. T. Turnbladh, *Central Pacific Drive*, vol. 3 of *History of U.S. Marine Corps Operations in World War II* (Washington: Historical Branch, G-3 Division, Headquarters, U.S. Marine Corps, 1967), chaps. on seizures of Saipan, Tinian, and Guam.

15. Ibid.: see "American and Japanese Preparations," 261; "Saipan: The First Day," 276–78; and "Northern Saipan: End of the Campaign," 339–42.

16. Thomas F. Stroock, letter to author, January 4, 1999.

17. Ibid.

18. T. D. Allman, "The Curse of Dick Cheney," *Rolling Stone*, August 25, 2004, www.rollingstone.com/politics/story/_/id/6450422?pageid=rs.Politics Archive&pag (accessed December 19, 2004); Nina J. Easton, "On the Campaign Trail, Cheney Works to Upgrade Image," *Boston Globe*, September 1, 2004, A34, http://www.boston.com/news/politics/president/bush/articles/2004/09/01/on_the_campaign_trail_cheney_works_to_upgrade_image?pg=full (accessed December 13, 2006). "Board of Land Commissioners Approve Modifications in Royalty Rate Structure," press release, State of Wyoming, Office of the Governor, Jim Geringer, March 8, 1996.

20. Stroock, letter to author, January 4, 1999; curriculum vitae, Presidential Appointments Staff, U.S. Department of State, Washington, D.C. (copy in author's files).

21. *Who's Who in America, 1997*, vol. 2, *L–Z* (New Providence).

22. David Todd, lobbyist and partner at Patton & Boggs, interview by author, January 27, 1995, Washington, D.C.

23. Mark Kirk, interview.

24. David Todd, interview.

25. Ambassador Thomas F. Stroock, cable to Secretary of State, GUATEM 02866, March 17, 1992, "Thirty Months in the Human Rights Trenches," 0299 (copy in author's files).

26. Ibid., 0303.

27. Ambassador Stroock quoted in Lewis H. Diuguid, "U.S. Recalls Ambassador in Rebuke to Guatemala on Human Rights," *Washington Post*, March 8, 1990, A35.

28. Ambassador Stroock, cable, "Human Rights Trenches," 0304.

29. Anna Vinegrad, "From Guerrillas to Politicians: The Transition of the Guatemalan Revolutionary Movement in Historical and Comparative Perspective," in *Guatemala After the Peace Accords*, ed. Rachel Sieder (London: Institute of Latin American Studies, 1998), 218.

30. Mark Kirk, interview.

31. Former official of U.S. Embassy in Guatemala, interview by author, May 9, 1997, Washington, D.C. Stroock's perspective is often referred to as "American exceptionalism" or, to use H. W. Brands's term, "exemplarism." See H. W. Brands, *What America Owes the World: The Struggle for the Soul of Foreign Policy* (Cambridge: Cambridge University Press, 1998).

32. Former embassy official, interview.

33. Suzanne Patterson, interview by author, May 9, 1998, Antigua Guatemala.

34. John Hamilton, Deputy Assistant Secretary of State for Inter-American Affairs, interview by author, April 24, 1998, Washington, D.C.

35. Bernard Aronson, interview.

36. James Carroll, interview by author, March 25, 1998, Falls Church, VA.

37. Bernard Aronson, interview.

38. Ibid.

39. Mark Kirk, interview.

40. Stroock, letter to author, November 24, 1998.

41. Mark Kirk, interview.

42. James Carroll, interview; Suzanne Patterson, interview, May 9, 1998.

43. James Carroll, interview.

44. Ibid.

45. Mark Kirk, interview; Suzanne Patterson, interview, May 9, 1998.

46. Tim Weiner, "Tale of Evading Ban on Aid for Guatemala," *New York Times*, March 30, 1995, A1, A3; Sam Dillon and Tim Weiner, "In Guatemala's Dark Heart, C.I.A. Tied to Death and Aid," *New York Times*, April 2, 1995, A1, A6; also see Tim Weiner, "Guatemala Agent of the C.I.A. Linked to Killing of American," *New York Times*, March 23, 1995, A1; Tim Weiner, "Long Road to Truth on Guatemala Killings," *New York Times*, March 24, 1995, A1, A3; Tim Weiner, "A Guatemala Officer and the C.I.A.," *New York Times*, March 26, 1995, 6; Catherine S. Manegold, "A Woman's Obsession Pays Off—at a Cost," *New York Times*, March 26, 1995, E1, E4; Sam Dillon, "On Her Guatemalan Ranch, American Retraces Slaying," *New York Times*, March 28, 1995, A1, A5; Tim Weiner, "C.I.A. Director Admits to Failure in Disclosing Links to Guatemala," *New York Times*, April 6, 1995, A1, A3; Trish O'Kane, "A Guatemala-CIA Scandal Splits Army," *Christian Science Monitor*, April 6, 1995, 7; Clifford Krauss

and Tim Weiner, "Secret Guatemalan Military Unit, Linked to C.I.A., Dies and Is Born Again," *New York Times,* April 10, 1995, A6; Congressional Intelligence Oversight Board, *Report on the Guatemala Review,* June 28, 1996, 37–39, app. A (copy in author's files).

47. Suzanne Patterson, interview, May 16, 1998.

48. Bernard Aronson, interview.

49. Ibid.; Richard Nuccio, interview by author, March 6, 1998, Cambridge, MA.

50. Declassified CIA secret cable, Z-010, August 1990, 2, National Archives (copy in author's files).

51. James Carroll, interview.

52. State Department, secret memorandum to U.S. Embassy in Guatemala, December 18, 1990, X74975, "Stop Delivery of Military Assistance to Guatemala" (copy in author's files).

53. Jorge Serrano Elías, interview by author, April 2, 1998, Panama City.

54. Ibid.; James Carroll, interview.

55. Jorge Serrano, interview, April 2, 1998.

56. Stroock, letter to author, January 4, 1999.

57. David Todd, interview.

58. Ambassador Stroock, cable, "Human Rights Trenches," 0305.

59. David Todd, interview.

60. Ambassador Stroock, cable, "Human Rights Trenches," 0305.

61. John Keane, confidential cable to Secretary of State, GUATEM 12071, November 16, 1992, 4–5, 11 (copy in author's files).

62. James Baker, Secretary of State, confidential cable to American Embassy in Guatemala, 029485, January 1991, "Working with Serrano" (copy in author's files).

63. Ibid.

64. Ibid.

65. Stroock, letter to author, June 9, 2005.

66. Jorge Serrano, interview, April 2, 1998; declassified CIA cable Z-020, February 1991, National Archives (copy in author's files).

67. Jorge Serrano, interview, April 2, 1998.

68. Bernard Aronson, interview.

69. Jorge Serrano, interview, April 2, 1998.

70. Stroock, letter to author, June 9, 2005.

71. Ibid.

72. Jorge Serrano, interview, April 2, 1998.

73. Ibid.

74. Ibid.

75. Declassified CIA cable Z-020.

76. Ibid.

77. Tim Weiner, "C.I.A. Cloak: It's 'Liaison,'" *New York Times,* April 5, 1995, A8; Krauss and Weiner, "Secret Guatemalan Military Unit," A6; Tim Weiner, "More Divulged About C.I.A. in Guatemala," *New York Times,* April 25, 1995, A5.

78. Secret CIA cables Z-022 and Z-024, April 1991, declassified June 1996, National Archives (copy in author's files).

79. Weiner, "Tale of Evading Ban on Aid," A5.

80. Declassified CIA secret cable Z-022, April 1991, 3 (copy in author's files).

81. Schirmer, *Guatemalan Military Project,* 184.

82. Secret memorandum for Undersecretary of Defense for Policy, through ASD/International Security Affairs, from DASD/Inter-American Affairs, I-95–18771, April 14, 1995, "Talking Points for USDP Call to NSC."

83. Frank Smyth, "Has Guatemala Become the Cali Cartel's Bodega?" *Wall Street Journal,* March 10, 1995, A15.

84. "U.S. Puts Guatemala on Its Drug Blacklist," *San Diego Union,* April 1, 1990, 11; DEA Intelligence Division, "Worldwide Cocaine Situation," October 1993, 53, DEA, U.S. Department of Justice, Washington, D.C (hereafter cited as Justice Department).

85. State Department official Robert Blaud, former Desk Officer for Guatemala at the Bureau of International Narcotics Matters (INM), telephone interview by author, March 3, 1995.

86. "International Narcotics Control Strategy Report," March 1992, 156; and April 1994, 150, INM, State Department.

87. Suzanne Patterson, interview, May 16, 1996.

88. Krauss and Weiner, "Secret Guatemalan Military Unit," A6.

89. James Carroll, interview.

90. See secret CIA cables Z-022 and Z-024.

91. Francisco Perdomo, former Minister of the Interior, interview by author, April 2, 1998, Panama City.

92. Declassified secret CIA cable, Z-053, February 1993, approved for release June 1996, 2, National Archives (copy in author's files).

93. John Arndt, telephone interview by author, May 11, 1995. U.S. negotiators would respond that it was in Guatemala's interest to cooperate in the drug war because of the threat posed by narcotics trafficking to Guatemala's stability, a position President Serrano shared. Guatemala also had a stake in the war on narcotics, and therefore, the two issues, human rights and narcotics control, should not be played against each other. Jorge Serrano, interview, April 2, 1998.

94. Richard Nuccio, interview, June 11, 1998, Washington, D.C.

95. John Keane, Deputy Chief of Mission, cable to Secretary of State, GUATEM 12999, December 1992, "President Serrano: You Just Don't Understand," 3.

96. Edmond Mulet, interview by author, June 7, 1996.

97. Jorge Serrano, interview, April 3, 1998.

98. Ibid., April 2, 1998.

99. Haroldo Shetemul, interview by author, June 14, 1996; Fernando Hurtado Prem, interview by author, May 30, 1996; Francisco Perdomo, interview.

100. Francisco Perdomo, interview.

101. James Carroll, interview; Suzanne Patterson, interview, May 16, 1998.

102. Ambassador Stroock, cable letter reply to Senator Patrick J. Leahy, GUATEM 08131, August 4, 1992, WOLA file (copy in author's files).

103. Katharine Riker, interview by author, December 21, 1994, Cleveland.

104. Ambassador Stroock, cable letter reply to Senator Leahy.

105. Katharine Riker, interview.

106. Ambassador Stroock, cable to Secretary of State, GUATEM 07935, July 30, 1992, "Safety of AMCIT Katharine Riker," 0019–20 (copy in author's files).

107. Gustavo Meoño, interview by author, April 13, 1998.

108. Ibid.

109. Coroncho, former specialist, Guatemalan army intelligence, interview by author, June 15, 1996.

110. Ambassador Stroock, cable, "Safety of Katharine Riker," 0020.

111. Katharine Riker, interview.

CHAPTER 8

1. "Maritza Urrutia: No Fui Secuestrada," *El Grafico,* July 30, 1992, 1. "Becado por el gobierno de los Estados Unidos y a su labor docente."

2. *El Grafico,* July 31, 1992, 14.

3. Author's recollection; Edmundo René Urrutia, interview by author, December 20, 1994, Cleveland.

4. George Chester, e-mail message to author, September 25, 2005.

5. General Otto Pérez Molina, interviews by author, March 11 and 18, 1998, Washington, D.C. In 1995 Ambassador Stroock observed that the CIA was very effective in antinarcotics activities in Guatemala. Panel discussion at meeting of Latin American Studies Association, Washington, D.C., September 1995. The CIA station chief declined repeated requests to be interviewed for this book.

6. George Chester, interview by author, April 16, 1996.

7. James Carroll, interview by author, March 25, 1998, Falls Church, VA; former U.S. Embassy official, interview by author, May 9, 1997, Washington, D.C.

8. Former embassy official, interview.

9. Ibid.

10. James Carroll, interview; Suzanne Patterson, interview by author, May 16, 1998, Antigua Guatemala.

11. Former embassy official, interview.

12. Maritza Urrutia, declaration submitted to the Inter-American Human Rights Commission, Washington, D.C., February 24, 1993, 26.

13. Coroncho, former specialist, Guatemalan army intelligence, interview by author, June 13, 1996.

14. Maritza Urrutia, declaration, 27.

15. Maritza Urrutia, interview by author, June 26, 1995, Mexico City; and declaration, 27.

16. Maritza Urrutia, interview, January 12, 1995, Mexico City.

17. Pedro, interview by author, August 7, 1996; Juan, interview by author, January 27, 1996; and Olga Pérez, interview by author, February 20, 1998.

18. Pedro, interview.

19. Carlos Barrientos Aragón, interview by author, February 20, 1998.

20. Ibid.

21. Maritza Urrutia, declaration, 27.

22. Ibid.

23. Maritza Urrutia, declaration, January 12, 1995, Mexico City.

24. Maritza Urrutia, testimony, 28.

25. Ibid, 29; ODHA, *Los Mecanismos del Horror,* vol. 2 of *Guatemala: Nunca Más,* Informe Proyecto Interdiocesano de Recuperación de la Memória Histórica (Guatemala City, 1998), 201; UNOPS, "Torture and Other Cruel, Inhuman, and Degrading Treatment," in *Guatemala: Memória del Silencio,* Informe de la Comisión para el Esclarecimiento Histórico (Guatemala City, 1999), vol. 2, par. 706, http://shr.aaas.org/guatemala/ceh/mds/spanish/cap2/vol2/vi/2.html.

26. Letter from Héctor Aroldo Medrano Contreras, Segundo Jefe del D.I.C. y el Sub-Comisario de la Policía Nacional, al Juez Octavo de Paz Penal, Guatemala, July 24, 1992, court file no. 2038, Oficial Quinto, Juzgado Cuatro de Primera Instancia Penal, Guatemala.

27. Ambassador Thomas F. Stroock, cable to Secretary of State, GUATEM 08866, August 24, 1992, "Maritza Urrutia's Story," 0008 (copy in author's files).

28. "Maritza Urrutia Confirma Sus Declaraciones y Pide Amnistía," *Siglo Veintiuno,* July 31, 1992, 9.

29. Coroncho, interview, June 15, 1996.

30. Press conference, July 30, 1992; "En Dónde Estuvo Estos Días?" *El Grafico,* July 31, 1992, 5.

31. "Maritza Urrutia Viajó Ayer A Estados Unidos," *Siglo Veintiuno,* August 8, 1992, 6.

32. "Una Tormenta Llamada Maritza," *Crónica,* October 9, 1992, 23.

33. "Maritza Urrutia Se Acoge a la Amnistía," *El Grafico,* July 31, 1992, 1.

34. She added, "We have to leave!" Maritza Urrutia, interview, January 12, 1995, Mexico City.

35. Maritza Urrutia, interview, June 26, 1995, Mexico City.

36. Msgr. Próspero Penados del Barrio, interview by author, February 26, 1996.

37. Sister Tere Pineda Albizures, interview by author, January 23, 1996.

38. Maritza Urrutia, interview, May 18, 1996, Mexico City.

39. Claudia González, interview by author, January 26, 1996.

40. Maritza Urrutia, interview, January 12, 1995, Mexico City.

41. "Ay, siento que no estoy aquí!" Report on Maritza Urrutia case, September 1992, 8, ODHA file (copy in author's files).

42. Robert Kirschner, MD, interview by author, February 27, 1995, South Bend, IN.

43. Carolina Urrutia, interview by author, July 1, 1995.

44. Photos, ODHA (copy in author's files).

45. Carolina Urrutia, interview, August 1996.

46. Coroncho, interview, June 13, 1996.

47. C. S. Brenes and J. L. Font, "Ocho Días de Incertidumbre," *Crónica,* August 7, 1992, 24.

48. Ramiro de León Carpio, interview by author, May 11, 1996.

49. Ramiro de León Carpio, interview, April 7, 1998.

50. Carmen Aída Ibarra, interview by author, May 27, 1996.

51. Ibid.

52. Juan Luis Font, interview by author, February 24, 1998.

53. Ibid.

54. Maritza Urrutia, interview, January 1995, Mexico City; August 14, 2005, The Hague.

55. Ramiro de León Carpio, interview, April 7, 1998. In preparing his "Report on the Situation of Human Rights in Guatemala" (working paper, Economic and Social Council of the United Nations, E/CN.4/1993/10, 38, December 18, 1992), Christian Tomuschat, an independent expert, cites a written opinion published by the human rights ombudsman on October 6, 1992.

56. Coroncho, interview, June 15, 1996.

CHAPTER 9

1. Maritza Urrutia, interview by author, June 26, 1996, Mexico City.

2. "Estuvó o No Secuestrada la Señora Maritza Urrutia?" *El Grafico,* July 31, 1992, 14.

3. Ibid.

4. Ibid.

5. "Serrano: Es Obligación del Estado," *El Grafico,* July 31, 1992, 6.

6. "Ministro Ve Lado Humano: Su Familia Debe Tener Regocijo," *El Grafico,* July 31, 1992, 6.

7. Ibid. The defense minister assured the press that the army had the capacity and the obligation to guaranty Maritza's security, as well as her family's.

8. Robert Kirschner, MD, interview by author, February 27, 1995, South Bend, IN; Maritza Urrutia, interview, January 11, 1995.

9. Carmen Aída Ibarra, interview by author, May 27, 1996.

10. Ramiro de León Carpio, interview by author, April 7, 1998; Ambassador Thomas F. Stroock, cable to Secretary of State, GUATEM 08072, August 3, 1992 (copy in author's files).

11. Ambassador Stroock, cable to Secretary of State, August 3, 1992; George Chester, interview by author, April 16, 1996.

12. Ramiro de León Carpio, interview.

13. Ibid; report on Maritza Urrutia case, September 1992, pp. 9–10, ODHA (and copy in author's files).

14. Ramiro de León Carpio, interview.

15. Donald Knight, interview by author, April 21, 1998, Waterloo, IA.

16. Suzanne Patterson, interview by author, May 9, 1998, Antigua Guatemala.

17. Ibid.

18. Ibid.

19. Ambassador Stroock, cable to Secretary of State, August 3, 1992.

20. Ibid., August 24, 1992, Guatemala 08866, 0003.

21. Ibid.

22. Ibid., August 3, 1992.

23. William Robinson, telephone interview with author, December 30, 1994;

Anne Manuel, interview by author, January 26, 1995, Washington, D.C.; Bonnie Tenneriello, interview by author, February 11, 1995, Ann Arbor, MI; e-mail message from William Stanley to author, March 10, 1995.

24. Carlos Salinas, interview by author, December 19, 1996, Washington, D.C.

25. William Robinson, interview, May 30, 1995, Albuquerque.

26. Frank LaRue, interview by author, March 19, 1996.

27. William Robinson, interview.

28. Bonnie Tenneriello, interview.

29. William Robinson, telephone interview.

30. Bonnie Tenneriello, interview.

31. Heather Wiley, telephone interview by author, November 22, 1994.

32. "Country Reports on Human Rights Practices for 1991," February 1992, Department of State, Washington, D.C. (its yearly report to the Senate Committee on Foreign Relations and to the House Committee on Foreign Affairs complied with the Foreign Assistance Act of 1961); Secretary of State, cable to American Embassy Guatemala, "Final Version of 1991 Human Rights Report for Guatemala," 029455, January 30, 1992, section F, p. 14 (copy in author's files); "La Brida y la Espuela: Los Hilos del Espionaje Telefónico" and "Guategate," *Crónica*, June 30, 1995, 7, 17–20; "Temor Porque la Embajada de Estados Unidos Tenga Su Propia Red de Escuchas Telefónicas," *Siglo Veintiuno*, August 21, 1995.

33. Ana Gallagher and Wallie Mason, interview by author, January 27, 1995, Washington, D.C.

CHAPTER 10

1. Edmundo René Urrutia, interview by author, May 11, 1996.

2. Ibid.

3. Ronalth Ochaeta, interview by author, May 12, 1996.

4. Maritza Urrutia, interview by author, May 18, 1996, Mexico City.

5. Gustavo Meoño, interview by author, April 13, 1998.

6. Elaine Scarry, *The Making and Unmaking of the World* (Oxford: Oxford University Press, 1985), 35.

7. Gustavo Meoño, interview.

8. Ibid.

9. Ibid.

10. See declassified secret CIA cable, Z-124, November 1994, 3, National Archives (copy in author's files).

11. Gustavo Meoño, interview.

12. Miguel Ángel Sandoval, *Los Años de la Resistencia: Relatos Sobre las Guerrillas Urbanas de los Años 60* (Guatemala: Editorial Óscar de León Palacios, 1998), 27–49 and 51–53.

13. Miguel Ángel Sandoval, interview by author, August 19, 1996, Mexico City.

14. Ibid.; Gustavo Meoño, interview.

15. Miguel Ángel Sandoval, interview.
16. Gustavo Meoño, interview.
17. Miguel Ángel Sandoval, interview.
18. My thanks to Maritza Urrutia for this insight.
19. Manuel Conde Orellana, interview by author, June 4, 1996.
20. Ambassador Thomas F. Stroock, confidential cable to Secretary of State, GUATEM 7252, 22 July 1991, Political Section 327227, "Political Violence and Serrano's Administration," 1 (copy in author's files).
21. Ibid., 4.
22. Ibid.
23. Suzanne Patterson, interview by author, May 16, 1996, Antigua Guatemala.
24. Ambassador Stroock, cable, "Political Violence," 2.
25. Ambassador Stroock, confidential cable to Secretary of State, GUATEM 11861, November 22, 1991, "Guatemala Meets Most FMF Human Rights Benchmarks: Time for Small Steps in Response to Big Ones," 4 (copy in author's files). Indeed, two army colonels and a captain allegedly involved in the killing remained free. John Arndt, memo—talking points, confidential "Scenesetter," President's Meeting with Guatemalan President Jorge Serrano Elías, SEJRA 134, September 27, 1991, x71145, 1 (copy in author's files).
26. Ambassador Stroock, cable, "Time for Small Steps," 4.
27. Ibid.
28. Arndt, "Scenesetter," 2.
29. Ambassador Stroock, cable, "Political Violence," 2.
30. Ambassador Stroock, cable, "Time for Small Steps," 4; also see Ambassador Stroock, confidential cable to Secretary of State, GUATEM 6459, June 28, 1991, "Status Report on FMF Benchmarks."
31. "Country Reports on Human Rights Practices for 1991," February 1992, at 613 (see full cite in chapter 9, note 32). The same paragraph also described human rights violations committed by members of the URNG.
32. David Todd, lobbyist and partner at Patton & Boggs, interview by author, January 27, 1995, Washington, D.C.
33. George A. Chester, Jr., confidential memorandum to Philip B. Taylor, "Welcome Home," February 13, 1992, 1.
34. "Country Reports for 1991," 618.
35. In 1995, speaking at a panel during the annual meeting of the Latin American Studies Association, Stroock described the Guatemalan army as "the only institution that works throughout the country." Video recorded by Patricia Goudvis (copy in author's files). Also see Clifford Krauss and Tim Weiner, "Secret Guatemalan Military Unit, Linked to C.I.A., Dies and Is Born Again," *New York Times,* April 10, 1995, A6.
36. Anne Manuel, interview by author, January 26, 1995, Washington, D.C.; Thomas F. Stroock, letter to author, June 9, 2005 (copy in author's files).
37. James Carroll, interview by author, March 25, 1998, Falls Church, VA.
38. Ambassador Stroock, cable to Secretary of State, GUATEM 02866, March 17, 1992, "Thirty Months in the Human Rights Trenches," 0302 (copy in author's files).

39. Leonard Kusnitz, *Promoting Democracy or Protecting Human Rights?: Guatemala and the United States, 1993–95,* Pew Case Studies in International Affairs (Washington, D.C.: Institute for the Study of Diplomacy Publications, School of Foreign Service, Georgetown University, 1997), 2.

40. Ambassador Stroock, cable, "Political Violence."

41. Secretary of State James Baker, secret cable to American Embassy, Guatemala, 196964, June 26, 1992, "Demarche on IMET and Galvez Pena Assassination" (copy in author's files).

42. Ambassador Stroock, cable, "Human Rights Trenches," 0308.

CHAPTER 11

1. "URNG: Maritza Urrutia Es Militante Activa," *El Grafico,* August 2, 1992, 1, 4.

2. "Declaración Urgente de la Comandancia General de la URNG," July 31, 1992; *El Grafico,* August 2, 1992, 4.

3. Edmundo René Urrutia, interview by author, December 20, 1994, Cleveland.

4. My thanks to Maritza Urrutia for this insight.

5. "Oscar Conde, Asesinado," *La Picota,* January 27, 1960; "La Muerte de Oscar Conde," *La Hora Dominical,* January 31, 1960, 13, 20.

6. Manuel Rojas Bolaños, "La Política," in *De la Posguerra a la Crisis (1945–1979),* vol. 5 of *Historia General de Centro América,* ed. Héctor Pérez Brignoli (San José, 1994), 118.

7. Sonia Orellana viuda de Conde, interview by author, August 9, 1996; e-mail message from Manuel Conde, December 28, 2004.

8. Sonia Orellana v. de Conde, interview.

9. María Ortega viuda de Orellana, interview by author, August 3, 1996.

10. Sonia Orellana v. de Conde, interview.

11. Lección Inaugural, Universidad para la Paz, Dr. Jorge Serrano Elías, Presidente Constitucional de la República de Guatemala, San José, Costa Rica, March 18, 1991, 18.

12. Instituto de Relaciones Internacionales y de Investigaciones para la Paz, *Cronologías de los Procesos de Paz: Guatemala y El Salvador* (Guatemala, 1991), 34, 95; Jorge Serrano Elías, interview by author, April 2, 1998, Panama City.

13. General Otto Pérez Molina, interview by author, March 11, 1998, Washington, D.C. For a detailed analysis of these two attempted coups, see Jennifer Schirmer, *The Guatemalan Military Project: A Violence Called Democracy* (Philadelphia: University of Pennsylvania Press, 1998), chap. 9, "Contradictions of the Politico-Military Project," 206–34.

14. The formal title of the agreement was the "Peace Accord of Esquipulas II: Procedure to Establish a Firm and Lasting Peace in Central America."

15. Susanne Jonas, *Of Centaurs and Doves: Guatemala's Peace Process* (Boulder: Westview Press, 2000), 39.

16. General Julio Balconi Turcios, interview by author, February 24, 1998.

17. Amílcar Burgos, interview by author, February 26, 1998.
18. Ibid.
19. Jorge Serrano, interview.
20. Amílcar Burgos, interview, February 26, 1998.
21. Ibid.
22. Jorge Serrano, interview.
23. General Otto Pérez Molina, interview, March 11, 1998.
24. Amílcar Burgos, interview, February 26, 1998.
25. General Julio Balconi, interview.
26. *Cronologías de los Procesos de Paz,* 98.
27. Manuel Conde, interview by author, February 16, 1998, Guatemala City.
28. General Otto Pérez Molina, interview, March 11, 1998; Olga Pérez, interview by author, February 20, 1998; Jonas, *Of Centaurs and Doves,* 30–31, 62n4, 38.
29. Schirmer, *Guatemalan Military Project,* 235–60, 241.
30. Manuel Conde, interview, June 20, 1996.
31. Jorge Serrano, interview. Susanne Jonas describes how "ultra-right" sectors in Guatemala opposed any negotiated peace process and how certain sectors of the army considered the members of COPAZ to be traitors. Jonas, *Of Centaurs and Doves,* 31, 41.
32. General Julio Balconi, interview.
33. See Jonas, *Of Centaurs and Doves,* 62n4.
34. Anna Vinegrad, "From Guerrillas to Politicians: The Transition of the Guatemalan Revolutionary Movement in Historical and Comparative Perspective," in *Guatemala After the Peace Accords,* ed. Rachel Sieder (London: Institute of Latin American Studies, 1998), 216–19.
35. General Otto Pérez Molina, interview, March 18, 1998.
36. Richard Nuccio, former Senior Policy Adviser to Assistant Secretary of State and U.S. coordinator of "Group of Friends" to Guatemalan Peace Process, interview by author, March 6, 1998, Cambridge, MA.
37. See Jonas, *Of Centaurs and Doves,* 32, 40, 44–47.
38. General Otto Pérez Molina, interview, March 18, 1998.
39. Jorge Serrano, interview.
40. Miguel Ángel Sandoval, interview by author, August 19, 1996, Mexico City; also see Jorge Serrano, interview.
41. Manuel Conde, e-mail message to author, March 14, 2006 (in author's files).
42. General Julio Balconi, interview.
43. General Otto Pérez Molina, interview, March 18, 1998.
44. General Julio Balconi, interview.
45. Ibid.
46. Manuel Conde, e-mail.
47. Manuel Conde, interview, June 20, 1996; John Keane, cable to Secretary of State, GUATEM 13124, December 1992, "GOG Peace Commission Meets With ARA/DAS Maisto," 5; Keane, cable to Secretary of State, GUATEM 12999, December 1992, "President Serrano: You Just Don't Understand," 2 (copies in author's files).

48. Jorge Serrano, interview.

49. Richard Nuccio, interview.

50. Mark Kirk, former Special Assistant to Assistant Secretary of State for Inter-American Affairs, interview by author, March 23, 1998, Washington, D.C.

51. Richard Nuccio, interview.

52. Phillip Taylor, cable to Secretary of State, GUATEM 10396, October 1991, "GOG Delegation to Peace Talks Asks U.S. to Ease Up on Human Rights Criticism," 2 (copy in author's files).

53. Manuel Conde, interview, June 20, 1996.

54. Phillip Taylor, cable, "Ease Up on Human Rights Criticism," 3–5.

55. General Julio Balconi, interview.

56. Amílcar Burgos, interview, May 14, 1996; Manuel Conde, interview, June 4, 1996; Miguel Ángel Sandoval, interview.

57. Manuel Conde, interview, June 4, 1996.

58. Ibid.

59. Amílcar Burgos, interview, May 14, 1996.

60. General Julio Balconi, interview.

61. Jonas, *Of Centaurs and Doves*, 2–3, 41.

CHAPTER 12

1. Coroncho, former specialist, Guatemalan army intelligence, interviews by author, June 13 and 15, 1996.

2. Miguel Ángel Sandoval, interview by author, August 19, 1996, Mexico City.

3. Manuel Conde Orellana, interview by author, June 4, 1996.

4. Ibid.

5. Miguel Ángel Sandoval, interview.

6. General Julio Balconi Turcios, interview by author, February 24, 1998.

7. Miguel Ángel Sandoval, interview.

8. Maritza Urrutia, interview by author, January 12, 1995, Mexico City.

9. Ronalth Ochaeta, interview by author, May 12, 1996.

10. Maritza Urrutia, interview, January 12, 1995.

11. Ibid.

12. William Stanley, e-mail message to author, March 1, 1995.

13. Maritza Urrutia, interview author, January 12, 1995.

14. Ronalth Ochaeta, interview.

15. Suzanne Patterson, interview by author, May 9, 1998, Antigua Guatemala.

16. Ibid.; John Arndt, interview by author, May 8, 1997, Foreign Service Institute, Virginia.

17. Suzanne Patterson, interview.

18. Bonnie Tenneriello, interview by author, February 11, 1995, Ann Arbor.

19. Frank LaRue, interview by author, March 19, 1996.

20. Martin Ennals, "Amnesty International and Human Rights," in *Pressure Groups in the Global System: The Transnational Relations of Issue-Orientated*

Non-Governmental Organizations, ed. Peter Willetts (New York: St. Martin's Press, 1982), 80.

21. Carlos Salinas, interview by author, December 19, 1996, Washington, D.C.

22. Bonnie Tenneriello, interview.

23. Carlos Salinas, interview.

24. Mark Kirk, former Special Assistant to Assistant Secretary of State for Inter-American Affairs, interview by author, March 23, 1998, Washington, D.C.

25. Carlos Salinas, interview.

26. Bonnie Tenneriello, interview.

27. William Robinson, interview by author, May 30, 1995, Albuquerque.

28. Bonnie Tenneriello, interview.

29. Anne Manuel, interview by author, January 26, 1995, Washington, D.C.; WOLA file (copy in author's files).

30. Carlos Salinas, interview.

31. Edmundo Urrutia, interview by author, July 1, 1995. Edmundo would eventually send a letter to the press, thanking the organizations that had assisted his daughter. He did not, however, include the army in his list of benefactors!

32. Edmundo René Urrutia, interview by author, December 20, 1994, Cleveland.

33. Ibid.

34. Maritza Urrutia, interview, January 12, 1995.

35. Ibid.

36. See WOLA file, fax August 3, 1992.

37. Carlos Salinas, interview.

38. See WOLA file, fax.

39. Ibid.

40. Thomas F. Stroock, letter to author, January 4, 1999.

41. Ibid.

42. Ambassador Stroock, confidential cable to Secretary of State, Washington, D.C., GUATEM 08072, 3 August 1992, "Advisory Opinion: Visa for Maritza Urrutia" (copy in author's files).

CHAPTER 13

1. Maritza Urrutia, interview by author, January 12, 1995, Mexico City.

2. Haroldo Shetemul, interview by author, June 14, 1996.

3. Rony Véliz Samayoa, interview by author, June 5, 1996.

4. Juan Luis Font, interview by author, February 24, 1998.

5. Thomas F. Stroock, letter to author, November 24, 1998.

6. Ibid. Ambassador Stroock recalled that the head of the embassy's political section, George Chester, also opposed providing a U.S. entry visa to Maritza. George Chester strongly disagreed with this recollection and suggested that Ambassador Stroock could have had "some confusion in his mind" when he expressed it. George Chester, e-mail message to author, September 25, 2005.

7. Ibid. Also potentially at risk was a pending "open skies" treaty addressing commercial air access in both countries.

8. Suzanne Patterson, interview by author, May 9, 1998, Antigua Guatemala.

9. Jorge Serrano Elías, interview by author, April 2, 1998, Panama City.

10. Ibid.

11.. Stroock, letter. A meeting of the United Nations Human Rights Commission in Geneva was actually scheduled to convene a week later on August 13, 1992. While the main topic on the commission's agenda was the situation in the former Yugoslavia, Guatemala was also an item scheduled for discussion, and the commission issued a draft resolution about human rights in Guatemala near the end of that month. Situation of human rights in Guatemala: draft resolution/ submitted by Mr. Despouy, Mr. Eide, Mrs. Forero Ucros, Mr. Joinet, and Mr. Saboia. Geneva: UN, 25 Aug. 1992. N Document Symbol: E/CN.4/Sub.2/ 1992/L.37.

12. Jorge Serrano, interview.

13. State Department, INM, "International Narcotics Control Strategy Report," for March 1992, 159; and for April 1993, 154, 504.

14. Suzanne Patterson, interview; Haroldo Shetemul, interview; also see John Arndt, interview by author, May 8, 1997, Washington, D.C.

15. Suzanne Patterson, interview.

16. Ambassador Stroock, cable to Secretary of State, GUATEM 10041, September 23, 1992, "A Serene Serrano Surveys The Scene," 0087 (copy in author's files).

17. William Robinson, telephone interview by author, December 30, 1994; John Arndt, telephone interview, May 11, 1995.

18. Suzanne Patterson, interview.

19. Justice Department, DEA, Drug Intelligence Brief, "The Evolution of the Drug Threat: The 1980's Through 2002," www.usdoj.gov/dea/programs/foren sicsci/microgram/mg0303/mg0303.html (accessed April 16, 2005); Coletta A. Youngers and Eileen Rosin, "The U.S. 'War on Drugs': Its Impact in Latin America and the Caribbean," in Drugs and Democracy in Latin America: The Impact of U.S. Policy, ed. Coletta A. Youngers and Eileen Rosin (Boulder: Lynne Rienner, 2005), 3; Robin Kirk, More Terrible Than Death: Violence, Drugs, and America's War in Colombia (New York: Public Affairs, 2003), 86.

20. Youngers and Rosin, "U.S. 'War on Drugs,'" 3.

21. State Department press conference/statement presenting the "2005 International Narcotics Control Strategy Report," Paula Dobriansky, Under-Secretary of State for Global Affairs, and Robert B. Charles, Assistant Secretary of State for International Narcotics and Law Enforcement Affairs, Washington, D.C., March 4, 2005 (copy in author's files).

22. Justice Department, DEA and National Narcotics Intelligence Consumers Committee (NNICC), "The NNICC Report 1991: The Supply of Illicit Drugs to the United States," July 1992, DEA-92032, 7.

23. Ibid., 1, 2, 11; Justice Department, DEA, "Country Brief: Guatemala," April 2003, 4.

24. Justice Department, DEA, "Illicit Drug Trafficking and Use in the United States: Current and Future Trends," September 1993, DEA-93037, 7. From

1998–2001, in spite of continuing efforts at interdiction and eradication, cocaine prices remained stable in the U.S., although its average purity declined. "Illegal Drug Price and Purity Report," April 2003, DEA-02058, 1, 4. In a rather pathetic illustration of the limits of the drug war's success, the DEA concluded in 2001 that abuse of cocaine in the U.S. had "stabilized, albeit at high levels." "Drug Trafficking in the United States," September 2001, DEA-01020, 1. In April 2005 the White House Office on Drug Policy acknowledged that the availability of cocaine throughout the United States was stable, or slightly increased, while prices had remained stable and purity improved. Joel Brinkley, "Colombia Drug Fight Sees Mixed Results: Success There Doesn't Help U.S. Situation," *International Herald Tribune*, April 28, 1995, 5; to achieve these results, Brinkley noted, the U.S. spent three billion dollars to eradicate over a million acres of coca plants in Colombia.

25. "International Narcotics Control Strategy Report," March 1992, 157; Frank Smyth, "Justify My War: Why Clinton Eyes Haiti's Drug Trade and Ignores Guatemala's," *Village Voice*, August 2, 1994, 15–16. By 1998, DEA special agents in Guatemala formally accused thirty-one Guatemalan military officers of drug trafficking. Frank Smyth, "Still Seeing Red: The CIA Fosters Death Squads in Colombia," *Progressive*, June 1998, 26; Youngers and Rosin, "U.S. 'War on Drugs,'" 207. Drug-fueled corruption was so rampant in Guatemala during the subsequent Portillo regime (1999–2003) that the U.S. government estimated that members of a now defunct state agency tasked with Guatemala's counternarcotics mission stole more than twice the amount of cocaine legally seized in 2002. "Country Brief: Guatemala," April 2003, 5. While the government of current president Oscar Berger demonstrates greater willingness to combat trafficking and corruption, limited resources severely restrict its effectiveness. "International Narcotics Control Strategy Report," March 2005, www.state.gov/g/in/rls/nrcprt/205/vol1/html/42364.htm (accessed April 16, 2005). With corruption comes violence. Colombian traffickers often pay Guatemalan traffickers for their logistical support with cocaine instead of money. This obviates the need for large financial transactions, which are traceable by law enforcement agencies. In order for the local traffickers to recoup their investment, Guatemalan dealers convert the cocaine into "crack" cocaine and sell it domestically. This dynamic exacerbates increasing "crack" cocaine abuse within Guatemala, which in turn is a significant factor in the increase of violent crime throughout the country. "Country Brief: Guatemala," April 2003, 6.

26. James J. Gormley, "Reflections of a State Department Drug Warrior," *Foreign Service Journal*, June 1992, 31. In March 2006, however, U.S. government officials predicted that the price of cocaine would begin to rise in the U.S. and Europe during 2006 as a consequence of a six-year effort to eradicate coca production in Colombia. "UN Antidrug Officials Predict Cocaine Prices Will Rise," *International Herald Tribune*, March 16, 2005, 5.

27. Suzanne Patterson, interview.

28. John Arndt, interview, January 26, 1995, and telephone interview, March 22, 1995.

29. William Robinson, *A Faustian Bargain: U.S. Intervention in the Nicaraguan Elections and American Foreign Policy in the Post-Cold War Era* (Boulder: Westview Press, 1992), 161.

30. Suzanne Patterson, interview.

31. Ibid.

32. See Diocese of El Quiché, *El Quiché: El Pueblo y Su Iglesia* (Santa Cruz del Quiché, 1994), 241 (citing Puebla 42); Consejo Episcopal Latinoamericano, *La Iglesia en la Actual Transformación de América Latina a la Luz del Concilio II,* 2nd ed. (Bogotá, 1969), 75.

33. Susan Burgerman, *Moral Victories: How Activists Provoke Multilateral Action* (Ithaca: Cornell University Press, 2001), 69.

34. David Holliday, interview by author, October 20, 1995.

35. Ibid.

36. Memo to Maritza Urrutia File, ODHA, August 6, 1992 (copy in author's files).

37. Heather Wiley, Amnesty International USA, fax to Frank LaRue, CHRLA, Anne Manuel, Human Rights Watch/Americas, and Bonnie Tenneriello, WOLA, August 4, 1992, "Abduction of Maritza Urrutia," CHRLA file (copy in author's files).

38. Memo to Maritza Urrutia García File.

39. WOLA file; notes of Bonnie Tenneriello, August 1992, in author's files; William Stanley, e-mail message to author, March 5, 1995. And though Stanley does not specifically remember when he had this conversation with Edmundo René, he generally remembers its content. Notes and communications that refer to this telephone conversation indicate that it occurred on Tuesday evening, August 4, and that Edmundo René called a friend other than William Robinson (Stanley was the only other person Edmundo René called in the States during this period). William Robinson, interview, May 30, 1995; Edmundo René Urrutia, interview by author, December 20, 1994, Cleveland.

40. Notes of Bonnie Tenneriello, in author's files; Heather Wiley, fax to Frank LaRue, Anne Manuel, and Bonnie Tenneriello, August 3, 1992, in author's files.

41. William Robinson, interview, May 30, 1995.

42. Mark Kirk, former Special Assistant to Assistant Secretary of State for Inter-American Affairs, interview by author, March 23, 1998, Washington, D.C.; Richard Nuccio, former Senior Policy Adviser to Assistant Secretary of State for Inter-American Affairs, interview by author, March 6, 1998, Cambridge, MA.

43. Mark Kirk, interview.

44. Anne Manuel, interview by author, January 26, 1995; John Arndt, e-mail message to author, August 8, 2005.

45. Gonzalo Menéndez Park, interviews by author, May 2, 1996, and February 16, 1998.

46. Manuel Conde Orellana, interview by author, June 4, 1996.

47. Gonzalo Menéndez, interview, May 2, 1996.

48. Gonzalo Menéndez, interview, February 16, 1998.

49. Gonzalo Menéndez, interview, February 19, 1998.

50. Thomas F. Stroock, letter to author, June 9, 2005 (in author's files).

51. Juan Luis Font, interviews, February 24–25, 1998.

52. Juan Luis Font, interview, February 25, 1998.

53. Ibid.

54. American Embassy, cables to Secretary of State, GUATEM 08126, 08129, 08130, 08131, and 08132, August 4, 1992 (copies in author's files).

55. American Embassy, confidential cable to Secretary of State, GUATEM 08072, August 3, 1992, "Advisory Opinion for Maritza Urrutia" (copy in author's files).

CHAPTER 14

1. "Menéndez: Maritza Urrutia No Ha Solicitado Asilo en Embajadas," *Siglo Veintiuno*, August 5, 1992, 3; author's notes, August 5, 1992.

2. Suzanne Patterson, interview by author, May 9, 1998, Antigua Guatemala.

3. Ibid.

4. Dr. José García, telephone interview by author, May 1, 1995. U.S. intelligence officers collected impressive amounts of minutia about Guatemalan army officers. A cable (item 00050109) on February 7, 1992, reported that one brigadier general "drinks Johnny Walker Black," and his favorite food is "fish in garlic sauce." And according to a June 9, 1992, cable (item 00208551), another high-ranking officer was told to watch his cholesterol (copies in author's files).

5. Suzanne Patterson, interview; George Chester, e-mail message to author, September 25, 2005.

6. Ibid.

7. Suzanne Patterson, interview.

8. Ibid.

9. Thomas F. Stroock, letter to author, January 4, 1998.

10. Ibid.

11. See Carlos Salinas, Amnesty International USA, fax to Heather Wiley, Amnesty International USA, Frank LaRue, CHRLA, Bonnie Tenneriello, WOLA, and Anne Manuel, Americas Watch, "Conversation with Bill Robinson after he spoke with Dan Saxon of the archdiocese, 1:30 P.M. August 6, 1992," WOLA and CHRLA files (copy in author's files).

12. Jorge Serrano Elías, interview by author, April 2, 1998, Panama City.

13. Manuel Conde Orellana, interview by author, June 4, 1996.

14. Jorge Serrano, interview.

15. Tom Stroock, letters, November 24, 1998, and June 9, 2005.

16. Jennifer Schirmer, *The Guatemalan Military Project: A Violence Called Democracy* (Philadelphia: University of Pennsylvania, 1998), 251.

17. Tom Stroock, letter, June 9, 2005.

18. George Chester also recalled that President Serrano was concerned about the URNG's use of a "self-kidnapping" to sabotage the peace negotiations then under way in Mexico City. George Chester, e-mail.

19. Suzanne Patterson, interview.

20. John R. Hamilton, Deputy Assistant Secretary of State for Inter-American Affairs, interview by author, April 24, 1998.

21. Suzanne Patterson, interview.

22. George Chester, interview by author, April 16, 1996.

23. Tom Stroock, letter, November 24, 1998. When asked to comment about Ambassador's Stroock's reasons for delaying the issuance of Maritza's visa, former political counselor Chester replied: "I find Ambassador Stroock's explanation interesting, and much broader than my understanding of the issue at the time." George Chester, e-mail.

24. Suzanne Patterson, interview.

25. Tom Stroock, letter, June 9, 2005.

26. William Robinson, interview by author, May 30, 1995, Albuquerque.

27. Bonnie Tenneriello, interview by author, February 11, 1995, Ann Arbor.

28. With four exceptions (notes 29–32), the account of this afternoon's events—my exchanges with Jones, the meeting in the ambassador's office, and conversations that followed at the archbishopric—relies on the notes I took on August 5, 1992, and my memo of August 6, 1992, to the Maritza Urrutia García File, ODHA; also see Carlos Salinas's account of my phone call to Bill Robinson in Salinas's fax to the other NGOs (see note 11).

29. Author's notes, August 5, 1992; Heather Wiley, Amnesty International USA, fax to Frank LaRue, CHRLA, Anne Manuel, Human Rights Watch/Americas, and Bonnie Tenneriello, WOLA, August 6, 1992 (copy in author's files).

30. Suzanne Patterson, interview.

31. Fernando López, interview by author, January 26, 1996.

32. Ronalth Ochaeta, interview by author, May 12, 1996.

33. Heather Wiley, fax to Frank LaRue, Anne Manuel, and Bonnie Tenneriello.

34. Carlos Salinas, Amnesty International USA, interview by author, December 19, 1996, Washington, D.C.

35. Juan Luis Font, interview by author, February 24, 1998.

36. Carlos Salinas, interview.

37. Ana Pérez, e-mail message to author, October 13, 1994.

CHAPTER 15

1. "Maritza Abandona Hoy el País," and "Su Hermano También Se Marcha," *El Grafico*, August 6, 1992, 5.

2. Carmen Aída Ibarra, interview by author, May 27, 1996.

3. Rony Véliz Samayoa, interview by author, June 5, 1996.

4. Fernando López, interview by author, January 26, 1996.

5. Olga Pérez, interview by author, February 20, 1998.

6. George Chester, interview by author, April 16, 1996; George Chester, e-mail message to author, September 25, 2005.

7. Ambassador Thomas F. Stroock, cable to Secretary of State, GUATEM 02866, March 17, 1992, "Thirty Months in the Human Rights Trenches," par. 26; American Embassy, cable to Secretary of State, GUATEM 12066, November 14, 1992, "Serrano Administration Lashes Out on Human Rights: Critics Be Damned," pars. 4–7 (copies in author's files).

8. Ronalth Ochaeta, interview by author, May 12, 1996.

9. Acisclo Valladares, interviews by author, August 6, 1996, and April 13, 1998.

10. Ramiro de León Carpio, interview by author, April 7, 1998.

11. Ronalth Ochaeta, interview.

12. Fernando López, interview.

13. Ronalth Ochaeta, interview.

14. Fernando López, interview; Ronalth Ochaeta, interview.

15. Fernando Lopez, interview.

16. See Robert A. Pastor, *Whirlpool: U.S. Foreign Policy Toward Latin America and the Caribbean* (Princeton: Princeton University Press, 1992), 35.

17. Fernando López, interview.

18. William Robinson, interview by author, May 30, 1995, Albuquerque.

19. Ibid.

20. Carlos Salinas, Amnesty International USA, fax to Heather Wiley, Amnesty International USA, Frank LaRue, CHRLA, Bonnie Tenneriello, WOLA, and Anne Manuel, Americas Watch, "Conversation with Bill Robinson after he spoke with Dan Saxon of the archdiocese, 1:30 P.M. August 6, 1992," WOLA and CHRLA files (copy in author's files).

21. Bonnie Tenneriello, interview by author, February 11, 1995, Ann Arbor.

22. Ibid.; John Arndt, interview by author, January 26, 1995, Washington, D.C.

23. Bonnie Tenneriello, interview.

24. Carlos Salinas, Amnesty International USA, interview by author, December 19, 1996, Washington, D.C.

25. John Arndt, interview, May 8, 1997, Arlington, VA; and e-mail message to author, August 8, 2005.

26. Carlos Salinas, interview.

27. George Chester, interview.

28. Gonzalo Menéndez Park, interview by author, February 16, 1998; see "Yanqui Go Home," *Crónica,* August 21, 1992, 23. Ernesto Viteri declined to be interviewed for this book.

29. George Chester, interview.

30. Gonzalo Menéndez, interview, February 19, 1998. The government of Guatemala did not raise this issue with the U.S. Embassy until the following week, when Ambassador Stroock was in the United States. George Chester, e-mail.

31. John Arndt, interview, May 8, 1997.

32. John Arndt, telephone interview, January 26, 1995.

33. John Arndt, telephone interviews, March 22, 1995, and December 21, 1966.

34. John Arndt, interview, May 8, 1997.

35. John Hamilton, Deputy Assistant Secretary for Central America, the Caribbean and Cuba, interview by author, April 24, 1998, Washington, D.C.

36. William Robinson, telephone interview, December 30, 1994.

37. Maritza Urrutia, letter to Archbishop Próspero Penados del Barrio, August 6, 1992, ODHA file (copy in author's files); "Maritza Urrutia Viajó Ayer a Estados Unidos," *Siglo Veintiuno,* August 8, 1992, 6.

38. Mario René Cifuentes, interview by author, December 13, 1995.

39. Edmond Mulet, interview by author, June 7, 1996.

40. Former official of Government of Guatemala, interview by author, May 30, 1996.

41. Mario René Cifuentes, interview.

42. "Maritza Urrutia Viajó Ayer a Estados Unidos," 6; Maritza Urrutia, letter to Archbishop Penados.

43. Jorge Serrano Elías, interviews by author, April 2 and 3, 1998, Panama City.

44. Author's notes, August 6, 1992.

45. Robert Kirschner, MD, director of international programs for Physicians for Human Rights, interview by author, February 27, 1995, South Bend, IN.

46. Thomas F. Stroock, letter to author, June 9, 2005.

47. Ibid.

48. Ronalth Ochaeta, interview.

49. Acisclo Valladares, interviews, August 6, 1996, and April 13, 1998.

50. Guatemalan Ministry of Foreign Affairs, "Report Concerning the Case of Maritza Urrutia for Case 11.043 of the Inter-American Human Rights Commission," September 22, 1992, 5.

51. Francisco Perdomo, interview by author, April 3, 1998, Panama City.

52. Ramiro de León Carpio, interview.

53. Fernando López, interview.

54. Claudia González, interview by author, January 26, 1996.

55. Carmen Aída Ibarra, interview.

56. "Te vas, o no te vayas!" Maritza Urrutia, interview by author, January 12, 1995, Mexico City.

57. Ronalth Ochaeta, interview.

58. In 1980 members of the security forces tried to abduct Marco Tulio Collado as he was being escorted by the Costa Rican ambassador down the same corridor to a flight out of Guatemala. Collado's life was spared only after the ambassador immediately called the foreign minister and threatened to make an international incident over the matter. Sam Dillon, "Despite Change, Fears Linger in Guatemala," Miami Herald, January 14, 1986. I was unaware of this history in 1992.

59. Maritza Urrutia, letter to Archbishop Penados; El Grafico, August 8, 1992, 5.

60. Msgr. Próspero Penados, interview by author, February 26, 1996.

61. Carlos Salinas, interview.

62. Ibid.

63. Maritza Urrutia, interview, January 12, 1995.

64. Ronalth Ochaeta, interview.

65. Fernando Penados, interviews by author, August 15 and December 12, 1995.

66. Father Sergio Orantes, interview by author, August 5, 1996.

67. Maritza Urrutia, interview, January 12, 1995.

68. Father Luis Pérez, interview by author, May 24, 1996.

69. Fernando López, interview.

70. Father Sergio Orantes, interview.

71. Maritza Urrutia, interview, January 12, 1995.

72. Mass celebrated by Msgr. Próspero Penados, August 16, 1996, author's notes. The sacrament does not vary significantly from day to day or year to year.

73. Ronalth Ochaeta, interview.

THE AFTERMATH

1. "Maritza Urrutia Citada a Tribunal," *Prensa Libre*, August 7, 1992, 1, 8.

2. "MP Pide que Maritza Urrutia Comparezca a los Tribunales," *Siglo Veintiuno*, August 7, 1992, 3.

3. "Maritza Urrutia Citada," 8.

4. Acisclo Valladares, interview by author, August 6, 1996.

5. Rony Véliz Samayoa, interview by author, June 5, 1996; Carmen Aída Ibarra, interview by author, May 27, 1996.

6. Carmen Aída Ibarra, interview.

7. Ibid.

8. Ibid.

9. Maritza Urrutia, interview by author, June 26, 1995, Mexico City.

10. Maritza Urrutia, interview, January 12, 1995.

11. Ibid.

12. "Medical Aspects of Torture," *Danish Medical Bulletin* 37, no. 1 (January 1990): 31, 32; Maritza Urrutia, interview, January 12, 1995.

13. Elaine Scarry, *The Body in Pain: The Making and Unmaking of the World* (Oxford: Oxford University Press, 1985), 7. As Scarry explains, "This world unmaking, this uncreating of the created world, which is an external objectification of the psychic experience of the person in pain, *becomes itself the cause of the pain*" (45; emphasis added).

14. Jorge Serrano Elías, interview by author, April 3, 1998, Panama City.

15. Msgr. Próspero Penados del Barrio, interview by author, February 26, 1996.

16. Ibid.

17. Jorge Serrano, interview, April 3, 1998; Ramiro de León Carpio, interview by author, April 7, 1998.

18. Deputy Chief of Mission John Keane, secret cable to Secretary of State, GUATEM 8577, E2622A, August 19, 1992, "Charge's Meeting with Foreign Minister Regarding Political Counsel Chester"; Ambassador Thomas F. Stroock, secret cable to Secretary of State, GUATEM 9141, E2641A, September 1, 1992, "Government of Guatemala Continues to Complain About the Urrutia/Chester Affair" (copies in author's files).

19. Secretary of State, secret cable to American Embassy, Guatemala, 265174, E2804, August 18, 1992, "Vice Foreign Minister Villacorta's Meeting with Deputy Assistant Secretary Maisto" (copy in author's files).

20. Deputy Chief of Mission John Keane, secret cable to Secretary of State, 8426, E2615, August 13, 1992, "Government of Guatemala Requests Departure of FO-01 Political Counsel Chester"; John Keane, confidential cable to Sec-

retary of State, GUATEM 327226, E2616, August 14, 1992, "Urrutia Case: Government of Guatemala Request for Political Counsel Departure" (copies in author's files); John Keane, secret cable, "Charge's Meeting with Foreign Minister."

21. John Keane, secret cable, "Government of Guatemala Requests Departure of FO-01 Political Counsel Chester."

22. John Keane, secret cable, "Charge's Meeting with Foreign Minister."

23. Juan Luis Font, interview by author, February 24, 1998.

24. Jorge Serrano, interview, April 3, 1998.

25. Juan Luis Font, interview by author, February 24, 1998.

26. Mario René Cifuentes, interview by author, December 13, 1995.

27. Deputy Chief of Mission John Keane, confidential cable to Secretary of State, E2806, August 20, 1992, not sent, "Urrutia Case: Letter Delivered" (copy in author's files).

28. George A. Chester, Jr. Political Counselor, Embassy of the United States of America, letter to His Excellency Licenciado Gonzalo Menéndez Park, Minister of Foreign Relations, National Palace, August 20, 1992.

29. American Embassy, Guatemala, confidential cable to Secretary of State, 08785, August 21, 1992, 0144 (copy in author's files).

30. Confidential e-mail memorandum for Assistant Secretary Bernard Aronson's meeting with Guatemalan Foreign Minister Menéndez Park at UNGA September 24, drafted by George Chester on September 22, 1992, cleared by deputy chief of mission [Keane], and approved by the ambassador (copy in author's files). Tom Stroock declined to respond to the author's questions about this memorandum. John Keane replied that he did not recall the events mentioned. John Keane, letter to author, November 12, 2004.

31. George Chester, e-mail message to author, September 16, 2005.

32. Barbara W. Tuchman, *The March of Folly: From Troy to Vietnam* (New York: Ballantine Books, 1984), 5.

33. John Keane, confidential cable to Secretary of State, 08622, August 18, 1992.

34. "Embajador Stroock Rehusa Hablar Acerca del Caso de Maritza Urrutia," *Prensa Libre,* late September or early October 1992.

35. Thomas F. Stroock, letter to author, June 9, 2005.

36. Ambassador Thomas Stroock quoted in Lewis H. Diuguid, "U.S. Recalls Ambassador in Rebuke to Guatemala on Human Rights," *Washington Post,* March 8, 1990, A35.

37. Juan Luis Font, interview by author, February 24, 1998.

38. Primo Levi, *The Drowned and the Saved* (New York: Vintage International, 1989), 86.

39. John Keane, confidential cable to Secretary of State, 12066, November 13, 1992.

40. John Keane, confidential cable to Secretary of State, 12071, November 16, 1992, "Serrano: Let's Mend Relations."

41. John Keane, confidential cable, November 13, 1992.

42. Declassified CIA cable Z 064, November 1992, R222, approved for release June 1996, National Archives.

43. Francisco Perdomo, interview by author, April 3, 1998, Panama City; Jorge Serrano, interview, September 9, 1998.

44. Bernard Aronson, interview by author, July 20, 1998, Washington, D.C.

45. Ibid.

46. Jorge Serrano, interview, April 2, 1998; General Otto Pérez Molina, interview by author, March 18, 1998, Washington, D.C.

47. Secret, "Country Paper Guatemala," April 14, 1995, Classified by DIR, IA Region, 1 of 6, 1017.

48. Tim Weiner, "A Guatemala Officer and the C.I.A.," *New York Times,* March 26, 1995, A6.

49. Intelligence Oversight Board, "Report on the Guatemala Review," June 28, 1996.

50. Tim Weiner, "C.I.A. May Dismiss Chief Officer Involved in Guatemala," *New York Times,* September 28, 1995.

51. Jane Mayer, "Outsourcing Torture," *New Yorker,* February 14–21, 2005, 106–23.

52. "Leadership Failure: Firsthand Accounts of Torture of Iraqi Detainees by the U.S. Army's 82nd Airborne Division," *Human Rights Watch,* September 2005, http://hrw.org/reports/2005/us0905/ (accessed on December 31, 2005); Tim Golden, "Army Faltered in Investigating Detainee Abuse," *New York Times,* May 22, 2005, 1, 16; Eric Schmitt, "Congress Hears of Soldiers' Abuse of Afghan Villagers," *New York Times,* March 11, 2005; Reed Brody, "Justice at Abu Ghraib," *International Herald Tribune,* January 19, 2005; Neil A. Lewis and David Johnston, "FBI Agents Cite Abuses of Prisoners," *International Herald Tribune,* December 22, 2004; "The Road to Abu Ghraib," *Human Rights Watch,* June 2004, 4; Susan Sontag, "Regarding the Torture of Others," *New York Times Magazine,* May 23, 2004, 24–29; Steven Strasser, ed., *The Abu Ghraib Investigations: The Official Reports of the Independent Panel and Pentagon of the Shocking Prisoner Abuse in Iraq* (New York: Public Affairs, 2004), 103–6; "Injustice in Guantanamo," *International Herald Tribune,* August 23–24, 2003, 10; "Unjust, Unwise, UnAmerican," *Economist,* July 12, 2003, 9.

53. "U.S. Holding At Least 26 'Ghost Detainees,'" *Human Rights Watch,* December 1, 2005, press release at http://hrw.org/english/docs/2005/11/30/usdom12113.htm (accessed on December 31, 2005); Mark Danner, "What Are You Going to Do with That?" *New York Review of Books,* June 23, 2005, 55; "Patterns of Abuse," *International Herald Tribune,* May 24, 2005, 8; "Torture by Proxy," *International Herald Tribune,* March 9, 2005, 6; Douglas Jehl and David Johnston, "C.I.A. Given Free Rein to Move Prisoners," *International Herald Tribune,* March 7, 2005; Douglas Jehl and David Johnston, "Congress Killed Measures to Ban U.S. Use of Torture," *International Herald Tribune,* January 14, 2005, 4; Eric Lichtbau, "Gonzáles Excludes C.I.A. from Rules on Prisoners," *International Herald Tribune,* January 20, 2005, 8; "The United States' Disappeared," *Human Rights Watch,* October 2004; Eric Schmitt and Douglas Jehl, "Army Kept Dozens Off Iraq Prison Rolls," *International Herald Tribune,* September 11–12, 2004, 2; David Johnston and James Risen, "U.S. Memo Provided Basis for C.I.A. Coercion," *International Herald Tribune,* June 28, 2004, 6; Eric Schmitt and Tom Shanker, "Rumsfeld Ordered Unlisted Detention," *International*

Herald Tribune, June 18, 2004, 8; Jeffrey Smith and Josh White, "El General al Mando de las Tropas de EEUU en Irak Autorizó las Torturas en las Cárceles," *El País* (reprinted from *Washington Post*), June 13, 2004; Douglas Jehl and Neil A. Lewis, "U.S. Military Disputed Protected Status of Prisoners Held in Iraq," *International Herald Tribune,* May 23, 2004, 10; Strasser, *Abu Ghraib Investigations,* 32–33, 72–73, 96, 116–17, 154–57; Isabel Hilton, "Torture: Who Gave the Orders?" *Open Democracy,* May 13, 2004, www.opendemocracy.com/media_abu_ghraib/article_1904.jsp (last accessed June 15, 2005); Department of Defense, secret "Working Group Report on Detainee Interrogations in the Global War on Terrorism: Assessment of Legal, Historical, Policy, and Operational Considerations," March 6, 2003, 21 (copy in author's files).

EPILOGUE

1. *International Herald Tribune,* March 26–27, 2005, 4.

2. N. C. Aizeman, "Endurance of Corruption Shakes Guatemala Anew: Hopes for Anti-Drug Leader End with Arrest," *Washington Post,* March 11, 2006, A01, www.washingtonpost.com/wp-dyn/content/article/2006/03/10/AR2006031001928 (accessed on March 18, 2006); "Detenido por Narcotráfico el Jefe de la Lucha Anti-Droga de Guatemala," *El País,* November 18, 2005, found at www.elpais.es/articulo/2005111 8elpepiint_12/Tes/elpepiint/ (accessed on January 28, 2006); "El Comentario de la Semana: El SAIA Descabezado," *Prensa Libre,* November 20, 2005.

3. Thomas F. Stroock, letter to author, June 9, 2005.

4. "Los Restos del ex-Presidente Árbenz Recibidos con Honores," *Siglo Veintiuno,* October 20, 1995, 2; Edmundo René Urrutia, interview by author, October 1995.

5. Manuel Conde Orellana, e-mail message to author, June 20, 2005.

6. Sonia Orellana viuda de Conde, interview by author, February 19, 1998.

7. Jorge Serrano Elías, interviews by author, April 1 and 2, 1998, Panama City.

8. ODHA, *Guatemala: Nunca Más,* Informe Projecto Interdiocesano de Recuperación de la Memória Histórica (Guatemala City, 1998).

9. Francisco Goldman, "Murder Comes for the Bishop," *New Yorker,* March 15, 1999.

10. Francisco Goldman, "Victory in Guatemala," *New York Review of Books,* May 23, 2002, 77–83.

11. Goldman, "Murder Comes for the Bishop," 66–68.

12. Corte InterAmericana de Derechos Humanos, *Maritza Urrutia v. Guatemala* (San José, November 27, 2003).

13. Laura Aldana [de Pineda], interview by author, June 1, 1996.

14. Ester de Urrutia, letter to her daughter Julia Urrutia [de Castellanos], November 11, 1954, Argentine Embassy file, Guatemala City (copy in author's files).

Selected Bibliography
and Further Reading

THE 1944 REVOLUTION, THE 1954 COUP,
AND ITS AFTERMATH

Cullather, Nicholas. *Operation PBSUCCESS: The United States and Guatemala, 1952–1954.* Washington, D.C.: History Staff, Center for the Study of Intelligence, CIA, 1994.

De Atitlán, José. *Guatemala: Junio de 1954, Relato de la Invasión, de la Caída de Árbenz y de la Resistencia Popular* [Guatemala: June 1954, the Invasion, the Fall of Árbenz, and Popular Resistance]. Buenos Aires: Editorial Fundamento, 1955.

Gleijes, Piero. *Shattered Hope: The Guatemalan Revolution and the United States, 1944–1954.* Princeton: Princeton University Press, 1991.

Schlesinger, Stephen, and Stephen Kinzer. *Bitter Fruit: The Untold Story of the American Coup in Guatemala.* New York: Anchor Books, 1990.

GUATEMALA'S ARMED CONFLICT
AND PEACE PROCESS

Black, George. *Garrison Guatemala.* New York: Monthly Review Press, 1984.

The Black Book of Communism in Guatemala. Mexico City: Permanent Commission of the First Congress against Soviet Intervention in Latin America, 1954.

Castañeda, Jorge G. *Utopia Unarmed: The Latin American Left after the Cold War.* New York: Vintage Books, 1994.

Concerned Guatemala Scholars. *Guatemala: Dare to Struggle, Dare to Win.* Brooklyn: Concerned Guatemala Scholars, 1982.

Debray, Régis. *The Revolution on Trial.* Harmondsworth: Penguin Books, 1974.

Dillon, Sam. "Despite Change, Fears Linger in Guatemala." *Miami Herald,* January 14, 1986.

———. "On Her Guatemalan Ranch, American Retraces Slaying." *New York Times,* March 28, 1995.

Goldman, Francisco. "Murder Comes for the Bishop." *New Yorker,* March 15, 1999.

———. "Victory in Guatemala." *New York Review of Books,* May 23, 2002.

Grandin, Greg. *The Last Colonial Massacre: Latin America in the Cold War.* Chicago: University of Chicago Press, 2004.

Instituto de Relaciones Internacionales y de Investigaciones para la Paz. *Cronologías de los Procesos de Paz: Guatemala y El Salvador* [Chronologies of the Peace Process: Guatemala and El Salvador]. Guatemala, 1991.

Johnson, Haynes. *The Bay of Pigs: The Leaders' Story of Brigade 2506.* New York: W. W. Norton, 1964.

Jonas, Susanne. *The Battle for Guatemala: Rebels, Death Squads and U.S. Power.* Boulder: Westview Press, 1991.

———. *Of Centaurs and Doves: Guatemala's Peace Process.* Boulder: Westview Press, 2000.

Manz, Beatriz. *Paradise in Ashes: A Guatemalan Journey of Courage, Terror, and Hope.* Berkeley: University of California Press, 2004.

Martínez, Demetria. *Mother Tongue.* New York: One World, 1996.

National Security Archive. Guatemalan Death Squad Dossier. Washington, D.C. Available online at www.gwu.edu/~nsarchiv/NSAEBB/NSABB15/press.html.

Rojas Bolaños, Manuel. "La Política." In *De la Posguerra a la Crisis (1945–1979)* [From Postwar to Crisis]. Vol. 5 of *Historia General de Centro America,* edited by Héctor Pérez Brignoli. San José, 1994.

Sandoval, Miguel Ángel. *Los Años de la Resistencia: Relatos sobre las Guerrillas Urbanas de los Años 60* [Years of Resistance: Stories of Urban Guerrillas in the 1960s]. Guatemala: Editorial Óscar de León Palacios, 1998.

Schirmer, Jennifer. *The Guatemalan Military Project: A Violence Called Democracy.* Philadelphia: University of Pennsylvania Press, 1998.

Unidad Revolucionaria Nacional Guatemalteca. *Guatemala: The People Unite! Unitary Statement from the Guatemalan National Revolutionary Unity.* San Francisco, CA: Solidarity Publications, 1982.

Vinegrad, Anna. "From Guerrillas to Politicians: The Transition of the Guatemalan Revolutionary Movement in Historical and Comparative Perspective." In *Guatemala after the Peace Accords,* edited by Rachel Sieder. London: Institute of Latin American Studies, 1998.

HUMAN RIGHTS POLICY

Allman, T. D. "The Curse of Dick Cheney." *Rolling Stone,* August 25, 2004. Available online at www.rollingstone.com/politics/story/_/id/6450422?pageid=rs .PoliticsArchive&pag (accessed December 19, 2004).

Bacchus, William I. *Foreign Policy and the Bureaucratic Process.* Princeton: Princeton University Press, 1974.

Brands, H. W. *What America Owes the World: The Struggle for the Soul of Foreign Policy.* Cambridge: Cambridge University Press, 1998.

Brinkley, Joel. "Colombia Drug Fight Sees Mixed Results: Success There Doesn't Help U.S. Situation." *International Herald Tribune,* April 28, 1995.

Brody, Reed. "Justice at Abu Ghraib." *International Herald Tribune,* January 19, 2005.

Burgerman, Susan. *Moral Victories: How Activists Provoke Multilateral Action.* Ithaca: Cornell University Press, 2001.

Danner, Mark. "What Are You Going to Do with That?" *New York Review of Books,* June 23, 2005.

Dillon, Sam, and Tim Weiner. "In Guatemala's Dark Heart, C.I.A. Tied to Death and Aid." *New York Times,* April 2, 1995.

"Disappeared in Guatemala: The Case of Efraín Bámaca Velázquez." *Human Rights Watch/Americas* 7, no. 1 (March 1995).

Diuguid, Lewis H. "U.S. Recalls Ambassador in Rebuke to Guatemala on Human Rights." *Washington Post,* March 8, 1990.

Easton, Nina J. "On the Campaign Trail, Cheney Works to Upgrade Image." *Boston Globe,* September 1, 2004, http://www.boston.com/news/politics/president/bush/articles/2004/09/01/on_the_campaign_trail_cheney_works_to_upgrade_image?pg=full (accessed December 19, 2004).

Ennals, Martin. "Amnesty International and Human Rights." In *Pressure Groups in the Global System: The Transnational Relations of Issue-Orientated Non-Governmental Organizations,* edited by Peter Willetts. New York: St. Martin's Press, 1982.

Golden, Tim. "Army Faltered in Investigating Detainee Abuse." *New York Times,* May 22, 2005.

Gormley, James J. "Reflections of a State Department Drug Warrior." *Foreign Service Journal,* June 1992.

Greene, Graham. *The Quiet American.* London: Penguin Books, 1955.

Guatemala Ministry of Foreign Affairs. "Report Concerning the Case of Maritza Urrutia for Case 11.043 of the Inter-American Human Rights Commission." September 22, 1992.

Hilton, Isabel. "Torture: Who Gave the Orders?" *Open Democracy,* May 13, 2004. Available online at www.opendemocracy.com/media_abu_ghraib/article_1904.jsp.

"Injustice in Guantanamo." *International Herald Tribune,* August 23–24, 2003.

Jehl, Douglas, and David Johnston. "C.I.A. Given Free Rein to Move Prisoners." *International Herald Tribune,* March 7, 2005.

———. "Congress Killed Measures to Ban U.S. Use of Torture." *International Herald Tribune,* January 14, 2005.

Jehl, Douglas, and Neil A. Lewis. "U.S. Military Disputed Protected Status of Prisoners Held in Iraq." *International Herald Tribune,* May 23, 2004.

Johnston, David, and James Risen. "U.S. Memo Provided Basis for C.I.A. Coercion." *International Herald Tribune,* June 28, 2004.

Kirk, Robin. *More Terrible Than Death: Violence, Drugs, and America's War in Colombia.* New York: Public Affairs, 2003.

Krauss, Clifford, and Tim Weiner. "Secret Guatemalan Military Unit, Linked to C.I.A., Dies and Is Born Again." *New York Times,* April 10, 1995.

Kusnitz, Leonard. *Promoting Democracy or Protecting Human Rights?: Guatemala and the United States, 1993–95.* Pew Case Studies in International Affairs. Washington, D.C.: Institute for the Study of Diplomacy Publications, School of Foreign Service, Georgetown University, 1997.

Levi, Primo. *The Drowned and the Saved.* New York: Vintage International, 1989.

Lewis, Neil A., and David Johnston. "FBI Agents Cite Abuses of Prisoners." *International Herald Tribune,* December 22, 2004.

Lichtbau, Eric. "Gonzáles Excludes C.I.A. from Rules on Prisoners." *International Herald Tribune,* January 20, 2005.

Manegold, Catherine S. "A Woman's Obsession Pays Off—at a Cost." *New York Times,* March 26, 1995.

Mayer, Jane. "Outsourcing Torture." *New Yorker,* February 14–21, 2005.

McClintock, Michael. *The American Connection: State Terror and Popular Resistance in Guatemala.* London: Zed Books, 1987.

O'Kane, Trish. "A Guatemala–CIA Scandal Splits Army." *Christian Science Monitor,* April 6, 1995.

Pastor, Robert A. *Whirlpool: U.S. Foreign Policy Toward Latin America and the Caribbean.* Princeton: Princeton University Press, 1992.

"Patterns of Abuse." *International Herald Tribune,* May 24, 2005.

"The Road to Abu Ghraib." *Human Rights Watch,* June 2004.

Robinson, William. *A Faustian Bargain: U.S. Intervention in the Nicaraguan Elections and American Foreign Policy in the Post-Cold War Era.* Boulder: Westview Press, 1992.

Scarry, Elaine. *The Body in Pain: The Making and Unmaking of the World.* Oxford: Oxford University Press, 1985.

Schmitt, Eric. "Congress Hears of Soldiers' Abuse of Afghan Villagers." *New York Times,* March 11, 2005.

Schmitt, Eric, and Douglas Jehl. "Army Kept Dozens Off Iraq Prison Rolls." *International Herald Tribune,* September 11–12, 2004.

Schmitt, Eric, and Tom Shanker. "Rumsfeld Ordered Unlisted Detention." *International Herald Tribune,* June 18, 2004.

Schoultz, Lars. *Human Rights and United States Policy toward Latin America.* Princeton: Princeton University Press, 1981.

Smith, Jeffrey, and Josh White. "El General al Mando de las Tropas de EEUU en Irak Autorizó las Torturas en las Cárceles." *El País* (reprinted from *Washington Post*), June 13, 2004.

Smyth, Frank. "Has Guatemala Become the Cali Cartel's Bodega?" *Wall Street Journal,* March 10, 1995.

———. "Justify My War: Why Clinton Eyes Haiti's Drug Trade and Ignores Guatemala's." *Village Voice,* August 2, 1994.

———. "Still Seeing Red: The CIA Fosters Death Squads in Colombia." *Progressive,* June 1998.

Sontag, Susan. "Regarding the Torture of Others." *New York Times Magazine,* May 23, 2004.

Stover, Eric, and Elena Nightingale. *The Breaking of Bodies and Minds: Torture,*

Psychiatric Abuse, and the Health Professions. New York: W. H. Freeman, 1985.

Strasser, Steven, ed. *The Abu Ghraib Investigations: The Official Reports of the Independent Panel and Pentagon of the Shocking Prisoner Abuse in Iraq.* New York: Public Affairs, 2004.

Tomuschat, Christian. "Report on the Situation of Human Rights in Guatemala." Working paper for Economic and Social Council of the United Nations, E/CN.4/1993/10, 38, December 18, 1992.

"Torture by Proxy." *International Herald Tribune,* March 9, 2005.

Tuchman, Barbara W. *The March of Folly: From Troy to Vietnam.* New York: Ballantine Books, 1984.

"UN Antidrug Officials Predict Cocaine Prices Will Rise." *International Herald Tribune,* March 16, 2005, 5.

United Nations Centre for Human Rights. *Enforced or Involuntary Disappearance.* Human Rights Fact Sheet, no. 6. Geneva, 1989.

"The United States' Disappeared." *Human Rights Watch,* October 2004.

"Unjust, Unwise, UnAmerican." *Economist,* July 12, 2003.

U.S. Congressional Intelligence Oversight Board. *Report on the Guatemala Review.* Washington, D.C., 1996.

U.S. Department of Defense. "Working Group Report on Detainee Interrogations in the Global War on Terrorism: Assessment of Legal, Historical, Policy, and Operational Considerations." March 6, 2003.

U.S. Department of Justice Drug Enforcement Administration. "The Evolution of the Drug Threat: The 1980's Through 2002." *Microgram Bulletin* XXXVI, 3, March 2003. Available online at www.dea.gov/programs/forensicsci/micro gram/mg0303/mg0303.html.

U.S. Department of State. "Country Reports on Human Rights Practices for 1991." Report submitted to the Committee on Foreign Affairs, House of Representatives and the Committee on Foreign Relations, U.S. Senate, February 1992.

"U.S. Puts Guatemala on Its Drug Blacklist." *San Diego Union,* April 1, 1990.

Weiner, Tim. "C.I.A. Cloak: It's 'Liaison.'" *New York Times,* April 5, 1995.

———. "C.I.A. Director Admits to Failure in Disclosing Links to Guatemala." *New York Times,* April 6, 1995.

———. "C.I.A. May Dismiss Chief Officer Involved in Guatemala." *New York Times,* September 28, 1995.

———. "Guatemala Agent of the C.I.A. Linked to Killing of American." *New York Times,* March 23, 1995.

———. "A Guatemala Officer and the C.I.A." *New York Times,* March 26, 1995.

———. "Long Road to Truth on Guatemala Killings." *New York Times,* March 24, 1995.

———. "More Divulged About C.I.A. in Guatemala." *New York Times,* April 25, 1995.

———. "Tale of Evading Ban on Aid for Guatemala." *New York Times,* March 30, 1995.

Weschler, Lawrence. *A Miracle, a Universe: Settling Accounts with Torturers.* Chicago: University of Chicago Press, 1990.

Wyden, Peter. *Bay of Pigs: The Untold Story.* New York: Simon and Schuster, 1979.

Youngers, Coletta A., and Eileen Rosin. "The U.S. 'War on Drugs': Its Impact in Latin America and the Caribbean." In *Drugs and Democracy in Latin America: The Impact of U.S. Policy,* edited by Coletta A. Youngers and Eileen Rosin. Boulder: Lynne Rienner, 2005.

HISTORY OF THE CATHOLIC CHURCH IN GUATEMALA

Alfonso, Martin. *Relación Histórica Descriptiva de las Provincias de la Verapaz y de la del Manche, escrita por el Capitan . . . Año de 1635* [Historical Description of the Verapaces]. Guatemala City: Editorial Universitaria, 1960.

Chea, José Luis. *Guatemala: La Cruz Fragmentada* [Guatemala: The Fragmented Cross]. 2nd ed. San José: Editorial DEI, 1989.

Conferencia Episcopal Guatemalteca. *Clamor Para la Tierra* [Cry for Land]. Guatemala City, 1988.

Consejo Episcopal Latinoamericano (CELAM). *La Iglesia en la Actual Transformación de América Latina a la Luz del Concilio II* [The Church and the Current Transformation of Latin America in Light of Vatican II]. 2nd ed. Bogotá, 1969.

Diócesis del Quiché. *El Quiché: El Pueblo y Su Iglesia, 1960–1980.* [El Quiché: The People and Their Church]. Santa Cruz del Quiché, 1994.

Falla, Ricardo. *Masacres de la Selva: Ixcán, Guatemala (1975–1982)* [Massacres in the Jungle: Ixcán, Guatemala]. Guatemala City: Editorial Universitaria, 1992.

Le Bot, Yvon. *La Guerra en Tierras Mayas: Comunidad, Violencia y Modernidad en Guatemala (1970–1992)* [War in Maya Lands: Community, Violence, and Modernity in Guatemala]. Mexico City, 1995.

Lovell, W. George. *Conquista y Cambio Cultural: La Sierra de los Cuchumatanes de Guatemala, 1500–1821* [Conquest and Cultural Change: The Cuchamatanes Mountains of Guatemala]. Antigua Guatemala: Centro de Investigaciones Regionales de Mesoamerica, 1990.

Macías, Julio César. *Mi Camino: La Guerrilla* [My Path: Guerrilla Warfare]. Mexico City: Editorial Planeta Mexicana, 1998.

Oficina de Derechos Humanos del Arzobispado de Guatemala (ODHA). *Guatemala: Nunca Más* [Guatemala: Never Again]. Informe Projecto Interdiocesano de Recuperación de la Memória Histórica. Guatemala City, 1998.

O'Flaherty, Edward, S. J. *Iglesia y Sociedad en Guatemala (1524–1563): Análisis de un Proceso Cultural* [Church and Society in Guatemala: Analysis of Cultural Process]. Seville: Publicaciones de la Universidad de Sevilla, 1984.

Pinto Soria, Julio. "El Indígena Guatemalteco y Su Lucha de Resistencia Durante la Colonia: La Religión, la Familia y el Idioma" [Indigenous Guatemalans and Their Resistance during the Colonial Period: Religion, Family, and Language]. Centro de Estudios Urbanos y Regionales, Universidad de San Carlos de Guatemala, no. 27, September 1995.

Samandu, Luis, Hans Siebers, and Oscar Sierra. *Guatemala: Retos de la Iglesia*

Católica en una Sociedad en Crisis [Guatemala: Challenges of the Catholic Church in a Society in Crisis]. San José: Editorial DEI, 1990.

Stoll, David. *Between Two Armies in the Ixil Towns of Guatemala*. New York: Columbia University Press, 1993.

United Nations Office for Project Services. *Guatemala: Memória del Silencio* [Guatemala: The Record of Silence]. Informe de la Comisión para el Esclarecimiento Histórico. Guatemala City, 1999.

Wilson, Richard. *Maya Resurgence in Guatemala: Q'eqchi' Experiences*. Norman: University of Oklahoma Press, 1995.

ARCHIVAL SOURCES

Department of State. Cables, letters, and telegrams between Washington, D.C., headquarters and U.S. Embassy, Guatemala, 1989–92.

Embassy of Argentina Archive, Guatemala City, Guatemala. Documents from 1954.

Library of Congress. Manuscript Divison. Guatemalan Transcripts, special series (covering 1950s).

National Archives. Central Intelligence Agency. Studies and other records relating to the CIA's activities in Guatemala, 1952–54.

Index

Abu Ghraib prison (Iraq), 237
AFG (Guatemalan Women's Alliance),
    13–15, 17, 20, 242, 250n11
African National Congress (South
    Africa), 42
Agencia Nueva Nicaragua, 55
agrarian reform program, 14, 20
AID (U.S. Agency for International
    Development), 25, 30
Albuquerque (N.M.): and Edmundo
    René, 3, 30, 58, 98, 131, 144, 226;
    and Maritza in exile, 228–29; and
    pressure for Maritiza's release, 40,
    43–44, 58, 60, 128; and pressure for
    visas, 155, 187. See also Robinson,
    Bill; Stanley, William; University of
    New Mexico
Aldana, Humberto, 20, 242, 256n39
Aldana, Luis Arturo, 46, 242
Aldana, Rita Josefina, 46, 242
Aldana de Pineda, Laura, 20, 46, 242,
    256n39
Alemán, Juan Daniel, 214–15, 220, 226
Alonso Hernández, Juan, 75
Alpírez, Julio, 236
Alvarado, Pedro de, 14, 65
Alvarado Monzón, Bernardo, 28
American Academy for the Advancement
    of Science, 215
American Airlines, 218, 222, 224–25

Americas Watch, 56–57, 172, 183–84
amnesty: for Maritza, 36, 41, 87, 94–96,
    120, 122–25, 140, 147, 151, 172,
    207, 227; and URNG, 158
Amnesty International, *plate 23*, 57–58,
    89, 141, 171–72, 185, 202, 215–16,
    221, 229
anti-Communism, 5–9, 14–15, 20, 65,
    68–69, 74, 82, 156, 222, 251nn21,22
Arana Osorio, Carlos, 34, 41, 80
Arbencistas, 16–18
Árbenz, Jacobo, xix, 6–8, 13–16, 20, 28,
    60, 65, 68, 239–40, 242
archbishopric, 38, 61–62; and Gerardi
    celebration, 127–29, 137; refuge in,
    98, 121, 126–32, 135–40, 144–45,
    153–55, 166, 168–70, 173, 178–80,
    183–85, 190–91, 193–94, 196,
    200–202, 205–10, 214–22. See also
    ODHA
Archdiocese of Guatemala's Human
    Rights Office. See ODHA
Arenas Barrera, Luis, 48
Argelia (fictitious comrade), 22, 26, 36,
    85
Argentina, 13, 139, 263n9
Argentine Embassy (Guatemala City),
    xviii–xix, 15–17
Armas, Castillo, 15, 18, 20
Arndt, John, 59, 111, 188, 191, 211–14

Aronson, Bernard, 59–60, 98, 102, 104, 107
arraigo (court order), 207–8, 211, 215, 217–18, 226–27
Arriaga, Alex, 58
Asencio, José Luis, 162
assassinations, 15, 23, 88
Asturias, Rodrigo, 173
asylum, political, 119, 137–38, 172, 201

Baker, James, 103, 106–7, 148–49, 151–52, 192
Balconi Turcios, Julio, 159–61
Barrientos Aragón, Carlos, 11, 40–41, 48–50, 121–22, 224–25. *See also* Esteban (ex-husband)
Barrios, Rufino, xviii
Batista, 21
Batz, Domingo, 73
Bay of Pigs invasion, 250n4
Becker, Luis, 162
Berganes, Carmen Sofía, 131, 188–89
Berger, Oscar, 277n25
Bingaman, Jeff, 58, 60, 189, 262n22
The Body in Pain (Scarry), 145
brainwashing, 54–55, 115
Brands, H. W., 264n31
Buche, 86
Burgos, Amilcar, 158, 161, 164–65
Bush, George H. W., 99–100, 103–4, 107, 109–10, 149–50
"butcher of Zacapa." *See* Arana Osorio, Carlos

Caballo (pseud.; Horse), 86
Camila (pseud.), 26–27. *See also* Urrutia, Maritza
Camino Real hotel, 115–17, 120
Canada, 168–69, 187
Canadian Embassy (Guatemala), 168, 219
Cano, Victor Hugo, 122–23
Carlos V, King of Spain, 65
Carolina (sister). *See* Urrutia, Carolina
Carroll, James, 103–4, 110, 118, 151, 179
Carter administration, 99
Casariego, Mario, 68–71, 74, 77
Caso Franjul, Juan José, 262n22
Castillo Armas, Carlos, 6–9, 68
Castro, Fidel, 18, 21, 27–28
Catholic Action, 72
Catholic Church, xix, 38, 61–63, 250n11; and disappeared persons, 71, 73, 91–92, 113–14; history of in Guatemala, 65–79, 236, 260n31, 261n49; and "liberationists" (1954), 7–8;

masses, 68–69, 75–76, 82–83, 85, 88, 90–92, 190, 221; silence of, 234. *See also* archbishopric; ODHA
Catrín (pseud.), 24, 26
CEMACO, 36
Center for Human Rights Legal Action, 55–56, 239
Central American Forum for Political Dialogue, 239
Central American Parliament, 239
Central American Peace Accords. *See* Esquipulas II
Cerezo, Vinicio, 101, 148, 158
Chando, Don (pseud.; "fair-skinned man"): and amnesty for Maritza, 95–96, 118–20; concerns about outcome of Maritza's disappearance, 125, 128, 132, 166–67; and filming of video, 41–42, 52–53, 80–81, 85–87, 94–95; interrogations of Maritza, 22–27, 35–37; and Maritza's kidnapping, 5, 10; military career of, 238; and radio noise, 42; reaction to video, 115; and soccer games, 125, 128; and torture, 55; transfer of, 166–67
Che. *See* Guevara, Ernesto ("Che")
Cheney, Dick, 100
Chesperito (pseud.), 24, 26
Chester, George, 117, 131, 137–38, 191, 195, 206, 275n6, 280n23; and Serrano, 212–13, 231–32, 279n18, 284n30
Chino, El (pseud.), 5
Church of the Word, 77
CIA (Central Intelligence Agency), 8; and counternarcotics activities, 99, 109–11, 117, 180–82, 267n5, 276–77nn24,25; and Guatemalan army, 104, 108–11, 118, 235–36, 279n4; and "liberationists" (1954), xix, 6–9, 15, 17, 250n4; and Maritza's kidnapping, 117–18, 191–92; and visas, 174, 179–81, 191–92
civil patrols, 167–68
cocaine trade, 99, 104, 110–11, 181–82, 276–77nn24–26
cold war, 53, 68, 98, 101, 118, 151, 171, 236
Colegio Asunción, 38, 62–63
Colegio de Infantes, 82
Collado, Marco Tulio, 282n58
Colochita (nickname), 47. *See also* Urrutia, Maritza
Colombia, 99, 104, 110–11, 182, 239, 263n9, 277nn25,26
colonialism, 43, 66–67

Communists: and AID, 25; and Catholic Church, 68, 74, 76, 82; and "liberationists" (1954), xix, 6–7, 14–20; and Maritza's family, 14–21, 27–28, 250n11; and Sandoval, 146. *See also* cold war; Cuban revolution

Conde, Oscar, *plate 4*, 8, 15, 20, 156

Conde Orellana, Manuel, *plate 15*, 20, 156 57, 159, 161–65, 167, 239

Contra war (Nicaragua), 43, 158

COPAZ (Guatemalan Peace Commission), 155–65, 167–68, 173, 194–95, 241, 273n31; and human rights violations, 147, 155, 160–65, 167–68, 180

COPREDH (Guatemalan Presidential Human Rights Commission), 192–93, 197–98, 214–15, 234, 262n22

Coroncho (pseud.), 24–25, 37, 54, 88, 120, 132, 167

Costa Rica, 169, 187, 201, 207, 209

Council of Classes (Instituto Belén), 45

counterinsurgency, 34, 38, 40, 49–50, 71–77, 160, 167, 242

counternarcotics activities: and CIA, 99, 109–11, 117, 180–82, 267n5, 276–77nn24,25; and Guatemalan army, 104, 108–11, 151, 180–82, 238, 277n25; and U.S. government, xix, 43, 99, 104, 108–11, . 139, 151, 183, 266n93, 267n5, 276–77nn24–26

The Count of Monte Cristo (Dumas), 47

"country team" meetings (U.S. Embassy), 103, 179

court order. See *arraigo* (court order)

crack cocaine, 277n25

Crónica, 112, 131, 179, 189

Cuartel General, 173

Cuban revolution, 16, 21, 27–28, 46

Davis, Robert K. ("Bob"), 6, 250n4

"D-Day" (World War II), 99–100

DEA (U.S. Drug Enforcement Administration), 99, 104, 110–11, 174, 179, 181, 238, 276–77nn24,25

death penalty, 181

death squads, 29, 74

de León, Alonso, 67

de León Carpio, Ramiro, *plate 20*, 33; and archbishopric refuge, 129–32, 137–38; and *arraigo* (court order), 217; death of, 239; as Guatemalan president, 236, 239; and Maritza's disappearance, 97–98; and political asylum request, 137–38; and pressure for Maritiza's release, 90,

262n22; and travel preparations for Maritza and family, 218; and visas, 137–38, 179, 183, 185

Democratic Union Party, 239

Desfile de la Huelga de Dolores (USAC), 47

Deutch, John, 236

development poles, 77, 261n57

DeVine, Michael, 104–6, 109, 139, 149–50, 180, 236

Diana (pseud.; witness to kidnapping), 5, 30–31

The Diary of Anne Frank, 47

disappeared persons, xx, 53–54; and Aldana de Pineda, 46, 242, 256n39; and Catholic Church, 71, 73, 91–92, 113–14; and EGP, 31, 49, 114; and Guatemalan government, 60–61; and union members, 56; and URNG, 147; and USAC student association, 47, 78–79. *See also* Urrutia, Maritza

displaced persons, xvi, 71–75, 77, 261n57

Dodd, Christopher, 59

Domenici, Pete, 58, 189, 262n22

Domingo García, José, 41

The Drowned and the Saved (Levi), 234

drug wars. *See* counternarcotics activities

Dulles, Allen, 17

earthquake (1976), 261n49

economic assistance, U.S., 58–59

Edmundo (father). See Urrutia, Edmundo

Edmundo René (brother). See Urrutia, Edmundo René

EGP (Guerrilla Army of the Poor; the Organización): and Barrientos ("Esteban"), 10–11, 25, 35–36, 40–41, 48–50, 121–22; and Catholic Church, 72; and disappeared persons, 114–15; and license plate message, 84; and Maritza's kidnapping, 3–4, 11, 13, 25–27, 31–32, 85, 87, 127, 214; and Maritza's reappearance, 124; Maritza's work for, 3, 31–33, 47–51, 144–47; in Mexico, 32, 146–47, 169, 229–30; reference to in video, 95, 112–14, 116, 123

Eisenhower administration, 14–15

Ejército Guerrillero de los Pobres, 48

El Petén, 15, 157

El Quiché region, 62, 64, 71–78, 121–22, 236

El Salvador, 13, 99, 101, 156, 158

Enriquez, Mario René, 160, 162

Espina, Gustavo, 90

Esquipulas II, 158

Esteban (ex-husband), 10–12, 22, 25–

Esteban (ex-husband) *(continued)*
27, 35–37, 41–42, 64, 94, 112, 140,
166. *See also* Barrientos Aragón,
Carlos
Ester (grandmother). *See* Urrutia, Ester
Castellanos de
evangelical Protestants, 34, 62, 76–77,
261n49
exceptionalism, American, 101, 153, 237,
264n31

fair-skinned man. *See* Chando, Don
("fair-skinned man")
Falla, Ricardo, 71
FAR (Fuerzas Armadas Rebeldes), 27–29,
46, 48, 89, 146, 156, 256n39
Fat Man. *See* Gaspar, Don
Flickner, Charlie, 58
Flores, Carlos, 249n11
Flores, Gerardo, 78–79, 129, 131
Fogarty, Mrs., 192
Font, Juan Luis, *plate 21*, 131, 179,
188–89, 231–32, 234
"free" press, 189
Fuerzas Armadas Rebeldes. *See* FAR
Fulbright Scholarship, 30, 42

G-2 (Guatemalan army intelligence ser-
vice), 23, 40, 109, 122, 151, 154,
181, 214–15, 253n4
García Samayoa, José, 262n22
Gaspar, Don (pseud.), 23, 37, 128
Gaspar Ilom. *See* Asturias, Rodrigo
genocide, 75, 260n44
Gerardi Conedera, Juan, *plate 9*, 70,
72–75, 78, 127–28, 240–41
Gerhart, John, 58
González, Claudia, 127
Gospel Outreach, 77
Grafico, El, 37, 116, 120, 135–36, 154,
205, 228
Gramajo, Héctor, 160
Gran, José María, 73
Grandin, Greg, 77
Guantánamo Bay, 237
GUATEL, 39–40
Guatemala Coordination Group (Amnesty
International), 57
Guatemalan army: and Barrientos, 10–
11, 40–41, 121–22; and Catholic
Church, 71–79, 92, 113–14; and
CIA, 104, 108–11, 118, 235, 279n4;
continuing threat from, 121, 131–
32, 169, 207, 209, 228, 233–35; and
COPAZ, 158–60; and counternar-
cotics activities, 104, 108–11, 151,
180–82, 238, 277n25; and Edmundo

René Urrutia, 29, 33, 37–38, 89, 173;
and EGP, 31–32, 40–41, 50, 62,
114–15, 121–22; and FAR, 27, 29;
and Gerardi, 129, 240; and Human
Rights Committee (United Nations),
194; and "liberationists" (1954),
6–9, 14; and Maritza's kidnapping,
10, 12, 31–34, 37–39, 44, 64, 90,
114–18, 187, 191–92, 208; and Maritza's reappearance, 119–20, 136,
269n7; and media, 148, 179; and
military coup (1963), 156; and monitoring of airline flights, 220; and
October Revolution (1944), xv–xvii;
and ODHA, 61, 194; and ombudsman's office, 98; and peace negotiations, 147–48, 158–60, 167, 273n31;
propaganda campaigns of, 147–48,
154, 214; surveillance by, 3, 23–24;
and URNG, 147–48, 158–60, 167,
273n31; and U.S. government, 84,
98, 103–11, 118, 139, 148–52, 171,
174–75, 180–82, 231–34, 263n9,
271nn25,35. *See also* G-2 (intelligence service); Island (la Isla)
Guatemalan attorney general, 96, 122–
23, 147, 149, 262n22; and *arraigo*
(court order), 217–18, 226–27; and
press conference, 119–20, 124–25,
131, 137, 169–70, 189
Guatemalan Communist Party. *See* PGT
Guatemalan Congress, 37, 256n39
Guatemalan Constitution, 20, 172
Guatemalan Defense Ministry, 37–38,
83, 174–75
Guatemalan Department of Immigration,
121
Guatemalan Embassy (U.S.), 262n22
Guatemalan Episcopal Conference, 230
Guatemalan government: and license
plate number, 81, 84, 88–90; and
Maritza's disappearance, 84, 95,
116–17; and Maritza's reappearance, 135–36; and peace negotiations, 20, 89, 111, 146–48, 154–65,
167–68, 173, 180, 194–95, 236,
241; public/political pressure on,
43–44, 55–58, 89–90, 141, 262n22;
relations with U.S., 43–44, 55, 60–
61, 98–112, 149–53, 162–64, 211,
232–36, 266n93, 271n25; secret
"security council" of, 234–35. *See
also* Serrano Elías, Jorge
Guatemalan National Revolutionary
Union. *See* URNG
Guatemalan Peace Commission. *See*
COPAZ

Guatemalan Presidential Human Rights Commission. *See* COPREDH
Guatemalan Supreme Court, 39, 147, 256n39, 262n22
Guerrilla Army of the Poor. *See* EGP
Guevara, Ernesto ("Che"), 16, 18, 28, 45–49, 51, 242
Gutiérrez, Victor Manuel, 16

habeas corpus, writ of, 39
Hacienda Country Club (Panama City), 240
Hamilton, John, 102, 214
"handshake agreement," 194–97
Harkin, Tom, 58, 189, 262n22
Hernández Pico, Juan, 71
heroin trade, 182
Ho Chi Minh front, 10, 40, 50, 121–22
Holliday, David, 183–84
Hora, La, 84, 90–91
Hoyos, Fernando, 72
humanitarianism, xix–xx, 20, 101, 132, 177, 179, 195, 233
humanitarian law, 164, 171–72
Human Rights Committee (United Nations), 37, 194–96, 276n11
Human Rights Office (Archdiocese of Guatemala). *See* ODHA
human rights ombudsman, Guatemalan, 33, 81, 97–98, 120–21. *See also* de León Carpio, Ramiro
human rights organizations, 39–40, 43–44, 56, 78, 141. *See also* NGOs
Human Rights Watch, 56–57, 183–84, 258n26

Ibarra, Carmen Aída, *plate 22*, 129–31, 136–37, 219, 228
imperialism, U.S., 15–16, 18, 28, 60, 162
Independent Movement of the Masses (MAM), 36
INM (U.S. Bureau for International Narcotics Matters), 99, 110, 139
INS (U.S. Immigration and Naturalization Service), 170
Instituto Belén, 44–45
Inter-American Bureau (U.S. State Dept.), 59, 98, 171, 211
Inter-American Court of Human Rights, 55, 241
Inter-American Human Rights Commission (Washington, D.C.), 55–56, 98, 233–34
Iran-Contra debacle, 59
Iraq, 237
Iraqi Kurds, 138
Island (*la Isla*): concerns about outcome of Maritza's kidnapping, 125, 128,

132, 166–67; Maritza at, 22–27, 35–37, 41–42, 52–55, 63–64, 79–81, 85–88, 94–97, 115, 118–20, 253n4; reconstruction of, 166–67; soccer games at, 125, 128
Ixcán region, 48, 51
Ixil region, 40

"Jackal." *See* Arana Osorio, Carlos
Jeffords, James, 57–58
Jesuits, 71–72, 82, 113
John Paul, Pope, 77
Jonas, Susanne, 160, 273n31
Jones (U.S. Embassy staff person): and interviews with Maritza, 138–41, 170, 183; and security of U.S. citizens, 60–61, 81, 83–84, 112–13, 115, 139; and travel preparations for Maritza and family, 208; and video of Maritza, 112, 118; and visas, 128, 138–41, 155, 170, 183, 191; and visas, delay of, 193–94, 196–99, 206–11, 216
Juan (student), 82, 91–92, 97, 113, 121
Julia (aunt). *See* Urrutia, Julia
Julia (friend), 49

Kappy (fiancée of Edmundo René). *See* Riker, Katharine
Keane, John, 284n30
Kirk, Mark, 59, 171–72
Kirschner, Robert, 215–18, 222
Kurdish people, 138

Laguardia, Braulio, xvii
la lucha, 27–28, 48
LaRue, Frank, 55–56, 141–42, 171
Latin American Institute (University of New Mexico), 44
Law Against Communism, 15
Leahy, Patrick, 58–59, 189, 262n22
Leguizamon, Julio, 16
Levi, Primo, 234
"liberationists" (1954), xviii–xix, 5–9, 13–21
liberation theology, 69–73, 234, 236
license plate number, 81, 84, 88–90
literacy campaigns, 13–14
López, Fernando, 200–201, 205–6, 208–11, 217, 219, 223, 239
López, Hermógenes, 71
López, Mr. *See* Davis, Robert K. ("Bob")
"Love Song for Stalingrad" (Neruda), 14
Luis, Father. *See* Pérez, Luis
Lutheran Church, 138

Maisto, John, 213–14
MAM (Independent Movement of the Masses), 36
Manolo (pseud.). *See* Meoño, Gustavo
Manuel, Anne, 56–58, 172, 183, 188, 258n26
marijuana, 63
Maritza. *See* Urrutia, Maritza
market women. *See* vendors, women
Marroquín, Francisco, 67
Martínez, Victor Hugo, 75–76
Marxism, 7, 29–30, 50, 82
Maryknoll Order, 260n31
massacres, civilian, 72, 78
masses, 68–69, 75–76, 190; for Maritza, 82–83, 85, 88, 90–92, 221–22
Mayan population: and Catholic Church, 65–77, 91, 236, 260n44, 261nn49,57; and EGP, 48; and Guatemalan army, 63–64, 86, 167–68; and peace negotiations, 161, 167–68; in shantytowns, 241; and Spanish conquest, 14
McClenny, Lee, 118
McShane, Susanne, 40, 43
Medellín principles, 69–70, 72, 78
media: and Alpírez affair, 237; and Guatemalan army, 148; and "liberationists" (1954), 6–9; and Maritza's disappearance, 32–33, 37, 40–41, 44, 56, 89–90, 188–89; and Maritza's reappearance, 129–31, 135–37, 269n7; and NGOs, 137; and ODHA, 89–90, 129–31, 136–37, 168–69, 178–79, 205–6, 219, 227–28; at press conference, 123–26; and URNG, 154–55; and video of Maritza, 112–16, 121–22
Mega 6 department store. *See* Paiz Mega 6
Mein, John Gordon, 164
Meléndez, Licenciado José María, 262n22
Melville, Thomas, 260n31
Mencos, Axel, 75–76
Méndez Ruiz, Ricardo, 114
Menéndez Park, Gonzalo, 180, 188, 212–13, 232
Meoño, Gustavo, *plate 7*, 31–32, 114–15, 145–46, 229
Mérida Escobar, José, 191
Mexican Embassy (Guatemala), 15, 169
military assistance, U.S., 99, 104–11, 149–50, 152, 238, 263n9
Moran, Francisco, 66
Morán, Rolando, 229

narcotics trafficking, war against. *See* counternarcotics activities

National Defense Authorization Act (U.S.), 182
National Reconciliation Commission (Guatemala), 89
National University of San Carlos. *See* USAC
Nazi Germany, 234
Neruda, Pablo, 14
Neumann, Bernardo, 192–93, 197–98, 214–15, 220, 226, 234, 262n22
newspaper articles, 37, 84, 89–90, 116, 120, 136, 154–55, 179, 188–90, 205, 227. *See also* media
NGOs (nongovernmental organizations): and COPREDH, 192; and Maritza in exile, 229; and pressure for Maritza's release, 32, 43–44, 55–59, 89, 137; and pressure for visas, 141–43, 155, 171–74, 177, 183–85, 187–88; and U.S. government, 43–44, 55–59, 151, 171–72; and visas, delay of, 193–94, 196–97, 200–203, 208, 211–16. *See also names of NGOs*
Nicaragua, 13, 48, 99, 101, 146, 158, 187
Nicaraguan Embassy (U.S.), 43
Nicaraguan Foreign Ministry, 43
Nicaraguan News Agency, 43
nongovernmental organizations. *See* NGOs
Notisiete, 95–96
Nuccio, Richard, 58, 111, 162–63

Ochaeta, Ronalth, *plate 11*, 239; and archbishopric refuge, 168–70, 178–79, 184; and *arraigo* (court order), 217–18; and EGP, 144–45; and Maritza's disappearance, 38, 61, 81, 88–89; and media, 129–30, 136, 219, 228; and Serrano, 235; and travel preparations for Maritza and family, 208–9, 217–20, 222–24, 228; and USAC student association, 78–79; and U.S. government, 83, 88–89; and visas, delay of, 193–94, 201–2, 205, 207–11, 214, 216–17
October Revolution, Guatemala (1944), xv–xviii, 14, 16, 60
Octubre (PGT newspaper), 15–16
ODHA (Oficina de Derechos Humanos del Arzobispado): creation of, 78–79; and Maritza's kidnapping, 38–39, 60–61; and mass for Maritza, 82–83, 85, 90–92; and media, 89–90, 129–31, 136–37, 168–69, 178–79, 205–6, 219, 227–28; and pressure for Maritza's release, 81–84, 88–

90; reference to in video, 52; and Serrano, 230, 235; silence of, 234; students' views of, 97, 121; and travel preparations for Maritza and family, 191, 194, 196, 206; and URNG, 132, 155; and U.S. Embassy interviews with Maritza, 138–41, 171, 174, 183–86; and visas, 128, 141–43, 155, 171–74, 183–85, 190–91; and visas, delay of, 196, 200–201, 207–9, 215

Oficina de Derechos Humanos del Arzobispado. *See* ODHA

ombudsman. *See* human rights ombudsman, Guatemalan

"open skies" treaty, 276n7

OPERATION CADENCE, 110

Opinión, La, 8

Orantes, Sergio, *plate 12*, 82–83, 88, 90–92, 218, 221–24, 240–41

Orderly Departure Program, 138

Orellana, Alma América, 157

Orellana, Manuel, 7, 20, 156–57

Orellana, Maria, 157

Orellana, Sara, *plate 3*, 5–7, 9, 20

Orellana de Conde, Sonia, *plate 3*, 5–7, 9, 20, 156–57, 239, 251n21

Organización. *See* EGP (Guerrilla Army of the Poor)

Organization of American States, 43, 142, 239

ORPA (Organización Revolucionaria del Pueblo en Armas), 48, 70

orphaned children, 53–54

Paiz Mega 6, 52, 119

Parker, Susan, 203–4

passports, xx, 11, 121, 131, 138, 185, 193–94, 197–201, 203–4, 207, 209–11, 216, 219, 222, 224–25. *See also* visas, U.S.

Patricia (friend), 44–47

Patterson, Suzanne, 239; and Guatemalan army, 148–49, 181–82; and interviews with Maritza, 138–41, 170, 183–87, 191; and Stroock, 102, 179–80; and visas, 170, 177, 179–80, 191–92; and visas, delay of, 195

Paul VI, Pope, 69

Paz y Paz, Roberto, 14

Peace Commission (Central American Parliament), 239

Peck, Richard, 44

Pedro (student), 82–83, 91–92, 97, 121

Pellecer, Luis, 113–14

Peña, Luis Valdes, xvi

Penados, Fernando, 130, 205, 220, 222–23

Penados del Barrio, Próspero, *plate 10*; and archbishopric refuge, 98, 126, 129, 136, 139, 145, 169, 173, 190, 205, 214, 217–18, 220–22, 226, 230–31; and *arraigo* (court order), 217; death of, 241; and Gerardi celebration, 129; and human rights abuses, 77–79, 114, 223; and Maritza's disappearance, 62; and mass for Maritza, 83; and Medellín principles, 70; and peace negotiations, 173; and Sebastián, 145, 205; and Serrano, 230–31

Peralta, Otto, 80, 86, 135

Peralta Azurdia, Enrique, 156

Perdomo, Francisco, 217, 235

Pérez, Ana, 203–4

Pérez, Luis, 62, 83, 114, 218, 222–23

Pérez, Olga, 206

Perón, Juan, 18

Peter, Marian, 260n31

PGT (Guatemalan Communist Party), 13–19, 27–28, 46, 48, 242, 256n39

photographers, 179, 205–6, 219, 227–28

Physicians for Human Rights, 215

Pilar (mother). *See* Urrutia, Pilar

Pineda, Tere, 62, 126, 128, 178, 201, 220, 222, 225–26

Pinto Soria, Julio, 66–67

political prisoners, xviii–xix, 61, 207

Ponce, Jorge, 156

Ponce Vaides, Federico, xv, xvii–xviii

Prensa Libre, 37, 90, 227

Presidential Human Rights Commission. *See* COPREDH

press. *See* media

propaganda, revolutionary, 27–28, 44–45, 48–51

prophetic church, 72

Protestantism, 34, 62, 76–77, 261n49

pseudonyms, 5n, 27, 50

PUA (Party of Anti-Communist Unity), 8

Quezada, Rodolfo, 89, 159, 167–68, 173

radio broadcasts, 6–9, 14–15, 32, 40–41, 121–22, 251nn21,22

Radio Havana, 46

radio noise, 26, 42, 53–54, 63–64, 88, 96

Radio of Liberation, 6–9

Radio Sucesos (radio program), 8

Radio Universal, *plate 4*

ranchera music, 42

rape, fear of, 27, 63–64
Ravinel, Arthur, 221
Reagan, Ronald, 108, 181–82
Red Cross International Committee, 106
reducciones (towns), 66
Reuters news agency, 136, 205, 228
revolutionary theory, teaching of, 50
Richardson, Bill, 44, 189
Rieser, Tim, 58
Riker, Katharine (fiancée of Edmundo
    René), 239; in archbishopric refuge,
    126–27, 135, 139, 178, 185, 190–
    91, 201; concern for safety of, 34,
    60–61, 83–84, 98, 112–13, 115,
    117, 139–40; and flight to U.S., 222,
    224, 226; and Maritza's disappear-
    ance, 30, 33, 39–40, 44; at mass for
    Maritza, 93; at press conference,
    124–25; reaction to video, 112–13,
    115–17; and Sebastián, 53, 185;
    travel preparations for, 191, 196,
    218–19
Ríos Mont, Efraín, 77
Robinson, Bill, *plate 8*, 40, 42, 241; and
    Maritza in exile, 229; and pressure
    for Maritiza's release, 43, 55–58,
    128; and pressure for visas, 141–42,
    155, 171, 173–74, 177, 187–88,
    190–91; on U.S. foreign policy, 183;
    and visas, delay of, 196, 201–2, 215,
    220–21
Rodil Peralta, Juan José, 262n22
Rossell Arellano, Mariano, 7–8, 20, 65,
    68, 82, 222, 250n11
Rumsfeld, Donald, 238
Ruth (pseud.), 9–10, 26–27, 47, 168.
    See also Urrutia, Maritza

safe houses, 32, 48, 89, 229
Salinas, Carlos, *plate 23*, 141, 171–72,
    202, 212, 221, 241
Sánchez (investigator), 97–98, 120–21,
    185
Sánchez, José Ángel, 7
Sandinistas, 43
Sandoval, Miguel Ángel, 146–47, 229
Sandra (friend), 12–13
San Gaspar Chajul, 72
San Mateo Ixtatán, 67
Sapia Bosch, Alfonso, 108
Saxon, Dan: and archbishopric refuge,
    120–21, 126–27, 129, 132, 138–
    40, 144, 153–55, 166, 168, 179;
    and *arraigo* (court order), 218;
    and Edmundo René Urrutia, 116;
    and flight to U.S., 222, 224–26; and
    Maritza's kidnapping, 38–39, 81,

83, 97, 112; marriage of, xx, 241;
    and NGOs, 141–43, 155, 171–74,
    183–84; at press conference, 124–
    25; and pressure for Maritza's
    release, 141–42; reaction to URNG
    article, 154–55; silence of, 234; and
    Stroock, 197–200, 206–7, 209, 216;
    and travel preparations for Maritza
    and family, 191, 194, 196, 199–200,
    218–20; and U.S. Embassy inter-
    views with Maritza, 138–41, 174,
    183–87; and visas, 121, 131, 138–
    43, 185; and visas, delay of, 193–
    94, 196–204, 206–9, 219–21
Scarry, Elaine, 145
Schirmer, Jennifer, 77, 260n44
Schultz-Heim, Laurie, 58
Sears, Greg, 183, 185–87, 191
Sebastián (son): in archbishopric refuge,
    128, 132, 135, 137, 144–45, 185,
    190–91, 205–6, 216–17, 220, 222;
    birth of, 50; effect of mother's disap-
    pearance on, 53–54, 85, 135, 185;
    father of, 40–41, 224–25; and flight
    to U.S., 222, 224–25; Maritza's con-
    cern for, 12–13, 26, 42, 86, 186–87,
    229; in Mexico, 229, 241; passport
    of, 194, 197–99, 209–11, 216, 219,
    222, 224–25; and return to Guate-
    mala, 241; reunion with Maritza,
    128; surveillance of, 3–5, 9–11, 23–
    24, 63; travel preparations for, 191,
    196, 216–18; visa for, xx, 98, 121,
    128, 131, 137–38, 170, 175, 191; at
    Walt Disney Nursery School, xix, 4,
    10, 23, 31, 97
Secaira, Leticia, 123–24
Second Vatican Council. *See* Vatican II
Sergio, Father. *See* Orantes, Sergio
Serrano, Adan, 17
Serrano Elías, Jorge, *plate 14*, 17, 234–
    35, 240; and Catholic Church, 127,
    230–32; and Chester affair, 212–
    13, 231–32, 279n18, 284n30;
    defense of Guatemalan army,
    231–35; failed coup attempt of,
    235–36; and Ochaeta, 235; and
    peace negotiations, 155–65; and
    pressure for Maritza's release, 44,
    58–60, 89, 171, 262n22; reaction
    to Maritza's case, 136, 179, 230–
    35, 240; resignation of, 236, 239;
    and Stroock, 105–9, 111–12, 148–
    51, 162, 180–81, 183, 192–96,
    234; and URNG, 147–48, 157–
    62, 279n18; and U.S. government,
    105–9, 111–12, 138, 148–51, 162–

64, 170, 180, 231–35, 240; and
 visas, 180–81, 183, 188, 192, 231,
 235; and visas, delay of, 193–95,
 198, 212–15
shantytowns, 72–73, 241
Shetemul, Haroldo, 112
Siegel, Adina, 221
Sierra Franco, Raul, 16
Siglo Veintiuno, 37, 90, 129–30, 137,
 190, 205, 219, 228
silence, 234, 237, 240; vows of, 126–28,
 131–32, 142, 168
Silva Jonama, Mario, 28
sleep deprivation, 42, 54, 64, 95–96.
 See also radio noise
socialism, 28, 46, 49–50
social justice, 69–77
solidarity groups, Guatemalan, 56
Somoza regime (Nicaragua), 43
Sompopon (pseud.), 24
Spanish conquest, 14, 65–67, 74, 77
Stanley, William, 44, 187, 278n39
Stroock, Thomas F., *plate 13*, 99–103,
 238–39; and American exceptionalism, 101, 153, 264n31; and CIA,
 109–11, 117–18, 179, 266n93,
 267n5; and "handshake agreement,"
 194–99; human rights objectives
 of, 104–11, 117, 139, 152–53, 234,
 262n22, 271nn25,35, 284n30; and
 Saxon, 197–200, 206–7, 209, 216;
 and Serrano, 105–9, 111–12, 148–
 51, 162, 180–81, 183, 192–96, 234;
 silence of, 234; and visas, 174–77,
 179–81, 183, 188–89, 191–92,
 275n6; and visas, delay of, 193–
 200, 205–6, 208–9, 212–14, 216,
 280n23
Student Association (Instituto Belén),
 45–46
Student Association (USAC), 53, 78–80,
 86, 90–92, 135, 239
Sweeney, Jim, 58

Taiana, Jorge, xviii–xix, 242
Taracena, Marco Antonio, 160
Taylor, Phillip, 163–64
Tegucigalpa (Honduras), 5–9
telephone taps, 23, 34, 39, 44, 61, 142,
 173, 185, 194, 207
Teleprensa, 95–96, 123
television news, 89–90, 95–96, 112–16,
 118, 122, 132, 221. *See also* media
Tenneriello, Bonnie, 57–59, 82, 88–89,
 172, 211–13, 241
Todd, David, 100
Toj Medrano, Emilio, 114

Tomuschat, Christian, 202, 224–25
Torricelli, Robert, 162–63
torture, 53–55, 145, 231, 234, 237,
 283n13; EGP's views on, 48, 114,
 145–46, 230; of Maritza, xx–xxi,
 24, 53–55, 167–68, 189, 228, 230,
 237; NGOs' views on, 141, 215;
 and URNG, 147; and USAC student
 association, 78–79; and U.S. government, 237
tourist visas, 79, 169–70, 235
trago duro, 158
tribute, 66–67
Tuchman, Barbara, 233
Turcios (revolutionary leader), 28

Ubico, Jorge, xvii
Unidad Revolucionaria Nacional Guate-
 malteca. *See* URNG
United Nations: and Guatemalan army,
 119; and Guatemalan human rights
 expert, 202, 224–25; Human Rights
 Committee, 37, 194–96, 276n11;
 and peace negotiations, 162, 167;
 refugee agency of, 138
University of New Mexico, 30, 42, 44.
 See also Albuquerque (N.M.)
Urgent Action Appeal (Amnesty International), 57–58
Urgent Action request (ODHA), 39, 172
URNG (Guatemalan National Revolutionary Union): and amnesty, 158;
 and Human Rights Committee
 (United Nations), 194; as joint command, 48; and Maritza, 51, 55, 61,
 84, 140, 146–48, 154–55, 175, 184,
 187, 207, 229; and ODHA, 127,
 130, 132; and peace negotiations,
 20, 89, 111, 146–48, 154–65, 167–
 68, 173, 180, 194–95, 236, 241;
 reference to in video, 95, 112; and
 Serrano, 147–48, 157–62, 235,
 279n18; and U.S. government, 60,
 101, 148, 162–64, 175
Urrutia, Carolina (sister), *plate 5*, 11, 28,
 38, 41, 62–63, 85, 92, 121, 128,
 131
Urrutia, Edmundo (father), *plate 2, plate
 5*, xvii–xviii, 19, 27–29, 34, 239–40;
 and archbishopric refuge, 155; and
 birth of Maritza, 21; and Guatemalan army, 34, 172–73, 275n31;
 and Maritza's vow of silence, 128;
 marriage of, 46; at mass for Maritza,
 90; and media, 37, 84; and ODHA,
 61–62, 81, 84–85, 98; and ombudsman for human rights, 97; at press

Urrutia, Edmundo (father) *(continued)*
conference, 124–26; reaction to
video, 114; and Sandoval, 147; and
Sebastián, 31, 85; and subpoenas,
217; telephone calls to, 33, 42, 87,
96, 122
Urrutia, Edmundo René (brother), *plate
5, plate 6,* 239; in archbishopric
refuge, 126–28, 135, 139–40, 154,
178, 184–87, 190–91, 201–2, 206,
218–20, 222; and *arraigo* (court
order), 218; concern for safety of,
34, 60–61, 98, 112–13, 115, 117,
135–36, 139–40; and flight to U.S.,
222–26; and Guatemalan army, 29,
33, 37–38, 89, 173; ideological differences with Maritza, 49–51, 144,
166; interrogations of Maritza
about, 11, 22, 25; life as young
guerrillero, 28–29, 33, 59, 89; and
Maritza's vow of silence, 126–28;
at mass for Maritza, 92–93; and
media, 37, 89–90, 116, 135–36; in
Mexico, 30, 47, 49–50; and NGOs,
57, 174; nonconfrontational strategy
of, 40, 56, 89–90, 92; and ODHA,
38–39, 83–84, 89, 127–28; at press
conference, 124–25; as professor
at USAC, 53; reaction to URNG
article, 154–55; reaction to video,
112–13, 115–17; and Sebastián,
53; travel preparations for, 191,
196, 218–19; at University of New
Mexico, 3, 30, 39–40, 42, 44, 51,
58, 131, 187, 278n39; and U.S.
Embassy interviews with Maritza,
184–87; and visas, delay of, 201–2,
206
Urrutia, Ester Castellanos de (grandmother), *plate 1, plate 2,* xv–xix,
13–21, 27–28, 46, 242–43, 250n11
Urrutia, Héctor (uncle), 19
Urrutia, Julia (aunt), *plate 2,* xvii–xix,
13, 15–18, 113, 242–43
Urrutia, Manuel (grandfather), *plate 2,*
xv–xvi, 15–21, 242
Urrutia, Maritza, *plate 5, plates 16–19:*
in Albuquerque, 228–29; amnesty
for, 36, 41, 87, 94–96, 120, 122–
25, 140, 147, 151, 172, 207, 227;
in archbishopric refuge, 126–29,
131–32, 135–40, 144–45, 153, 166,
168–70, 173, 178–80, 183–85,
190–91, 193–94, 196, 200–202,
205–10, 214–22; and *arraigo* (court
order), 207–8, 211, 215, 217–18;

birth of, 21; and Catholic Church,
63, 65, 79, 82–83, 85, 90–92, 126,
221–22; childhood of, 27–28, 31;
and decision to speak out, 229–30,
233–34, 240; education of, 44–47;
and EGP, 3, 31–33, 47–51, 144–47,
229–30; fear of being killed, 22, 27,
35–36, 86–87, 95, 97; and flight
to U.S., 222–26, 230; and Guatemalan offers of protection, 173,
214–15; ideological differences with
Edmundo René, 49–51, 144, 166;
illness of, 88, 118–19; interrogations
of, 11–13, 22–27, 33, 35–37, 47,
52–54, 63, 94; at the Island *(la Isla),*
21–27, 35–37, 41–42, 52–55, 63–
64, 79–81, 85–88, 94–97, 115,
118–20, 253n4; kidnapping of,
xix–xx, 5, 9–13, 17, 20, 23–24,
30–34, 97, 124, 215, 241; and
letter to Tomuschat, 202, 224–
25; and makeup, 52, 80, 94, 112–
13; marriage of, xx, 241; medical
examinations of, 144–45, 215–17;
in Mexico, 12, 35, 38, 41, 47–51,
140, 229–30, 236, 241; newspaper
articles concerning, 37, 84, 89–90,
116, 120, 136, 154–55, 179, 188–
90, 205, 227; in Nicaragua, 48;
passport of, xx, 121, 131, 138,
185, 193–94, 197–201, 203–4,
207, 209–11, 216, 219, 224; and
peace negotiations, 146–48, 154–
55, 163–65, 167; and photograph
with mother, 228; and political
asylum, 119, 137–38; prayers of/
for, 62–63, 87, 90–91, 226; press
conference of, 119–20, 124–26,
131, 137, 169–70, 189; reading of,
46–47, 50; reappearance of, xx,
119–26, 135–36, 214–15; and
return to Guatemala, 241; sleep
deprivation of, 42, 54, 64, 95–96;
surveillance of, 3–5, 10–11, 23;
telephone calls from, 12–13, 24–26,
33, 39, 42, 56, 61, 87, 95–96, 112,
122; travel preparations for, 191,
196, 199–200, 206, 208–9, 216–
20; and URNG, 51, 55, 61, 84, 140,
146–48, 154–55, 175, 184, 187,
207; and U.S. Embassy interviews,
138–41, 170, 174, 183–87, 189,
191; and visa, 98, 128, 137, 139–43,
148, 155, 170–72, 174–77, 179–84,
186–89, 191–92, 275n6; and visa,
delay of, 193–204, 207–17; vows of

silence, 126–28, 131–32, 142,
168
Urrutia, Miguel (uncle), 19
Urrutia, Oscar (uncle), xvi, 242
Urrutia, Pilar (mother), *plate 5*, *plate 19*,
21, 46–47, 51; at archbishopric
refuge, 228; and Maritza's kidnapping, 12, 25–26, 30, 33; and Maritza's vow of silence, 128, at mass
for Maritza, 90; and media, 84; and
ODHA, 98; and Sebastián, 85; and
subpoenas, 217; telephone calls to,
12, 25–26, 33
USAC (National University of San Carlos),
29–30, 32–33, 47, 63, 67; and Father
Sergio, 82; and Maritza's disappearance, 90; and Ochaeta, 78; School of
History, 82–83, 86, 90–91, 97, 113,
121, 135, 206; Student Association,
53, 78–80, 86, 90–92, 135, 239
U.S. Agency for International Development (AID), 25, 30
U.S. Bureau for International Narcotics
Matters. *See* INM
U.S. citizens, 60, 83–84, 104–6, 109,
113, 139. *See also* DeVine, Michael;
Riker, Katharine (fiancée of Ed-
mundo René); Saxon, Dan
U.S. Committee for Refugees, 214
U.S. Congress: and peace negotiations,
162–63; and pressure for Maritza's
release, 43, 55–59, 89, 262n22; and
pressure for visas, 171–72, 174,
189; students' views of, 97; and U.S.
military assistance, 106, 149–50;
and visas, delay of, 212, 214, 221
U.S. Congressional Human Rights
Caucus, 58
U.S. Department of Defense (DOD), 83,
105, 110–11, 174, 236, 238
U.S. Drug Enforcement Administration.
See DEA
U.S. Embassy (Guatemala): and Catholic
Church, 78–79, 83; and counternarcotics activities, 139, 180–82,
276–77nn24,25; distrust of, 61;
human rights objectives of, 98–103,
105–11, 148–53, 163–64, 232–34,
284n30; and interviews with Maritza, 138–41, 170, 174, 183–87, 189,
191; and Maritza's kidnapping, xx,
33; and peace negotiations, 163–64;
and political asylum, 119, 137–38;
and pressure for Maritza's release,
56, 59–60, 141–42; reactions to
video, 117–18; reference to in video,

52; and security of U.S. citizens, 60,
83–84, 104, 112–13, 115, 139–40,
194; and Serrano, 231–33; students'
views of, 239; and travel preparations for Maritza and family, 194–
96, 218–19; and visas, xix, 98, 128,
137–42, 155, 168, 170–71, 174–77,
179–88, 191–92; and visas, delay
of, 193–200, 202, 206–14, 216
U.S. Embassy (Mexico City), 229
U.S. government: and counternarcotics
activities, xix, 43, 99, 104, 108–11,
139, 151, 183, 266n93, 267n5,
276–77nn24–26; human rights
objectives of, xxi, 60, 98–111, 148–
53, 232–34, 266n93, 284n30; and
"liberationists" (1954), xviii–xix,
14–15, 17–18; and Maritza's disappearance, 43–44; and peace negotiations, 162–64; relations with
Guatemala, xx–xxi, 43–44, 55,
60–61, 98–112, 149–53, 162–64,
211, 232–36, 266n93, 271n25. *See
also* CIA
U.S. House Appropriations Committee,
59, 152
U.S. House Committee on Western
Hemisphere Affairs, 58
U.S. Immigration and Naturalization
Service. *See* INS
U.S. Marine Corps, 99–100
U.S. Senate Foreign Operations Subcommittee, 58–60, 152
U.S. Senate Western Hemisphere Committee, 59
U.S. State Department: Bureau for International Narcotics Matters (INM),
99, 110, 139, 182; human rights
objectives of, 98–111, 148–52, 162–
63, 192; Inter-American Bureau,
59, 98, 171, 211; and peace negotiations, 162–63; public/political
pressure on, 43, 56, 58–60, 141–
42, 171; and Serrano, 231–35; and
visas, 138–41, 155, 170–71, 174–
75, 185, 187–89, 191, 196, 201;
and visas, delay of, 197–98, 203,
208, 211–14, 216

Valenzuela, Atala, 14
Valladares, Acisclo, *plate 18*, 96, 119–20,
122–23, 147, 149, 217–18, 226–27,
262n22
Vatican II, 68–69, 78
Véliz Samayoa, Rony, 136–37, 205–6,
227–28

vendors, women, 4–5, 13, 21
Vendrell, Frances, 167
video, *plate 16*, 112–15; making of, 41–42, 52–53, 80–81, 85–87, 94–96; as propaganda campaign, 154, 164, 189, 214–15; reactions to, 112–18, 120–23, 137, 140–41, 145, 147, 170–71
Villa de Voto (Argentine prison), 19
Villanueva, Faustino, 73
visas, Mexican, 169
visas, U.S., 79, 98, 128, 131, 137–43, 148, 155, 169–72, 174–77, 179–89, 191–92, 275n6; delay of, 193–204, 207–16, 219; and EGP in Mexico, 229
Viteri, Ernesto, 212–13
Voice of Liberation, 9, 251n22

Walt Disney Nursery School, xix, 4–5, 10, 23, 30–31, 63, 97, 124

Washington, D.C., 30, 43, 55–60, 82, 88–89, 102–3
Washington Office on Latin America. *See* WOLA
Weschler, Lawrence, 55
White, Virginia, 60
White House Office on Drug Policy, 276–77n24
Wiley, Heather, 57–58, 89, 185, 202, 229
WOLA (Washington Office on Latin America), 57, 59, 82, 88, 172, 241
Women's Alliance (AFG), 13–15, 17, 20, 242, 250n11
women's rights, 13, 21
World War II, 99–100

Ydigoras regime, 156
Yon Sosa, 28

Zacapa province, 156–57
Zimbabwe liberation movement, 42–43

Text:	10/13 Sabon
Display:	Franklin Gothic
Compositor:	Integrated Composition Systems
Indexer:	Sharon Sweeney
Cartographer:	Bill Nelson
Printer and binder:	Thomson-Shore, Inc.